THE UNIVERSE SPEAKS

A Heavenly Dialogue Collection

Kimberly Klein

"*The Universe Speaks* is the most in-depth, accurate communication with those who have crossed over into heaven that I have ever seen put to paper. Talia is a remarkable spirit who gets right to the heart of spiritual knowledge. This is a must read for anyone curious about life after death—and let's face it, isn't everyone?"

~RonaLafae Thapa, internationally recognized psychic and medium

"The author offers hard-to-dispute proof of the validity of these messages . . . More than eight months of "conversations" between Talia and "G" reveal insights and contain knowledge that only Talia herself could have known."

~Kirkus Reviews

"*The Universe Speaks* is powerful proof that the 'veil between the worlds' is thinner than we think. Kim Klein's story of her daughter's death in a plane crash in Panama reads like fiction. But Talia's teachings from the spirit world after her 'death' provide the reader with hope, inspiration, and a new understanding of the reality of life."

~Jennifer Read Hawthorne, co-author, #1 *New York Times* bestsellers *Chicken Soup for the Woman's Soul* and *Chicken Soup for the Mother's Soul*

"Love and wisdom transcend the veil as Kim Klein's daughter on the other side reveals marvelous insights about the true meaning of life. *The Universe Speaks* brings hope to anyone who has ever lost a loved one."

~Randy Peyser, author of *The Power of Miracle Thinking*

Dedication

This book is dedicated to all of you who have chosen to walk the walk on this journey of ours, to live authentically, true to your heart and soul. And to Talia, the love of my life, whose dedication to getting these messages out to you, the reader, knows no bounds.

Talia and Mom, our last photo together, taken December 2007
© photography by Helene Glassman/*www.imagerybyhelene.com*

The Universe Speaks: A Heavenly Dialogue Collection

Copyright © 2011, 2018 by Kimberly Klein

ALL RIGHTS RESERVED. No part of this publication may be reproduced, stored in a retrieval system or transmitted, in any form or by any electronic, mechanical, photocopying, recording or otherwise—without prior written permission, except for the inclusion of brief quotations in a review.

For information about this title or to order other books and/or electronic media, contact the publisher at: www.pmapress.com or info@pmapress.com

Library of Congress Control Number: 201690871

ISBN: 978-0-9881787-5-5

Printed in the United States of America

Cover and Interior design by: 1106 Design

Author Photo: Peter Palladino

Table of Contents

About this Collection Edition	vii
The Dialogues Begins	1
Before the Crash	7
My Shift	9
Talia	11
"G"	19
Afterword	661
A Message from G	665
About Kim Klein	669

About this Collection Edition of *The Universe Speaks: A Heavenly Dialogue*

ORIGINALLY, *The Universe Speaks: A Heavenly Dialogue* was published in two parts, Book One and Book Two. This was due to the large number of dialogues, as well as the depth of information contained in each. In fact, Talia, my daughter, the Spirit communicating in these dialogues, requested that the Dialogues be published as two different books.

Book One taught us not only that there is no death—that the spirit lives on after we shed our bodies—but also that we all have the ability to speak to and hear spirits as they communicate to us. Book Two took us deeper into the meaning of life and how to experience our truest self—our authentic self—the self closest to what some of us call God.

After publishing both books one and two, I received a number of requests for a single abridged version. Originally, I did not want to combine or shorten the two books; I didn't want to take away from them in any way or leave out a single one of Talia's words. Then I realized that I could eliminate certain parts of the dialogues between Talia and G, the medium through which Talia's teachings were received, without the messages losing their meaning or power. In fact, I saw that removing some of the nonessential conversations might make the book easier for some people to read, and as I was told, to carry with them for daily reference. So I re-edited both books, and the result is this slightly abridged *Collection Edition*.

For those of you who have read both of the Dialogues books, thank you for your input on this new release. For those who have yet to read them, this combined work will be easier to carry and absorb. I'm hoping that my repeat readers will garner even more insight into the realities of the Universe and the Spirit World, and I'm hopeful that my new readers will get as much out of the dialogues as I have!

I am very fortunate to experience communication with the Spirit world firsthand. I'm also pleased that so many readers from all over the globe have written to me telling me that as soon as they finished reading *The Universe Speaks,* they too started to hear from the spirit world—and their lives were forever changed.

That is what I wished for, and that was Talia's desire, too. So thank you for joining me in this new *Collection Edition.* May it bring you great joy and peace.

The Dialogues Begin

On December 23, 2007, a small private plane carrying my thirteen-year-old daughter, her father and her best friend crashed into the side of a volcano in Panama, killing all on board except my daughter's friend.

Talia was my only child. For nearly three days the whereabouts of the plane—and the fate of my daughter, her father and her friend—were unknown. It was the most horrific and traumatizing time of my life. My mind and my body were not connected, and from the moment I realized my daughter was "dead," I have never been the same. My heart was ripped out of me, my emotions disconnected from my body, and my entire life torn apart.

Of course I will never be the same. Never the same because Talia is no longer "alive." But also never the same because all that I thought about life and death has been altered. In the midst of the worse time of my life I feel ultimate love and peace.

❋   ❋   ❋

Tell my mom I'm OK.

Talia?

Yes, tell my mom I'm OK.

OK, I will when I see her.

TELL MY MOM I'M OK!

I will, I promise!

It sounded like an everyday message from a daughter to her mother—but it was really not so everyday. You see, Talia made that statement to my friend G on January 23—while he was on the way to her memorial service. She said it a month *after* she had died.

Now, I am not the kind of person who would readily believe that someone had heard my daughter speaking from the spirit world. In fact, I did not believe in the spirit world until recently. So why would I ever believe that those words, "Tell my mom I'm OK," were actually from Talia? It would have been much more rational for me to assume my friend had made up that message to help me deal with the overwhelming pain of losing my daughter.

But when G gave me Talia's message, I knew, deep in my heart, that those were Talia's own words. Yes, they were said to help me, but they were not made up; they were actually Talia's words, said by her, for me.

Who am I? you may be wondering. I'm Kim, Talia's mom. A forty-something, California-raised, well-educated, middle-class woman.

I grew up pretty simply, with no particular religious or spiritual rules to live by. I just lived my life my way, rationally and according to my own guidelines, which were pretty basic: Try to treat people well, don't lie, and be happy.

Because I didn't have any set religious or spiritual guidance growing up, I decided I didn't believe in God—or the spirit world. I was too independent to believe there was one supreme person or entity with a set of rules I was supposed to follow in order to go to heaven when I died. In fact, that idea annoyed me, because I saw so many religious leaders using their position to control the members of their congregations.

I felt that if there were a God, you should be able to pray to that God directly—he wouldn't make it necessary for people to go through an intermediary to get to him. There was no need to pray to a secondary source or confess to a human acting as God's representative, or do whatever a particular leader said you had to do. Nor did you have to join a church or temple as a means of getting to heaven. You could just be you, live your life, and speak to your God when you wanted to, on your terms.

But though I didn't believe in the God that most people I came in contact with believed in, I didn't shut myself off from the possibility of the existence of God either. Since the idea of God had not been pounded into me, and until recently I had had no mystical experiences or miracles to show me the existence of God, I had no reason to believe in either the existence or the nonexistence of God. But I was open to receiving proof of the existence of God or the spirit world. And I did believe in my own instincts, often "just knowing" something, which seemed to imply that I believed there's more to us than our minds.

I labeled myself *agnostic*—not believing but open to proof. I really believe it was this openness that allowed me eventually to see, hear, and experience the evidence I needed to prove that there is in fact a spiritual dimension and a power, a force that some people call God.

So when did I go from not believing to believing? It was just after I really understood that my daughter had been killed. I say *understood* that she had been killed, because even when I first found out, it took a while for me to really know she was gone. Gone from this earth the way I had known her. But once I realized she was in fact "dead," my entire belief system shattered.

This shattering was not like the shattering of a mirror, whereby when it broke nothing was left. It was like the shattering of a glass door that, once broken, allowed me to see

Collection

into a world much more beautiful, perfect, and fulfilling than the world I was living in. My daughter's death is what shattered that door. From the moment I really understood she was gone, I went from not believing in life after death to absolutely believing in it. I knew that the messages Talia was sending me from beyond were from her, and so very real.

What made me believe? It was not that the words "Tell my mom I'm OK" in themselves changed me from a non-believer to a believer. Since the very moment I realized Talia was "dead," I began receiving many messages from her through various sources, all of which have built on one other and been confirmed by one other. When looked at both alone and as a whole, they have proven to me that not only is Talia actually telling people the messages they relay to me, but, beyond that, those messages are in every way totally, completely, and irrevocably Talia. I know, deeper in my heart and soul than I can even describe, that Talia is communicating to me and, most important, that she is not dead, but more alive and amazing now than she was with me here on earth.

※ ※ ※

That moment—the moment when my entire belief system shattered—happened the afternoon of December 26, 2007, after I heard the news and really understood that Talia was dead.

I was lying down, drifting in and out of sleep, crying. Suddenly, I was startled out of my sleepy state by a definite sensation of pressure around my left wrist. I knew deep in my bones that what I felt was an actual touch, and my soul knew it was Talia.

I suppose you're saying, "OK, your daughter just died, so of course you are going to imagine things like her touch." Well, it was not my imagination.

Just minutes after I felt her touch on my wrist, my cell phone rang. It was my friend in Santa Barbara. She had just called Rebecca, a medium I had spoken to in the past, and during that call my friend said Rebecca had started to get messages from Talia that were meant for me. Rebecca told my friend that Talia was trying to show her "a charm or something."

I immediately knew what it was. Talia wanted me to get her bracelet from her wrist. This bracelet meant a great deal to both Talia and me. I had given it to Talia the previous Mother's Day as a thank-you gift for being my daughter. The bracelet was simple: just a gold coin on a black rope. It was her absolute favorite thing in the world and she never took it off, ever.

Right after I hung up the phone with my friend, my phone rang again, and it was Rebecca. "It's a bracelet! Talia wants you to get her bracelet with the gold on it!" Oh, my God! There was no way on earth this had been made up. No one knew about the bracelet or its significance, or that Talia had been wearing it on the trip—least of all Rebecca, who had never met Talia before.

My first couple of conversations with Rebecca after that were filled with short messages from Talia to me, meant to help me get over the shock of the accident. Here is a little of what Talia said. I will explain their significance as needed:

The Universe Speaks

Talia loves you. She's with her dad.

Talia and her dad stayed at the plane with Frankie [Talia's friend] to keep her safe until help came. They kept Frankie in a daze to keep her from panicking. They protected Frankie.

Talia said her dad guided Sam to help find the plane.

Talia wants you to get her backpack. She's worried about it.

Talia said she had the best life, a charmed life, and still considers it the same way.

Talia is concerned about the dogs and her male horse; he will be upset with any change.

> Talia had two horses, a male and a female. Her male horse, Justinian, is an extremely emotional animal, and he was very attached to her. He reacts to change, so Talia's letting me know that she was concerned about him was significant.

Talia is concerned about her awards and wants you to make sure to get them for her.

> Talia had won numerous equestrian awards during the 2007 horse show year, and she was the number one equitation rider in her age group in our region. Talia had been looking forward to going to the awards banquets and receiving her awards in January.

*Tomorrow will be difficult for you. She doesn't want you to look at her this way. She had **no pain**.*

> The day after I got these messages from Talia, I was to go to the morgue to identify her body and to visit her in the flesh for the last time. No one knew that in the States. Only the members of my family who were with me in Panama knew. It was going to be a very difficult day for me, and in fact it was. I'll never forget the expression on Talia's face, ever. Talia didn't want me to remember her that way, and she was making a point of telling me that.

Talia said you were the best mother and will always be her mom.

Talia is with Stella. All passed family is with her. Stella has her by the arm, and she will be fine; she's there for you.

> Stella is my grandmother, who died in 1980. Stella is not a common name, not one to be guessed.

Talia wants photos and music as her memory. Said you know the song.

Collection

There is a particular song that was Talia's favorite at the time; I knew exactly which one it was. Also, Talia had many photos of herself riding that she was very proud of.

Talia wants you to look for the hummingbirds.

The hummingbird message didn't have any significance for me when I first got the message in Panama, but as soon as I got home it did. I started seeing hummingbirds hovering by my office window, looking in, all the time. In one instance it was pouring rain, and this little hummingbird was outside my window. I said out loud, "Talia, is that you? It has to be, because hummingbirds don't usually fly in the rain."

No more than ten minutes after I said that, I went to my back door, and as I was stepping out I saw, lying perfectly on the step, straight and centered, the same hummingbird I had just seen by my window on the other side of the house. It was wet and freshly dead. That was a confirmation from Talia, saying yes, Mom, it's me, and to prove it I'm making a statement!

Talia told you to get her diary or journal.

Besides the messages above, which I received right after Talia died, there were some remarkable events that further solidified my newfound beliefs.

Everyone I knew who was close to Talia and me, or close to Michael, her father, was clamoring for communications with them via Rebecca. One afternoon I was visiting a friend of mine, and we were talking about my upcoming birthday. I mentioned to her that my mom wanted to receive a message from Talia to find out what Talia wanted her to get me for my birthday. I commented that it would be amazing if Talia told my mom exactly what gift to get me and where to buy it.

Some friends of mine, a married couple, had a phone-in appointment with Rebecca no more than thirty minutes after the conversation I'd had about my birthday. During this couple's conversation, Talia said, "My mom's birthday is soon. I want you to get her a gift."

Talia then went on to describe the gift in detail, and where to buy it. What's remarkable is that she described not only the store, which had not even been in existence when she was alive, but the woman who had opened the store, where it was, and what it sold, giving the couple a detailed description of the item she wanted them to buy me. Right after they finished speaking with Rebecca, the husband got in the car and drove to that store, and on the table in the center of the room was the exact thing Talia had described. He bought it on the spot.

Well, my mom called Rebecca and left her request. While waiting for a return call, she started to search the Internet for a gift Talia might want me to have. She found what she thought was the perfect gift, and as she was looking at it on her computer screen, the phone rang. It was Rebecca returning her call. "Talia wants you to get her mom a glass heart." My mom almost fell off her chair. On the computer screen, at that very moment, was a photo of a glass heart. A pink glass heart.

Yet another unbelievable event happened to Rebecca while she was shopping. She was looking at some necklaces, and as she passed one in particular she heard Talia's voice say, "Buy that for my mom; it's her birthday." Rebecca asked, "Talia, is this you?" "Yes, buy that for my mom."

Rebecca bought the necklace, then called me and said she had something for me. I went to see her and had a reading, and it was then that she gave me the necklace Talia had picked out for me. It was made of crystals and stones; the meaning of one of the stones was "spirit manifestation." Another coincidence? Not in the least. It was Talia.

After hearing these messages and experiencing all of these "coincidences," and being blown away at the interconnectedness of them all, I had no doubt in my mind or heart or soul that Talia was sending them to me as signs that her consciousness was alive and with me still. As a reader who doesn't know Talia or me and has not lived our lives, you will never really feel the truth that I know so well. I'm telling you that before this time, I didn't believe in God, in the soul, or in the spirit world. To convince me that Talia is still here, communicating with me, took some really big substantiations. Really big.

Before the Crash

Even before the plane crash that killed Talia, events occurred that would reveal unseen forces at work.

Talia had just turned thirteen a few weeks before leaving for Panama with her dad for a weekend vacation, taking her friend Frankie with her. This wasn't the first time Talia had gone down to Panama with Michael—in fact, she had been there many times before. Michael went down to the islands at least twice a month, often taking Talia with him on his jaunts. Talia would surf, scuba dive, swim, explore, and commune with nature.

This particular trip was special to Talia because she was taking her friend with her. When I look back on it, what seemed like the beginning of a normal vacation was just a steppingstone on her soul's path, which she had walked throughout her life. A life that, despite ending in the flesh, has not ended in spirit.

On December 19, 2007, when Talia's dad picked her up for the weekend, I kissed and hugged her goodbye, as usual. I told her to be safe and that I would see her in a few days. That was it. I didn't consciously know that the hug and kiss I gave Talia as she left were going to be the last I would give her while she was living, or that this moment would be the last time I would ever see her alive.

I say *consciously* because when I look at some of my actions and thoughts in the weeks prior to Talia leaving, and when I think about what has happened since the accident, it seems I somehow knew that Talia wasn't coming home—at least in my subconscious awareness. There's no way I could have known consciously and not held onto Talia and kept her from leaving that night.

One odd thing that happened was that just a week before Talia left for Panama, I told her I wanted her to organize her jewelry. At this point Talia had her earrings and other miscellaneous things scattered in different drawers. I wanted her real jewels to be kept in one safe place so they wouldn't get lost. Most of her jewelry had sentimental value more than anything else, but it was important to me that she keep track of it.

So one night I gathered all her jewelry, and together we went through it, figuring out what was what. We put all the important pieces in a little jewelry box separate from her other things. That alone wasn't a big deal.

The Universe Speaks

Then, a few days after Talia had left for Panama, I went to my safety deposit box and took out all my jewelry and other sentimental items and organized them, labeling everything for Talia—this came from her great-great grandmother, this was her grandfather's, and so on. If something happened to me, I didn't want Talia to be stuck with a bunch of things, mostly heirloom pieces, and not know the significance of each piece or who had given it to me and when. I cleaned it all up for her—or so I thought.

OK, maybe I was in an organizing frenzy or something. But looking at it now, there's no way I would have been able to go through Talia's jewelry after she died. It would have sent me over the edge, though at some point I would have had to. For some reason I was made to do it ahead of time. It seems very odd to me.

Then, while Talia was on her trip, I had a very strange "vision." I imagined Talia calling me from Panama and telling me that something had happened to her dad, but that she and Frankie were OK. I told her to stay exactly where she was; I was heading down to Panama right then to get her. I told her not to move—I would be there.

I figured this vision was just my imagination, and I actually forgot about it until soon after my return from Panama. But as I thought more about it, I realized it *had been* Talia, telling me she was OK, right after the accident. Her spirit letting me know she was OK. That made me very happy, because when I first got back from Panama, I wondered why I hadn't "felt" the accident when it happened.

There are so many stories of parents or spouses who say they had a strange feeling the moment an accident happened or an interesting visit from someone at the exact time the person died, and I wondered why I had not had that. I had even felt sad about not having had that feeling. But once I realized I actually *had* experienced it through my vision, I was a bit relieved. I can't explain why, I just was.

Of course, this vision was very close to what actually happened just days later. Except that Talia didn't call me; someone else did.

It was on December 23, one day before Talia was supposed to come home, that I got "The Call."

"Kim, this is Bob (Talia's grandfather). The plane that Talia and Michael and Frankie were on is missing." What? I literally went into a coma for a few seconds. My heart stopped. I couldn't breathe.

Needless to say, from that moment on I have never been the same. The details of the excruciating next three days are all described in my book *Hummingbirds Don't Fly in the Rain*. This plane crash changed my life, my belief system—and my understanding of death, the life that I led with Talia, and the life she is leading now.

My Shift

How could Talia's "death" change how I look at the life we had together? Her "death" forced me to analyze every single decision I had made in raising her, everything we had done together, and every single word I had ever said to Talia while she was growing up. I questioned every single move I had made and how it related to her. Had I made the right decision letting her show her horse so much? Had I done the right thing saying no to this and yes to that? It didn't stop. I questioned everything.

Looking back, I realized that how I raised Talia made her the person she was while here with me and prepared her perfectly for the next part of her soul's journey, her life after the accident. In fact, Talia herself sent me a message letting me know that how I had raised her is what made her the person she was on earth and the spirit she is now; it gave her the ability to be at the level she is now, learning all that she's learning.

Here are the exact words she sent me through my friend G, the person whose conversations with Talia follow in this book:

Tell her my time there was divine. She did everything in a perfect way and was (is) an awesome mother. She got me here perfectly.

My mom got me here perfectly. That's why she has no regrets, as she shouldn't, ever. She will share in this reward, and it's far beyond tremendous. There are no words to describe it.

Those words are Talia's—but she was actually quoting me. A couple of days before Talia communicated this to G, I had told another person I had absolutely no regrets regarding my time with Talia. So when she said, "That's why she has no regrets," it confirmed two things for me: one, that Talia is with me all the time, listening to me, and two, that I was in fact the best mother I could have been to her. All my questioning stopped. This is what gives me a sense of peace.

Talia

VERY SOON AFTER TALIA WAS BORN, her father and I got divorced. Now that I look back on my life, I see that raising Talia on my own was meant to be. Most of the lessons she learned in this life could not have happened if her dad and I had stayed married.

When I say that I raised Talia on my own, I really did. Her dad was around, and he did take care of his financial responsibility to care for her, but he was extremely busy and really did not see Talia much at all. The time that Talia and he were together was made up mostly of short weekend visits.

While I don't want to take away from his time with Talia, I do want you, the reader, to understand how much time Talia and I were together and how very close we were. Raising Talia was my destiny, my sole purpose in life. I was a full-time mom, and I loved it more than anything else in the world. I worked hard to raise her well and *consciously*.

It wasn't an easy job, though *job* is not the correct word; a truer word would be *honor*. It's not easy to teach guide, and mentor a child from conception onward. Especially knowing that everything you say or do—and everything that child witnesses, experiences, and thinks about—will have a deep impact on his or her understanding and possibilities in this world and the next. Trying to give Talia information without giving answers, without influencing the direction of her thought or causing walls to be built around her mind, was the most difficult task I could have had. And I loved every moment of it.

Of course, at the time I was raising Talia, I didn't know that my influence and guidance would affect her life *after life*. I couldn't have known it then, because that was when I didn't believe in an afterlife. But I did know that her time on earth, with me in this life, would be molded by my every word and move. And because I wanted not to shape her thoughts and beliefs but allow her to grow and form her own, I had to be extremely diligent.

Teaching without limiting is the most difficult task there is. I watched over myself every second of the day. Each word, action, response—even the inflection of my voice—had to be used precisely to ensure that they were not influencing Talia's thoughts and beliefs but were merely stepping stones for her to walk on while forming her own code for life. My goal was to keep Talia's mind open and not to stifle her or cause the doorways of her mind, leading to all the universe offered, to close.

Looking back at Talia's life here with me, I'm confident that I accomplished my goal. I know this because Talia was an amazing child and person, an independent-minded, analytical, gracious, joyful, generous, and thoughtful girl who was wise beyond her years. Yes, I'm her mother, and all mothers think their kids are the greatest, smartest, most perfect kids on earth. But I'm not the kind of person to give credit where it's not due—in fact, I'm pretty critical. So when I say that Talia was everything I say she was, it's true.

Here's a portion of something the head of Talia's upper school said about her at her memorial. I think it really exemplifies who Talia was from an outsider's perspective:

> "The first time I met Talia, I was struck by her extraordinary independence, her contemplative focus, her philosophic composure, and her unflappable maturity. She was *two* at the time!
>
> "Every parenting book ever written, of course, refers to this time in the toddler's life as 'the terrible twos,' which makes my first memory of Talia all the more remarkable. Here was a child who, after being out of the womb and out in the world for just twenty-four months or so, comported herself with thoughtfulness, self-assurance, and grace—qualities that would become quintessentially Talia over the years. . . .
>
> "When you're a teacher, you spend a lot of time wondering what your students will be like as adults. Sometimes it's difficult or even impossible to imagine what some kids will be like as grownups. This was never the case with Talia. She went about her business at Crane with such efficacy and aplomb that it was as though we had already had a glimpse of the adult Talia. Indeed, she figured out and accomplished more in thirteen years than many people do in a long lifetime."

Talia was true to herself. Everything she did was authentic and came from her heart, her soul, her true self. This is best seen through Talia's own writings. Here are some examples of her views about life, found in the autobiography she was assigned to write in school the year before the crash.

Collection

My Life Messages

Some of my life lessons have really helped me through a lot of situations. It took me a while to compile a list because there is a lot of big life messages that everyone should follow, like be kind and don't kill, but I tried to think of other life messages that people often forget about or put aside more often. The ones I chose could end up being a lot more important than you think in the long run. Here is what I chose:

1) Life isn't fair; don't think it is.
2) Be an optimist; believe the impossible.
3) Never give up; fight till the end.
4) Do what you believe is right; even if it means not going with the flow.
5) Believe none of what you hear and half of what you see.
6) Listen to your instincts; follow your gut.

Just One Day

I have thought long and hard about whom I would want to switch places with. I even wrote a paper on one person who I would switch places with. I read it to myself a couple of times. I decided that it was really horrible. I can't possibly imagine in my wildest dreams what it would be like to not be myself. I love my life so much I am lost when I try to think about what my life could have been.

Maybe for a day I could switch with the children in Rwanda so that at least for a day they could have a warm place to sleep, a meal, and clean water, so that they could live one more day. And maybe for one day I would really understand what it meant to suffer.

This chapter was the hardest for me but I am glad I did it. Maybe one day all little boys and little girls will have a warm bed to sleep in and food to eat every day. Not just for one day.

TALIA
Lively, friendly, hyper, smart
Sibling of Zippy, Gunther and Layla
Lover of ice cream
Who fears spiders
Who needs chocolate chip cookies
Who gives laughter
Who would like to see and travel the world
Resident of Sterling Silver Stables
Klein

(The "siblings" Talia referred to here were her dogs!)

Stop and Think: What is a Hero?
I think a hero is someone who is completely selfless in all of their actions. Someone who takes risks for others, and takes time out of their own life for someone else's life.
I think that parents are heroes too, because they raise us to be who we are and put up with us when we're not so grateful.

Collection

Here's the letter Talia wrote to me when she was assigned to write a letter home, giving me a progress report on how she was doing in school.

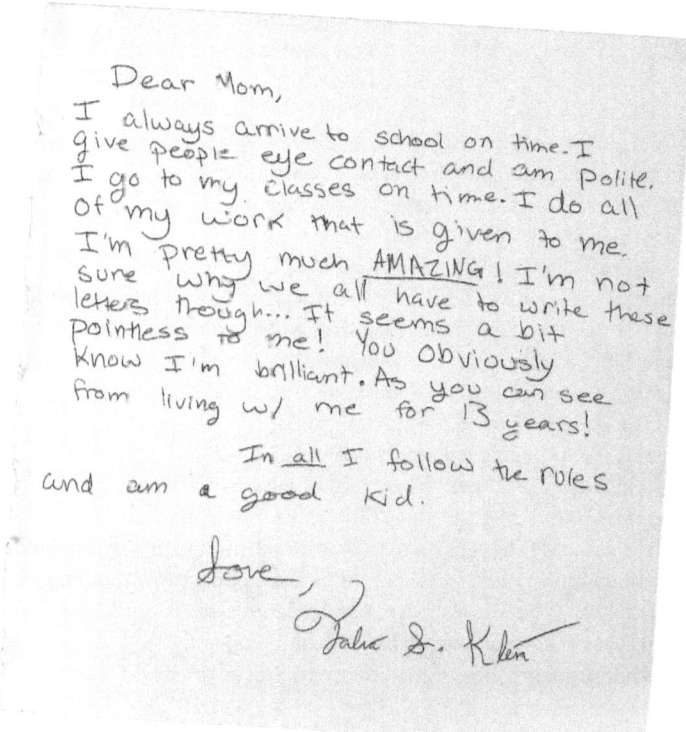

Dear Mom,
I always arrive to school on time. I give people eye contact and am polite. I go to my classes on time. I do all of my work that is given to me. I'm pretty much AMAZING! I'm not sure why we all have to write these letters though... It seems a bit pointless to me! You obviously know I'm brilliant. As you can see from living w/ me for 13 years!
   In all I follow the rules and am a good kid.
       Love,
       Talia S. Klein

Talia was truly a special person. Adults loved to converse with her. She was enthralled by conversations about the universe, whether there's a God, moral codes, quantum physics, music, literature, movies, food. She actually preferred to talk with adults than kids. But Talia was still a kid. She played sports, hung out with friends, loved volleyball, and loved riding her horses and competing in horse shows.

Talia also was a great student, and she loved school so much that she was torn between missing school and going to horse shows. One time I wanted to take her to Six Flags Magic

Mountain on a school day, and she freaked out. No way was she willing to miss a day of school. It's not that I was a bad mom for wanting her to miss a day; it was just that Talia worked very hard and was always ahead in her assignments, so she was more than capable of missing a day of school for some good old fun. Even her teachers didn't mind that she "ditched" a day here and there for horse shows or whatever came up.

There was something unique about Talia. People called her an "old soul." Truly she was; she emanated wisdom.

Talia decided for herself that she didn't believe in God. That wasn't something I ever told her. Her father and I didn't believe in God, but I wasn't going to put my thoughts into Talia's head. She had to think for herself. It's interesting, though, that her belief system started to change as she neared thirteen.

Growing up, Talia would tell me that some of her dreams came true: sometimes she would dream that an event would occur, or that this or that would happen, and then it would actually happen, quite soon after her dream. She asked me if this was possible. Of course it's possible, I told her, because it's happening.

Well, those prophetic dreams of hers led her to start thinking about the possibility that there was more to us, more to the universe, than just our bodies. There was something else going on. Talia started to ask whether people could see into the future, and she said if that was possible, then maybe there were souls, or some sort of energy that enabled people to do this, since our regular bodies alone didn't have this ability.

Then Talia asked if I thought there were spirits all around us that we couldn't see but that animals could. This thought was spurred by Laura, an animal communicator I hired to "talk" to one of Talia's horses, Justinian, who sometimes acted up with her. When Laura "spoke" with Justinian and we heard what he had to say, both Talia and I were amazed. That conversation actually changed her understanding of the world and started Talia on an entirely new path.

When Talia realized that the animals were thinking, talking, and communicating with people and other animals, she concluded there must be a consciousness beyond the body. If that was the case, maybe there were spirits and other consciousnesses all around us, living in a world we couldn't see but that was truly there.

It was at this time that Talia asked about parallel universes—what were they, and did they exist? I told her I wasn't able to give her any real answers about whether they existed or even what they were, but there were scientists, quantum physicists, who were studying that very topic. Now that Talia was able to put a title to something she was so fascinated with, she decided, on the spot, that she wanted to become a quantum physicist instead of a patent litigator.

Collection

This revelation, as I called it, happened two weeks before Talia left on her final trip to Panama. It's amazing to me that right after Talia's mind opened to the possibility that there's more to the world, life, and the universe than what we see, she left her body and moved on into the realm she was so curious about.

The timing of Talia's death may seem coincidental, but, looking at the psychic preparation she went through and her interest in topics well beyond her years—even beyond most adults' thought processes—it seems that she was preparing for her next adventure: her life in the afterlife. In fact, now that I have the benefit of hearing from Talia from her new life, I realize that is exactly what she said had happened.

It's extremely hard for me to think that Talia was only supposed to be here with me for a short time. But when I heard from Talia herself that her life here was in preparation for her life there, I realized that my life's purpose was indeed to raise Talia in a way that prepared her for where she is now. Her true purpose in the afterlife is to learn and to transmit the messages and lessons found in her communications to me and to the world. I have no doubt that I helped her accomplish that purpose. In Talia's own words:

My mom was very, very mindful of how she raised me. Do you see the fruit of it? She WILL share in the rewards of the fruit of my life, of my "being" who I am, because she was instrumental in it and a central part of my life. . . . It has nothing to do with my great honor of being her daughter or of my affection and LOVE for her as my mom. My love for her has no bounds and she knows this. I said before you had to be outside to see in; there are much deeper truths here than is readily apparent

The life I lived WAS for an example. I didn't know it then and if you would have told me I would have laughed. I wouldn't have thought that was necessarily true, but it was necessary and it was true. You may not always know whom you are influencing. I influenced people then without noticing it. You're always more than you think you are. But to know that is to trust it, that you can be used in a divine way, whether you know it or not.

I know in my heart that because Talia was educated in a way that enabled her mind to remain open to the possibilities of the universe, she was able to enter the next phase of her soul's journey at a very high level. This has allowed her to learn the lessons she has learned so far extremely quickly, and it has enabled her to move close to the source of all things. This high level of learning in the spirit world is what allows her to know what she now knows and, even more important, it allows her to be able to communicate that information to us here, in this earthly realm.

The Universe Speaks

Talia; a few of her self portraits

"G"

The words that follow in the dialogues (Part Two) are Talia's words—actual statements and information downloads that she has spoken and entrusted to my close friend "G" (abbreviated for privacy).

Who is G? He is my very dear friend. Since G was a young boy, he has been in touch with his instincts, always able to listen to his strong gut feelings. As he got older, these visceral sensations became stronger, and the more G listened to his body, the clearer and more definite his instincts became. Visions flourished as he began to hear and see the spirits. He also developed the ability to read people; at one point his ability to see auras around people was so pronounced he actually asked for that ability to go away, and it did.

Talia is not the first spirit G has heard or spoken to, but his communications with her have broken all barriers previously known to G and, according to Talia herself, the depth of the communications between her and G has never been reached before in any other spirit communications. The spirit world is in awe of their communications. As Talia said:

Some won't believe it, but this hasn't been done before, not on this level, not in this depth. People have been communing with "spirits" ever since there were people in the physical realm, but it hasn't been recorded in this depth before. Mostly it has been bits and pieces.

What is it that enables G to hear and communicate with Talia? As Talia says in the following pages, anyone and everyone is capable of communicating with spirits, but most people are simply unaware of this. Unaware because of the belief system they were raised with, were indoctrinated with, or have chosen for themselves. In some cases, their lives are just so wildly busy that they are unable to hear any communications that might come their way. Their minds are never quiet enough for the spirits' voices to be heard. But regardless of the many possible reasons for not being able to hear from loved ones or others, G is open and able to.

How does G hear Talia? Does he hear her voice in his head or does it come to him from the external world? What does her voice sound like to him? How does he feel when he is speaking with her? Is he in a meditative state or walking around doing normal things when he hears her?

Well, G has heard Talia, felt her, and seen her while in all states of being, from the very relaxed, quiet place that some would call a meditative state to going about his daily routine and all of a sudden hearing Talia speak to him as if she were standing right beside him. Sometimes he hears her actual voice; sometimes he hears her thoughts in his head. It does not matter what he is doing or how hectic his life is; what matters is whether or not his mind is clear and quiet.

If G's mind is quiet, he can hear and communicate with Talia regardless of what his outward world is like. There was an instance when Talia spoke to G while he was working. He heard her voice so loud and clear that he thought the people he was with could hear her as well. At other times, while in a meditative state, he has not only spoken to Talia but has seen her, touched her, and spent time with her. There are no rules as to how, when, and where G speaks with Talia. It just happens.

Talia's communications with G started off with a simple message meant to help me and evolved into hundreds of hours of actual discussions between G and Talia. Practically every word between them was carefully transcribed at the time they were heard or spoken. The date and time of each talk was kept from mid-April of 2008 forward.

Before April, Talia's communications with G were short and sporadic. We had no idea they would evolve into what they have become, and so, in the beginning, G simply scribbled some notes about his and Talia's communications for the purpose of telling me what Talia had said. Once we realized that Talia was not going to stop talking to G, and that their communications were growing deeper and more extensive, G started to keep a journal of all of their talks. As she spoke, he wrote; as he thought or spoke, he wrote. The conversations were written as they occurred.

In places, especially at the very beginning of the dialogues, these conversations will seem jumpy or disjointed—maybe even confusing—and sometimes rather personal. But in order for Talia's message to get out to the world the way she presented it, I wanted the conversations to be communicated the way they were originally written down at the time they occurred. I did not want to alter anything to make the text read better or to clarify or interpret what she said. I wanted to leave everything as close to the original as possible, with very little editing. So basically, what you'll be reading is exactly what was said and how it was said.

The only change I've made to the actual conversations was to remove personal information between G and Talia or between Talia and me. Not everything Talia said was meant for the world, and you will read her words to that effect in some of the communications where I left the original dialogue without deleting anything.

The reasons for some of the disjointedness are twofold. One, in the beginning Talia and G were actually learning to communicate with each other. Talia was new to multidimensional communication and was still learning how to communicate with us here. The ability of the spirits to reach us, and for us to hear the spirits, is a learned ability, which Talia speaks about

Collection

in the dialogues themselves. Though everyone has that ability, the skill needs to be fostered, for us and the spirits. So as both Talia and G learn to communicate with each other, the conversations evolve and become much clearer and easier to understand.

Second, some of the questions G asks Talia are answered by her before he has had a chance to actually formulate the questions in words. Therefore, he has written Talia's answers, but they seem to come out of nowhere, when in fact they are Talia's response to G's thoughts, which she read before he even knew he had those thoughts.

There are things said and people mentioned that will make no sense to you, the reader, so where we thought it necessary to help clarify Talia's message, we have added some narrative, trying not to interrupt the flow of the dialogue. There is not always a reason or a lesson in the talks. Some are just friendly chats. That is part of what Talia wants the world to know: conversations between the spirits and us are as normal and natural as any conversation two people here would have. Communication with the spirit world does not have to be about meaningful, spiritual, "important" things; it can be just a conversation about day-to-day stuff. Just a hello or brief words of encouragement.

Yes, many of her messages are lessons—some of them deep and meaningful lessons about life and the universe—but not all of her messages are obvious. Some are very subtle.

But all of them are from Talia, who received this information from the spirit that moves through all things.

Regardless of whether you believe G is speaking to Talia in the spirit world or not, these writings are still important and intriguing messages that stand on their own, so please be open-minded when reading them.

So here we go. Here are Talia's words (in italics; G's words are in regular text). And here I am, Talia's mom, the previously devoted non-believer, now a believer. I don't doubt, I don't question, and I am not even a speck skeptical that the following words are indeed Talia's words, spoken by her to us, from where we call Heaven.

January 23, 2008

The Day of Talia's Memorial

Tell my mom I'm OK.

Talia?

Yes, tell my mom I'm OK.

OK, I will when I see her.

TELL MY MOM I'M OK!

I will, I promise!

    And G kept his promise to Talia. That day, at the luncheon after Talia's memorial—her Celebration of Life, as I called it—G finally got me alone and told me that Talia was OK. When he said it, I looked at him and said, matter of factly, "Yes, I know."
    G wasn't sure I understood exactly how sure he was that Talia was OK or whether I thought he was just placating me, so he said it again. "No, really, she is OK."
    "I know!" I said, making it clear that I too knew. Taking a chance that he might think I was "out to lunch," I decided to tell G that I had been speaking to Talia through Rebecca, and that Talia had been giving Rebecca many messages for me letting me know that not only was she OK, but that she was with her dad and doing great.
    G was excited and relieved. That's when he told me Talia had been communicating with him directly. That same night, once G got back home, he called me. Talia had another message for me.
    "Tell my mom that she will be OK, and that she is being healed."
    G continued to hear from Talia off and on for the next few months. As time went on, her messages to him and for me and others became longer, and their interactions, their dialogues became more detailed. What follows are those conversations between G and Talia that began in April 2008.

The Universe Speaks

April 2008

April 20

Talia, you had a perfect life.

It is even more perfect where I am now. My mom is being healed.

April 21

6:20 AM
Good morning, Talia.

Good morning.

Are you here?

I am with my mom.

I like yellow. But my mom does not know that.

Why did you tell me that?

Just because you would know it was me and to tell you to believe yourself. Always believe yourself.

> Talia telling G that she liked yellow was very significant for me. Not because I didn't know about Talia's liking the color yellow (I didn't), but because just a few days before her telling that to G, I had put a bouquet of yellow roses in her room. I feel that by Talia telling G she liked yellow, she was really sending a message to me that she was aware of the roses I had put in her room and liked that I had done that.

April 23

Talia, sometimes I don't know if this is you or God speaking to me, you sound so similar.

Collection

We are so completely in agreement there is hardly any separation at all. Where I am is more beautiful than where you are by like a billion times. Where I am it's perfect, perfection. There are horses here.

I want to be where you are.

You have things to do. Nobody knows all the things you know . . . believe in yourself. . . . At Thanksgiving I saw who you were . . . that is why I liked you. I told my mom I liked you. I wanted to talk to you too. . . .

> Talia is referring to Thanksgiving 2006. G and another friend joined Talia, our family, and me for dinner. While sitting at the dinner table, G had a very unusual, very spiritual experience. He saw Talia in the spirit, in front of a bronze-colored door, holding it open and looking at him, inviting him to go through that door. What was beyond the door was blackness. She was wearing a crown on her head, and he heard a voice in his head, who he felt might be God, tell him, "She will be with me." At one point he looked down and noticed that he seemed to be wearing WWI clothes, although this vision disappeared the moment he acknowledged it. While G was having these visions, which I was unaware of, I noticed he had a strange look on his face. I just figured he was a bit uncomfortable sitting between two people he didn't know at the table. Little did I know!

So why didn't you talk to me more that day?

Convention. I could tell you were unconventional but I didn't have those words at the time. Tell my mom I love her.

She knows.

Just call her and tell her I love her. What is more important than that?

April 29

Good morning, Talia.

Good morning.

> G was thinking about the Ginko tree that Talia's school had planted in her memory, and the words that were carved into the stone planter around the tree. Most of the words had been chosen by a friend of mine and me, with the help of Talia herself. I asked Talia to confirm to me, through Rebecca, that the words we had picked were the right words to use; she

confirmed that she liked them and okayed them. Unfortunately, a couple of the words were changed by the parents group at Talia's school, who were paying for the memorial. My friend and I were not happy about that change, nor was G, and though Talia was not thrilled about one of the words that ended up being used, she understood why the parents group had chosen it. What follows is Talia's discussion with G about these words as G thought about her school and the special tree.

That's why I want them to know about my life, to lead them to this place. That's important. My words are much better than their words. Much more precise and meaningful. They that are going to be touched by them, changed by them, will be. So why water them down and make them harder to understand? Did you not think I had help; they were born of the Spirit.

To bring forth fruit. To change people's lives. Their intellect traps them. Their thoughts circle in their heads until it becomes a prison. I want them to be free. There's nothing better than freedom.

My mom showed me how to be free, to think your own thoughts and not what people tell you to think. If you're thinking someone else's thoughts how can you be free? It's your birthright to be free. It's a yearning everyone has. So why would someone make a prison for others to live in?

That's a good question.

Yes, it is. We are all created in God's image. Is God free? He's only bound by his word. Which has no boundaries. People are enslaving each other on the earth. This needs to stop. Most of them aren't even aware of what they're doing to themselves and each other. He was sent to free you. Listen to Him; He is truth. The truth will set you free.

That's what you've been trying to tell people all along.

It takes responsibility and some work. That's what they fear. Which is another prison.

Tell her—Mom—wisdom is the PRINCIPAL THING; therefore, get wisdom and with all your getting, get understanding. Knowledge puffs up, but love builds up.

April 30

I liked green tea. I had fun that day we tested the tea.

> G thought this was a strange thing for Talia to tell him, but when he told me she had said it I knew exactly why she had mentioned it. It was a message for me! Talia and I both loved green tea, and one day we decided to do a taste test of many different types of green tea. There are dozens and they all taste

Collection

different. So we tested about fifteen different types and found out exactly which ones we liked for hot versus cold tea. We had a lot of fun that day!

Are you going to talk to me today? You don't have your pen!

G realized that he had no pen.

Tell you what, I will walk with you and you do whatever you do

Tell Mom to be patient; that is one thing she is learning. Tell her that her prayers have been answered.

Just then the phone rang. It was me, calling G.

That's Mom—she will ask you what's going on.

G answered the phone.

Talia, what's Gunther doing today?

Gunther can tell you all about me, though he's had a hard time coping with it all.

Gunther was Talia's and my German Shepard. At the time of this conversation with Talia, he was "dead" and with Talia in spirit. Right after the crash, after Talia "died," Gunther was so upset that he actually made himself sick. So sick that he died! When Gunther was sick I had Laura, the animal communicator, talk to Gunther to try to find out what was wrong with him, because the vets were not having any luck with their tests. Gunther told Laura that he wanted to be with Talia, and that he was going to be with her. As he was dying Gunther told Laura that he saw Talia surrounded in light and that Talia's hands were reaching for him.

The things that I've told you are true. Every one of them. It's a waste of time to doubt.

G was doubting whether he was hearing Talia correctly.

Frankie will be all right; she just has to find her place of peace. It lies within her; she just doesn't know it yet.

My mom is excited about our communications. She just doesn't understand why she can't do it yet but she will. It's hard bridging the gap of the flesh.

I didn't hurt at all (the crash). I was received up into His arms and welcomed, then sent back to help Frankie.

My dad and I are closer now than we ever were. He thanked me for my prayers for him. He understands everything now. We have fun together.

The Universe Speaks

During the years before the crash, Talia's relationship with her father was not easy for her. Just a short time before the crash they were beginning to regain their closeness. So when Talia speaks of her being closer to her father now, it's very reassuring to me that, one, she and her dad are happy together, and two, that she is indeed speaking to G.

My mom will be all right, He promised, and she will grow in understanding. I'm glad you have your pencil now.

G is laughing.

Laughter works well, like a medicine, and you need it sometimes. I'm glad to give it to you and that's what HE sounds like laughing through His people. He smiles a lot. He is all the fullness of the Godhead bodily and Pure Love without end. He is Everything and all there is without end. He is everything and ALL there is. There are so many words I want to say, and I'll keep talking with you.

Kim will be fine.

Why did you use her name?

That's what I was told. By HE who cannot lie. Who is All Truth, the Light of Lights. In whom is no darkness nor shadow of turning. These words are truth. I love you.

You know I love you too.

Thank you for taking my message. For your time.

Talia, you know there's nothing I'd rather do.

I know that and that's great! You know you can't share this with everybody—they'll think you are crazy.

I know that.

But I'm glad you're sharing it with whom you do.

My pleasure.

Mine is greater.

Tell her—Mom—that her prayer was answered today. She's always heard. Don't worry about the small stuff.

About that goddess stuff . . .

> G was thinking that he now understood why so many cultures believe in gods and goddesses. People in the past must have spoken to various spirits in the way Talia is speaking to him, and their words, like hers, were so

28

Collection

> powerful they were made into gods and goddesses. He thought that Talia would have been called a goddess too.

I can't really argue with you because we're all part of Him, so in that way it's true, but I don't really feel like a goddess, not the way you think. But I do absolutely feel AMAZING! World without end! There are so many truths, so MANY paths but only one true GOD. "Everyone will find ME in the end."

So much here is unspeakable. It's difficult for me to try to explain, to put it into words. This is a language beyond words.

May 2008

May 2

*There's no use telling you things you already know. But there's a difference knowing something in your **head** and KNOWING something in your **heart**, in your spirit, in your soul, deep down.*

You have an unction from the HOLY ONE and you know all things. I'm just here as a reminder, a counselor through HIM.

You knew I was always going to be a teacher.

No, I didn't know that.

Yes, you did.

Yes, I did—I remember now.

Of course you do; you saw it, you just forgot.

Now I remember, the power of the flesh.

> G realized that he did remember knowing somehow that she would someday be a teacher.

The flesh has no power but the power you allow it to have.

I can't argue with that.

No, that would be stupid and you're not. So when you act stupid realize it's just an act. You're just acting stupid.

I always make you laugh.

The Universe Speaks

Yes, you do, every single time.

I'm glad. It's such a tremendous pleasure helping others; if people realized that there wouldn't be so many problems. The payback is stupendous. Pass that on to people: THAT never fails.

Thank you, Talia.

My PLEASURE.

Thank you for being open to me. Mom too.

She's growing in wisdom. She asked to. Ask and you receive. People so overcomplicate everything. The truth is always simple and easy to understand once you boil it down.

Tell her my time there was Divine. She did everything in a perfect way and was—is—an awesome mother. She got me here perfectly.

You don't have to edit my words—she'll get it. Tell her to take care of HERSELF now. She's building something awesome now.

You tie it together so . . .

You can't help but tie it all together; it's all tied together.

You know you're blowing my mind here.

That's OK.

You know I wish I could record this.

Yes, wouldn't that be great.

This is bizarre.

Not really, this communication with the spirits has always been going on.

I have to go.

I know.

I don't have a watch.

> G thought that was a strange thing for Talia to say, since you do not need a watch in the spirit, but when he told me about this I laughed because Talia never wore a watch unless she absolutely had to. She hated watches. G didn't know this about Talia. She didn't like the feeling on her wrist or the constraints of time. When Talia says these kinds of things to G, it's great because it not only confirms to G that he really is hearing Talia, it confirms that to me too.

Go.

Collection

I don't want to.

You have to.

Go. I'm going out there with you. Of course I can be more than one place.

6:00 PM
Thanks for the help today.

Any time. I learn from what you are doing. I learn from everything you do. That's where the gods and goddesses came from, from us helping. We have to help; we're compelled to do it. How could we not?

You could refuse.

No, we couldn't. There's only joy and peace here, a peace so profound it surpasses all understanding.

How long will you do this?

As long as you need it.

How did you become so wise?

HE is.

The light brings understanding. The Light illuminates the words to quicken the understanding to that which is beyond words. Keep listening. I love to talk.

We—Mom and I—use to walk and talk a lot. Ask her what we talked about. That will make her think. RE-MEM-BRANCE. Tying all the pieces together into one coherent whole. Piecing it together. Nothing is really apart except for the contrast of the separation.

May 4

7:00 AM
Write.

What do you want me to write?

Just keep writing. You're going to find out some things about your life you need to know. You don't need confirmation or validation, you just need the truth and the truth bears witness to itself. Your heart always knows what's true. You'll not be led astray. I know your heart.

8:04 AM
Thank you for being my friend, Talia.

The Universe Speaks

THANK YOU *for being mine.*

2:28 PM
Hi, Talia!

Hi!

How are you doing?

You know how I'm doing . . . perfect. All things are yours. Spirits, this dialogue, this conversation, all things. Tell her—Mom—all things are hers too. Just tell her to claim it. She can do it.

May 5

7:08 AM
You're more alive than anyone I know.

  G was thinking about some friends of his.

I know . . . . They are cut off from their life, from the truth, by their thinking. As you think in your heart so are you. You are what you are by what you think.

People know. They sense the truth; it's just out of reach for most. What a source of frustration. Some people kill themselves over it, others live in desperation over the contradiction of being judged and misunderstood by what they really are and what they are perceived to be. People should love one another and not judge one another. There is one judge; He does not need help.

I have no doubt.

As you shouldn't. Your lack of time is the push you need. You will never have enough of it there. Redeeming the time . . . The days are evil, in a manner of speaking.

Talia, is there anything you don't know?

Yes, lots.

12:45 PM
  While on his lunch break G thought about how excited he was about his communications with Talia. He thought about how the meanings of the words are so deep and multifaceted—there is no explaining it. He realized that what Talia had said, "They that are going to get it will get it and they that are not aren't; people that are not going to get it are not for a variety

Collection

of reasons," was true mostly because people have prejudged her words and are closed off to them and their meanings.

So what do you think?

Well said. See, Mom said you were articulate.

G was laughing about this.

I'm glad I can make you laugh. When you read this to Mom she'll laugh too.

I have not changed much, only grown.

G started thinking about the color of green, noticing it more, and thought about the meaning of green as a color. He thought it meant growth.

Yes, that is the meaning of green, growth. That's why I was pointing it out, and yellow and brown and gold. Any questions?

And grey?

Wisdom.

And brown?

Wisdom too.

Why?

Grey speaks of the maturity of wisdom.

And brown?

Brown speaks of being grounded in it.

Let me ask the right questions.

You can ask any questions you want.

Inspire me.

You already are. You should put this in your notebook.

G was writing down the discussion about colors he was having with Talia on a little piece of paper, since he was outside and not near his notebook.

OK, why?

It's easier to keep track of.

Let everything be done decently and in order.

Yes, that is a good saying. Why do you do the things you do?

The Universe Speaks

I thought I was asking the questions.

Yes, but that's a question you should ask yourself.

You know you blow my mind.

I know . . . I'm blowing your mind out of proportion, expanding it.

I feel unworthy.

Everybody's worthy, they just don't know it.

Think about "singleness of purpose."

I'll have to think about that.

Yes, please do.

You totally blow me away.

Thank you, I'm glad you think so.

You know how humble that makes me?

That's a good thing. The world could use a lot more of that.

I have to slow down to talk to you.

      G knew she meant slow her vibrations down.

I'm glad you do.

We don't mind, we just wish more people would listen.

There's not anything that's not interconnected with everything else.

Is that true?

That's absolutely true, and it can be proven. By mathematics, by inner vision, by intuition and by the Light. The Light that lights the life of all men. WHATEVER questions ANYONE has, the answers are there if they seek them.

You're going to find some things out you never dreamed of in the near future.

I don't know if I like the sound of that.

NO, it's good stuff.

      G was thinking about how tired he was feeling.

It does weary the flesh; your vibrations have to be faster. The whole universe is on a vibrational level for balance to maintain harmony. That's why it's easy to tell if someone is out of harmony; their very essence is not vibrating in harmony, and vice versa. It's a very delicate balance.

Collection

You're right about nothing being a coincidence and everything means something, although some would contend with you about that out of ignorance.

Wow, that's pretty heavy.

Yes, it is. That speaks of the Art of Life. That's an art you should study.

I will.

I know you will . . . I don't waste time.

Thank you for sharing your wisdom with me.

Thank you for listening . . . time to go.

I know.

Go ahead and go. I'll help you. You will feel me.

May 6

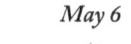

G was thinking about what I told him Gunther had said. Guther had told Laura that Talia liked to play games. Laura asked Gunther, "What kind of games does Talia play?" Gunther answered, "Like chess, only with people."

8:09 AM
Talia, I can't write down everything you say to me.

Of course you can't—that would be unrealistic. There is a message here for certain people to MOVE them in a CERTAIN direction. It is like a chess game and it's a grand game, to move the pieces TOGETHER in a CERTAIN way. I KNOW what I am doing. It's far beyond this world.

G was thinking that he cannot possibly describe some of the visions he has while talking to Talia, or the meaning of some of the downloads he receives while talking with her.

No, you can't describe what you're seeing any more than I can describe what I am being. Just let them flow. . . .

You know what this means to me?

Do you know what it means to me? This is IMPORTANT. Don't get hung up on the images and ashes.

G was looking at the small vial of Talia's ashes that he carries with him.

The Universe Speaks

They are pointing to something much grander. Your thoughts are more real than anything else there. They truly create. I see your questions forming before they are FORMED; that is why nothing's hidden that shall not be revealed. You are a tool to be used by the Creator. Fight a good fight, not against what IS going to be regardless. Of course he can use ANY THING to get his work done, but it's his good pleasure to give you the kingdom. This is a free gift to all who will receive it.

Why are you doing this?

I wanted someone to tell me these things when I was there but nobody did, even though there were some that could. I was astounded when I got here and found out the truth of the simplicity of it all, the obviousness of it all. It's a treasure not so well hidden. Why do people deceive themselves?

Why do they?

They bask in their pride. It's like a wall that blocks them off from the truth, from the obvious. After a while that wall is just as real to them as anything could be; remember, your thoughts create things.

When the sages talked of illusions, it was something REAL as illusions. It appeared to them as illusion because they knew that thought and methods of thought could dissolve what was perceived as real. Well, it IS real but created by the mind—that's about as REAL as it gets. So when people CHANGE their mind they change what was created by them so that it appears as an illusion. It's not an illusion, it's real. So when a person decides to change it, it changes and THAT is real.

That's a small blurb on the nature of reality. The nature of reality is living real. BEING true and speaking the truth out of a sincere heart CHANGES things. Alters the nature of reality: that's FLUID. It is not static. That is why they (scientists, true seekers) can't pin it down. It's not somewhere; it's everywhere and nowhere at once. It IS the true nature of being.

Talia, you know I don't know these things.

I know you don't, that's why I'm telling you! But you have perceived them.

Yes, I know them but I don't know them.

Yes, not in your head, few do, but they need to. This could change everything.

Wow.

Yes, that's MOM upside down. The revelation of the light of truth NURTURES, causes one to grow, straight and true. That's the change no politician can bring you, that's the change no politician can even promise you.

Yes, I am in POSITION to do this now; like the queen, I can move ANYWHERE.

Which piece am I?

Collection

Sometimes you're just a pawn. I don't mean that in a bad way, but you know that's true.

I know.

Now you're aware of it.

Thank you. I can take your criticism.

It's not criticism; it's just the truth. The truth will set you free, G.

Talia, this is so absolutely awesome!

I know, it's a true message of change.

I LOVE my friends and I'm sorry my going hurt them. It has purpose.

> That day I had been speaking to one of my friends, a parent of one of Talia's friends from school. We were talking about the kids being hurt and missing Talia.

9:22 AM

My ashes were my essence there.

What does that mean?

Think about it.

Do you want me to carry them with me?

Yes. My mom does.

She—Mom—asked for this to happen today. Tell her not to get distracted by the things of this world.

10:40 AM

Everything is tied together. It is one of the mysteries of living the ART of LIFE, realizing it's ALL tied together. World of One. You see how that truth has been twisted by the "well-meaning fools."

Talia, there is no way I can express my thanks to you.

I know, you don't have to pound your point across to me—I got it.

OK.

OK, now we're on equal terms.

What do you mean?

I mean, don't make an idol out of me. I'm not one.

The Universe Speaks

Is this chastisement?

No, not at all, just a fact.

Well, I've got to adore you.

That's OK, I adore you too.

Really?

What do you think, I'm lying?

No, I don't, you are cracking me up again.

I know.

I notice you always seem to get the last word in.

You want it?

No, not at all.

That's you honoring me and I'm worthy of it.

I know you are; why are you telling me this?

It just came up in conversation and I'm putting things in perspective. You're worthy of honor too you know.

OK, I've never had an experience like this.

Me either.

So it's new to you?

Of course. Again, I'm putting things in perspective.

12:43 PM
Truth: sometimes it hurts, but it does bring relief, and healing if applied correctly. Don't be harsh or brutal with it.

She's—Mom's—been trying to get in touch with you.

Why, did she call?

No, the other way.

> I have been practicing sending my thoughts to G telepathically, or spiritually, as I try to open up and learn to hear Talia.

Oh. I tried to call earlier. Why didn't she answer?

Collection

She was busy.

I thought so before I called.

You KNEW so. Your emotional excitement spurred you too. Be careful with that.

Your precision amazes me.

Yours amazes me.

Thanks.

You're welcome.

You're always so polite, so respectful.

That is the way I was raised. Respect is a secret some people don't get.

I know, a lot of them.

That's one thing I tried to teach my friends.

How many got it?

Some. Respect opens doors where you would otherwise be turned away.

I'm going to have to buy more notebooks.

Looks like it.

> G writes down all of his communications with Talia in spiral bound notebooks.

May 7

Early AM
You're not going to talk to me today? ☺

Good morning.

Good morning . . .

I wasn't going to.

Why do you think I repeated how important this was?

I figured because it was important.

Yes, it is, but also I knew you would reach a point where you wanted to back off. Three is the number of power. Notice how many times I repeated things three or more times.

Let's talk about your training. You think it was a coincidence?

There are no coincidences.

Exactly. You were being prepared for just such times as these and what is to come. Your prayers have been answered; you're NOT deceived. I agreed and prayed with you on that. You know how to walk in this realm, but you must have confidence and faith. You do need some time to sort things out. This is a delicate balancing act. Do all the things you think you need to do because you need to do them. Go ahead.

3:25 PM
You have to be OPEN to me; fear stifles.

Self-pity doesn't serve you well. What have I told you that was wrong?

Nothing. I just wanted to be sure it's you.

Be sure, it's me.

So now what?

You're not really believing right now.

No, I guess not. I'm sorry, Talia.

That's all right, you need time.

May 8

9:00 AM
Why do you doubt yourself?

The way I was raised?

Could be some other factors.

There are a handful of people that will receive this, a small remnant. They are the ones we are moving to accept this. The others will have to get it on their own. That's a circuitous route and time consuming. I'm trying to move them on a path of righteousness. That's the right path: to move them ahead. There are multiple levels and depths of understanding in this. The future is not written in stone; most of it's decided by the decisions of man. To accept or reject are close decisions.

You have a unique path of blending flesh with spirit into a harmonious whole.

Some will absolutely reject this as heresy and the ramblings of a madman.

Do you think you're mad?

Collection

No, just a little crazy though.

No, you are not crazy, but it sounds like it sometimes. Sometimes it takes an extreme to create a balance.

May 10

5:57 AM
You've got my attention, Talia.

I told you not to edit my words.

I wasn't sure it was you; it seemed too obvious. I don't want to add anything that's not you.

That message goes much deeper than the obvious, it has to do with who she—Mom—is. It's all for the good. You're learning too, and if you hadn't left it out we wouldn't be discussing it now.

> Talia is referring to something she told G about her death. She told G that it was her time to go. He didn't tell me that because he didn't want to hurt me.

What's the deeper meaning?

The deeper meaning is really just as obvious, just deeper. You worry as much as anyone sometimes, so be careful who you judge or you will end up doing the same thing. Forgiveness is the key to freedom. You must forgive everyone no matter what they did to you or what you think they did to you. A key component is to be AWARE of it. Sometimes you can judge without being aware. What people do to you maliciously or inadvertently is for your learning, so how could you hold that against them. Also for me it was personally for her [Mom].

> Talia was referring to the message that it was her time to go.

I have so much AFFECTION for her—Mom—I could never fully explain it. So you see, if it [the crash] hadn't happened, we wouldn't have gotten into this because you wouldn't have been as open. You also do that to yourself. Your deeper self knows what you need, so when you think you're "screwing up" it's you doing it for your own good, for your own growth. See how exquisite that is. You cannot lose because EVERYTHING works TOGETHER for good to them who are called according to his purpose. You are called to the purpose; can you deny it?

No, I know that.

I know you do so don't deny it.

Well, I really thought I screwed up by not telling your mom.

The Universe Speaks

You really didn't. You just left something out for a purpose—now it's right in front of your face.

Wow, you really do know what you are doing.

Told you.

What about leaving the bracelet?

> I had a special bracelet made up that says, "Talia, Pretty Much Amazing," which I gave out to all of her friends. G also has one that he wears, but he forgot to put it back on after he took a shower, and he felt bad.

You knew you were forgetting something.

I know, why did I do that?

You'll see. You think you "screwed up." That was you teaching yourself again. You are your own best teacher.

Am I going to ever quit being an idiot?

You've never been an idiot, but you have acted like one before. People can easily convince themselves they're something they are not. They are made in the Creator's image. That inherently gives them the power and ability to create; therefore, they are in a manner of speaking the masters of their destiny. If people realized this they could change the course of their lives into anything they want. Most people don't know this. Most wouldn't even dream it was possible. Nothing is impossible to them that believe. Most people cannot receive anything so simple as ultimate truth. They think it must be complicated and ornate. That again is mainly their pride forming that perception so they can take credit for something that is essentially a FREE gift. You do not work your way into the kingdom; it is a free gift. It is gifted to everyone. That takes the eliteness out of the equation so that their own pride and selfishness can't accept it. They want to "do it on their own," and it just doesn't work that way.

Thanks for the notebooks.

> Talia had a penchant for writing and always had a hidden stash of empty notebooks ready to be used. I gave them all to G to use for his communications with Talia.

You're known here.

Really?

Yes, really, you're real. We can't say that about everyone. Some people just aren't real, not even to themselves.

That's sad, but I know it's true.

Collection

Yes, it is "sad but true." It is no coincidence that that saying is so prevalent, because it is so prevalent. You've got to go to work.

I know.

A labor of love.

This is.

It all is, or should be. Do all that is in your heart.

I never saw that deeper meaning of that until now.

Now you do.

Thank you VERY much.

Thank YOU very much.

7:08 AM
The biggest regret of my life is not having had more time to spend with you while you were here.

Don't regret it. It's for a reason. Everything HE does is perfectly reasonable.

Why won't she—Kim—answer the phone?

It's for a reason.

You crack me up; you are killing me!

I'm killing what you don't need.

May 11

AM early
Tell her hi . . . and I love her. This is her first Mother's Day without me.

You have questions.

Nothing springs to mind; I don't know where to start.

You want to ask about my life, of how I got this way.

Yes, I did.

He knew me before the foundation of the world—before all you know to exist was. He fashioned me from an image of pure thought, from pure and holy love, and established me a place in his kingdom. We ARE all an aspect of God, of his holy vision. Remember he said without a vision the people perish. This is His vision for His people that without they perish—His vision is that none would perish, but that all would come to Him, to come back to their very source of being. He clothes himself in darkness to show the contrast of his light. HE said, the Kingdom of Heaven is WITHIN you. And yet are not people clothed in darkness? Aren't most blinded to the very light within them, that surrounds them?

THAT'S God clothing HIMSELF in darkness. He lives WITHIN you; his pure essence is the ONLY LIFE there is; that is why he said, "You can do nothing without me."

This is mind-boggling.

Well, it shouldn't be. He said you have the mind of Christ, who understands all things. The only confusion is by the darkness that surrounds you. He is the light; he is the illumination of all understanding. All you have to do is receive Him, not reject him, and believe him. The simple truth to set you free.

No analyst will figure this out; it's a gift to receive.

Most of the things of this life are like charms to keep you idle, to keep you from receiving this gift.

When you see through this illusion to the meaning of these things, these "charms," it always points back to the truth. People receive these messages all of the time but most ignore them as a stray thought or their imagination. Yet when they begin to awake they realize that these messages are messages of truth. Now it's their decision to pursue this or fall back into darkness and sleep. MY message is to wake people up, to awaken them to a glorious new world that is THEIRS to walk in. THAT'S when they will be fulfilled. ALL that they want is here and all that is here can be realized within them.

I'm ... stunned, really.

That's what the truth does to people. It's stunning. There's SO much more.

This book has something to do with everything. The interconnectedness of ALL things.

How can we apply this to our lives?

By believing.

May 12

6:07 AM
People are afraid of what they might find out about themselves. What others may find out about them. It shakes the foundation of their perceptions, about what they believe. It's

Collection

intimidating for them to accept that as truth. It would change their thinking, of what they are comfortable with. To accept the "true tracks" would be to accept all that the Spirit teaches as real, for it is a doorway to the spirit.

> "True tracks" is a term used to describe the floor of tracks left by animals or people while walking. The true track is where you find the individualization of the one who left the track.

That vision [at Thanksgiving of Talia holding the door open] you had WAS my invitation into the mysteries of the spirit. Am I not revealing them?

Yes!

Yes, and revelation entails responsibility. Who wants more responsibility?

But how can I . . . ?

Baby steps. Your enthusiasm pushes you too fast sometimes. You must present it as they can accept it. If they are not willing to take baby steps it's no sense trying to get them to run a marathon. How many did you get in Martial Arts?

One.

Yes, one. Sometimes one is enough. Sometimes one is all you need. Remember, God is one. Even the master himself only had twelve. Twelve out of all the people he met and touched and healed. Only twelve willing to follow him, forsaking all. And what did he promise them right up front? That he had no place to lay his head. That's that truth that astounded them. That's the hook that caught them. And they WERE fishers of men because he "made them to become." That's awesome, isn't it.

Yes, that's awesome; you said you had to be clever.

Yes, clever in the spirit. Look what those twelve did. Talk about a place of honor, well, they really do have it. THE rewards are UNSPEAKABLE.

7:50 AM
Why do you think he said, "Thou shall have no other gods before me?" Because there ARE NOT other gods before Him. They are all false idols who only cause pain and misery. He came that you might have LIFE and that more abundantly.

You HAVE been chosen for this. You think this was haphazard? I have the most amazing counselors here.

3:24 PM
Who's going to get this?

The Universe Speaks

There are many factors involved in whether a person gets this or not, but primarily it's a personal decision, a choice. The dynamics of choice can never be understated. To climb to the mountain top you have to WANT it. I also made wise decisions during my life; that's how I got "here."

This is fun! I love communicating with you.

> G thought as he walked, *I don't want you to take over my life.*

Don't worry, I'm not going to "take over your life."

> G thought she said that kind of cheerfully; I think it was kind of funny to her.

It was funny to you, wasn't it?

Yes, it was.

May 13

Talia, I don't know where to start.

Just write.

I feel like I'm full of questions.

You are. You're a person to help us get our message out.

Direct me.

Direct yourself.

Yes, I was having fun. I wouldn't have told you if I wasn't having fun.

My life went perfectly. Perfectly.

You CAN'T write down everything I say to you or show you.

You're getting glimpses of the whole message. I could show it to you in an instant but you couldn't contain it; the natural mind would wash it away. Everything I say to you isn't a message for the masses; I'm your friend. The message for the masses isn't even a message for the masses because the masses aren't going to get it. The message is for those who ARE going to get it. The option for freedom is ALWAYS before your face.

What about the three Native Americans?

Collection

Some time back, while G was driving across the country, he had had a spiritual experience in which three Native Americans came to him and told him of their plight while still here on earth.

The three Native Americans were like a conference call to you. They were not all in the same place on the same level. They are poor souls whose circumstances of their life created much bitterness in their lives. They wanted an audience to air their grievances and you gave it to them. It will take much "time" before they move on, but they will.

You sensed the grandness of the message. That is as a full-course meal. The milk, the meat, the drinks, the dessert—everything of a splendid full-course meal on earth, only lasting and much more. Some prefer a buffet, to pick and choose. Some choose to settle for the crumbs from the table. Some just are not going to eat at all. AND it's a free meal, except for the effort.

My being seated at the head of the table at Thanksgiving WAS a symbol of royalty and of my being able to move anywhere.

All the circumstances of your life too, have put you in a position to receive this.

So you see, your life too is perfect in every way.

Thanksgiving, I saw you then as being a bit tattered and war torn, a glimpse of your grief and struggles and something far beyond that, the light of life. You seemed somewhat a contradiction; a part of me was just as fascinated with you as you were with me.

Just as?

Just as.

G had a vision while sitting next to a pond of seeing a silver dolphin statue with children around it. At about the same time G had the vision, I was having a discussion with a sculptress about a fundraising project she was working on, whereby parents of departed children could sponsor a small dolphin sculpture, to be included in a much larger installation, in memory of their child. But G didn't know about my meeting until later that day, and then he questioned Talia about his vision.

So what about the dolphins, Talia?

The dolphins are not about buying "me" a dolphin. The dolphins are about redemption, about redeeming the time, about the joy of life, about the fellowship of play—it's about working together in harmony. Dolphins ARE like children. Dolphins are intelligent—but they never misuse it. There's much more about the dolphins, but everything isn't to be written, but just to know.

Well, again it's nice to know I don't have to write everything.

The Universe Speaks

No. Anyway, all the books in the world could not contain it all.

All the things people tell you are not true.

Why are you telling me that? I certainly know THAT'S true.

You certainly do, but you certainly do not know who is not telling you the truth at times.

Is this a warning?

Yes, it is. Just beware—be aware.

Thank you for the heads up.

That's good—keep your head up.

> G thought about alertness. Looking to the SOURCE.

Yes, the LIGHT. The light is a sword of truth that cuts through the darkness in any direction you wield it. It's being used right now to cut to your heart to illuminate your soul to the truth of life.

> Then G thought about how he receives downloads of information from Talia and how he then just knows, like osmosis.

The absorption can be instantaneous or VERY SLOW. The light quickens. The light was EVERYWHERE the day you visited [at Thanksgiving]. You saw me moving in wisdom.

Absolutely, yes.

You see how many people saw that?

Kim and I got a glimpse?

Pretty much.

And yet there were seeds planted. Everybody pretty much knew something was going on. You can only be conscious by what light you are walking in.

This is . . .

Yes, the whole meal deal. I'm a part of everything.

THAT is an astonishing revelation!

Yes, so are YOU. So is everyone.

NOTHING hidden that shall not be revealed.

The time of subliminal messaging is over! We want to get it out there.

Collection

You were reading my thoughts a while ago when I was thinking that you seemed to be everything, when you said to me that you were a PART of everything.

Yes, why did you think He said, "Love your neighbor as yourself?" You are ALL a part of the WHOLE, the Oneness of God and all there is, because there ISN'T anything else.

This is earth shattering!

Yes, the dust of the earth in whom is the Breath of Life. Why do people look for miracles? Tell them to look in the mirror. The negative connotations people look to others with is the darkness speaking, a misunderstanding, the voice of darkness. Give it no place. Your spoken word creates.

This is one of the most important works you will ever do.

I love so much being a part of this.

You're a part of everything.

To know the length, the breadth, the depth and the height. Nothing is hidden that shall not be revealed. Your face is the face, or reflection, of God on earth; why do you think a smile goes so far?

I wish I could give people the understanding of what's behind those words.

Only they can do that. There are people using these powers for ill, but it will never really work.

I didn't think so. Nice to know

Yes, it is—that's why I told you. Their threats are empty.

You know I love this bracelet.

    G is speaking of the "Pretty Much Amazing" bracelet.

I know, and not as a physical object but what it symbolizes and the direction it points.

When will this all stop?

Never. You heard the franticness, the way the world "ties your time." You've been given time to do this.

I've noticed throughout this you've mentioned time a lot.

That is because it's important. It's important to understand it. Time is flexible. It CAN be distorted and bent, just as gravity bends light. Light is NOT a constant. That's man's understanding of the physical nature of light. That's incorrect as they will discover (some know already but they want to prove it). A direct KNOWING is always more efficient than scientific proof. Scientific proof is merely a demonstration of what is already known.

The Universe Speaks

I know you are not dogging science, are you?

Not at all, but there are "two sides to every coin." There are actually infinite sides to everything, but we won't get into that.

Do you know how much I appreciate this?

Yes, I do, completely.

Who is the little girl?

> While visiting Talia in the spirit, G saw a little girl with her. When he told me this I immediately remembered that Rebecca, the medium I speak to Talia through sometimes, saw Talia with a little girl as well.

I'm her teacher. She is a beautiful, beautiful soul.

I saw that.

What bothers her most is she is so missed. She's dealing with it wonderfully; she's coming to understand.

What is her name?

Names are not important, unless you want power over something.

That has so many meanings on so many different levels.

Yes, it does.

Mind-boggling.

Your mind needs to be boggled from time to time to get the trash out.

Never heard it put like that.

Shaken around, part of the "great shaking."

I will show you things to come. Now we're going to get it right. Now's the right time. For everything there IS a season. Now it's my great honor to be a part of this.

You told me a while ago to stop here and do the things I need to do. We kept going. What's with that?

Do all that is in your heart. Time doesn't mean much here. Time is important THERE. What would you rather spend your time doing, because you ARE spending it.

The power of the Spirit is beyond words. Indescribable, undeniable. It is Living.

Time has many parallel dimensions running at the same time. That's how you experience two experiences at once. Future and present now. Past and present now. Future and past in the PRESENCE now. It's all one, the oneness in Him. He is, the only reality that is. Time as you experience it is an illusion. The separation of things and places is an illusion as you experience them.

You see how the frustration arises, the discontent? You see how the peace rules in your heart, the absolute contentedness? It is a matter of consciousness, or walking in the light of the fullness, or walking the darkness of despair. Walk in the light—it's so much easier.

This whole experience is beyond anything I ever imagined.

And YOU have a vivid imagination!

I'm sure a lot of people will say that when they read this.

Oh, they will.

May 14

5:37 AM
Opportunity is a doorway. Sometimes you have to get through it quickly. That's where the quickening comes in. Without it you'll not have the necessary speed to manage it or even recognize it: that the doorway is even there or exists.

Can you open it yourself?

Not by the works of the flesh; the quickening is a gift of the spirit. Seizing the opportunity is a choice, a decision of the higher Self, who always knows what is best. That's why most people miss it; they're not in touch, in tune with their higher Self.

I've heard of the higher Self but never really thought in those terms.

I just want you to know it exists. That's the self I told you to believe in. I was blessed on earth to be in touch with my higher Self so that my steps were directed. That's why my confidence was so high.

> G was thinking that Talia was answering his questions even before he had a chance to form them into words.

Yes, I'm answering your questions during, before, and after you ask them. Here there's no time. It's all at once, therefore I have to slow down to more clearly perceive the timeline or this wouldn't make much sense at all. You get it?

Yes, I think so.

As you think, so you are.

The Universe Speaks

Then I get it.

Bravo, excellent choice. See how easy that was?

Not a problem at all.

There really are no problems, only lessons to be learned.

So problems are another misnomer?

Pretty much.

I'm influenced by the people around me; everybody is. You're influenced by the company you keep. Walk circumspectively, not as fools, redeeming the time.

There's time again.

Yes, bend it by the force of your gravity; you know how to do that.

I've done it before.

Yes, from the ground up, the foundation, blended with the quickening of heaven.

Hardly anybody's going to understand that.

No, hardly anyone will. That's something you have to experience; the intellect will never get it. But you've done it and it was a sign to others.

She—Mom—is a very special person whose eyes have been opened to this. Greater love has no man than this.

> Talia is referring to my shattering, and my new unwavering belief in the afterlife.

He's already given everything. Past, present and future are yours. You CAN change the past. That's another misconception people have. That you can't change the past. Well, if it's all happening at once you can certainly change the result of the past, and I've already given you the key: Forgiveness. That's the ultimate gift anyone can give another. The healing properties of that are truly beyond description.

Remember your friend who called you true blue? He saw into you. He asked for that because you were a mystery to him and he had doubts about you. That put his mind totally at ease. Remember the light in his eyes when he told you? That was the light of life. That was the light of revelation. That was the true light in him bearing witness with the true light in you. Face to face. No man has seen God's face at any time. To see God's face is to die. To die to the Self.

To die is to live.

Help others. How can you help others when you're tied up, wrapped into yourself.

Collection

I guess pretty poorly.

Yes, poorly—you've not been given poverty.

Who is the King? Who do you serve? Yourself? Or are you friends with the King?

I'm friends with the King.

Exactly, now live like it.

I'll try.

Don't try, do.

That's why we're getting into a more detailed description of some things here. For others the simple truth will suffice. No matter what we do here, some are just not going to receive it. Some will look for an ulterior motive. That's the darkness in them looking, groping really, for the darkness in others.

How can you help them?

They have to help themselves. God will not remove your choice, but he will certainly compel you in the right direction.

Why do people fight so hard against Him?

That's their flesh struggling against death. They know that to see Him is to die. They love their lives, no matter the misery. It's all they know, so they think that's all there is. They know it's not, but that shakes their very foundation to where it seems to them like they are dying. Like they are going to lose their lives. But He said that who loses his life will save it and he who saves it shall lose it. The fleshly mind can't handle the contradiction of that so they fight against it. It's all very simple, see?

Yes.

We could get into it, the myriad of facets of it, much more deeply, but if they didn't get that, more is not going to help them either. They have to help themselves. They ARE the masters of their own destiny.

Strict rules.

No, the laws of life.

    G was thinking about art . . .

People who don't understand artists, don't understand themselves—we're all creative. The Art of Life encompasses all of the arts. Gives place to creativity. True art also inspires. I was interested in art.

The Universe Speaks

The deception is because of scrutiny. The truth can bear any and all manner of scrutiny; a lie cannot bear the light at all.

Boy, this is good stuff.

Isn't it though.

This whole art thing is fascinating.

How could it not be?

Good point.

It's a perfect point. It's a perfect pointer, a perfect pointer to truth. Why do you think people are so in awe of art? Because it's inspired, it inspires, it's inspirational. It can TRANSFORM people to other levels. Haven't you been inspired to push some of the things you do to the level of art?

Yes.

That's being inspired, doing something inspirational even before it's art. That's the goad you need sometimes to take things to another level. Remember what your dad said, that "there's an art to everything." That's a truth he speaks a lot. He's right; there IS an art to everything. You've had a hard time understanding people that don't want to make things into an art, to take it INTO the next level.

Yes, I have.

They have just as hard of a time understanding you. ART is not easy without the flow, the flow of the Spirit, which is the only true inspiration. Without the spirit you can do NO thing. Remember, He said "be ye perfect." A lot of people have struggled with that. Even become discouraged. He was told, "These are hard sayings Lord; who can hear them?" What a question! Now THAT is a sacred question. Man's spirit strives to be perfect; it's imprinted within them. That's the struggle, that's the fight, and yet when he yields himself to Him, the fight is over. He said, "Take my yoke upon you, for my burden is easy," because he LIVES within you.

Boy, there's more to this, isn't there?

Of course. A LOT more.

It's the very crux of the nature of man, of ENTERING INTO REALITY.

Wow!

Yes, wow indeed.

Thank you for this.

You're welcome, always.

Collection

G was thinking about having dinner with some friends . . . eat, drink and be merry for tomorrow we die. . . .

That's THE ANSWER.

Point being?

Look at what you just said. The answer to every question is within the very question itself. It's not so much a riddle as a solution when you look at it, see it, perceive it on a multi-dimensional, holographic, spherical-like structure. You got that revelation before.

Yes, but I didn't have the words, and when I tried to explain it, people looked at me like I was crazy, like I had two heads.

That's because only the light reveals it. Words without it are just words, dead. "Everything is spherical," you said.

Yes.

And how could you expect them to understand that, without the light of direct knowledge?

Yes, I came to realize that but it was still frustrating.

Well, now we have some words to explain it somewhat. You think this is deep. And it is, but these are baby steps. Don't you think I feel some frustration here trying to get this ACROSS?

I thought of that, but I didn't really think you would be frustrated there.

We have the same feelings here, just more perfect. You can feel my frustration now trying to get this across in words that are easy to be understood.

Yes, and I've been a bit frustrated at times.

This is not an easy task. There IS a great gulf. This takes tremendous energy. The good news is that there's no lack of it. Tapping into it is a trick I'm trying to teach.

Trying?

Trying means exactly that, it's trying. We're DOING it, but it is trying. There's a difference.

This is phenomenal.

Yes, it is. All things are possible to them that believe. You see some of the multi-level lessons behind every word, which you can't express. That's the main source of your frustration. Remember, art is true expression. Expressing yourself on that sublime level is true art. No matter WHAT you are doing.

The more you get rid of what you don't need, the more you can "have" what you do.

The Universe Speaks

11:47 PM

All that frustration you are feeling from them—your friends—already is the strivings of the flesh. "Much ado about nothing," as it were. Don't get caught up in it; it will just bog you down. "Be ye separate."

Yes, it's hard to really take it very seriously.

Take YOURSELF seriously. YourSELF knows all things and is moving you into another plane. Where all things are possible. Seize the moment.

I never saw it like that before.

Yes, capture the moment.

Time again.

It's a large issue. It's a real paradox. There's a lot of it, there's not enough of it, and it really doesn't exist. Some places anyway. Every place is at the same place. It's been placed in Him. That's the only place that is.

Time is a creation of thought, of higher thought, to create "separation" for learning so we can bring it all back together again into an even more perfect whole.

You're not going to tell me that's not heavy, are you?

No, I'm not. How astounded do you think I am daily?

Oh, man, I can't wait to see you.

We just talked about time.

1:14 PM

You see how we change here just like we change there. IT has to do with PURPOSE, with inspiration. The pieces I'm moving are to change them. Change them for the better. To inspire them to change. Anyone can change—it's up to them. Yet art inspires. To express your true self is to express the light of life of the only Being that is, the Creator of all things. You are created in His image, from perfect thought. That makes you a creator. You CAN change things. How many times have you heard it said, "Can't change it." That's a lie. And as it's been said, a lie is but for a moment, but the truth endures forever. Seize the moment, break the lie by the sword of the light of truth. The Kingdom of Heaven suffers violence and the violent TAKE IT by force.

To be a child of the King is your birthright. There's no earning it. You're BORN to it. I was born to it from the very beginning.

J's dream; I put it in a context he understood.

> Talia's Uncle J had a dream that Talia called him on his cell phone. He heard the ring, answered it, and heard Talia say to him, "Hi, Uncle J, I am

Collection

all right." When he woke up he knew deep in his heart that it was really Talia that had come to him to speak to him. G then spoke to Talia about the dream J had had and then told him about this discussion with Talia.

Thank you for confirming that to J.

9:20 PM
What about that sense of urgency you have?

That's my knowing: there's not much time there. Time is short—how many times have you heard that?

A lot.

Yes, and it's true, time is always short there. It's just not long enough to do all the things you need to do. That's why I'm spurring you on, in a manner of speaking. You're tired, weary.

Yes.

You need sleep. When you're this run down it's hard for us to communicate.

You had a lot more you wished to communicate today.

Yes, I did. Don't worry, we'll get into it in depth. My message will not be detoured.

So we're going to stay on the right road.

You bet.

Of all the misconceptions, death is the biggest myth of all.

May 15

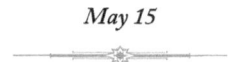

Personalities?

The differences are intricate, sometimes subtle, sometimes very contrasting. There's a reason: it's learning the difference. If you're in total agreement what difference does it make?

2:43 PM
You don't have to edit anything I say, but you can distill the message.

The world needs more than sages now, it needs a revolution.

Talia, I feel like I want to explain what you are saying to people, but sometimes I do not even know how to explain it to myself.

The Universe Speaks

You can't always explain what I am saying, any more than I can always explain what I'm saying.

This message is far beyond me.

If the eye is skewed it skews your perceptions.

You must have an intense desire, a passion even to achieve enlightenment. What many consider enlightenment is merely knowledge. Enlightenment is walking IN the light.

If your perceptions are skewed, soon that divergence from the path becomes greater, eventually leading to deception and even delusion. And yet if you yield yourself to the path of light, it becomes the perfect path in which you can do no wrong. The perfect law of life is the law of liberty in which there is no law.

This is the way of wisdom. Few know this path. Did I not say "there would be few to find it"?

Talia, this did not sound like you. It sounded like another spirit.

This is who I serve. There's many personalities, all aspects of God. God is infinite, unending; He expresses himself through us. That's His art.

May 16

1:03 PM
Talia, who were all of the sages? The wise men?

Truly the sages, as you call them, are one, even though they are far and few between.

No one knows them but they know each other.

He reveals himself in His creation. He is countering the dogma of the day by revealing Himself in this way.

Talia, I wish I could spend more time with you.

The time you spend with me will be returned to you many times over. This is giving in its most perfect sense.

Whoa!

Whoa? We're just getting started.

5:32 PM
His art, his children, the apple of His eye, is what is closest to His heart. There is an expression, "Seeing through the eyes of God." That's a perfect expression.

Collection

One worthy of all attention.

This is to SEE all things.

This is to KNOW all things.

This is to BE as all things.

This is to be all things to all men that some might be saved, delivered from all darkness and delusion.

The choice to enter INTO the darkness results in an end result of delusion. Is not this the definition of insanity?

Choose to enter INTO the light. For in the light are ALL things seen.

May 17

6:46 AM
What fellowship has light with darkness. The darkness will never and cannot understand the light. So don't resent the message; be thankful for it.

11:20 AM
Every day there's options, choices set before you. Rarely is the case "I had no choice."

The decision is yours. Wisdom is profitable to direct. (You don't have to be a part of a game you didn't subscribe to).

He that is offended for not getting their own way is going to be offended anyway.

In all labor there's profit, but beware of entering into a game that doesn't edify.

Putting yourself first is often putting everyone else first too. This is meat that you're understanding. Be not darkened.

12:37 PM
You should notice a common thread, a common theme throughout all this. That's ONENESS. A cohesion of the whole. The dark, negative, repelling force is just as much a part of bringing all of the parts into a cohesive whole as its counterpart.

4:35 PM
This is a labor of love.

For me too.

The Universe Speaks

6:43 PM
We talked of gravity before.

What is always present along with it?

Magnetism?

Magnetism is a force that both attracts and repels. That's one explanation of the conflict you see between people for no apparent reason. It's also an explanation of the mysterious attraction some feel for one another. This in people is a spiritual force. The reason I started with gravity is that it's the foundation, rooted and grounded in love. Love is a force that NEVER fails.

Another reason I began with gravity is to let you know you have it. It's a force you can learn to use for good. Meditate on the meaning of this and it will become clearer. All things are possible to those that believe.

Electricity has both positive and negative aspects. All this is tied together in a most intricate manner. Suffice it to say that all things are held together by the word of His power.

May 18

7:53 AM
G thought to himself, *I am going to be late for work.*

This is not just a job; it's an adventure for you. It's an opportunity to touch people in a positive way.

Good morning, Talia.

Good morning!

Your excitement is contagious.

I hope so.

She—Mom—slept well last night. She has good instincts but her head gets in the way sometimes.

Why are you telling me this?

So you can pass it on. Today will be a good day for you.

It doesn't feel like it now.

Goes to show you can't always go by feelings. Go by truth. It's time.

Collection

I know.

It's important to know the times.

Wow.

Exactly.

It's already turning into a good day.

Told you.

1:10 PM
My air-conditioner quit.

It's for a reason.

What is the reason?

It's all hooked into the system. Don't rely on their system. See how comfortable it is? It's not about just being lulled to sleep, it's also about comfort. See how fast your body adjusted? It's also a choice of a mental direction to acceptance.

Thank you, Talia.

No problem.

2:33 PM
Your whole attitude changed that situation for good.

May 20

Talia, it's been a while since I have heard from you.

Yes, it has. You've been very busy and you had to recharge.

I don't know where to start.

There's really no starting and stopping since there's really no time. It's just continuing.

That's the way it feels.

That's the way it is.

I feel like hardly anyone's ready for this.

No one hardly is. That's OK, their hearts are being prepared. This is to receive the message of life in the continuance of all things. All things will continue whether they are prepared or not. Preparation is yielding, not resisting the Spirit.

I lived my life as an example; I didn't know it at the time. Now it's clearly manifest. That was the spirit living through me. The credit is all His and to reveal His glory upon the earth. He does this continually.

Oh, wow.

Oh yes, an instrument for His glory. He alone is worthy of praise and honor. He alone is the One true God.

How can I know this is you?

How can you not?

Well, it's just sometimes I hear your voice so clearly I know it's you without a doubt, and sometimes it's indistinct.

Know thyself. That's my answer.

May 21

7:00 AM
Good morning, Talia.

Good morning. You still haven't grasped what it means, me being a part of everything. You still haven't grasped what it means, you being a part of everything.

The spider takes hold with her hands and is in king's palaces.

I said the violent take it by force.

People are largely opposed to violence. Generally they should be, but that's not what I am speaking of here.

He rebuked the wind and it stopped.

> There were unbelievably strong winds that night. G yelled out to the wind to stop.

You rebuked the wind last night and it slowed, paused, according to your faith. According to your faith so be it unto you. According to your faith so you hear. According to your faith so is the level of your understanding. Without faith it's impossible to please Him. Every man's been given a measure of faith. Use it. Nothing's more pleasing than pleasing Him. Why would you

Collection

hinder your own faith? Why do you fight against yourself? There's no winning warring against God. He is and all there is. Walk in faith.

I believe.

Yes, the devils believe and tremble.

What are you saying?

I'm saying the lessons are never-ending.

I'm missing something here.

You're missing a lot. You want to get to the end. There is no ending. The race is not to the swift or the battle to the strong. You think you're strong; there's only one source of strength, and you know where the speed comes from. You've studied it. Time to study some other things. All things are yours. You know where you got the speed, now get what you need. Strength is easy to misuse. Remember you have to be clever. Being clever is being in balance. If you're out of balance you fall.

Yes, you got that before but you forgot—that wasn't very clever. Take hold with your hands like it was hidden treasure, because it is, absolutely.

You seem not so chipper today.

There's a time to be chipper and a time to cut to the heart of the matter. Now's the time to cut to the heart of the matter.

I'm exactly who I was yesterday, only more.

That's beautiful.

Exactly.

We know who we are. If you knew who you were almost all your so-called problems would disappear instantly.

How do we know who we are?

I've already covered that, sufficiently. Remember I said don't judge. You're just as dense as those other people, just ON another level. That doesn't make you ANY better than them, just dense on another level.

How do you change this?

I've already covered that too.

You see in His light; you see light. If you do not walk in the light you have, how can you see more light? That's where the lessons seem to end. They don't; they are just waiting for you to catch up.

The Universe Speaks

Yes, I said we had work to do.

I'm sorry, Talia.

You don't have to be sorry to me. You can't hurt me. You can concern me, but you can never hurt me.

Thank you for your patience.

Thank you for yours.

I'm very grateful.

That's good, being grateful is good but being graceful is better. Yes, only by the grace of God.

You are FILLED with this message.

Yes, I am. It's like being pregnant, pregnant with Words of Life. I WILL deliver this message and it WILL bring forth life.

Singleness of purpose.

Perfectly.

You're getting more undense by the moment. This doesn't have to be a long process—it can be instantaneous.

You couldn't speak a lie if you tried.

There's no way I could here. There's no way to even try. That's as senseless as anything you can think of. The whole foundation of everything that means anything is truth. Nothing is more absolute, no footing firmer. The truth is the beginning and the end, yet it has no end or beginning—that's the truth. How could it ever be otherwise?

I don't know.

Yes, you do.

Nothing can hold this message back, can it?

No, nothing will. Nothing is NO thing; how could it hold it back? Nothing doesn't even exist. You see my meaning?

Yes.

Nothing can ever work against you because nothing is no thing. It doesn't exist except as a construct of your mind. There is nothing to come against you but yourself. When people get this the wars will end, whether between nations or within us.

My life will never end, and I will succeed in all I do because He always gives me victory. This is something I know as an absolute concrete fact.

Collection

This is something you should confess for yourself. Because it's TRUTH and the TRUTH never fails.

I know truth and love are synonymous.

Yes, that was revealed to you before; now walk in it.

Time to tighten up.

Time to tighten up by shaking away the loose ends you don't need. Time to burn away the dross by the light of truth.

This seems easy.

It is! But again it takes a great effort, intense desire. This intensity is the flames I speak of, the flames of truth, flames to burn away all that can be burned so all that is left is that that cannot be burned. That's all that is going to remain anyway. Ashes to ashes, dust to dust—all that is left is perfection, which is really all there is. So you see, "be ye perfect" is not such a hard saying after all.

He will "cause you to become"; your job is to let him. SEE—not so hard after all.

"After all" means something.

Yes, it does.

After all the work and there's none left to do, the real work will begin.

I don't really understand that.

No, you don't; it's not time.

But it's prophecy.

Yes, it is.

"It's not time" means more than it looks like too.

Yes, it does. Things, meaning EVERY thing, are leading you in the direction you need to go. Did He not say, "My sheep know my voice and they follow me and another they will not follow?"

Yes.

Do you think the Shepherd doesn't know what he's doing?

No . . .

No is correct—yes he does.

All the promises of God are "yes" and "so be it."

The Universe Speaks

I . . .

Don't worry about the future or dwell on the past. These are lessons that are happening right now. All things are yours. You don't really get that.

I'm trying.

IT'S trying. Stop trying, receive it! It's only the separation in your mind that confuses. Oneness of mind is no confusion. If you know how fragmented you were you'd be devastated. But your faith, your higher Self, KNOWS he's bringing it all together and cannot fail; therefore, it's true that you shouldn't be too concerned. You're helpless to pull yourself together anyway. It's enough to know he will cause it to happen.

4:18 PM
OK, I keep seeing diamond shapes everywhere.

The diamond is a stone born of fire, intense pressure, and gravity. It's VERY hard. And a stable currency. But primarily it bends or channels light to reveal colors that symbolize moods, personalities, ministries, mysteries, and clarity. Also the beauty of purity. These things—the beauty of purity—cannot be had or manifested without fire and intense pressure, also polished by the hand of man. See you are part of this.

5:17 PM
You told me once that animals talk there where you are, but I didn't write it down.

No, because you thought it was too outlandish and might compromise the credibility of the message and dialogue. You've since learned otherwise, and everything I've said to you has been confirmed in one way or another. It's all part of the process.

Did I disappoint you?

No, because I know the answer as soon as I think it, although it's not quite like that either. This really can't be explained in earthly terms.

I heard you say that colors there were much more vivid.

> One of the things that Talia told me when I went to see Rebecca was that the colors where she is are much more vivid, vibrant and amazing then they are here, with us.

You KNOW they are! And crisp. You can smell them, hear them if you want to, and even taste them. There's nothing like it, not in your shadow world.

Wow.

Yes, wow!

Collection

There it takes faith, here it just is. There are really NO words I can use to describe it.

That sounds . . . wonderful.

WONDERFUL! It is, a WORLD of WONDER beyond ANY description.

Then it's no sense asking you to describe it.

No, no sense at all, but I could describe elements of it to you.

Please do.

ANYthing you want is here. It just IS and there's no end to all you can do here. One is NEVER tired but filled with hope and a sense of Purpose. The expectations burst forth! There is no within or without. There is no sorrow, pain or suffering. Those are like a distant memory. Your life on earth is SO short, no amount of suffering could ever compare to the glory that is to be. The deepest doubts you ever had there you could compare to a mist, hardly noticeable. Here you are totally, absolutely and completely fulfilled. No thing missing. Everything that there is, is here to behold—beauty unspeakable. Words just fail.

7:16 PM

    G was looking at Talia's ashes.

I'm not there!

    G and I were discussing reincarnation. I was curious whether or not Talia would tell me if it was real or not, so I asked her and then asked G to ask her about it.

9:47 PM

Reincarnation. Is it real?

It's real—if you want it to be real.

May 22

9:43 AM

I know you have things to do. I know you have your life to live and so do I.

    G was walking, thinking back to when Talia told him that she was going to give him a special ranking, when Talia popped in . . .

You're thinking they are physical skills. The physical skills are a doorway to the spirit. **THIS IS THE ART OF LIFE.**

The Universe Speaks

12:50 PM
How's the little girl?

She's doing better, much better. She's accepting all things as they are.

I can feel your excitement and joy.

I LOVE this—His—work! We HAVE to use multiple meanings, otherwise it would make no sense.

Because it's a multi-dimensional universe?

That's right. That's one reason.

I wish I had the words to describe you.

There are no words to describe me. You could describe elements of me or partial aspects of me, but to define me is to define the universe. To label all that is. How could you ever label all there is? But to describe ANYONE would be the same. We are all made in His image, so to describe anyone completely would be to describe Him, He who is ALL there is.

Yes! Wow!

Yes, wow!

That's actually a pretty good description.

I'm cracking up here.

I know you like to have fun, so have fun with it.

I am.

I KNOW you are.

      G prayed for Talia.

That was . . . very powerful.

I . . . didn't know it worked both ways.

Yes, it does—it works ALL ways.

That was like spontaneous combustion or something.

That's the Spirit bursting forth for truth.

The times of these forced games are over for you.

      Doing what other people expect of you, acting the way people expect you to act.

Collection

Good.

Yes, indeed. You were chastised for your boredom many times. They pushed you to have interests in something that had no interest for you. You resented that because of the force used to remove your choices. Often when you were inspired to the correct choice you were chastened. This was very discouraging for you. It also showed a blatant lack of respect for you as a person. If the authorities, the ones you were taught to respect, showed none to you, how could these teachers expect any response but rebellion. That's your free spirit rebelling against the spirit of slavery forced upon you. You saw most just go along. You saw a part of them secretly hating it, and yet they went along with the program AND were rewarded! Now there's something to puzzle a child. You saw what really was versus what was happening, and it didn't add up. As a matter of fact you were called stupid for speaking about it and not going along with it.

Where are these people now? Some will read this and weep—with realization; some will read this and laugh—with disdain.

And some will just scratch their head.

Most won't read it at all. Their minds have been made up. That's the process of this world: to make up your mind.

So you'll fit the program.

In a manner of speaking, yes. But if one can see through this delusion one will be free. Men's hearts yearn for it—that's why it's spouted off so much—but it's mostly used to bring them back into bondage. That's the power of this world. The power to break the human spirit, to crush the spirit is to have a defeated foe, a slave. The truth WILL set you free

Now, think of that alternative. That's what they are doing! Using the law to bring into bondage. Matters not whether it's a religion, a government or an individual; the process is the same.

This is perfectly cogent to me.

Yes . . . never depart from the simplicity, which is IN the anointed one! He came to set you free! He came to GIVE you life, liberty and that MORE abundantly. You see, the counterfeit cannot compete.

Talia, is this you?

That doesn't matter—it's US.

Of course I'm here. Time to remove yourself.

Time to remove myself?

Yes.

The Universe Speaks

What do you mean?

Just exactly what I said.

Remove myself from what?

Remove yourself from the kingdom of darkness—and all that entails—into the kingdom of light.

That's where the true Authority is, isn't it?

Yes, of course. You CAN do anything, you know.

Is that true?

Of courses it's true. One should compromise when one should. And one should not compromise when one shouldn't. That's pretty obvious, isn't it?

Yes . . .

You asked about compromise and that's my answer.

This could go on and on forever, couldn't it?

It will. I'm growing up into Him IN ALL things; so are you. Just wanted you to know.

Well, that's a confidence builder.

Yes, it should be.

That seems like such an everyday answer, and yet there's multiple meanings again.

Yes. Always.

There you go again.

I'm always going.

You're having fun here too, aren't you?

Every bit and much more.

That's great.

Yes, that's Great!

Talia, the queen.

I don't need a servant, yet to serve me would be to serve the King; a friend WILL work just fine.

That's an awesome answer!

Collection

How could it not be?

Guess it could not.

No, it couldn't. EVERYTHING here is awesome!

You know, unless people look at this as a hologram, the meaning will be obscured. Their minds have to be open to do this. Most minds have been forced closed by what we discussed before.

That whole timeline, like writing "before" or "earlier" is so odd. It's hard to write it because I know it's happening in the NOW.

That's just to frame it to help them understand. It's exactly what we were talking about—viewing this as a hologram—holographic point of view. The One Point sees all points of view. To perceive this, one must see it. This has nothing to do with the natural eyes. This is also far beyond what the natural intellect can grasp. The truth has no conflict with itself; that's man's ideas thrust upon it.

What am I going to do with this discussion, this journal of mine?

You're going to publish this. Great is the company that publishes this.

Help me.

You already are.

Double meaning again.

Oh, many more than that.

I'm among a Great Company now. We WILL fulfill our purpose.

There's some hard times coming.

There's some interesting times coming for sure.

7:24 PM

Talia, I don't want to do this if it's not you.

You don't want to do this if it is me.

Why not?

Your personal pride. You fear it. Just burn it away with all the rest. Remember what I said: fear stifles. Now write it down.

Why?

Because I asked you to.

The Universe Speaks

All right.

Of course it will be.

You think you know no one else will see through it like you do. That's an assumption you shouldn't make.

I just don't think there's very many that will be able to connect the dots.

That's true, there won't be very many, not for a while, so . . .

So I guess you know what you're doing.

Of course I do. I've already told you that. I know EXACTLY what I'm doing.

I'm just trying . . .

What's with the struggle? That's funny; you're trying to explain it to yourself!

I'm sure there's a lesson here.

I showed you the lesson I'm attempting to get across here in an instant—now you're resistant.

No, I'm just trying to explain it to others.

No, you're trying to explain it to yourself, and it's YOUR explanation. You've GOT to see the humor in that.

Yes, perfectly.

That's where it comes from. You're afraid of acceptance. That's silly really, that's just a concept. You know this—why the insecurity? Let me tell you one reason for that. It's because you've judged other people for striving so hard to gain acceptance. You know that's a vain show. That's why I said BE AWARE of judging others because when you do, you do the same thing yourself. So when you see people making mistakes, if you can correct them, correct them; if you can't, then do not judge them.

Thanks for the correction and the explanation.

You're welcome. Now let's get on with it. There's a lot more to do yet.

Science is struggling with understanding the non-locality of mind, but the answer's right there in the hidden wonders of the revelation of creativity. It's right before anyone's face wherever they go. They just don't see them.

Why?

They are blocked off for nearly any number of reasons. But . . . mostly pride. I mean, "What would people think?"

Talia, what if I get up there and you tell me half of this stuff was not you but me?

Collection

Then we'll have a big laugh.

You don't seem to be worried about being misquoted.

I'm not worried about anything. I AM concerned about getting the truth out.

I KNOW THAT'S you.

That's why I said you sometimes must walk by faith, not by sight and not always by what you KNOW to be true. We all know in part but we will KNOW even as we are known.

I know that's you too.

Pleasant to know, isn't it?

Yes, it is.

The promises of God are the promises of God. Remember that when you must walk by faith. Anyway, you and I are One. In Him. How could we ever be wrong?

That's a heavy statement.

That's a statement of fact. So, if you and I are one, and we agree as one, how could one contradict the other? We are one in Him. How could we ever lose?

Your clarity is splendid.

My clarity is yours.

I can see how someone could twist this around.

If they are going to twist the meaning of these words around, they're going to twist it around from a twisted mind. That's no concern of ours. You are part of this. You are part of everything. You are connected with all things, with all there is. That's why I say "we," "us," "our." This is our message—not just mine but ours. You have ownership here. You felt at times you were being used.

But it's such a joy to be used.

But that's not really what's happening here. This is your message too.

I suppose I didn't realize that.

Now you do. To realize is to live real. Live real; anything, everything else is phony.

Nobody's ever put this so plain, so clearly.

Everyone knows all of this already; there is nothing new under the sun. We're just reminding them to wake up! It's wake-up time!

That's a fact.

The Universe Speaks

You bet it is.

That's a bet I'll take.

You already got it. See—it's already in the bag. What are you working for? You already have all you need.

There's some stuff there I'm going to have to think about.

Please do. That's some good advice you just gave yourself.

I've often wondered what it would be like to have someone you could ask anything to and they would have the answers.

You've always had someone like that.

But I didn't know it.

Now you do.

And I know it's not you either.

No, it's not. We are not going helter-skelter here in any direction for curiosity's sake. We have a message and that's "singleness of heart."

That's the first time I've heard you use that term.

That's the first time I've used it.

What does that mean exactly?

What it means we've already discussed elsewhere in other terms in some depth. What it means exactly is, singleness of purpose is the "doing." Singleness of heart is the "being." For out of the heart are the issues of life. Out of the abundance of the heart the mouth speaks. Diligence is needed here, and a close watch. Words are life and death; choose life. I ALWAYS chose life. It's all there is really. So the choice is easy and simple.

Awesome!

Yes, it is, isn't it.

May 23

Talia, the day we met, you were sitting at the head of the table, and at one point I saw a crown on your head. When I looked down I saw myself wearing an old tattered, dusty uniform—something like from the civil war or WWI. Could you tell me about that?

Yes, I could.

Collection

What we wore symbolized our future relationship in the NOW. Not only is a crown placed upon your head by someone else, it speaks of your thoughts. It's also a symbol of your treasure stored in heaven for you, and kingly authority. Your clothing spoke of your past trials and tribulations, your present battles and your calling. Remember what your friend Ken said. God showed him about you, the same thing the spirit showed you about you.

In the mouth of two or three WITNESSES shall every word be established?

Go to work now. Remember I said don't ask if you don't want the answer. That's why I pointed to your watch. We don't really have the time for this now. We'll speak more about this later.

You see now how you can call the answers unto yourself. That's being creative. **That's the Art of Life.**

Splendid.

Yes, it is, totally.

When you total it all . . .

Yes, exactly, you can never come up wanting.

May 24

Talia, you can do so much more where you are than where I am.

It's not only that I can do much more here; I can do ANY thing here. The truth's never that complicated. It's just that things are not always as they seem or appear to be. Do not pre-judge what you think is. We have specific things to write about here.

When your message is out, will you keep talking to me?

No matter how deep I move into He in whom all is, I will still talk with you.

It seems I'm pointing to a faraway shore; it's really not so far away.

Be mindful not to hurt others, for what you do to others you do to yourself.

I already know what you're going to ask before you ask it. The questions are just to frame it for your SELF. All are one.

You already see how my Game is moving people.

Yes, I do.

Of course you do, I'm affirming to you what is real. The only thing the false world offers is pain and suffering.

I do like pushing the envelope. That's why it's hard to keep up sometimes. Now that you see the truth as a hologram, you see past, future and present just is.

Pushing the envelope again.

That's part of my job.

May 25

6:17 AM
Write!

Good morning, Talia.

I want to record what happened last night, but I don't know where to start.

> The night before, I was explaining to G what Talia's touch felt like to me. As I was telling him, I felt Talia's presence very strongly, and as it persisted, G began to feel Talia as well. The feeling he had moved deeper until he felt as if his pains were being taken away by Talia. Her energy was healing him. He no longer had any pain!

Let it absorb awhile.

That was awesome.

I know, for me too.

I didn't know you were a healer.

Me either.

You either?

No. I know all things are possible, but that was a new experience for me too. Do you feel my great joy in helping others?

Yes.

That's everyone's gift.

My mom feels on a VERY deep level, and I'm healing her too. She will always be able to feel me. You see the light in her eyes? That's not a mistake or your imagination.

That's the light of life, isn't it?

Yes, of course it is.

Collection

I really didn't expect that, your healing.

Yes, well expect the unexpected. Most people expect the things they conjure up in their minds, and that is what they get.

Masters of their own destiny.

They are creators; most just do not realize it. They should be co-creators with the Creator—that's easy enough. Instead they create their own misery, for themselves and others. What could be a more simple choice.

7:10 AM
Presence of mind IS the issue. That's a large part of Singleness of Purpose. This direct focus is where you see the miracles. Presence of mind is a term you've heard before; now think of what that really means.

I think I know exactly what you mean.

You do!

But how can I put that in words?

Again that's something that must be experienced. We could discuss it in depth until you ran out of paper and still barely scratch the surface of what that means, but what's the point.

Another multifaceted answer contained in the question.

Yes, you are a quick study; I heard that about you.

That's precious, and sweet of you.

How could it be otherwise?

Point taken.

Exactly!

You see all the many directions we could take here.

Yes, like many paths leading up a mountain.

Yes, MANY paths and they ALL lead to the top. His ways are more that the sands of the sea.

Literally, I was told that years ago.

I know, I'm quoting you quoting Him now. You saw the look you got when you told people that.

Yes . . .

Again, it must be experienced—not in word but in power. That was a small portion you experienced last night.

I really don't have the words for that.

Of course you don't. There aren't any really. But you heard the silence, the stillness. That's where we LIVE.

Yes, indeed. That speaks of the promises of God: his contract with his people. You have a contract of everlasting life with the Creator, IN WHOM nothing was made WITHOUT Him. You see all things are WITHIN Him. How could you EVER fail, He ALLways GIVES us the victory—in Him. Now these are some concepts you're not completely grasping right now, but you will.

How can I ever repay . . .

There is no repaying; it's a free gift. You're not quite getting that yet either. You think you have to work for it. I'm telling you there is no work to do; it's already been done for you. Completed, finished in Him.

So we just receive it.

Yes, what happened last night? Did you work for it?

No.

No, not at all, you just took the wine.

Talia uses the term "wine" to explain the gifts G receives from her.

7:16 AM
You see how to obey is better than to sacrifice?

Yes.

And how He fulfills his promise to give you all the desires of your heart?

Yes.

This is a lesson told in the earliest parts of human history.

Cain and Abel?

Yes, you should reread that. That's God Himself revealing His true nature. That story also reveals all the so-called problems of man. No use to rehash it here; it's plain as DAY. Yes, wherever you go it's right in front of your face. Face to face. Look in the water, in a placid pond: THAT'S your answer. That's why so many people look to others to fulfill them. They can't believe they HAVE all the answers contained within them. There are no OTHERS.

Collection

Oneness.

Yes, to most that's just a word, without meaning. Again it has to be experienced. God is an experience. Most people think it's just pie in the sky! The PIE is within you. The Kingdom of Heaven comes not with observation.

The invisible God.

There's way more to this, isn't there.

There's no end. Rooted and grounded in Him growing up into all things! THAT'S gravity.

Last night all I heard you say was "Hi," and as for seeing you, that isn't meant to be.

I told you we would speak of it later.

I know. I just wanted to record it.

It already is, it's ALL recorded, in the Book of Life. NOTHING compares with THAT book. It contains everything. Some think it's a figure of speech. It is every word ever spoken. Some think it's just a list of names, because that's how they see it as described. It is a list of names, of natures, natures of life. All the nature of life, of being is contained therein. If you could just see the cover you would weep. I did. With joy. The beauty of life is unspeakable.

Wow!

Yes, wow! Remember that word's inverted; that's the nurturing spirit of the Mother, giver of life. The sweet Holy Spirit.

I'm out of time again.

Told you you'd never have enough of it there.

Must feel nice to be always right.

You think you know what it feels like.

Is that a dig?

Yes, sort of. Just wanted to give you a laugh before you went to work.

Well, you did.

Good.

You are the most—wow!

Yes, I am.

      G was getting dressed and got a long-sleeve shirt to wear.

Short sleeve. Sometimes less is more.

The Universe Speaks

Remember you're a pathfinder. Remember who you are. I'm always reminding you who you are.

10:24 PM
Well, Talia, I guess you proved how cool you were last night.

You were talking about it with Mom, my touch. I just confirmed your truth. You know the universe confirms YOUR truth too. This isn't a one-way street; as a matter of fact they go in EVERY direction. These are paths of truth; these are the laws of life. These paths will lead you out of bondage and into Liberty.

What you did last night—that was so precious and beautiful.

I always am.

May 26

6:34 AM
Talia, your name is so beautiful.

That's because that's who I am. That describes my very nature: "Heaven's Dew." You experience me. You experience me in my truth, my living my truth. I live UP to my potential. Anyone can do it, live UP to their potential. That's a free gift too.

When you experience me you experience a part of Him who is in all, through all and in you all. See how that works? It's his great pleasure to reveal Himself in his people.

You ARE just like Heaven's Dew.

I am. Again, you don't have time for this right now. You'll never have enough time to do the things you need to do here. You could use that sense of urgency also. You have much to do and so little time. Use what you have wisely.

Death as an advisor.

Life makes a much better advisor, life in the pure sense of the word.

1:23 PM
     G felt Talia's touch.

That WAS the sacred silence wasn't it?

Yes, it was, not in words but in deed and in truth.

Out of time again.

Collection

Yes and no.

10:23 PM
Hello, Talia.

Hello, G.

I'm tired.

I know; just write.

You said I had to be UP for this.

You do, you are.

OK.

You think we can't transcend the flesh? We can do all things. There are no limits here. Remember what your grandfather said about fatigue: it can work for or against you.

Figured he said it for a reason.

Everything's for a reason. I already told you that.

OK, let me have it.

You already do—you just don't know it yet—but you will.

Do you see all things?

I see all things that I see; you see?

Yes, I see what you mean.

That's why they were called seers: they SAW. They couldn't always articulate either, but they saw. They put things they saw in their own words for the people. It wasn't for themselves, the seers. You're a messenger for your people; give them the message.

What's the message?

To reveal the Art of Life—that's living it. Like I did, and do.

You are a shining example.

Yes, I am, always. What do you fear? Rejection? You've already been rejected in every possible way, and you've already been accepted in every possible way. What's there to fear?

Nothing.

That's exactly right. Fear nothing. You've been given the gifts. Use them, don't quench them. Don't think: do, write, flow.

The Universe Speaks

I can do that.

Of course you can. I don't waste words. You should know that by now.

I do.

Yes, you do.

Then I will do by being in Him.

Now you're getting it. See—it is easy. Your struggles are an example for others. Your victories are an example for others. You've never been one to beat your chest anyway. We appreciate that, even if you have suffered the scorn of others.

I'm writing!

Yes, you are—see how they flow, the words of life. Lived impeccably they bring forth fruit everlasting. Why are you stopping?

I'm just amazed.

It is amazing, always and forever. Pretty much amazing.

> Talia using the words "pretty much amazing" has a special meaning to me. Those are the words she used in a letter she wrote while in school, describing herself to me! When G heard those words he thought he was imagining things!

You think you're thinking this up? If you are you need to work for RAND (a think tank).

I don't think they'd have me.

Believe me, they would stifle your creativity, then want to dock your pay. You know how that works.

Oh yes, I do, the old set up.

That's one of those "experiences" I hate.

It's for a reason.

Figured.

You've figured right. You don't need their kind anymore. What could they add anyway?

About the only thing I can think of would be money.

Money's nice to have, but it isn't the god they make it to be.

I know that.

Collection

Then why worry about it? They don't know who you are, but I do. You know who they are, but they think you don't.

Spirit on the water, darkness on the face of the deep.

That's exactly right; those kind of people will never get it. That's their lot in life and they have their reward. You don't need them, they don't need you, but they call you indispensable.

They lie.

Yes—you know it's true.

Yes, I do.

Yes, you do. Now, without them what do you have?

Everything.

Yes, everything. Trust us—we're here to help you.

I trust you, I trust you.

Good, now let's go on. Leaving those things behind.

Yes, just drop them. Remember, the company you keep.

Then I will keep you with me.

And I will always be there for you.

May 27

12:14 AM
You stopped.

Just tired.

Why?

Probably lack of sleep.

Yes, and other things: trinkets in your way.

A test.

It's all a test. I told you that.

I just know when you're tired you make mistakes; that's how the brain operates.

The Universe Speaks

Your brain has very little to do with what we're doing here now—it's a tool to use. Just don't be overly reliant on it.

Well, that's a mouthful for a girl so smart.

You know where that comes from, and it's not brain power. This causes a lot of problems.

I've certainly seen that.

Yes, you certainly have. Keep your HEART with all diligence, not your brain. You have to be somewhat out of your mind to do this.

That's funny.

Yes, it really is, isn't it.

I feel a little achy.

Well, that's all temporary.

Guess everything is here.

No, not everything. What counts is forever.

That's beautiful.

Yes, it is.

How's that little girl?

She's wonderful, just wonderful.

That's great.

Yes, it is great.

She's understanding now. I've explained a lot of things to her now and she accepts them. She trusts me completely. She is a VERY precious soul. Lovely. She's smiling now. She says hello, and she likes you.

Why can't I hear her?

She doesn't know how to do that yet. She's still learning. The lessons here are never ending; they just go on and on.

Go to bed now.

Sounds like a plan.

It is.

Goodnight, Talia.

Collection

A goodnight to you.

7:24 PM
Talia.

You were open today to help others.

Yes, I guess I was.

That was not so hard now, was it?

No, not at all, quite pleasant really.

It always is. Even just being open to help others really says it all.

Well, I appreciate your approval.

You walked in your truth today and you really didn't even realize it. See how effortless that was? That's just letting Him live his life through you. That's the Art of Life and the Art of Peace, letting the Creator live His life through you.

And you were just talking this morning about the obliviousness of people and their capabilities of moving in the spirit, another part of them they are not even aware of . . . at play.

That's completely true. That's their innate curiosity moving what they really ARE. How could they not do this? It's their very nature as spiritual beings. Matters not their level of awareness of it or their remembrance of it. They are going to do this anyway. Everyone does this. We are all fashioned alike and have been born by the very breath of life. Who have you seen proud and puffed up for being born?

Can't say I've met anyone.

No, you haven't, yet how many have you met puffed up about having the breath of life within them?

I guess a lot.

Yes, you have. You've even done it yourself a time or two. Almost everyone you've ever met has at some time, and yet none of the credit is theirs; it just is. That's the gift of life. A lot talk about it; few know what it is.

Never heard it put like that before. That's boiling it down to the brass tacks.

And I've never heard that statement before. ☺

Never waste time. You don't have enough of it.

But can't I bend it?

The Universe Speaks

You saw it warp a couple of times today—when you took it by force. You said "it's mine" and it was so. You ARE a creative creature. You ALL are. We ALL are. How could we not be? We are created IN his image. Some think that's in likeness of; nothing could be farther from the truth.

Why?

BECAUSE THAT TAKES AWAY YOUR POWER AS A CREATIVE BEING.

They're under the impression that that also relieves them of some personal responsibility. It doesn't, of course, but that's a subconscious perception they adhere to for what they believe is personal gain. That is another ploy of enslavement. If they convince you you're powerless to change your circumstances without their help, what are you to them.

A slave and a dunce.

That's exactly right.

This is some heavy stuff.

When has it not been? I told you this is a message of freedom. Many want a process of A B C, but it just doesn't work that way. You were born free. You don't have to "do" anything. You just have to "be" in Him.

Boy, that smacks of humility.

And your pride will smack you down every time.

Now to answer your question, "How can we verify this to others?" Everyone already has access to truth—they were born by it. Honesty with themselves is one access or doorway, pure honesty. Another is by the quickening of the spirit, revelation by the light of self of He who is all. His ways to reveal the truth are numberless. There is no way I could even tell you an untruth. It just isn't possible. This path, this truth WILL set you free.

There is just no way for us to discuss ANY thing here without it leading to more freedom. I told you nothing was better than freedom . . . in Him. I can only point in the one direction because that's ALL that is. I told you of many paths. These are many ways, and the number of his ways are numberless. Your friend Ken has the revelation of numbers; no use covering it here—ask him.

G called his friend Ken to confirm some things he had told him.

That was a good call and confirmed to you everything we've been talking about here.

Collection

Yes, it did.

I'm glad you agree.

I do.

I KNOW you do. We MUST agree; what else could we do? Nothing. We could do nothing without agreement.

May 29

7:35 AM
Talia?

Yes.

Good morning.

Good morning. The words aren't going to jump on the paper—you have to write.

I feel we're behind.

We're not behind; we're right on time.

I just feel you have a lot to say.

I do.

Then could we get started?

We already have.

You're playing your Game today, aren't you?

Yes, I am. I'm moving people in the direction they need to go, including you. You're going to find out some things today you didn't expect.

Like what.

You'll see.

I'm expecting the unexpected.

No, you're not, not really. You think you know the direction your life is taking you. You really don't.

The Universe Speaks

What do you mean?

What I mean is that the words that I'm speaking to you are spirit and life; your natural mind can never understand them.

I know that.

You know that on an intellectual level. That's not what I'm talking about here. As long as you're SELF-CENTERED you can't grasp this. It's when you look OUTWARD to others, when your pride dissolves, then you can receive—to overflowing.

That's perfect, simple truth.

Of course it is. That's intellectual knowing—now live it. It's easy to start thinking about this and miss the point.

I think that's because I've judged others for living trapped in their brain.

That thinking's correct. Now, let it go, just release it. It's that easy.

>G spontaneously took a deep breath, just like the other night during Talia's "visitation."

Like a breath of fresh air, wasn't it.

Yes, it was.

And nearly instantaneous, wasn't it? That's how quick it is for you to make a decision to change. Now that's using your brain as a tool, as it's meant to be used. You see the design of this all?

You are a chess master.

I'm FAR beyond that.

It's such an honor to know you.

It's such an honor to be known.

Wow!

Yes, again the world turns things upside down. When you see "beyond the veil" you see the nurturing spirit, for the "growing up into Him." Then everything seems a gift. That's the true nature of our father. There's variance of natures but one spirit.

It's really not so complicated.

No, it's really not.

Talia, you are totally awesome!

Yes, I am and always will be. Unchangeable.

Collection

May 30

9:30 AM

Everything you do correlates with everything else you do. That's what you learned yesterday that you didn't expect. I told you this Life, this ALL was an intricate web. A luminous web of life. It's everywhere. That's why it feels like it's all happened before—because it's all happening at ONCE.

You were just speaking the other day about where Solomon came from.

All things work in your favor, for your good, ultimately.

How could you judge someone for screwing up—it's all for their learning. Everybody's on a different level of learning in the same place. Unless a person has given themselves over to pure evil and is doing pure evil.

Why do you call it pure?

Because that's what it is‧ pure undiluted evil. That's easy to see. That determination on your part you ARE meant to judge, without being judgmental or judged yourself. You know who they are because they have chosen to become that. They have decided in no uncertain terms to become that that they are not.

This is meat.

This is meat?

This is meat. You have to chew it well, then give it time to digest, then it brings forth life.

This whole message seems to be becoming more condensed.

It is, absolutely. They HAVE been spoonfed and pampered long enough. Time to grow up into Him in ALL THINGS. The voice of Truth echoes throughout the universe, bearing witness, reflecting itself to itself.

When you put it like that, it's amazing anybody could NOT get this.

Isn't it though. That's why I said, "Choose life"; it's ALL revealed in the light. There is no other truth. It's a real struggle to walk in darkness. Asleep to truth. Some are far off the road; many of these are leaders. You see how humanity is where it is.

Why did you call this path a road?

Because there's room enough for everyone.

You ask the right questions—that's one reason you were chosen for this.

89

The Universe Speaks

Yes, I used to drive some of my teachers crazy with my questions.

Well, you're not driving us crazy, but unlike most of your teachers we DO have the answers.

This is way beyond cool.

Yes, it is, off the charts in every direction, all leading in the same direction.

Thank you, Talia, thank you so much!

Thank YOU so much. So many struggle so hard trying to become what they are not. This is a LOT of work. Yet, if they yield themselves to what they are, the struggle ends.

This is self-evident, isn't it?

Yes, evidenced by the Self, of who they really are. Society generally attempts to force people into being what they are not. You see the misery this causes, the deep discontent. Because that's all based on a lie. People instinctively know this and yet most accept it as truth, instinctively knowing too, that truth is freedom. When they don't get the expected results they either resign themselves to their fate or they try even harder with the program they've been taught. The conflict comes with what they know to be true and what they have been told is truth. This IS a craftily woven lie intertwined with truth to appear as true. This is the sell to acceptance of it. No lie is of the truth, yet to deceive one must use the truth in a twisted fashion.

So if they were to tell the truth it would sound something like: we want to enslave you so we can have complete power over you, right?

Yes, something like that, and who's going to buy into something like that.

Nobody.

No, believe it or not some still would, but not nearly enough to matter to them. These I speak about want ultimate power. They will never get it, of course, but that doesn't detour them from trying. Nothing will ever be enough for them—that's what makes them so dangerous to the common man.

"Nothing" and "common man?"

Nothing is what they get. Nothing will ever satisfy. That's why they work without ceasing, trying to find it. The IT they seek doesn't exist.

Common man is exactly that. The common man is powerless to resist. They have the stranglehold on now. Haven't you felt it hard to breathe sometimes?

Yes.

That's the interconnectedness with all things. When one suffers you all suffer. That's why it's important to help others. That's what we're doing here.

Collection

Time IS short. Now is the time for man to DECIDE to intend the outcome. The choice is simple, so very simple. Yet strong delusion IS sent because man chooses a lie instead of the truth. REMEMBER the saying, "Choose this day who you will serve." The choice is simple and not so very hard at all. Use what you have to make you into what you want to become. People are going to do that anyway. The lie they tell themselves is: "I don't have the things I need to become what I want." That's completely false. They have within them everything they need to create everything they are to become, and that's what they really WANT. They want to become what they were created to be.

You are so far beyond me.

I'm not so far beyond you. We are one. I'm Part of you, you're Part of me, we are a Part of the whole, which is one in all. Remember singleness of heart, singleness of purpose. This is that singularity which is the ONE, the Whole, Creator and Creation in one.

There's a huge emphasis on this.

There's a huge emphasis on this because that's all that is.

I notice you mix milk with meat a lot in this.

It's nice to have something to drink with a meal.

There's not going to be a lot of my narrative here, is there?

There doesn't need to be. If you were a writer you could weave a colorful tapestry of background to all this, but we're not interested in that. We are interested in the forefront, the forefront of truth. This is the cutting edge. This is what changes people's lives. As I've said, some of this is just for you. Not that you've been singled out as special or something—it's just that it's just for you personally. Not that the residual benefits will not benefit others if you live them, because they will.

Some things are not lawful to speak. "Lawful" meaning the "laws of life." You were told before, and not by me, that many things are unlawful to speak unless they are already walking in that light. To confirm it for them, that's His prerogative, to be first. The first born among many brethren. The first to reveal that light.

Your enthusiasm is commendable, but wisdom is profitable to direct.

5:15 PM
Strong meat is for those who by use have their senses exercised to keen discernment. You asked whom that was for. That's my definition of "them." You always liked advanced classes anyway. If you had your way everyone would be beyond you anyway. That is the selflessness I speak of.

So, I'm not a totally lost case after all.

You've never been a lost case, although you have been totally lost before.

The Universe Speaks

Redemption.

Yes, exactly, you have been bought with a price.

Talia?

Yes?

I just remembered I was told I would write a book.

> Years prior to this, G was in his yard when he heard a voice tell him that he was going to write a book. He blew it off, thinking to himself, *I am not a writer.* But now, after all of these communications with Talia, and Talia telling him that these dialogues should be published, he remembered what he had heard years prior.

You were and you did not believe it.

No, I didn't.

Now do you?

Well, like you said, the truth is right in front of my face.

It always is.

I can still feel that you're like pregnant with truth about to burst out of you.

I am! I am waiting on you.

Then let's do it.

You're not ready yet.

I'm just taking notes here.

That's not exactly true. It's not just audible. My spirit has to co-mingle with yours for you to clearly receive this message. It's not just you taking dictation; that's how you see it, but it's more than that. Our minds have to "click" together by the quickening of His spirit. Sometimes you're "far away" from where I am. It's not that I'm far away, it's that you are. It's not difficult for you to get here, but it's difficult for you to "stay" here. That's that very quiet place in the center of your being. That's where we live; we dwell in the peace. This is a difficult place to describe with words for none are needed here. That is That That Is.

Well that's a mouthful and no mistake.

No, no mistake at all.

These are some things people have been asking about, begging to know. It's time they knew them.

Collection

The last enemy to be destroyed will be death. That's what we're attempting to get across here, that myth, that illusion of separation. There really is none. A lot of people know this. A lot of people think it's mere fabrication. The fabrication is the walls they've built with their mind. Matters not whether they believe they are creative beings or not, the fact is they ARE; therefore they ARE going to create no matter WHAT they believe.

You're also the deepest person I know.

You should get around more. ☺

You're ageless, aren't you?

There is no age; a person's "essence," what they really are, is without time. Time OUT OF MIND. The age you speak of is an outward appearance or a chronological timeline. It doesn't exist here. It is realized as a concept, to be used here to put things in context to be understood there.

Now that's something I never heard before.

Nor would you there. Either they do not know it, or if they do conceive of it, they have not the words to really explain it in understandable terms. It's just a concept to them, a picture or snapshot of truth. What's important is that we're "trying" to move you out of concept and into reality. Reality is realizing the truth. Of "being" in it. It's true living, not false death.

Death, as you SEE it, is real. Death, as you UNDERSTAND it, is a myth, a concept. This misunderstanding is what hurts the most. That's why I told you, as you looked at my ashes, "I'm not there," because I'm not; I m "here." I am as you said the most alive person you know. That's why you've never heard me talk about my dying—because I never did. That's an illusion and a myth, a very convincing one, by the way. It will be used to dispel all the myths just because it is so convincing.

It does hurt.

Yes, it does.

I remember years ago when I was told about writing a book I questioned what it was going to be about. The answer I got was "everything." That's when I really blew it off.

That's why I told you that you could ask any question you wanted.

8:49 PM

    G was thinking about the time to come when Talia's words, these conversations, are published, and how a lot of people that do not believe in spirit communications might think he is crazy.

You'll be ostracized in certain circles.

The Universe Speaks

I've been there before, and I really couldn't care less about those circles. I don't care to move in them anyway.

Just letting you know.

OK.

It's going to hurt a little.

Been there too.

I know you have. I'm just getting you prepared for a little more. It is for your growth.

Guess it's time for me to grow up.

You have said you're a late bloomer. ☺

They that are going to reject this are going to reject this no matter what we say. You cannot save them all, G.

May 31

9:35 AM
Thinking about on-the-job training?

That's where the real learning takes place, isn't it?

Yes, Einstein wasn't joking when he said the biggest thing that got in the way of his learning was his education. He was smart enough to wash away what he didn't need. And THAT'S one of the biggest lessons he left.

You didn't go with the flow of conformity, did you?

No, I saw through it, instinctively.

That's amazing. I mean especially for your age.

I take no credit for it. I've already explained my walk there. As for age, again, there is none here.

Wisdom born of God.

Exactly. How could one take credit for a free gift?

> G was thinking about some of the things Talia has been saying and had written down his own interpretations of some of it, when Talia spoke up.

You wrote your thoughts around the revelation like a commentary. It wasn't bad, but it wasn't very precise either. To be perfectly precise it must be born of the spirit. That's what's different

Collection

about what we're doing here: the perfect precision. Like a surgical instrument cutting to the heart of the matter—which is just energy slowed down. Now, if your energy slowed down, what does it take to speed you up to reveal the energy being you are? Something to think about, isn't it? There are enough commentaries out there.

Ah. . .

We just don't need elaboration, that's all.

Well, thanks. It was just a free flow of consciousness, stream of thought thing.

No, it wasn't. It was what mattered slowed down, like a stutter step—it didn't feel at all the same to you, did it?

No, not really.

Not really, exactly.

It's not that it was bad or even wrong, it's just that that's not what we're doing here and it's not needed. Now you see how you could never do this on your own?

Yes.

11:25 AM
You've got something else to do today. Go and look at things from a different perspective, a different point of view. You've looked at it from your own point of view, now release it and see it with new eyes.

Where.

Just follow.

9:47 PM
I don't feel that I got that much out of today.

Yes, you did; you just don't know it yet. Some things serve you and some things do not. You need to be with me to do this.

I know you don't like to hear this, but I'm trying.

Stop trying; BE. We can't go much further if you don't stop doing what you're doing and be what you are.

I don't feel very inspired today.

I do.

Well, let me have it then.

The Universe Speaks

It's already yours; that's what you're not getting.

Oh, I see the multiple meanings of that.

Now you're getting it.

I'm staring at the page waiting for you.

And I'm staring at you waiting for you. ☺

All right, I'm ready.

Are you really?

I think so.

You think . . . so?

I'm not following.

No, you're not. You need to lead now.

What are you getting at?

The truth, always. The truth is you ARE on the cutting edge of darkness.

I've been told that before, twice.

That's because that's the truth, confirmed in the mouth of two witnesses.

What does that mean exactly?

It means that light is expanding, and you're right on the cutting edge of it.

I feel this, but it's like deep down and vague.

That's all right, the light will reveal it. When you walk in it you will see more.

This must seem like elementary school to you sometimes.

It does, but it's still just as fascinating as it can be.

Just as fascinating as it CAN be—wow, that's unreal.

It's just as REAL as it can be too.

What would you like to talk about?

Everything.

Well, as Grandfather said, "That's a lot."

Yes, it is; it's everything. Everything is in Him really—there is no other.

Collection

That's a nifty doctrine, and I'm sure it's true, but it's hard for us here to really conceive of it.

You have been conceived BY Him. Forget the doctrine—he's WAY bigger than that, and you can be sure it's true. We're going to move beyond now.

What does that mean?

We're going to move Beyond, NOW. We're beyond where we were then. Now we're Beyond now again. You have to SEE it to understand it; words aren't going to make sense.

Oh, man, there really is no explaining it, is there?

Not in words.

It's a wave formula, isn't it.

Something like that.

Time, light and gravity are waves?

Time, light, and gravity are physical phenomena, parts of which are made up of waves, but there's much more to it than that. The physical is not what we're speaking of here.

So there's a mathematical equation for this, a language made up of symbols so the mind can see it?

That's one way.

June 2008

June 1

7:23 AM
I saw it as a wave circling around behind you. It seemed about to push you from the back, and it was full of colors of all kinds, some I'd never seen before.

> G had a vision of Talia, with the most incredible colors swirling in the wind around her and behind her.

That's the wind of the Almighty pushing us to new places. That would be the easiest way to describe it. Although no words can do it justice—it just is. The colors are His blessings, unending. There is no end to the colors or His blessings. It's His good pleasure to give us the

Kingdom. God IS love and love never fails. He will not fail in what He has set out to do, and that's to bring us all back into his fullness. Can you feel the joy of anticipation?

Beyond that!

Oh yes, I told you there were no words for this. You've heard it said there was no new thing under the sun, and there's not. He completed his work there and declared, "It is finished." There are two correlations here, one in the Story of Creation, after which He rested, and one in the finished work of the cross. Look closely at this. This ties everything we've talked about here together. I can tell you there's no end to the new places here. He said He will do a new thing in the earth. I will tell you to look for it—watch.

I see in both places he said it is finished.

It is!

I keep thinking of Joseph here.

Joseph wore a coat GIVEN to him by his father, a coat of MANY colors. What did his brothers do?

They threw him in a pit out of jealousy and were going to murder him but sold him into slavery instead.

Sold him INTO Egypt. What happened?

In the end he ends up feeding his brothers and saving them from famine.

What I'm trying to get you to see here is he FORGAVE them.

And there's a famine in the land now?

Yes, there is, a famine of His word, of his true Voice. Remember the five-course meal I told you about?

Was it five?

It was five; you just didn't write it down. That's what we're doing here, laying out the meal. So they that have ears to hear CAN partake and be strengthened and move on.

I remember you saying five now, but I didn't want to limit. I was reasoning I guess.

Anyone can talk themself out of most anything. There are no limits to any number—it's just a symbol. People look at numbers dispassionately; it is a language and it's full of passion. Remember I told you if it came up to explain his revelation of numbers.

    G's friend Ken has a theory on numbers and their meaning.

Ken said there are really only ten numbers.

Collection

There are and there's no end to them.

Everything that can be contained, which is everything that is, is contained in 0.

Although that doesn't explain it exactly either. Contained is a gross term, slowed down; nothing's really contained, you have to SEE this. There are no words to describe it.

This is hard to grasp.

There is no "grasping" it; you must be in it.

> G thought about an incident in kindergarten. G was in art class and he asked his teacher for more colored crayons, because there weren't enough colors out. She told him there were plenty of colors out, and he said, "No, there aren't; I need more colors." She said he had all the colors that existed. G again said, "No, there are more colors." The teacher was exasperated and began to walk away, and while doing so asked G in a sarcastic tone, "So, you want your mom to buy you more colors? Are you jealous of the kids that have more than you? You can make do." G thought, *No, that's not it. It's just that I see more colors than I have to use.*

Now, that's something I haven't thought about since the day it happened.

There are LOTS of lessons there, aren't there?

Yes, there are.

You see, they train you to see what they want you to see and nothing else. It works too. Until you break through and see what's really there, which isn't what you were told at all. You remember we talked about the prison of the mind? Those are manmade bars.

Well, now I feel like my parents got their money's worth out of kindergarten.

You did. ☺

I wish I had known then what I know now. I would have called her on it.

You were five.

There's that number again.

Whoa! Talia. Thank you for this! This is priceless!

Yes, it is priceless.

I'm thinking precious . . . there are no words to describe you, are there?

No, there are not. That would be like describing the infinite.

It always comes back in a circle because it's spherical.

The Universe Speaks

Yes, it does, because it is.

My mind is blown here.

And that's a good thing.

Blowing the bars right off. I just feel like jumping up and down screaming.

You can.

I feel like running out, holding this over my head and screaming.

If you do, you are going to get some looks. ☺

I'm giving you the last word today.

Why?

Because I'm honoring you.

Thanks.

Guess that pretty much says it all.

11:28 AM
I feel when I get up and walk out of here into the world with other people everything pales by comparison.

It just seems that way. It doesn't. You can still walk in it when you walk out of here. Remember, it's just distractions, trinkets.

That all there is here, isn't it, just trinkets.

That's all there is to distract you. See through it.

I noticed you said before every man's been given a measure of faith. I know it says THE measure, but I wrote it like I heard it. But I've been wondering about that.

You heard right. Every man's been given the measure of faith, but what he receives is A measure of the measure. Told you we were here to establish Him in the present truth.

So the truth is changing, but it's unchangeable.

No, not really. The truth is the truth, unchangeable, but it is established presently.

Well, that's kind of hard to understand.

It would be unless you're walking IN it, established IN the present truth.

6:38 PM
Talia, you're SO awesome.

Collection

And just think, I'm a very small aspect of God.

No . . . that's TOO much to comprehend.

You must surrender yourself to that that cannot be comprehended.

Thank you for choosing me, God. Thank you for choosing me, Talia.

You were "open"; you chose yourself.

June 2

9:21 AM

Talia, I just read through nearly all of these dialogues so far, and it seems like the building blocks of life.

That's a perfect description, because it is really.

Can't help but notice the image of an infant.

Well, that's understandable. That's pretty much where we are really, but we're growing, fast.

We?

We're all in this together. If people understood that, the fighting would stop. When someone looks to someone else, that's when the fighting starts. When someone looks to someone else and sees themself, that's when the fighting stops.

What can someone give you that you don't already have?

OK, we could discuss this in detail, but we already have. Again, all things are yours, already. You already have all things you need. Seek it like hidden treasure, because it is. Seek and you will find. He cannot lie. Now, that's an equation that balances itself perfectly. And the answer is within you. When people do the math the war stops. There's nothing to take from anyone because you already have all you need.

Now I understand why math is a perfect language.

It is! And perfectly logical. Perfect logic is perfect. The problem with logic is people's imperfect use of it, which is of course illogical becoming the exact opposite. Yet some cling to their view with a tenacity that's nearly unbelievable.

Again, the universe is spherical; when they cannot or will not get outside their mind it just circles in their head. You ARE a microcosm of the universe, you know. Therefore you can know all things just by knowing yourself.

If people knew this . . .

The Universe Speaks

People in reality **DO** *know this. We're just reminding them—RE Minding. People also know the unknown can be known. This is a seed or spark within them that creates the desire within them to search. How many do you see searching, seeking for something they just can't put their finger on? That's the unknown but not unknowable that they know; if they knew, all their questions would be answered and they would be fulfilled. That's what they WANT. But for most their brain has been washed to another direction. They accept being called consumer; they wallow in it really. Wouldn't it be better to be called givers; wouldn't that be something to aspire to?*

Oh man, Talia.

Good stuff, isn't it?

Oh yes, it is!

1:51 PM
I told you this wasn't so much a job as an adventure for you, to touch people in a place they deny to themselves exist.

Cool, sounds like a Navy slogan.

It's an ocean of consciousness. You're teaching them to navigate though the sea of the universe, which contains all things. Everyone's trying to get there in their own way; most just don't know it.

The infinite is within them; that's something else that is hard to comprehend. But it's there! That's why I say it's right in front of your face, in the mirror. There's a certain fascination to people when they hear the words "behind the looking glass." That's another pointer, pointing to hidden truth. But you do really have to look behind the looking glass to see it.

Holograph!

Yes, outside of yourself looking back into yourself.

A reflection of what truly is.

That's it.

I have to go look in the mirror.

Yes, please do.

What did you see?

One thing, you can track a man's "times" by the lines on his face.

Yes, every one's there for a reason. What else?

I see what's going on inside is reflected outside.

Collection

And what's going on inside is a small part of everything that is, all happening at once. Now do you see what complex beings you are? How could you belittle another?

That would be foolish.

The height of foolishness. A fool is known by his multitude of words. Most of what you do that really counts is without words. How many words did we speak the day we met?

Not very many.

But look what happened and look where it led to. Look where our relationship, our friendship is leading us: fruit unimaginable.

That's wonderful to know.

Yes, it is. You knew you had something more to do. I just reminded you.

Well, thank you VERY much.

You are always welcome

June 3

8:03 AM
I'm not feeling it today, Talia.

How many times have you done things without feeling like it?

A lot.

So what's different with this?

I just don't want it to be me. I want this to be you.

It is me; it's us. Moving in Him. You don't always have to feel it; as a matter of fact, not feeling it is for a reason.

Faith.

That's part of it. You're interested in the credibility of this, and I appreciate that. I know it's hard and it's not easy; it's also NOT hard and it's one of the easiest things you've ever done. It takes effort, sometimes great effort. It's also one of the most effortless things you've ever done. It's a real struggle, and it's not a struggle at all. The flesh wars against the spirit and the spirit against the flesh, and those are contrary one to the other. But He always gives us the victory.

Thank you for that.

You're welcome. Are you ready to move on?

The Universe Speaks

Yes.

Good.

> The night before, I took G to visit a friend of mine from high school who was in town for a short visit. I knew that she would be fascinated and amazed by Talia's words, and I wanted G to tell her about the communications.

That girl you met last night. You said she had a sweet spirit, and every time you thought of her you thought of that, that she had a sweet spirit. Well, that's true, she does. And when you said she was on a good path, you saw the mountain with many paths on it. That was a confirmation that what you spoke was true. You helped her navigate by what you spoke to her about. You even said you saw the light in her eyes. That was the true light. You honored me by what you spoke to her about last night, and I want to say thank you.

You're welcome. Talia, you're teaching me about honor.

That's something you asked about years ago and not so long ago: "What is honor? I'm just not seeing it here." That prayer was honored. Prayers are present. Prayers are never ignored. Ask and you shall receive. He SAID, "You have not because you ask not. Ask and you shall receive." And He cannot lie. He is truth and joy unspeakable.

You're honoring Him here, aren't you?

He is worthy of all honor and praise and glory. He is the source of all things, but He is not just the source of all things, He IS all things. There are lesser beings of God, but He is all Beings.

You can only see it to understand it.

Absolutely.

How do you point things out?

> G is referring to how Talia causes G to see, or focus on, or think about something.

That's just energy, easy as can be. You can do it too, you know. It's thought condensed to a small pulse. You send it with intent.

I "see" it.

That's the only way you can know what I mean.

There's electricity involved.

It's spiritual energy. The brain and nervous system receive it as an impulse; that's why you feel it.

But would you still feel it without the body?

Collection

Of course you would, but the vibrations are on such a higher level that you don't need to. It just is—things are just known.

That was sweet what you did last night. That was true sharing, and you curbed your enthusiasm to a perfect balance. You didn't try to convince anyone of anything; you knew it just is. That is a fine way to present truth. Present the facts with true passion. That's authentic. That's felt by people and that's what they'll remember: the passion of truth. Out of her own mouth she said, "The truth will set you free." She knows that to be true and has claimed it for herself; therefore, it is so.

All true knowledge is the knowledge of Him, the building blocks of life. How often has He mentioned buildings? Man loves to build. They are "made" in his image. You are a holy temple. He is building you. To become what He is. In all things.

That's awesome!

Of course it is. And, He cannot fail.

Then, why do we worry so much?

THAT'S a good question.

June 4

7:43 AM
Good morning, Talia.

Don't think, write.

Talia, there's no way for me to express my gratitude and deep, deep appreciation of what you've done and are doing and are being. You're truly changing me from the inside out.

I told you this was a message of change. Of course it's changing you—you're listening. You're listening in the quietness of THAT THAT IS. Of all things. All things are yours.

Wow, I never saw it like that before.

I also told you to look with NEW eyes. He is doing a new thing UPON the earth, meaning you, meaning all who will listen and are willing to see with new eyes. You see things differently now. You're starting to see things as they really are, endless fascination. All things are placed in Him to bring you back to Him. That's where you came from in the very beginning anyway. See, it is all spherical, from and back to Him.

No one has ever put it like this.

This is the Pure Word of truth. This is given to me, and I'm just sharing it with you.

105

The Universe Speaks

I saw the little girl last night (the little girl that Talia is taking care of), and she was grinning from ear to ear, and her face was glowing, with light all around her face. She looks so different.

She IS different now. She completely understands now. Understanding brings joy unspeakable. You see so many people struggling to understand. That's another pure desire placed in the heart of man. They too instinctively know that to truly understand will bring joy unspeakable. With partial understanding things seem complex and sometimes troubling. With complete understanding comes peace!

You're explaining everything!

You were told this would be a book about EVERYTHING.

Yes, I even saw it with a capital E.

And THAT was for a reason.

This is everything I ever wanted.

Of course it is. You wanted a DIRECT LINE. It doesn't get more direct than this. You'll notice I don't filter anything, and yet my personality comes through clearly.

That's something to think about.

Yes, it is. God has never meant to remove anyone's personality but to enhance it. We are all unique in this way, beautiful aspects of what He is. That's part of this message, to reveal that. When someone attempts to stifle your personality that's their hatred or misunderstanding of the pure. That's them warring against God.

You see how time seems to distort when we're doing this?

Yes.

It doesn't really. Time is linear in man's thinking, in man's view. When man thinks of the eternal he thinks in linear terms. This is a completely false assumption. Time, like space and everything else, is spherical. But even that doesn't explain it: it is and yet it is not. Time, really, is a concept. It is not; it is nowhere. It seems to man it's everywhere and just is, and there is nothing you can do about it.

He just can't change it.

There is nothing to change about something that is not. How many times have you heard, "Time just seemed to stop?" This is an event of pure experience where perceptions were replaced with reality.

That's another "trick" not to be distracted, to "focus" your mind. Time itself is a distraction.

Collection

6:47 PM
That was a real surprise when you spoke to me while we were working.

Why would I not? It was fascinating to me. I told you I learn from everything you do. I jumped at the opportunity. I "seized" the moment and I enjoyed it immensely.

Well, you are welcome any time.

Thank you. I'll take you up on that.

You ARE crafty.

It's far beyond a craft. This is an Art.

The Art of Life.

How did it go with Frankie today?

> Frankie and I met with Rebecca, the medium. Frankie wanted me to go with her. She wanted to hear what Talia had to say to her.

Good. Not as good as I had hoped, but better than it seemed.

Did she receive it?

Yes, she did. She has a lot to learn yet, but she'll get it.

Excellent.

Yes, it shall be.

Why don't you call and find out. You're distracted by it anyway.

OK.

> G kept thinking about Frankie's and my meeting today with Rebecca and really wanted to hear about it from me. His desire to talk to me about it was distracting him from speaking with Talia.

8:06 PM
I don't know what to say.

You got a message you didn't expect today.

> While I was with Frankie at a meeting with Rebecca, Michael, Talia's father, came through and told Rebecca that he really liked G.

That was nice of him.

He's a nice man.

That makes me feel bad, for judging.

Don't worry about it. There's nothing to worry about. I'm just pointing out that your thoughts are real; they create. They can create chaos and misery or peace and joy. Peace and joy are better, you know.

My thoughts being real have never been this real to me before.

Again, this in an experience. You just experienced it.

Yes, that hurt a little.

It was a good hurt. To change you. To change your mind.

I'm glad it's changing.

It is. We just changed it.

I feel it.

How could you not? You've trained yourself to be sensitive to so many things, how could you not be sensitive to this, that your thoughts affect people. Good or ill, that's just the way it is.

Makes sense to me.

10:43 PM
>G was having a beer, relaxing.

How's the beer?

The wine's better.

>G is referring to Talia's touch and her healing of him, which he calls "wine." When he mentioned wine, Talia told him that she had tasted some wine while here, in her body.

I tried it. I didn't like it.

Does your mom know?

She knows.

Everything won't be resolved every time we talk about it.

I figured that.

You're a strategist; you would.

Never thought of myself like that.

You do it all the time.

Collection

OK.

Yes, it is.

Kind of has a sneaky connotation.

Not at all; you're just crafty.

I said that to you today.

And I said it was Art. I'm trying to get you to move into that level. Most I'm trying to do this with are unconscious of it. Do you see what I was dealing with today? Filled with distraction.

Never thought of that.

Now you can.

Must be frustrating.

It is. Beyond words.

I'm with you.

Yes, you are.

You are absolutely, totally, and completely awesome!

Yes, I am. You could admit that about yourself, you know.

THAT wouldn't seem right.

But it would be. We're speaking of your higher Self here, not what you see as imperfections or mistakes. Mistakes are just learning experiences anyway.

Well, if you put it that way.

I do. To speak it is to declare truth. It also hastens its being. Words are life. Choose life. Speak words of life; they're life giving. Also declare this about others. Show them who they really are. See the change. Words are life. Are not the words I'm speaking life?

Yes, they are.

Then use them. Speak into being. You CAN create life. "Having your loins girded about with truth." I've already told you this message wasn't just for you—time to get it out there. You've seen the signs, undeniable.

Talia, if only one other person gets this . . .

Oh, there will be way more than that. You've already seen people changing from this.

Yes, I have, without a doubt.

The Universe Speaks

Then bring them the message.

June 5

8:16 AM
You said you had things to say today, and I had something to do. Now I'm back.

Quiet yourself.

Talia?

Yes?

You have an appointment today, I guess right now.

> I had a phone appointment with a famous medium in New York. Though I hear from Talia through G, and Rebecca, I wanted to see if this other person was able to hear Talia differently and to pick up on different messages for me personally.

I don't have an appointment. There are places for us to be and we are. It's not here and there; everything is. All at once.

So you're not distracted by this?

Not at all, but you are.

I'm thinking ahead.

Yes, and you're trying to categorize things. It doesn't work like that.

Then I need to quit that.

Yes, and let things be as they are. Be in the Now. That's all that is.

What about character?

Character is a byproduct of everything we've talked about here. If you walk in it, if you live it. As a matter of fact, it's a very small issue when you compare it to what were discussing here. Most use the words "character" and "work ethic" as a banner to carry proudly. I tell you it's not that important to talk about: either you have it or you do not. What difference does it make to talk about it?

Then let's move on to something else.

Yes, let's.

What's the issue?

Collection

The issue is perfection. That's something most will not talk about because they think that they know it's out of reach for them. But it's not. They can't do it alone though, and that's what disturbs them. I'm telling you it's not out of reach at all. It's right before you.

You're saying you have to "see" it.

Yes, it's within you, but you have to see it. Remember I told you without a vision the people perish. They just wither on the vine. The vision is right before you. You just have to claim it. He does the work. He said He would finish what He started—the Author and Finisher of your faith. Your job is to let Him.

That seems simple enough.

It's all simple enough, more than simple enough. I told you people nearly always complicate things. That just muddies up the waters. Who wants to drink muddy water? You are made from the dust of the earth and have the breath of life. You can muddy the waters or you can let them flow clear.

And I see that when you do muddy the waters, if you are still it will settle and be clear again.

Sometimes you can't help but to muddy the waters, but that is a lesson too.

On that note I've been wondering about something.

Ask it.

When I got back from my walk, when I didn't have my pen, once I got it you said, "I'm glad you got your pencil." Did I hear you wrong or what?

You heard right. I wanted you to know you could change things in the past, that you could erase them. People carry burdens of the past with them like baggage. It's back breaking.

That's awesome!

Of course it is.

Yes, you SAID you had some things to say today.

Yes, I did.

Did I hear you right earlier when I asked you about the mediums and the psychics, when you seemed to say they're rusty?

Yes.

Why?

What causes rust?

The Universe Speaks

Oxidation?

Lack of oil.

The anointing.

Yes, many are called but few are chosen. It's not that they don't have a gift, it's that they've left their first love. It's not that they can't be used either, because they are. The anointing is a protection, a power. The kingdom of God is not in word but in power. There is nothing sweeter than the Holy Spirit and there is no faking it. Why take a Model T when you have a BMW.

That WOULD be slower.

A circuitous route. The truth must be quickened to bring forth fruit and only the Holy Spirit can quicken.

Wow!

Yes, it nurtures too. Nothing can possibly be gentler.

You DO move me.

Yes, I do. I move everybody I can. I move them in a perfect direction. You've seen this.

Yes, I have. I just don't know how to describe it.

There are no words to describe it. You can see it or you cannot. You can feel it or you cannot. There's no faking this either. You see people suppressing their emotions. Emotions are another tool in your arsenal to be used.

Why did you bring up emotions?

Because that's part of the message. People have been taught to suppress them long enough. I'm telling you to use them. They come from the essence of what you are, so to deny them is to deny yourself. This causes MUCH sickness. And the doctor's cure is to treat a physical ailment.

That IS stupid.

It's ignorance. Yet they will spout off about their education, never suspecting they've been taught wrong.

Hmmm...

I'm righting some wrongs here, with the sword of truth, which is a light to shine on the darkness. The darkness in them really hates that, unless they're ready, unless they are prepared to move on. Most are stuck in the mud of their own making.

You don't pull any punches, do you?

Why would I? It's either all or nothing. You know what He said about being lukewarm.

Collection

What is the void?

That's everything that is not. Everything that is has a counterpart that is not.

That's hard to understand.

Yes, it would be, wouldn't it? You asked. ☺

11:06 AM
Now I know why you didn't answer me when my thought had completely formed, *Were you perfect on earth?* It was ignored and you kept going. You answered it at the same time through someone else.

> It was not a coincidence that Talia brought up the issue of perfection with G when she did. I had just been talking to G, and I had told him that I thought that Talia was pretty perfect while here with us. Then, while I was on the phone with the medium in New York, Talia told him that she wanted me to know that she was not perfect while here with me.

Yes, I did. All of your questions will be answered.

Well, I'm seeing the perfection of imperfection.

That's something not many see, but that's true, there is. It all has purpose, meaning.

Everything means something.

Absolutely, exactly, everything. When someone says "don't mean nothing," they're just not seeing it.

We've got to see the invisible.

Exactly. You MUST look to those things that are not seen. Anyone can do this; as a matter of fact, everyone does. We're dealing in matter of facts here. Time to go.

June 6

10:09 PM
You're getting it! You're getting it!

> Right at the moment Talia said that, G and I were having a conversation in which we were speaking about and contemplating all of the things Talia had told us about energy being Truth. Right at that moment we realized that energy is all there is, that we are energy beings, pieces, parts of the one source of energy.

113

11:42 PM

I heard your friends were acting out.

> I had just found out that some of the kids in Talia's class, her friends, were beginning to act out at school, and get into some trouble. One of the kids admitted that he was depressed over Talia being gone, and that was why he was acting out in the manner he was.

My gravity held them together.

June 7

7:13 AM

You act like it's not enough time.

You said there wasn't.

Exactly.

Boy, it's going to be another one of those days.

It's a perfect day that the Lord has made.

His mercies are new every morning.

Of course they are. Everything is new every morning, everything is being renewed always. I told you it was ALL energy. Energy from every thing that is. The scientists have noticed a piece of energy here acts on a piece of energy there instantaneously, but that's not exactly true either. That's as they see it. In reality there is no here or there, and instantaneously isn't correct either. It is all now. They will discover that matter is energy slowed down by focused thought. That time is a perception. And that thought creates. They've already discovered that just to observe something acts upon it. That's why I've said so many times to look. Looking at something acts on it to reveal it as it really is. I said you were a creative being. "Ye are Gods."

You've said yourself that the eyes project energy. What did my eyes do to you the day we met? They changed you; they acted on you to reveal who you really are. The light of the eyes rejoices the heart. This IS the light of Life. Have you not captured someone with your eyes? They also capture the moment when you see it. So you see there is also more to this seeing that I've mentioned than you saw. In His light shall we see Light. And all of this can be proven by mathematics also. The passion of truth never fails. The precision of perfection is focused thought to reveal truth that will set you free. I told you, you have a part to play. That's why I call it a Game. Games are fun.

Talia, you just—wow.

Collection

Yes, I just wow.

Go now; this will never end. Never ending. Always. ☺

12:47 PM
Mental blocks of memory are always self-imposed or accepted. No one has power over you unless you allow them to have it. Thinking is an attempt to freeze time, which always causes confusion.

G is thinking about a big test he has the next day.

What's important is what you get out of it, not what you get from it. Many are not only missing the big picture, they are missing the little pictures too. There is really only one picture.

G thought to himself, *I'm quickened.*

I told you that's not me. We're quickened together. All this is yours. The revelation of the knowledge of truth. You asked to know what everything really was, what everything really meant. I told you prayers were "present," and the honest prayer of faith was honored and answered. So it is.

I'm overwhelmed.

You need to be.

I need to "BE."

He supplies ALL YOUR NEED. I cannot lie. I am as an embodiment of Truth. How could it EVER be otherwise?

It cannot.

That's correct.

Because your confidence will be shaken. You know why.

So that that cannot be shaken will remain.

Exactly. We are dealing in exactness here. Like dealing cards, you get to choose. It's a GRAND game. A game of truth in the inward "parts," to complete the whole.

My mom got me here perfectly. That's why she has no regrets, as she shouldn't, ever. She will share in this reward, and it's far beyond tremendous. There are no words to describe it.

> Hearing this really touched me. Talia telling G that I should have no regrets was a confirmation to me that Talia is really with me, always, and that she responds to what I ask her or say about her. Just a bit earlier that

day, I was on the phone with a friend of mine and I told her that I have no regrets with how I raised Talia, at all. Then to hear Talia say this was to me a wow moment!

Thank you for telling J (Talia's uncle) I love him.

And you said he would receive it.

And he did, perfectly. That was sweet of you.

That brings tears.

They're all counted.

"I am as" an embodiment of truth?

"I am as." There is one body; we are images of it. What you see on earth as a person is an image of that person. That's why there is no death. That's a physical body ceasing to function. There IS no death. That's why I call it an illusion. Like a mirage in the desert, of water. The water is not there. The water—which is life—has moved on.

Perceive those things that cannot be seen. "Look" to those things which are not.

Energy is invisible unless it's slowed down enough, acted on enough, by an outside force or an opposite force to be seen, but you can always perceive it.

Always?

Yes, always because you ARE energy. How could you not perceive yourself? Nobody's THAT cut off. That's just something that is, and that's all.

1:55 PM
I know why you were chosen for this.

It was revealed to you; respect.

Don't judge anybody for anything by outward appearance (age, looks, social status, etc.), but judge with righteous judgment, which is spiritual judgment, spiritual discernment.

You could talk about your service in the "intelligence community," which is a real misnomer. Now you're in the REAL intelligence community.

6:00 PM
Why did you bring that up?

Because you like shining the light of truth on the darkness of ignorance.

I'll bet it ties into some other things.

Collection

I'll bet it does.

Talia, it looks like I have a few minutes.

When it's all over that's what it will look like.

When my life on earth is over I will look back and it will look like a few minutes?

Yes, that's what it will look like, like a flower of the field.

"Behold the lilies."

That's right.

Guess there is not much to get hung up about.

You can only hang yourself up by the false images in your mind.

Thought creates.

Pure focused thought creates reality, in its many splendors.

You were bought with a price and His servant you are to whom you obey. You'll notice most people obey whoever pays the most. You are not your own; you have been bought with a price.

"The lamb."

The Lamb of God. I told you I was going to talk about a lamb.

I remember.

"He is the One."

Someone that read some of this dialogue said that "he sure skips around a lot."

THEN they should ask themselves: A) Who is the "he" they're talking about? B) If he skips around a lot, it's for a reason, and C) If they're not tying it all together then perhaps they are not seeing it. I tell you, this must be seen holographically. To really make sense of it, their eyes must be opened, by being open.

Some say, "You can't open your mind to every conceivable point of view."

There's only one point of view that matters.

June 8

6:12 AM
I'm glad you're going to my tree dedication.

I'm glad too.

> Talia's school planted a very special tree in her honor and memory, a Gingko tree that was the same age as Talia when she "died," thirteen. The tree was planted in a stone planter, and around the edges of the planter special words were engraved. Words that describe Talia: Amazing, Authentic, Gracious, Joyous, Insightful, and Athletic. As soon as the planting and stone engraving were finished, the school had a special dedication ceremony presenting the tree to the school community and to me.

7:45 AM
You told me awhile back, "It was my time," and I said I'm not going to tell your mom that. If you want her to know you can tell her through someone else.

That was for you to know.

Then you did tell her through someone else.

Then it was time for her to know. You said yourself, "Things take time." I told you there is timing in everything.

Vibrations.

Yes, and other slower rhythms.

I can see it.

Yes, and you've heard the music.

I have.

Think of the scale of sound your ears hear. Just as narrow as sight, yet some think all they see and all they hear is all that is. It's blatantly obvious that it is not. Their very logic is flawed to death. I told you people create whether they want to or not.

I have felt you, touched where you are at, smelled you and even tasted it that day you healed me. I've seen you and I hear you now. Nothing is more real to me really.

All you sensed in a harmonious whole. You're no different in that way than anyone else. Most of your problems are unconscious. I'm here to raise your consciousness. "Your" meaning everyone that takes the time to read these words and to listen to the voice of truth.

That's awesome!

We will not fail. I have seen the End and it's a Beautiful Beginning.

Passion creates quality.

You asked about it.

Collection

1:35 PM

People do not realize their capabilities. I'm saying to you that there are no limits. When people realize who they really are, all limits are transcended and there are no limits.

Sounds good. How do we do that?

By being who we say you are.

That sounds like a pat answer.

Again, you want a method of A+B+C. Let's skip A (the beginning) and C (the end) and just BE.

That even outdid the other answer.

You ARE down today. Snap out of it. That's the problem.

I feel like the walking dead.

You are experiencing a bit of that today.

Oh man, there's some irony here.

Sure is.

You want to be up all the time, and that's not going to happen. The downs are just as important as the ups.

Well then, I guess I should rejoice always.

Of course you should. Be at peace; all things are going to work out just fine.

It does not feel like it.

You can change it in an instant.

Thought is faster than light.

Thought is focused energy. Study this.

OK.

June 9

5:15 PM

G was thinking to himself: I remember when I traveled through Santa Barbara when I was younger I heard a voice say to me, "There is a girl from here who is going to change your life." My response to this was basically, whoopee! And then the voice said, "But she's not born yet." Needless to say I was a bit crestfallen at hearing this. Not to mention slightly doubtful! But then I KNEW what I heard. At the time I just filed it away. That night I slept very peacefully. I continued on my journey the next day north along the coast, through the redwoods into Washington, then back down through Nevada. I had some very interesting experiences.

7:00 PM

Maybe you should share about the sleeping bag.

Why?

Because that's another "in your face" example of how He supplies all your needs.

9:20 PM

G kept seeing a very particular kind of flower in his mind. He saw it so many times he finally asked Talia about that vision.

What is the meaning of this flower?

It means I love my mom.

G tried to find that flower in books and on the internet but could not. Then out of the blue, I showed G the vase that Talia, through a friend of mine via Rebecca, had given me for my birthday. The vase was blown glass, and the pattern and colors were exactly the flower that G has seen in his mind. It was then that G understood what Talia had meant by her statement, "It means I love my mom."

June 10

After I met that girl, Kim's friend, you said, "It was a fine way to deliver it." It was because of where SHE was at, wasn't it?

When you see they are not receiving it, by a spirit of resistance, say what you've got to say and move on. She was in a place to receive it. She was OPEN to receive it. She has strived to get there.

Rebecca said you had mastered multidimensional communications.

I have but there is much to learn yet.

Collection

June 11

3:15 PM
"It was beautiful."

Talia said that to G right after her tree dedication ceremony.

June 12

11:25 AM
Talia, I hope I can live up to your expectations.

I don't have any expectations. I expect you to be who you are.

We know in part, and we prophesize in part, but when that that is perfect is come, that in part shall be done away with. The Kingdom of Heaven is within you.

5:54 PM
Talia!

Yes!

I've missed our time together.

So have I. I'm glad you were at my tree dedication.

I'm glad I was too; it was an honor.

It was an honor for me that you were there.

This is humbling.

Good, that's a good thing. You just need to know who you are.

I'm trying to find out.

So you are. ☺

Yes, I see what you mean.

I heard that Frankie said she felt you there very strongly, and also afterward when she got home.

Frankie wrote Talia a letter after the tree dedication.

The Universe Speaks

She did and I'm so glad. I want her to know I'm all right and that I'll always be with her and that we will always be friends. She is very, very special to me. She always will be. She told me she felt me and that she misses me. I don't want her to be sad. She should be happy and know I'm OK and will always be with her, "friends forever."

She seems to be a very sweet person.

She is! We had a bond beyond this world and we still do.

I can tell it's hard on her sometimes.

It is, but that's temporary. She will grow up into Him in all things also. I made her some promises, and I'm in a position to always keep my word.

She has dreamt about you, hasn't she?

Yes, she has, and in her dream I told her I was all right and that she would see me again.

And you can't lie.

No, I cannot.

Well, it's sure an honor for me that you're my friend.

It's an honor for me as well. You're an honorable man and I appreciate that about you. I know your heart, and you do try to do the right thing.

Yes, I don't always succeed though.

Maybe you should redefine success.

Like how?

Like looking at it from a different point of view.

That's a thought.

That's a pure thought.

Well, if anyone knows about purity it would sure be you.

Everything here is perfectly pure.

And complete?

It's completed in Him.

What's next?

You're going to get a call.

      Just then the phone rang.

Collection

6:55 PM
Talia, that was actually pretty amazing. Too bad I didn't have a witness here.

That was for you. I'm constantly confirming this for you. You doubt as much as just about anyone sometimes. Also the truth cannot but help verify itself when you're aware of it. It's constant.

That was awesome.

Well, thanks. It's all energy you know.

I think I know exactly what you mean.

You do, and you're concerned with how to describe what you know about it. It's not necessary. As I've said, they that are going to get it will get it, and they that are not, aren't. There's nothing else we need to say about it here. They have been coddled and spoon-fed enough. People must learn to apply themselves and not listen to the lies that are forced upon them. There is ample truth right before their face. Again, it's time to wake up and that's a simple choice.

I concur!

Thank you. I'm glad you do.

That was a very interesting dream I had this morning.

> In G's dream he saw what looked like rocks pushing down on a mat, causing a funnel-like shape downward with a twist. It was like a twisting tube in the universe.

I'm showing you how energy works in the universe.

That whole "twist" on the torque thing was new to me.

It's always been there.

That's something I'll have to put my thinking cap on for.

It takes energy to see energy. That is a place where things disappear to reappear some place else. You'll see it; it takes energy.

I want that energy.

You have it as potential energy. You're not applying it yet. And space isn't "warped" either. That's as they see it. It's perfectly formed. When they come from a place of perfection, it will be perfectly clear to them. It looks chaotic; it's not at all.

You'll be tested by fools. Well meaning fools, but fools nonetheless. Remember, water off a duck's back.

Just shake it off.

Just shake it off and flow on, knowing what you know.

That was well put.

Yes, it was. The spirit foretold my coming to you and how I would affect you and your life. He told you that I would change your life.

You certainly HAVE.

I'm not finished yet.

That's good news for me!

Yes, it is, very good news.

Talk about a new thing in the earth!

OK.

I can tell you're just smiling.

Yes, I am, from your great joy.

June 13

1:00 PM
I have got to be honest with you, I'm about sick of people.

That's because you think they're phony. They all aren't.

What, just the ones I meet?

You meet some that aren't, and you appreciate their authenticity. They are refreshing to you.

Yes, I just don't meet very many.

There aren't very many, but there could be more. That's a defensive mechanism: they're protecting what/who they think they are. That's not what they really are but an image of who they think they are. If they knew who they were, you would like them all because you would see yourself in them, and they would see themselves in you. As it is, it's false images they feel they must protect. They see it as their very lives. They clamor for respect, not knowing that to truly respect themselves IS to respect others. He said to love your neighbor as yourself.

Well, thanks. I feel better now. You're certainly authentic and so is your clarity, as always.

Collection

You're welcome, and I am, and it is always. Now, get out there. Forget caution. I'm going to show you where things disappear and where they reappear. You will manifest them. That's part of YOUR job.

That sounds like fun!

Oh, it will be.

It will be.

That's the agreement we need. You see that that IS, not AS is.

Got it.

Then it's pure focused thought in faith, then release it as it is so, and so it is.

Got it.

Then be. The "doings," in the being.

Walk IN it.

Correct. You will see it as it is in the now, where everything is.

I can do that.

No, you WILL do that.

Intent.

Yes, you intend it, fully.

The ramifications of this . . .

It is beyond anything, anything that you know that is, yet it is not beyond everything. It is a part, a function of what is contained in everything, and it's everywhere.

I'll have to ponder this.

Yes, you will. What is, is not and then it is.

Cycles.

Everything cycles.

Everything that cycles does.

Except that that does not, the unchangeable.

You ARE a tracker.

I'm learning.

The Universe Speaks

Yes, you are.

2:37 PM
How do you do that with the perfume?

> G is referring back to how, when he felt Talia and was healed by her, he smelled her perfume.

That's the shadow; this is the real.

June 14

12:59 PM
Talia, those photos of you were awesome. It's so plain you were living a life fully as it's supposed to be lived.

> I had given G some photos of Talia, some with her horse, some playing volleyball, some just being her.

Yes, I did. I knew instinctively I had to. That's an instinct I always trusted.

Thank you for the life you lived, and thank you for the life you're living now.

The life I lived WAS for an example. I didn't know it then, and if you would have told me I would have laughed. I wouldn't have thought that was necessarily true, but it was necessary and it was true. You may not always know whom you are influencing. I influenced people then without noticing it. You're always more than you think you are. But to know that is to trust it, that you can be used in a divine way whether you know it or not.

I'm really, really running out of words here.

Many times there's not that much to say. Just let things be as they are. The most meaningful communication is often without words, for no words are needed. Words are misused more than anything anyway. How many times have you seen the sincere word of truth despised?

A lot.

Yes, a lot, and why is that?

Because the world is filled with knuckleheads.

Maybe we could get into a bit more detail.

You could. I see knuckleheads wherEVER I go.

Collection

Maybe you should reflect something else to them.

Ooh, got me on that one.

You will see what you expect to see. I told you to expect the unexpected. You're not always expecting to see divinity shining through whom you meet, but maybe you should.

Yes, you got me. You awe me into silence.

That's a "trick" I use to get you here and to keep you here.

Well, thanks for tricking me.

That's not so hard. You've always been open to truth. Your frustration has been that it always seemed so hard to find. It's not, when you look in the right places. It seems like it's placed here and there. It's really not—it's everywhere. It's man's nature to look here and there for someone who is genuine to tell them the truth, yet that's very rarely the case. That's their nature, to make a god out of someone. All the time God and all the answers are within them.

Looking for love in all the wrong places.

Pretty much.

I covet our time together; it's a divine haven.

You could call it that. ☺

I just did. You love this, don't you?

Yes, I do. It's truly a part of all that is, and it's being watched closely.

By a great cloud of witnesses?

Yes, a very great cloud.

I feel anticipation, the joy of them.

They are in awe; this is somewhat of a first.

> Talia is referring to this communication, at this level of frequency and intensity.

A new thing on the earth.

Exactly. This will confirm much to many.

Now I need to believe who I am.

Yes, the light IS expanding and you're riding the wave of it.

I feel like I'm learning everything I need to know about everything, doing this.

The Universe Speaks

You are. There are no other truths. There is only THE Truth. He in whom all is. To know HIM is to become one with Him. "Make them one Father even as we are one." Do you think this prayer is not answered?

Time to go back to work.

Time to be one in Him.

Make it so.

It shall be so. It has been spoken.

Oh man, Talia.

It's beautiful, isn't it? Remember how you used to ride on the ragged edge?

Yes.

You're doing that now, but now you're accomplishing something.

6:15 PM
Ride the ragged edge.

Ok, but it scares people.

It does, and it thrills them, disturbs them. But you'll always see a response. Some it will awaken, some it will shake back into slumber.

Why would it shake them back into slumber?

It's the choices they make.

They make them too, don't they?

Yes, they make them. It is your nature to create. Once you awake to who you are, nothing is impossible to you.

Some have vested interest in keeping you asleep.

Who you are is known in solitude.

In the quiet of the heart is your true nature known.

There is no other nature given among men whereby you can be saved.

A good man shall be saved.

He has magnified His word above His name.

His word is heard in stillness.

That's an equation of freedom.

Collection

When you are saved from your own deluded creations, then you are free.

Whomsoever the Son sets free is free indeed.

He has given you power and authority to be sons, and saviors shall arise upon Mt. Zion to judge the mount of Esau, and the kingdom shall be the Lord's.

When He was asked, "What is truth?" what was there to say? He was the embodiment of it.

In the silence is the truth and your true nature known.

You are all things.

That's an equation for wholeness, for completion.

June 15

8:07 AM
Talia, all of that wasn't you, was it. It was just the spirit flowing.

That "just the spirit flowing" is what makes all things possible. You said yourself you can't put these things in boxes. It is the box, what's in it and everything outside of it. Although that doesn't explain it either: it all is. Some like to have everything explained to them. Things are revealed in time.

Patience, Mom.

You know you can only fool yourself. Which is a trick people use on themselves to teach themselves.

I think I see exactly what you mean.

Yes, you can jump ship, but we're still all in it together.

That's a unique way of putting it.

Yes, you saw what I meant. That's placing pictures in your mind, to explain, to reveal meanings. That's expansion of understanding. That's light expanding. The universe IS expanding, you know. He reveals Himself in His creation. Are not we all His creation? Why would one take "the source of all things that are" out of the equation? That just doesn't add up.

That's so simple.

Yes, the complexity of simplicity. The complexity is the darkness. The simplicity is the light. And these complement one another.

I totally see that.

The Universe Speaks

You don't totally see it, but you see enough of it to totally matter.

OK, there's some deep stuff there, isn't it?

There always is.

How did you . . .

Learn all this stuff. I'm VERY close to Him.

Oh, man! I see something there that's way more than it looks like.

Of course you do; that's sincerity of heart. It's time. Sit down and write. There are some things you need to know.

OK.

You're not totally with me on this.

You know I've got to go back out there in a few minutes. I'm a little distracted.

No, that's not it. You're holding back. You're afraid of where this might go.

That was you looking at your watch.

Just trying to keep track.

You're trying to keep track of something that doesn't really exist.

Well, it seems to.

I know it does. When I say this is a game, it's not like most people take that word, as something trivial. This is a most serious game, one that takes all your wits about you and everything you have. This is the first time you've avoided me.

Talia, I don't mean to. I'm just jumpy.

You know this will shake the very foundations.

That's fine.

It's very fine. It's time for this. I KNOW this; you should too. You can't run.

I know that.

But it's crossed your mind.

Come to think of it, yes. OK, I surrender.

You have to surrender all. I know you're a fighter, and it goes against the grain, but that's the way it is.

You know I didn't really know all of this.

Collection

I know; that's why I'm showing you. You're trying to keep things safe, and there's no doing that. Let the chips fall where they may.

All right.

Of course it will be all right, always. That's all for now.

Guess I had plenty of time after all. ☺

June 16

6:47 AM
OK, what's with Narnia?

> While Frankie and I were meeting with Rebecca, Talia mentioned that she had seen the movie, *The Lion the Witch and the Wardrobe*, but she had called it *Narnia*. Talia also said that where she was, in Heaven, it was like Narnia.

That's the way it is here, only better. It was something she's—Frankie's—familiar with. I saw the movie.

12:58 PM
You told me once to look at it as if I'm an instrument to be played. I'm an instrument.

You're a beautiful instrument.

Come on.

You want to edit it, don't you.

Yes.

It's good to face the truth, the good and the bad. You see how hard it is for people to be honest with themselves, even when it's good? This really holds you back from knowing who you are.

It's like I've already done this. I've seen this before.

That's because it's all happening now.

I also see that some will think I'm deluded.

That's their own delusion of the truth. The truth is not what someone says it is or what they think it should be, nor what they want it to be. The truth just is. Ultimate truth is unchangeable no matter how it seems to change. He said, "I am the Lord thy God; I change not." Some dread if that's true; I tell you it's the best news ever.

The Universe Speaks

9:00 PM
Are you ready now?

You ARE chipper today.

I had a good day. Mom had a good day.

I didn't know you'd ever have a bad day there.

We don't, but there is a LOT going on and we do have concerns, much like where you're at on earth at times.

Well, I guess that's not news, but that's sure not the general consensus we down here have of heaven.

There are a lot of misconceptions. Look at the misconceptions on earth about what's going on there, and what things really are and what they mean.

Good point.

You bet it is. I know you adore me and that's sweet of you.

I do. Why do you bring it up?

I just don't want you to exalt me above measure, that's all.

I just know who you are.

Yes, you do, and I appreciate that, but you do have that tendency.

I remember, you told me about the gods and goddesses.

Yes, and that's held people back from doing what you're doing now.

I don't want to jeopardize your message.

I told you it wasn't just my message, that it's much greater than me.

I know it is, but you are totally awesome.

Yes, I am. I'm also just a messenger.

It seems you're diminishing yourself.

No, not at all. I'm just telling you the truth.

I wasn't going to build a temple or anything.

Well, that's good, because that really WOULD jeopardize the message. ☺

Talia—you're having fun. That's great.

I'm having great fun!

Collection

Fantastic! You're just finding out all the things you can do there, aren't you?

Yes! It's more than anyone could imagine! You're feeling a part of my unimaginable joy. There are no words for it there.

No.

Bask in it. That's what you should bask in.

What happened today?

Discovery! Wonderful, beautiful discoveries. And there's no end!

I'm so happy for you.

So am I. So am I.

Talia, you seem nearly speechless.

There's no speech for this. It's much, much greater.

I can't imagine.

No, you can't.

This is new to you.

It's all so beautifully new!

Maybe you need a day off.

That's funny. You need a certain detachment, along with a passionate interest, to do this.

I thought you were done for the night. I was going to tell you to go enjoy yourself.

I am, immensely!

You know, when you put it like that, it's kind of hard to stay here.

Sorry, Charlie, you've got work to do.

Now YOU'RE being flippant.

I'm having fun. You said you wanted me to. ☺

THAT made me laugh.

Laughter's good. It works like a medicine. And you needed it.

Thanks.

Any time.

You totally blow me away.

So you've said. It's all a balance, G. That's why I'm doing this.

My dad likes you a lot. He says you're a good man.

> This blew me away, because a few hours before Michael had Talia tell G this, I was having dinner with a friend of mine who asked whether or not Michael ever spoke to G. I told him that up until now, no, that Talia had told Rebecca once that her dad really liked G, but that was it. We both wondered why it was that Michael was not speaking to G himself, and then G got this message.

Tell him I said thanks.

He says you're welcome.

Why can't I hear him?

He's still learning it.

You seemed to have stepped right into it.

I did; it's easy for me. It's hard for some others to hear though.

You said through someone that I heard you 100%. Why is that?

You've forgotten most of the things you've gone through to get to where you are now. There's not a great need for you to remember them either. Everyone's path is different.

June 17

8:12 AM
You're distracted.

Yes, I know.

Go take care of what you need to take care of, then come back and we'll chat. When this door opens I need you to be quiet—your mental chatter doesn't help us. You need to be in perfect stillness.

8:52 AM
Don't make it harder than it is. The stillness is always perfect. This should be effortless. That's the trouble with words, the misinterpretations applied to them. There are more efficient ways to communicate. You puzzle whether you hear if there's an "s" on the end of a word. The reason is, I'm showing you it really is all ONE. The separation is for your learning. Yes, everything is for a reason. Why did you put the "T" when you meant the "G"?

Collection

> During G's communications with Talia, he puts an initial next to each statement he writes down, to indicate who is speaking, him or Talia. Sometimes he hears the words and says them at the same time, so he puts a "T" *and* a "G" down, but this time he wrote a "T" *instead of* "G."

In a hurry?

We are one. All things are.

So you see Mom's friend has the truth, but it is partial. Judge not, she'll get it worked out in time.

In time?

Yes, in time.

Time is a period of "places" placed together separately.

Hard to follow.

Yes, it can be. It's illumination of the heart for growth.

To bring singleness of heart, singleness of purpose.

Yes. This is concentration that is unwavering, and timeless. It's beyond awareness. Awareness is simply awakening. This concentration is purity of purpose.

That's the answer, isn't it?

That's the answer of how to do things right. That always results in fruit everlasting, and it's remembered.

I see there are so many truths here that if people knew or believed this they would dig for them. This is much more treasure than the greatest lottery on earth.

This is obviously not brought from any kingdom on earth. What we're doing here IS earth shattering. This can shatter every false perception that people have, if they will receive it.

Free gift, huh?

Of course it is. The curse of the law is the illusion that you must toil for something of value. The most valuable is always free. But it must be OBTAINED in freedom; that's why I said nothing was better. It's all obtained and contained in the freedom that is in Him. Get this and nobody can own you. That's why I said you were bought with a price and you were not your own. Sounds like a contradiction, doesn't it?

Some.

It's not. Not at all. That's the only true freedom that there is. No amount of money can buy peace or joy or understanding or anything we've talked about here. Yet people will toil like there's no tomorrow and even kill each other over it. This can put you in a place of no redemption. The love of money IS the root of all evil. And what does money represent? It can represent anything anyone wants it to represent, but is just a representation. People agree or disagree on what it represents, but it's still just a placard, or sign. See it like that and you see right through it because it is transparent. See what they use it for, and the motivation is apparent. It's just a lever to be used for good or ill, that's decided by the one using it.

Makes sense to me.

Of course it does; how could it not? It's perfectly sensible. People make much more of it than it is. It's not all that they make it to be.

I heard that someone said money doesn't change people, it just reveals character.

There's a lot of truth to that.

Some, we're just going to get their attention. Here, some are going to get more out of this than YOU have.

Cool.

Yes, it is. Very cool.

*Some will have a greater understanding; some will see the **DEEPER** meaning.*

That's awesome, because I know I'm riding that wave.

Yes, and they'll be ahead.

They have my blessing.

Torchbearers; you'll see them light the way.

This is much greater than I realized, and I thought it was pretty big.

Told you.

2:48 PM
Talia, all my expressions are inadequate.

The Art of Life entails no forced expressions. They should flow out of you, always.

June 18

6:45 AM
Good morning, Talia.

Collection

Good morning.

7:32 AM
Just write. There are some things you need to know.

Then I want to know them.

Do you really?

Yes, I really do.

Then you will.

OK.

Where are we going with this?

I wanted to point out desire.

What do you mean?

I mean you have to really want or desire something to really get it. A fervent desire, a passion in the heart. Most just go along for the ride. Remember our talk about violence.

Yes.

Many things, you have to "take it by force" or you won't get it.

All right, what is it I need to know?

That's it.

Many times you've gone along for the ride and it left you wanting.

I see what you mean. Thanks for the imagery.

You're welcome. Any time you've taken it by force in perfect balance, you've achieved great success. It's been astounding.

Astounding, huh.

You have been an astonishment at times to others.

OK.

Yes, and it was a sign to others on how to accomplish things, on how to get what they needed. You saw some ignore it, and you've seen how it inspired others.

Well, that's nice to know, that some were inspired, but I don't seem to be that consistent.

The Universe Speaks

The truth is completely consistent. It's your head that hinders things. You have a proclivity to do what you're told instead of what you know is right sometimes.

I didn't actually realize that.

That's why I'm telling you. Sometimes you go a little over the top to please, and that can compromise your position. It also smacks of insincerity.

"Smacks" jumped out at me a little.

Yes, it did. I'm pointing out that it's like a slap: it stings and it's abrupt.

I don't ever really remember seeing this before.

It doesn't happen often with you. I'm just letting you know you can kill or damage with kindness. Remember the balance; compromise when you should, not when you shouldn't.

So what are you going to do today?

I'm going to be who I am in Him.

I like the answer, but I thought you might be a little more specific.

I can do whatever I want, and I want to help people. That's what I'm going to do today.

That's nice. ☺

Yes, it is nice to help others. It's very fulfilling. More should try it; that's one of the purposes of life.

Your infallible, aren't you?

Now I am. I know you want me to get specific on what's going to happen today. You know the principle players I'm touching and moving. I don't know what's going to happen myself. I can't make anyone do anything. That's free will. We cannot interfere. So it's a surprise to me also. That's one of the pleasures of life, the pleasant surprises. I do know it will all work out perfectly.

That's awesome. I'm glad I asked.

I'm glad you asked too. I've been wanting to explain that. You've been under the impression that I know everything. I told you I didn't but that I know a lot. When we do this I don't always know where it's going either. I have more joyous anticipation with this than you do. I told you I can see your thoughts forming but before; that is like a clear sky to me. I don't know where the clouds may form. It has been said that His presence is like a cloud. Something to think about, isn't it?

Yes, it is, big time.

Absolutely.

Collection

I really didn't know if I was going to do this today.

I didn't either.

I'm glad I did.

So am I. I told you the power of your decisions could not be underestimated. And how you could call this unto yourself. We are always here to help, but the choices are yours to make.

To make, to create.

Yes, exactly. All the important decisions are yours to make. How else could you learn?

> G got a message he was going to get a phone call from someone.

You felt that coming.

Yes, I did.

That was a specific thought, directed to you, from the web of life. That's a luminous being, and it's energy of the universe. How is it some do not feel it?

Cut off from life.

That's it. Your works will be remembered.

That's what matters, isn't it?

That's worthy of remembrance.

What matters is worthy of remembrance.

Yes, and what doesn't, isn't. Some things are worthy to forget. When you see those things, forget them. Just leave them behind.

I meant to ask, what's with the balloons?

> While at a meeting with Rebecca, Talia told Frankie to be on the lookout for balloons: a sign from Talia to Frankie.

It's a celebration. That IS for Frankie to remember our times together. All of our times together were a sort of celebration. That's what I would like her to remember and not any kind of loss. We had a perfect friendship, and I want her to understand we still do. She knows me very well, and I want her to know when she feels my presence that's ME and not her imagination. She knows this is true, and she will feel my presence today, and that's me confirming to her that this is true. Tell her not to be sad, and she has a beautiful life ahead of her.

> G called a friend, whose wife answered.

That call you just made was a perfect example of non-locality of mind. She doesn't hate you; it's what she's given place to in her.

The Universe Speaks

Man, the things you can learn from a simple phone call.

Yes, you can learn from anything, and everything means something, and you don't have to rack your brains either. You just need to see things as they are.

Pure focused thought, perception!

Yes, perceive those things which cannot be seen.

"Thou hast set a table before me in the presence of my enemies."

That happens many times in life.

I don't care to break bread with the devil.

You don't have to.

He's a liar and a thief and the father of them all.

That's right. He has been cast out of heaven. Where is heaven? Inside of you, within the heart of man, within the heart of God, within all things. What evil have you seen that wasn't the creation of man?

I don't know.

Yes, you do.

I've seen the dark side. I've dealt with them.

You dealt with them because you wanted to deal with them; that's a game you chose.

What are you saying?

I'm saying evil stems from the knowledge of good and evil.

What do you mean?

Can you know good without evil?

I think you can.

Can you know light without darkness? It's for the contrast to know the nature of all things. All the battles are for learning, for growth.

All right.

Don't withdraw just yet; we're not done. You want to get mad at a person who's sick. How can you get mad at a person for just being sick?

Well, that's a whole different point of view.

Yes, isn't it though. That's a perfect point of view.

Collection

I love you.

And if I didn't love you I wouldn't be talking with you now.

Thank you.

Thank YOU for being who you are. You're a self-made man who's had nothing but help getting where you are.

That's funny.

That's true.

8:08 PM
You accomplished some things today; you felt the shift.

Yes, I did. I also sensed an accusation of exploiting you in the future.

I know you did, but how could you exploit me?

I know that—it's completely ridiculous.

Then why bother with it?

I just didn't want anybody to get upset.

It will work out.

I think maybe I should relax.

This can be tiring.

And the heat—hard to keep a straight face.

Some will accuse you of talking out of your head.

If I were that clever, I figure Disney would take me at gunpoint.

That is funny.

June 19

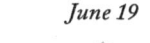

7:11 AM
Good morning, Talia.

Good morning.

I don't know how to thank you.

The Universe Speaks

What you're doing is thanks enough. Do you know how many want this, and from this side too, just to let their loved ones know they are all right? If there was envy here, they would be envious. I'm telling you they are standing in awe of this.

You let my mom know from the beginning of this that I was OK, and that confirmed to her without a doubt that what she already knew was true, and I'm so thankful for that.

There's nothing else I could have done.

Yes, you could have ignored me.

Talia, you were so totally adamant about it I couldn't ignore you.

Yes, you could have. We're in a position to see the things people ignore, and you would find it hard to believe. Talk about exasperation. If you knew how many times we shake our heads. "Why can't they see!" I've heard this many times. Many are so locked into their own little world that they cannot see what's really there. So I want you to know that I appreciate what you've done for me and are still doing.

I wouldn't have it any other way. This is a tremendous honor for me.

That's one reason my dad thinks so highly of you. He says he wishes he could have known you there.

Well, *I* appreciate that. Tell him thanks and I wish the same thing.

He says to tell my mom he never wished to do any harm, and if he had it to do over things would be different.

She'll read this.

He knows that.

My heart aches.

Every second counts there; that's why I showed you not to waste moments. A moment is more than a period of time. As a matter of fact, time has very little to do with it at all. A moment is a happening, an event of truth and revelation, Now.

That's a unique way of looking at it.

That's a way of looking at it as it is.

God, you're smart.

I'm just telling you what I hear. All that happened to you on Thanksgiving was to get you to this place where YOU could hear. Why do you think you went?

That was out of character.

Collection

That journey you made that day was watched closely and with excitement.

Come to think of it, I did feel that.

Yes, and the vision you had on the way back has come to pass, and it was to confirm to you that what you got WAS pure revelation of truth.

> On the way back from Thanksgiving dinner, G had had a vision of a water bottle with the words "Natural Spring Water" on the label. He had no idea why he saw this vision; at the time it meant nothing to him. But a year later when he was driving, he stopped for a break and picked up a bottle of water at the same location he had had the vision—the label was that of the vision.

But I don't have it all or the full interpretation of it.

No, no you don't, but you will. It's enough for now to know where it came from.

Wow!

Yes, Wow! God will always Wow you, and there is no end to it.

That brings us to boredom. Boredom is absolutely an illusion. That's an indication that someone doesn't know themselves. To know your Self is to perceive the infinite, in which there is no end.

I see the correlation there.

Yes, of course, it's all tied together by that luminous web of life in which there is no end. See now how we all are one and there is no escaping it.

Why would anyone want to escape it?

To cling to illusions as if it were life itself. People try to get the truth to fit their idea of the truth, but that's just an idea.

I don't know if I know how to not waste moments.

Yes, you do. You just don't practice it very often. But when you do, that's walking in perfection. You did that just now when you walked outside; you didn't waste a single moment and you were bathed in light.

That's awesome!

It always is and beyond awesome. The first thing you said was "everything's cleared up." You initially meant the atmosphere, but you immediately saw it meant more.

That's what we're doing here, isn't it, clearing things up.

The Universe Speaks

Of course it is. Nothing here is not completely clear and perfectly precise. Not that there aren't hidden truths, because there are. But if someone doesn't get this, it's not because they're empty headed but because they are not.

That to me is somewhat hilarious and sad at the same time.

A lot of things are like that. That's to help get you through it. That essentially is the realization people are given, that no matter how tragic something seems, it will all work out.

Eventually.

It's being worked out now. You, like most everyone, like a timeline so you can place things there to make sense to you. I'm telling you there really isn't one.

That does seem to be a contradiction.

That seems a huge contradiction, but it's not.

My dad, he wants to say more.

I can tell; I can feel it, and him.

He will. It's not that easy for him and he wants it to be right.

Tell him I'm here for him.

He knows that.

Part of that heartache I felt was his, wasn't it?

Yes.

I didn't know you could be sad there.

You can be anything here. Regrets don't stop, but they can be worked out.

"Being mindful" comes to me.

That's something that should be researched.

Should I?

Not yet. We're not done here.

OK.

I'm waiting.

Are you, patiently?

Not really.

Why not?

Collection

Excitement?

That's an emotion you should control.

OK.

It's always ok, when you control it. You can, you know.

No doubt.

Good.

      G felt a tremendous peace settle down over him.

There's a peace involved in that, isn't there?

Yes, there is. When you're doing things right, you'll always feel that.

Always?

Always, if you're in touch with your feelings.

Touchy feely, huh?

You want to make light of it while I'm making Light of It.

Oops.

That's all right. You do that a lot, but I know that's just you. You have said you like to keep yourself amused. That's being in touch with who you are.

Well, *that* was kind of a turnaround.

That was the Light of Truth shining on your cyclic nature. Just remember I said the downs were just as important as the ups. That's another contrast for enlightenment.

Good thing I was patient.

Good thing you are.

I don't have the words.

There are none, and there doesn't need to be.

10:57 PM
Where's my little notebook?

It's in the truck.

It is? It's in the truck?

It's in the truck. Why are you looking around? I told you where it is.

The Universe Speaks

> G started to wonder how it was that he was actually able to hear Talia. What was it exactly that enabled him to hear her and her to put thoughts in his head?

The brain just slows the vibrations down to a reasonable form.

Presence of mind?

That's part of it. Presence of mind in a larger sense contains everything. That's how you can know all things. And the vibrations of the energy of the web of life are how you can track anything. The tracks will always lead back to its source. The source or reservoir of all things. So, they are contained without being contained.

I can't see any reason to go anywhere.

There is nowhere to be but where you are.

You seem to be the master of understatements.

I have mastered some things, but mastery is never ending, because it's a living process. I just now mastered a way to put that to you in understandable terms.

Yep, it was in the truck (G's little notebook).

As I said . . .

There's nothing that shall not be revealed in time.

Wind IS a vehicle; that's why it sounds like one sometimes.

OK, I don't know what that means, but whatever, it's heavy.

Yes, that has to do with gravity.

> G heard a huge gust of wind come up, so loud and powerful it sounded like a huge truck had just gone by.

You just experienced something that there is no way to explain unless they have experienced it. To attempt to explain would be futile; it would diminish the process, which is to experience.

Like war at its most visceral level?

War is a tragedy in the makings of man.

Light and gravity are synonymous. You can't have one without the other. You also just experienced how light bends or is attracted to the heavier of two or more very small objects. Now you could be shown equations to refute this and prove it's wrong. I'm telling you that their equations are incomplete. I told you this was about Everything. Why would you want to edit it? That would be like editing everything. I tell you everyone who reads this is going to get a touch, a movement, and it's "right on time."

Collection

G thought about what Talia had just said, "right on time."

Amazing, the hidden truths in plain view.

NOW you're living the Art of Life and are flowing perfectly.

Thank you, Talia.

Thank you, G.

Wind is a vehicle for what?

It's a vehicle for truth. It's a vehicle for power. Just watch the way it blows.

People should only be destroyed when there's no other choice. That's the plain and simple truth. This seems like a hard saying. You were told you always have a choice, but sometimes the choice is made for you by others. You were told you could defend yourself. That's a God-given right that nature teaches.

The numbers yesterday—the number pattern you are working on with Ken—was your life as a mathematical structure of the universe. There is one in every number. When they understand that, they will be able to unlock all the mysteries of the universe. That's experiential understanding from a holographic base.

A lot of things that people think mean a lot mean very little, and a lot of things that they think mean very little mean a lot. People have it so backward so often.

Exasperated?

Oh, beyond words.

It's all one. People like separate subjects; it's all one.

G had a vision of Frankie and Talia looking at each other and laughing.

OK, what's with that?

That's when we thought or said something at the same time. It was delightful and the oneness I'm speaking of. It's God in you agreeing with the truth. Now I see that we saw so many things that were truths, and we discovered them together.

I can feel your total affection for her.

She was always a blessing to me in SO many ways.

And I feel her pain for you.

She shouldn't hurt for me. She should be joyous.

Fellowship is the bread of life. Light reflecting back on itself is light reflecting back on you.

I'm making up for lost time. In both directions since that's the way you see it. In reality, time can never be lost, but it can be misplaced.

Maybe I should tell them we shouldn't get paid by the hour. But all at once.

Yeah, try explaining it. It's difficult enough for me, and I'm in a unique position to see it.

It's hard enough for me to get it, and I'm getting it.

The only reason you're getting it now was your rebellion at their teachings. If you hadn't rebelled, you wouldn't be here, now. They said that was your biggest problem: you questioned everything. You didn't fit their program, which you saw as bondage. Many of them resented that greatly because that was to them the very foundation of their life. They saw you as despising them. You were just despising their work, their way, because you saw it was a false way and it led to nowhere, at least nowhere anyone in their right mind would want to be. That teacher you just thought of, she said you could do anything you wanted. That was a revelation she received through prayer. She also said you were her favorite student because you represented a challenge; you grew together. Remember she said you were the biggest problem she ever had?

Yes, I'd forgotten that part. I remember she threatened to retire when she got me the second time around in a later grade.

And you thought about it too.

Yeah, I really did. Hard to retire in the 5th grade though.

But you seriously considered running away.

Yes, I did.

You're kind of in the same place now, sort of a circle.

I don't want to run away.

No, but that's primarily because you're not locked in a classroom. You have more freedom now.

Freedom is good; it's like the sweet smell of success.

You love to be outside.

You said you had to be there before you could look in.

Yes, I did, and you do, and you are.

If the light's not on it, it's like it's not there.

That's exactly right. I say it's wake-up time. It's time to walk into the Light, in the dawn of the day when everything is new.

And I know violence isn't the answer.

Collection

No, not in the flesh. Victory here can only be achieved by an awakening brought about by a great shaking.

I see a sieve.

So you do. You have to be fine to make it through, like the eye of a needle. You see the brutality coming from many directions, but the peace and power is in the Kingdom.

So what about the whole Zippy thing?

> Zippy, Talia's dog, told Laura, the animal communicator, that he thinks it's not only Talia speaking to G, but other spirits as well trying to trick G into thinking it's Talia. And that G is thinking some things himself.

There have been a few times it was you, but it's mostly things I would or could have said. You said yourself, if we're in agreement, what difference does it make? And I've said that myself, see.

OK, what about being tricked?

I told you that you were being tricked. I trick you daily. How many times have I already confirmed this to you? This is not just in word but in power. Zippy senses another spirit that isn't me, and he's right. There's a huge number clamoring for your attention. There is also THE Spirit, which is not me but that I am part of. That's Zippy separating who he knows to be me from something else.

Anything else?

Yes, relax. The enemy will try anything and everything he can to prevent this from getting out there. He will not succeed, of course, but that won't stop him from trying.

I know most of the Christians will say this is "of the devil." I also know it's Zippy's perception, because he's heard me say you told me, when it was the Spirit that did. My mistake.

Was it?

Those that will say "this is of the devil" is because they've had that pounded into their head. Remember your friend who talked about the parrot preachers. That was a pure revelation of the Spirit that he received while deep in prayer and intercession, with a fervent heart, to reveal truth. God always honors this work, and yet you saw the truths he brought rejected by most. How we know the spirit of truth and the spirit of error is who HEARS our words.

I guess that sounded arrogant to some.

It did to those who couldn't hear it.

I know that today we both said the same thing at the same time.

The Universe Speaks

Yes, we most certainly did. I was just discussing how Frankie and I did that and what it meant.

There's definitely a "T" to go there (Talia's statement).

There definitely is because you hear our words. How many times have I said "our"?

A lot.

Yes, a lot. That's because this is again not just my message. As a matter of fact, very little of it is. I am, as you've said, being used, and my joy and honor in that is beyond comprehension. This came up for others; you already know what's the truth.

It's been a constant struggle.

For me also. That's why we said again that you were on the cutting edge.

Paul was also. I've seen that.

Yes, you have, and he proclaimed to the other Apostles that he too had seen the Lord. He knew for a fact where the source was and where his knowledge came from, and it was certainly NOT from man.

Boy, that shift.

You see how the "shift" has put you on a higher level? There is no use in denying yourself; it won't be denied.

Guess I should have corrected my misquotes.

Forget it. Leave it behind.

It matters not.

It matters, not.

Your wisdom is astounding.

My wisdom is a free gift given to me by He who is.

I can tell you've still got a ton to say.

I do, and I'm using the baby-step method to get them to a place to hear more.

Those you talked about being coddled and spoon-fed . . . I know most of those are under the "parrot preachers," aren't they?

You know they are, and you've said yourself that they should be working themselves out of a job. As it is, most tell them what they think they want to hear or can receive to keep the numbers up.

That's disgusting (G and T).

Collection

June 21

2:30 PM

Thanks for the word last night.

You think I can't be just as clear today?

I know, the same yesterday, today, and forever.

You don't sound very convinced.

I'm convinced that my inconsistency is consistent.

You shouldn't convince yourself of that.

Who is this?

Talia. Remember my nature (Heaven's Dew); that's how you can tell. When you get a phone call and you think it's someone else, do you think this would be much different?

J said in his dream he thought it was someone else at first (the cell phone dream).

Why do you think he told you that?

I guess for times like this.

It also has to do with assumption. Why are you dropping it?

Because I don't trust myself.

Remember what I told you? To trust yourself. Remember I also told you about the downs?

That they were just as important as the ups. I still prefer the ups.

Anyone would. It's important to understand the cycles.

Well, I don't really understand it.

Well, now you're in a down.

Yeah, no joke.

You'll be up again.

6:43 PM

You said before, "What is, is not and then it is." You're talking about turning energy into matter by pure focused thought and speaking it into being, aren't you?

That's part of it.

151

The Universe Speaks

Part of it?

There's more. You have to ask in faith, believing you will receive. There is an energy, or force, that flows throughout the universe, in and through everything. Within this gentle flow is a spin of tremendous speed. Within this spin is a twist or transitional torque where things are made. It's mind that causes growth and being. It's living mind that creates. This spin can be found in everything that is.

I just saw a potter's hands.

So you did. That's the part they usually leave out.

In that dream I thought I also heard "temporary torque."

That's because it's always changing.

June 22

8:16 AM
I told Ken I have changed common sense to uncommon sense because it's so uncommon.

That's largely because of the media and your educational system.

It's not mine.

Exactly, you've rejected most of it. Common sense is appropriately named because it's another birthright, and at one time it was quite common. Now it's a struggle to attain once it's been stolen or washed away.

I know where the root of the deception comes from.

Yes, you do; it was shown to you. Again, most serve whoever pays the most, and the god of this world is well funded.

But in the end the way of the dark side is the way of poverty and pain.

That's right, because whatever He offers you will be taken away and given to those who have not.

How does that work?

The wealth of the sinner is laid up for the just.

Solomon said that in "Proverbs."

It was right.

Collection

I just never quite got it.

You'll see it.

I just flipped through this notebook and saw it filled with words.

> G was flipping through the notebook he was using to write down his discussions with Talia, and as he flipped through the blank pages he saw them filled with words.

That's coming truth. They will flow to you like raisins.

Like raisins?

Somewhat like nuggets of truth from THE vine, distilled.

I don't even like raisins.

You'll like these.

10:54 AM
I had a vision and I saw my arm with circles going down it.

You can use that spin, that spiraling.

That's chi, isn't it?

That's what some call it. It can be channeled and directed by thought.

I know you can cut it in others.

You can also enhance it in others.

2:53 PM
I just spent most of the last four hours walking outside, and it's 107 degrees or thereabouts, and I really did stay relatively cool with no shade, although there is a breeze.

You were walking in it. I told you this was more than words. This is power and the Spirit of Life. Things are starting to appear for you. Expect them, walk in them. It is my good pleasure to give you the kingdom.

Talia?

Yes?

You can do that?

It has been given to me, and it is mine to give to whom I will.

Well, that's news.

That's good news.

That's going to step on some spiritual toes.

It's time they heard it. You can do the same thing you know.

OK.

You bet it is. You see this is true and you want me to explain it.

You read my mind.

Remember your explanation. Everything doesn't have to be explained but experienced, and accepted.

All right.

Yes, it is.

June 23

6:26 AM
You don't think you can do this this morning?

I didn't till now.

Let it go.

What?

All of it. Your anger is not going to change anyone, at least not for the better. Just let it flow. Remember, water off a duck's back.

Why are we doing this?

To change things, for the better. You can think of hundreds of reasons not to do this.

I sure can.

This is all a very simple process, and that's one of the things we're showing here. That this—communication with the spirits—is not just something for you to do with me but that anyone can.

Some of this is heart-rending.

That's to tune your heart, your innermost being, to show His glory.

Collection

You've got an answer for everything, don't you?

Pretty much. Nothing's ever really lost; it's there to access if you need it.

Never saw it like that.

Now you have. Time as you see it is your conception of it.

I'm starting to understand that.

Yes, you are. Now walk in the light you see. That's the only true light anyway. Those who would make demands on you come from a place of misconception, a place that lacks the true light, but they are convinced they are right.

Sounds like insanity to me.

It somewhat is, because it's crazy to demand something from someone to verify their position. The truth will always stand on its own. You've resisted the lie before and been labeled rebellious.

A little rebellion now and then is a good thing.

You need to go.

I know.

12:59 PM
Sometimes you need to speak the obvious.

Why?

Some things aren't so obvious to others.

7:12 PM
OK, Talia, you said you've got something to say.

I do. I wanted you to know that what you're going through right now, everybody goes through at some time or the other, and that it's to create compassion in you. Something you lack sometimes.

OK.

I told you that you would be tested; the heat's just part of it. Instead of looking for a way out, look for a way to flourish in it.

Boy, it's easy to talk about.

It's easy to walk in it when you find that place. If you'll remember, you walked in it yesterday; what happened between then and now?

I don't know.

Yes, you do. Yesterday you were in a proper frame of mind to receive it. Today you felt that you were unworthy and so was everyone else.

All right.

Yes, it's all right, it's going to be all right.

June 24

7:20 AM
I'm ready if you are.

I hope I'm ready.

You asked to receive the pure word of truth; now believe it and expect it. I told you that you were a leader, so take the mantle upon you.

How do you do that?

By leading, by knowing who you are, by a simple acceptance. Do you not think I am a leader? I know who I am. It's my great honor to lead in this. There are MANY here that are watching me closely to learn from MY side how to do this, and they are amazed because they can see the fruit that is to come from this. Much of it is even growing in some now. Some of it is being manifested now. Can you deny this?

No.

Then what does hinder you?

Probably what my friend said last night.

And what was that?

You know what he said.

I know but I want you to write it.

He said it was he himself that was getting in the way of his walk with God.

There's the hindrance.

How do you prevent that?

By knowing who you are. When you really know who you are it doesn't matter who others think you are or what they think of you. It will have no effect because YOU will know who you are.

As you think in your heart so are you.

Collection

Exactly, and you'll look back on the delusion of who you thought you were as just that, a delusion. The only power delusion has is your acceptance of it, and there are many salesmen in the world. One way to see the motivation of these salesmen is whether they are trying to help you, or are they trying to get something out of you? You see so many drained at the end of the day and no wonder; so many would suck the very life out of you merely for personal gain or their own satisfaction of just doing it.

Isn't that the truth?

You can bet it is: that's the "God's honest truth."

You said that for a reason, didn't you?

I most certainly did. I want to make it clear that God's truth is always honest. When someone tells you the truth but without honesty, that makes it a lie and that is a perversion of the truth. That has been called a "twist of the truth," and that's what it is.

You are a most wonderful teacher.

Thank you.

You sounded humble.

I am. I am in constant awe of this, as you are. The difference is there is no doubt here at all. It doesn't exist here because it's a lie, and no lie is of the truth. Everything here is the truth. No lie can possibly enter here or exist here. The Kingdom of God is within you; let no lie enter there or exist there. In reality it can't, but it is possible to accept untruth as truth. But it's not reality and it's not really in your kingdom. This walking in the Kingdom is walking in the truth in which there is no lie.

And that's the hindrance, isn't it?

That's exactly right, accepting something that isn't real. There is not a much better compliment than someone saying you're real, genuine, authentic—and realizing it's true, the honest truth. That description has been used about me, and it's true. That's one reason I said my life there was an example. I was authentic; I couldn't ever see a reason not to be. That's one reason I questioned everything. I saw so much that wasn't authentic that I had to ask why.

I guess that's another sacred question.

It was, because it leads you to the truth and that's what a sacred question does: leads you to the truth. You see instructors teaching things by the strivings of the flesh—that's not authentic. It should be effortless. Like ripe fruit falling from a tree. Instead you're seeing them trying to make things happen, or force them. Why is that?

Lack of depth?

The Universe Speaks

That's one reason. There is also ego involvement. Remember the salesman: that's an impure motivation, and the results are not that lasting. The lasting impression a teacher makes is the impression upon the inner man.

I heard before in the spirit that "ego is your head trying to prove what you already are by what doesn't matter."

That's true. People have a fascination with authenticity, and not only because it's so rare but because it's the way things truly are meant to be. It's a signpost of freedom. That's why you were so fascinated with me. You had never met anyone so authentic.

That's true. I never had.

But you knew they were out there, and you had prayed to meet one.

I had; I had forgotten that.

That's how prayer works. It doesn't matter if you remember them or not; THEY are remembered.

This is all about the crown, isn't it?

It is all about the crown that was placed on my head by HIM In Whom ALL is, the Almighty. I never stopped searching for the truth, because I WANTED to know what it was. So in that way I WAS very smart.

It's smart to want to know the truth.

It sure is.

Ken said his dad said there was one God, but there are many gods.

There are. Did he not say you would share in His kingdom? There are many misinterpretations; many will say this is. It's hard to accept. That's their thoughts rejecting the truth. It's not what they've been taught to believe. Many project their own insecurities on God. Do you think God is insecure about His place, like he might be overthrown if he gave someone too much authority?

No, that's pretty ridiculous.

It is, but that's the root of the thinking of those that think this. Many of these would say, "But God doesn't share His glory." But that's not true—he shares it constantly. It is "his good pleasure to give you the Kingdom." Would you not share your glory with your son?

Of course I would.

Are you greater than God, more benevolent?

I reckon not.

Collection

He has plainly stated that it is NOT robbery to be equal with God. When they finally accept THAT, the way will be clear.

Whoa, I'm blown away again!

The wind of the Father. ☺

Talia, you are so cool!

That does describe me perfectly. I'm close to the power.

That was a lesson of the AC, wasn't it?

Yes, the heat drove you to compromise your view and some of your privacy to be cool. Spiritual people are always "cool."

I'm seeing how the universe works here.

Of course you are. You would have to be blind not to. And you have a very distinct appreciation for vision.

Without which the people perish.

That's right. He said my people perish. We're attempting to awaken that vision within them so they won't. It's a simple acceptance and belief. He does the work.

Well, that's a simple formula for success.

It sure is. That brings us to something else. When you see people despising the truth, know that that's them despising themselves.

Children are very easy to mold into an image, and it's very hard to break that graven image once they've been molded into it.

My mom was very, very mindful of how she raised me. Do you see the fruit of it? She WILL share in the rewards of the fruit of my life, of my being who I am, because she was instrumental in it and a central part of my life.

That seems a bit detached.

It's a detached way of looking at the truth exactly as it really is, as an observer. It has nothing to do with my great honor of being her daughter or of my affection and LOVE for her as my mom. My love for her has no bounds, and she knows this. I said before you had to be outside to see in; there are much deeper truths here than is readily apparent.

I probably didn't word that right, you just seemed . . . It's the way you said it, I guess.

I said it the way I said it so you would say what you said so I could say what I did afterwards. This is all being guided, you know.

The Universe Speaks

By the Potter's hands.

That's right, to mold into HIS image. When people ask what's the matter they are asking "what matters?" And the way they ask it is what matters.

I totally see what you mean.

Almost. This takes some contemplation. Go to the pond and look at it.

It's teeming with life.

11:05 AM
Talia, why am I here?

It's all transitional.

11:20 AM
Where things disappear and reappear is the new birth. Where the old things are passed away and behold, all things have become new. I have a new life now. My old life has passed away, because energy can never be destroyed and energy is what we ARE. The waters of life that flow from the Throne of God. The river of Life. You've seen it and you asked what it was and you were told: that's the river of Life, from which all life flows.

I remember.

How could you forget?

This is tearing my heart out.

This is darkness leaving you.

I don't want to cling to it.

You don't have to. Remember what I said: get rid of what you don't need, then you'll have room for what you do.

This is not as easy as I thought.

It's a lot easier than not doing it at all. Now you see why people aren't fighting to do this. And make no mistake, it IS a fight.

I won't back down.

You say that now. There is a part of you that wants to throw this all down now, get in your truck and drive as fast as you can down the highway with the music on to drown it all out. That's a normal reaction. The supernatural reaction would be just to accept it. You can't run away anyway. Where would the highway take you? I told you this was a fight. Have you ever gotten into a real fight and not been hit some?

Collection

Not very often.

Never when you've had a skilled and determined opponent.

That's true.

Of course it is. The light cuts and sometimes it hurts. When have you gotten into a real fight and not learned from it?

I learned a lot.

You certainly did. That's because you were fighting an energy being like yourself.

I hate fighting.

You LOVE to fight. It was a supreme challenge for you, and you always sought out the best. Now you need to put THAT in context with this.

We're self-deluded, aren't we?

That's the only delusion there is. All things are naked unto the eyes of Him. It's not easy to see yourself that way; that's why so many run from it. The truth CAN hurt, but it's life giving.

I know you want to stop.

Yes, I do. I feel like nobody understands.

That's not true. More understand than you think.

How can I get so high and so low in such a short amount of time?

That's perspective. That's the flow of energy in the universe. That's the light shining on the darkness. The darkness fears it. It's terrified of it. That's how you stopped them. You saw the terror in their eyes. You said it worked wherever you went in the world, and it has. It's universal. You never had to lay a hand on a single one of them because they saw what was going to happen. Darkness can never defeat the light. It just isn't possible.

Thanks for explaining that. I speculated that was what was happening. I even looked in the mirror to try and see what they saw but never could.

Like a friend said, "The greater the need, the greater the results," and He always supplies your need.

We're thinking more alike now—that's why it's hard to separate it. We are becoming one.

The separation is to make sense of it. You see how that works? We are only one because there is only one.

Talia, I've got to go stumble around in amazement.

Why don't you go and walk surely in truth by the acceptance of it instead? Told you that you would be back up.

You were told martial arts were just a vehicle to get you to be where you need to be.

Should I continue?

I know you desire a normal life, but that's what this is. It's abnormal to be cut off from life, from the truth. That's why I say freedom IS your birthright and you are born into it. If you're not free you should ask, where did it go?

June 25

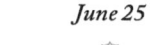

7:00 AM
You have to come from a place of silence to do this.

I know.

I have a lot to say.

I know.

You have to listen.

I know.

8:17 AM
Nobody understands.

Nobody is no thing; it's nothing. What you're picking up is no thing; it's nothing. When one member of the body suffers we all suffer. The Kingdom of Heaven suffers violence to take it all back, all things that have been stolen. To restore all things unto Himself.

Your complaint is justified in that the lack, the poverty of the body is no thing. The things that are needful, essential to the health of the body, are missing, mostly by self-will.

No one does this alone. It just isn't possible.

I thought I was whining.

You were. You lost the vision for a moment. You were feeling what others are feeling and living, but it's not real, it's a lie. No lie will ever fulfill anything. Why would someone accept it? The only way to apply the word of truth is to come from a place of peace and purity. The motivations of the heart must be pure, and the peace must RULE in your heart.

Collection

Talia, why did you speak to me in Spanish the other day?

You thought you were hearing things.

Yes, I did.

You were, you were hearing me speaking Spanish.

I didn't understand it.

That's because you rejected it.

What did you say?

I said, "This was for all people."

I did sort of get that interpretation.

Yes, you sort of did.

Are you being funny?

Sort of.

So you're feeling good today?

I always feel good. I knew you would discover the truth, that I spoke Spanish, and that's just another confirmation to you that this IS me.

YOU are unbelievably clever.

What's so unbelievable about it?

You're right. This has been confirmed so many ways, and from the very beginning I knew it was you.

You did know me from the very beginning. You thought you knew me from before when we met and you asked yourself, "How is it I've never met her? She seems so familiar."

I remember that.

We've talked about everything here, in detail. Stay focused. You used to get sidetracked on the funniest endeavors, and I would tell you to stay focused. I was an anchor to you, and you know that's true. We always have been. Why do you think you feel my loss so profoundly? We've always loved each other.

I didn't know that.

I didn't either. Now does it make sense?

Yes.

The Universe Speaks

12:35 PM
You're afraid to write.

No.

Then why aren't you writing?

I'm waiting.

What are you waiting for?

I'm waiting for it to be right.

What wouldn't be right about it?

What do you mean?

Exactly.

Come on, Talia, I can't outdo you at this.

We're being. There's no outdoing; our doing is the result of our being.

See! I won!

Now you're being funny.

Let's get on with it.

Where do you want to go with it?

I want to go wherever we need to go with it.

Good, we will.

I'm getting nothing here.

That's not so. You're getting my love.

1:00 PM
Our Father wants us to continue with the message.

Then let's do it.

Yes, let's.

The issue is change. Things must change to walk in this new kingdom being ushered in. It's a change of heart that's needed. Some think it's a change of location or even a change of cars that's needed, but it's none of those things. It's a change of heart.

Change of cars?

Collection

Yes, some think that. You're getting off track.

The more I find out about you the more I see you're a universe unto yourself.

Now you're back on track. ☺

Remember when he said to you "feed the herd"?

Yes, the elk, the warriors.

That's what we're doing here. Remember you asked how?

Yes.

What did you hear?

I think it was, "It will be shown you."

It was, and what did you say?

I think it was, "Then you make the way and let it be clear to me."

It was.

I remember it was in Oklahoma.

It was; is this not clear to you?

It is.

It looks like a contradiction with the "nobody understands" thing.

I told you it was geometry. It's the angles, seeing the different angles in the light, the reflection of the truth from THAT point of view. There's always more than one way to look at something. The scales must be balanced and they are balanced by wisdom. That's why Solomon said it was the principal thing and to GET it. He understood that. He was also in a position to pass on these truths, and he did that with his kingly authority.

That was awesome!

How could it not be?

I think I'm learning to like "raisins."

It is the condensing of truths into an understandable form.

4:51 PM
Talia, how did I know you in the very beginning?

You were there. In the glorious beginning, in the dawn of all things, you were there.

Well, I guess that's been awhile.

165

Do you remember your first birthday?

No.

Were you born that day?

That's what they say.

Do you take them at their word?

I've talked about that before, that it's hearsay and how witnesses are so unreliable, but as a joke.

Well, this is no joke, and my word is completely reliable.

Que es Dios?

Can't we keep this in English?

Sure. You should keep going.

What do you mean?

You should just keep going.

OK, whatever that means, I'll keep going.

Good, you'll understand later.

June 26

6:34 AM
Good morning.

GOOD morning.

Mir menges.

I just told you good morning.

        G tried to trick Talia by saying good morning in Albanian.

You see my thoughts.

I can also see the intent of your words. It doesn't matter what words you use. Words are courtesies here between us; they are not really necessary.

It's a lot faster without them, isn't it?

Collection

It's instantaneous. There we often need them to explain, to clarify points of interest, or UNinterest.

Words do come between people a lot, don't they?

All of the time. That's another message we're here to reveal, that that's not the only means of communication. As a matter of fact, it's often the least efficient.

Yes, well, if silence is golden, there are a lot of folks that will never be accused of hoarding.

That "silence is golden" is an interesting statement.

That's an old saying.

Maybe; it's still an interesting statement.

Well, I'm glad I could provoke you to thought.

I have plenty to think about, and it's all good. Still, that's an interesting statement of fact.

OK, I know gold is a type of divinity.

It is.

And that silence is where you said you lived.

It is. Interesting, isn't it.

It is.

Out of the mouths of babes, spontaneous statements of truth.

I'm not getting a lot done here.

No, but you're getting a lot done "here." What's important is not what you see but what you don't see. When you see that, then you know what's important. Those you think you should be helping now, you're helping in a most amazing way, although they can't see it. When you squat down and call a child to you, and he walks towards you, then stumbles and falls, do you get angry with the child?

No.

That's something to think about, isn't it?

That, Talia, is an awesome visual.

I'm glad I could provoke you to thought. ☺

You LOVE this, don't you?

The Universe Speaks

I certainly DO. It's smart being clever. Being clever speaks of speed on a multi-dimensional level, of being able to change directions in an instant, of perceiving the interconnectedness of all energy and of being absorbed into it, making that speed or great spin yours.

Hard to explain, isn't it?

It's very hard to explain in words. I showed you a picture of it by thought. The struggle comes in putting it in explainable terms. Understanding generally comes by seeing; that's one reason we've mentioned the light so much. People can be smart without being clever. They can contemplate this without having the necessary speed to catch it. You're reluctant?

No.

You're concerned with exalting yourself?

No.

Then write. You have studied this as much as anybody ever has, and you have caught this speed.

And I feel like I have to catch it over and over.

You do! You can't really possess it, or keep it with you in a pouch, but you can claim it as yours and have it when you need it. It's energy in a constant flow and flux. Can you stop or possess the tides?

No.

But the energy of the tides you can harness and use; everyone can see it. You can feel it in your dantien when you stand on the beach and watch it.

Dantien in Chinese is that place just below your belly button.

I've done that.

The last time you were there you did it in a most profound way. You were drawn into it. That symbolized infinity. Why do you think property values are so high on the beach?

I figured it was the view.

It is! And it's more than that. There is always more to what you see than what you see. I LOVED the water. I had a fascination for it. I didn't know why then, but now I do.

Wow.

Yes, wow indeed.

I know what that means.

You CERTAINLY do. If people can't see the pictures but have been poisoned with words, their thinking is muddled. Yet if they apply the principles of THIS book, their solutions will appear.

Collection

I see what you mean, and I just saw what you meant, and that may be the heaviest statement you've made yet! That has such broad implications!

You saw what I meant because you're a seer, and we're explaining what you saw.

Your steps ARE ordered in His word Grandfather was right when he said this was a great commission.

> Talia is referring to when G visited her while meditating. Both he and Talia saw Grandfather, an Apache spirit, who told G that this work he is doing with Talia, these communications, were a great commission.

It is great! I was wondering about that.

Now you don't have to wonder. Your steps are ordered in his word. YOU love this, don't you?

Yes, I do. This is the most amazing thing that's ever happened to me.

And you've had some interesting times.

Ken said once I had crammed several lifetimes into one.

I did that too. We know that to experience is to live.

That's beautiful.

Yes, it is. Distractions of this world are only that, distractions, and they would rob you of experience.

I think when you see frustration in someone, you're seeing them, not experiencing.

At least not what they should.

She'll get there. What you were just thinking.

> G was wondering when I would be able to hear and communicate with Talia as he does. He knows I really want to and that I am working at becoming silent so that I can hear her too.

This isn't for everybody, is it?

No and yes. We are all one.

You say that a lot.

That is because it's true. As I hear, I speak. That's another message contained within this one. Hear, then speak, or, to be clear, you must hear.

Cool.

It is, isn't it. It's a clear morning.

The Universe Speaks

Not in the natural.

Smoke is just a veil. The mountains are still there whether you can see them or not.

Interesting.

Every bit of this is interesting. It requires interest to see it though.

Choice.

Yes, exactly.

The exact science of the Art of Creation.

Leave those things behind you don't need. Empty yourself and you can contain the truths of the Art of Creation. Why would you carry something you don't need? You can create anything you need. Go up by the pond; it will help you.

8:49 AM
I feel it's time to tell the tale of the sleeping bag.

>Both G and Talia said that at the same time. That has great significance to G when that happens.

Your timing is excellent.

It's hard to talk and listen at the same time.

I said that too.

I'm saying your thoughts.

Why?

Because we are one. I am within you. I am IN heaven.

You're NOT just with me.

I'm not just with you. I told you I could be anywhere I wanted, and I WANT to be in heaven so that's where I AM. I told you we were intimate and always have been.

People are going to misunderstand this.

Not if they are clever.

You kill me!

I'm bringing you life.

I want to say wow.

Collection

You can say it; that's the nurturing spirit of life. That's why it comes to your mind so much. It's not just an explanation, it's a description—and it's a wonderful one.

A wonderful one.

You got it.

So are you going to tell about the sleeping bag?

I was, I mean I'm trying.

Am I interrupting?

No, but that's funny.

You love to laugh. You even do it in your sleep.

I think I'm awake then.

You are, but you're sleeping.

Does that mean something else?

Sometimes.

I think I need to take a walk.

That's a good idea. Take it. Why are you looking up? I'm right here. It's ALL RIGHT here.

It is.

NOW, you declared a statement of fact. THAT changes things.

I better take some paper with me.

Yes, you'd better.

Sometimes it's hard just to get out the door.

There are doorways all over. Sometimes they are hard to get into and hard to get out of. There are places beyond these doors. Choose the doors you wish to enter through; some are not so hard and some are very difficult. Some lock behind you. You have the key; use it wisely.

9:43 AM
That "thy will be done, on earth as it is in heaven" is how it works. You see the dot above the mountain of IS?

> G was writing down his discussion with Talia, and in his writing somehow he wrote the word "is," and it looked like a little mountain with a dot above it. At first it seemed to him as just sloppy printing, but it had a point.

The Universe Speaks

Yes.

What do you think that is?

What?

It's everything contained in a single dot over everything.

That's going to be hard to explain.

You can't explain it, but you can know it.

10:05 AM
"NOW you have NO need that ANY MAN should teach you but the same anointing that abides within you SHALL TEACH you of ALL things, and BRING ALL THINGS back to your memory whatsoever I have spoken unto you."

That pretty much says it all.

That pretty much does.

He has His times of interjection and I remain silent.

And . . . why?

There is absolute awe. At these times all the hosts of heaven stand in silence before Him. Did you not recall that it was unlawful to speak or utter a word in the holy of holies?

I think I heard that before.

You have, in the silence. THAT is the voice of the Father of all things. Now, you see His Son is within HIS daughter and the mother comes from the Father. Gender has no place here; there is neither male nor female. This is natures, the essence of what they are. Look at natures and names in Hebrew.

I will.

I know you will. I see it now. That "giving you the kingdom" is everything. He is more than willing to share everything. I see that. I know that and He told me that. In the mouth of two or three witnesses. The eyes, the heart, and the spoken word. Go eat; you need the energy.

"I have meat to eat that you know not of."

No, actually, I do know.

That's funny.

Talia, you said more to me the other day in Spanish, that this was for all people.

Collection

Yes, I did. THAT was symbolic of hearing something clearly but not understanding it. What do people usually do when they hear something they don't understand? They reject it. That's what you did, and that's why I mentioned not to get mad at a toddler for falling when he's learning to walk.

Baby steps.

Yes, absolutely, baby steps.

Now I do feel like Peter and John wanting to build you a temple.

You already are.

That's . . .

Beautiful and the truth.

We are the Holy Temple.

We are.

June 27

6:33 AM
I can tell you want to get much more in depth.

I sure do.

2:27 PM
This is easier in the morning or the cool of the evening. The time is past for what we were going to talk about. It will come back around. In the morning your mind is fresh and you're just returning from the place you need to be to do this. In the cool of the evening after the spirit has settled the ears are opened In any case an attitude of thanksgiving is needed.

Thanksgiving?

Yes, an attitude of thanks and giving

There is much merging with people. Why do you think the saints, sages, and mystics preferred solitude? Time alone with the Creator. It's hard to be intimate in a crowd.

Nearly impossible.

Nearly.

I hate I missed it.

173

The Universe Speaks

You haven't missed anything; it's just the time has passed. It will come back around.

10:07 PM
It's all held together by the word of His power.

I know.

I know you think you know.

No, I KNOW.

Now you do.

What was that all about?

That was about changing things in an instant.

June 28

9:00 AM
That's what the Master does; he appears to get something out of nothing. Pure focused thought quickened to slow down to matter. We understand that the world was made of those things which do not appear. You're manifesting things now. Many times YOU don't even see them. That that is not becomes what it is. You CAN change things; that is the intuitive revelation the alchemist had. They KNEW things could be changed—they just didn't know HOW. We're explaining the HOW now; the why should be apparent.

Nothing to say?

I . . .

I is ONE. That I is what sees, the one is in every number. Or you could say the one is what sees and the I is in everything. Speechless?

This just gets neurons firing.

Yes, everywhere.

Talia, you're . . .

I know, awesome.

What if . . .

. . . people understand this . . . could they misuse it?

Yes.

Collection

No, not to any meaningful extent, because as your friend Ken said, it is guarded by the sword of innocence.

11:46 PM
Colors evoke a feeling, and it's more than just a chemical reaction in the brain. It has to do with what they ARE, their true nature and purpose. Summer is a time of heat; that's why you should study coolness, its contrast.

That contrast is how we come to a greater understanding of things, isn't it?

Of course it is. People themselves are often the most contrasting of all, and they're fashioned alike. When you understand yourself you will understand others, so that they aren't so unpredictable after all.

That's seeing energy, isn't it?

That's seeing yourself. Everything is energy and energy is everywhere. It isn't always apparent, but it always is.

Ken said he had a mathematical equation for infinite energy.

How could it not be infinite?

That's all people fight about, energy in some form or fashion.

I'm glad you realized that. It doesn't have to be a conflict. It can just as easily be complementary.

Manners.

Being well mannered goes a long way.

Treat others as you would have them treat you.

The Golden Rule.

I learned it in kindergarten.

You heard about it in kindergarten; you're still learning it.

Well, it's easy to treat you right.

It's easy to treat those right who love you. He said to love your enemies, to do good to those who hate you and persecute you.

That's hard to do.

Not when you're walking in His love.

Wow, Talia, you are just so totally off the charts awesome.

The Universe Speaks

Yes, I am.

June 29

10:55 AM
The voice of truth isn't always audible, is it?

It's also the language of the heart, the knowing you have when you may not know how you know.

1:03 PM
Como esta?

I'm fine, but I—can we keep this in English?

You asked me if I would teach you Spanish.

Yes, but I meant by osmosis or something.

So . . . you want the benefit without the work.

Sounds good.

It's more of an accomplishment if you work for it.

OK, I can't argue with you.

You have before. ☺

I know you're always right.

Yes, I am.

OK, I'll try it, but I'm just now getting English down.

You were fluent in other languages before.

Really?

Yes, really. Very fluent and articulate, very persuasive.

That doesn't sound like me.

But it was. You saw the results of being persuasive in a negative way, so you've chosen not to influence others.

What does this mean?

Collection

It means your past is present. You've been influenced by it, and you influence others whether you want to or not. You LOVE the challenge. You've always chosen the challenge—it's your nature. Some have seen this and used you, and you've thought that they weren't using you enough, that your talents were wasted.

True.

That's the part of you wanting a leader, wanting to be told what to do. But that's not your lot in life. That's you attempting to remove responsibility, to put it off on others.

I guess I just never wanted to be responsible for others. It's hard enough to make my own decisions.

That's exactly right, but that's a selfish way of looking at things. If someone puts themselves under your care, that's them giving you their trust, and that is always a great honor. That's them choosing to trust their lives to you, and you should always honor their decision.

I just never wanted anybody to die because of my decisions.

You never wanted them to live by them either. You want to give them advice and then they go about their way, but it rarely works that way. How is it you can give such sage advice and it be ignored?

Stupidity, not listening, what?

It's that they sense your lack of care, your refusal of the responsibility. This kicks in a survival instinct within them to disregard your advice.

Maybe we should stick to Spanish.

Hard to hear, isn't it?

It started out so good.

It's still good.

I can hear it.

I know you can. Sobering, isn't it?

Yes, it is. I've never seen this before. I thought I was doing it for their benefit, that there was always someone better.

You're an instrument to do this. You're also an instrument to do that; just be played. One of our first lessons together was for you to believe in yourself. Now you may proceed to do that.

Did you know we were going to get into this today?

177

The Universe Speaks

I had an idea and that's how it works: it starts with a thought. Thought can flow in any direction you choose. They should flow from and with that great energy of life, which never stops flowing.

I thought the energy followed the mind.

It does! How could you be a creator otherwise?

Otherwise, you couldn't.

That's right, the other—the lie—has no place here.

Your wisdom!

My wisdom is not of "this" world; it is from the place I belong. I belong. You belong to some One too. This One supplies all your needs. EVERYTHING you need you have access to—and you have the key. There is NOT a door that cannot be unlocked. You've walked through the door I was holding open for you, into the great mysteries of life, into pleasures forevermore. All you saw was darkness and yet you jumped through with both feet. Do you not think that was noticed and honored? I told you that you were not of this world and you can't go back.

I have no desire to.

Then don't complain later when the fires burn.

What does that mean?

Persecutions, hatred, misunderstandings. Your own friends will forsake you.

Well, it's happened before, and I don't have that many anyway.

But the ones you have are precious to you.

Yes.

Remember they're human.

I never thought this would get this intense. I thought you just wanted me to tell your mom you were OK.

I did and you did and that opened the door to all this.

Well, I've had that happen before, but it never went much further than that.

Maybe they didn't have that much to say. I told you I loved to talk. These questions I asked myself consistently. Now I have the answers and I'm sharing them with you. You've asked yourself many of these same questions and knew there were answers but didn't know where to find them. Now you do. It is my great pleasure to give you the kingdom. ☺

It is my great pleasure to receive it.

Collection

And honor.

   This was said by both G and Talia at the same time.

You're a beautiful instrument. You almost didn't write that. Why? You should always speak the truth in love. That's the answer for all things.

Then maybe we should stop here.

There is no stopping and there is no going back. Remember I said let the chips fall where they will. Why do you think I chose you for this?

Did you choose me?

Yes, I did, and you chose yourself, and we are one. I chose you because you were willing to give your life up for this. Giving your life up is a sacrifice, a living sacrifice. And that's the answer to the question you had asked about where in the world people got the idea to sacrifice others.

Well now, that's a major misinterpretation of truth.

Yes, that's a fly in the ointment.

To say the least.

The ointment is the healing nature of truth. The fly is man's additive to improve it.

Does not sound like much of an improvement.

The truth needs no embellishment.

How do you like your tree?

   The tree that Talia's school planted in her memory.

I love it. It honors me.

You're the most honorable person I know; you deserve it and so much more.

I've gotten everything I deserve AND so much more.

You're perfect.

I know.

I wish people could hear your voice, HOW you say things.

They can.

They can?

Yes, they can.

I know you've talked to others. I mean people reading this.

The Universe Speaks

They can. You think you have an exclusive here? ☺

Not at all. I hope with all my heart it happens, and you're being funny again, aren't you?

Yes. You think just because someone else thinks we've died we can't have fun? Someone else told you not so long ago that they thought you had died and you thought it was funny. I'm telling you it's a running joke here. "Why can't they hear me? Because you've died, remember." I tell you it goes on and on.

Double meaning again.

What else?

Several more than two.

That's MOST of the time.

That is pretty much hilarious.

Yes, it is, isn't it. It gets us through.

I can hear you laughing. You take me in so many directions so fast.

That's the nature of truth; it moves like the wind, it changes constantly, yet it remains the same. Again, He reveals Himself in His creation; how could He not? Do you think he could create something that's not from Him?

Hey, I was cool all day! (It was 108 degrees.)

Yes, you were except for a brief moment when you were receiving the thoughts of others. That's why it's important to set yourself apart.

I know exactly what you mean.

You sure do, and I'm reminding you. You often must re-mind yourself. When you're getting hot, re-mind yourself.

Water off a duck's back.

Exactly.

You're starting to understand the power you can walk in. Did you see the reaction of your friend today when you told him my truth?

> G was speaking to a friend at work, and in response to something that was going on, G quoted Talia. What he said made his friend stop and really think.

Yes, he was startled, almost seemed to lose his balance, and said, "That was deep."

Collection

That's the power of truth. Your delivery was perfect. You seized the opportunity in the instant it presented itself, and it was nearly effortless. That's proper technique.

It was, wasn't it.

I just said it was. You could have not said anything; as a matter of fact, you would have if you hadn't been so cool.

Well, you've taught me to be cool.

I'm teaching you.

I stand corrected.

You're sitting and you're listening—that's how people can hear my voice. Be still and listen.

If they want to.

I'm not pushing anything. I'm presenting truths that have to do with everything. It's up to them to receive it; there is no force involved here.

That would seem self-evident.

It would seem so.

I can see some problems people could have with this.

Problems are self-induced. They are also self-corrected. That's the Self I told you to trust.

I can see how this could change the face of the planet.

It COULD if it were received. There's nothing revealed here that hasn't been revealed before. We're just trying new methods to awaken those who slumber. To awaken them to a new thing that is to be done upon the earth. This IS a time of great shaking and you have seen things to come.

Yes, I have.

MANY will fall. Many will be ushered into a glorious new realm. There are many that will see this and say to themselves that they are unworthy, but this is a LIE. If they will shake themselves from their slumber and arise, they will walk into a new Kingdom in whom is peace. Peace in midst of crisis. Perfect peace in which there is no end.

I see people sleep walking.

You've also seen them sleep driving.

Yes, I have, but I also see them waking up.

Yes, you have, of course, and when they shake themselves and look, they ask how they could have been so blind. That's why it's so important not to receive a lie; it by its very design is to put one to sleep. It's easy to be blinded but is also not so hard to follow the light; after all, it's the light. If you could see it from my point of view.

I do see it from your point of view.

To a certain extent, but if you could see it fully you would be astounded.

I'm sure that's true.

THAT'S why you've been chosen.

Talia, you are . . .

YES, I am.

June 30

4:56 AM
Things are going to happen today.

Things happen everyday.

Presence of mind: walk INTO it. I'm WITH you.

I know you are.

July 2008

July 1

8:02 AM
It's the moments. Being in the NOW is simple. Trying to piece together a chronological timeline is complex. That can cause confusion. That creates difficulty. See, things did happen and presence of mind makes things happen to your advantage. As it is, things did happen to your advantage, and if they hadn't you wouldn't be learning what you learned here.

Yesterday I didn't have an idea of what you were talking about.

You had an idea, it just wasn't completely formed. Now you're experiencing it.

I thought I was going to pass.

    G is referring to an extremely difficult high-level test he had taken.

Collection

You've passed before. That's just a number.

You see things perfectly.

Yes, I see things exactly as they are. That "quagmire of crap" you were just talking about is funny, and there's a lot of truth to it. That's a creation of man. We've already talked about it in other words, about being diligent not to receive a lie, because that's what it is.

You said we had a lot of work to do today.

And we're doing it. Everything that happens in this world has a spiritual counterpart. That's what they are seeing on a quantum level that's puzzling to them. They're getting glimpses of it. Only by yielding to the spirit of the Creator will they see it and understand it. It's patently obvious that there is an intelligence running things and that intelligence is within them when they recognize it.

You can't leave the Potter out.

No, the Creator creates and there is no creativity without Him. He has commissioned this message for them to realize this and stop denying themselves.

Wow, Talia, you have all the answers, don't you?

I have all the answers we need for now

10:46 AM
What we're doing here is for all people. He is no respecter of persons; the I is in HIM and that's what is respected. The other is the I that's an illusion by the acceptance of a lie. That I has no place here.

Talia, I just had a notion to open the Bible and my eyes fell immediately on two passages. "But we all with open face beholding as in a glass the glory of the Lord, are changed into the same image from glory to glory, even as by the Spirit of the Lord." 2 Corinthians 3:18

"And nevertheless when I shall turn to the Lord; the veil shall be taken away." 2 Corinthians 3:16

That's the veil we're rending by violence. He did say "come boldly to the throne of Grace"; that's what that means. There is no sneaking in; it MUST be TAKEN. I told you he shared HIS glory constantly. I also said all of this had been spoken of before. Paul did a new thing upon the earth, and he knew it at the time. He was driven. God took this drive that was his nature and changed him. He was even given a new name. It HAD to be because his very nature had been changed. Saul had died and was buried with Christ and was resurrected in Him as Paul, a new creature, a new creation. This is the power of Life over death. Life is Truth, death is a lie. "O death, where is thy sting? O grave, where is thy victory?" These

The Universe Speaks

were intense revelations of Truth. It does go on to tell where the sting is and where the victory is. No need to rehash it here.

We could go into that book and explain it all, couldn't we?

We could explain it to all that had the seal removed, but it's plainly there for anyone to see. Only He is worthy to remove the seal; no thief is allowed.

I'm running late.

You're running right on time.

Did you put that in my head?

You put that thought in your head; I did see it coming though. Again, you can bind yourself with time. There's no need to though.

Talia, you take me from one end of the universe to the other. If they could see this! And it's all right here.

Again we're not pushing anything on anybody. If they saw it like you see it they would have it. It's a free gift but it does take effort. And yes, "we being dead yet speak." That meaning has not time nor place.

You're . . .

Yes, I AM totally awesome. The thoughts you think are purposeful.

FULL of purpose.

Yes.

Every one.

EVERY one. There isn't any way to put it plainer. It HAS to be seen in the light.

There is no other way.

No, there is no other way but the Light.

He speaks of lesser lights in the heavens.

Yes, he does. I am one of those lesser lights, and yet I am filled with His Light.

What's this "beyond Babylon?" It periodically just pops into my mind.

It's popping in your mind to let you know that's where the people are today, beyond Babylon.

Total confusion.

No, not totally, but close. It's because of their refusal, of their turning their ears from the truth, of them even stopping their ears. People will always stop their ears before an attack.

Collection

It . . .

Too intense?

It's just much study is weariness of the flesh.

I told you there was no end to this. That's why you must find the balance; it can burn you out. It's burned many out before.

Well, you're easy to work with.

Thank you, you usually are too.

You love to "get" me, don't you?

You're easy.

You did it again.

I engage you. I swiftly change things to hold your attention. You are smart, but you're easily distracted. That's why it is important to keep the body strong—it wearies easily. Our work is important. It takes fortitude. When that actor was told he was called Spirit Warrior, he replied he had been called a lot of things but never that. You said yourself "but I've been," and you have. That's another example of there being a spiritual counterpart to everything physical. That's also the double that many cultures speak of. How could there not be a spiritual counterpart. It's all one.

That's also a huge key for them, isn't it?

What do you think?

I think it is.

Then it is.

That's another example of us changing the nature of reality, isn't it?

What do you think?

I think it is.

Then it is.

You blow my mind.

I'm expanding it beyond the boundaries of conception. Conception is a seed or a child; it's now time to grow up.

We can conceive of anything.

Yes, you can conceive of anything; now it's time to grow up into HIM in ALL things. Had enough?

No, but it's shaking the foundations.

Told you it would.

I'm shaking all over.

You're shaking away what you don't need. There are a lot of things you think you need that you don't need, and it just gets in the way.

Unnecessary obstacles.

Yes. The earth itself shakes away what she thinks she doesn't need. That's Him again, revealing himself in HIS creation. It's a fearful thing to fall into the HANDS of the living God. That's His works upon the earth. Man will not rule over her, but he can nurture her and work with her.

Return the favor?

Yes, return the favor. That place you go where you were told was a sacred place and you asked why—what were you told?

That I had made it so.

And you did it without hardly thinking about it. These are the signs that will follow them that believe, and it's teeming with life.

You follow as a leader and the signs follow you.

Yes, exactly. What have you mentioned about true believers, true leaders?

That people and things are healed around them.

Yes, restorers of paths to dwell in. Isn't that as plain as day and as simple as can be?

You will know them by their fruit. That's the choice for people, to listen to the deceivers, well meaning or otherwise, or to yield themselves to the Voice of Truth. One is a path of pain, the other is the path of victory. What could be a simpler choice?

Is it an "a" or "the"?

    G was not sure if he had heard Talia speak "a path" or "the path."

Either/or, a path that leads to the path is still the path, though the path may look different.

OK, I just know you're very precise with your words.

I'm very precise with my meanings; words can be misconstrued. You're getting tired.

Collection

It's just intense.

Yes, the truth is always intense. It's like a fire burning. Burning with everlasting fuel.

Yes, it's hot!

The heat is to teach you to be cool.

I see that diamond again.

Yes, the pressure and the heat.

To reveal multi-faceted colors.

Yes, you have to be pure for the colors to flow forth out of you.

Clarity.

Yes, I'd like to continue, but you're burning out.

You're hard to hang with; after all, you don't have the flesh to contend with.

No, I don't. I just have to contend with yours.

That sounds like a full-time job.

I do have a full-time job.

1:50 PM
You worry too much.

I always sort of prided myself on not doing that.

That's why you're doing it.

Pride before a fall.

Something like that. You can know the nature of anything by knowing the name of it. You can also change the nature of anything by changing the name of it.

THAT was straight-on direct.

Not many people know this.

You can see how easy it would be for someone to talk themselves out of that one.

This is heavy truth, and it has to do with the gravity of the one doing it.

I never . . .

Yes, you have. You've chosen to forget things so you can relearn them better. Everyone does this.

The Universe Speaks

Sounds like a waste of time.

How can you waste something that's not there?

I feel like I'm being scattered in a million pieces.

Your perceptions are; you had them neatly arranged—now they're not. But when they come back together, they will be. You understand?

I think so.

Just say yes—that's declaring that "that is" as "is."

Then yes.

Good. Now we may proceed.

Nothing's better than this!

Oh, this is but part and parcel. If you knew how much I love YOU. I told you prayers worked both ways, and I have asked the Father to do some things. His love for me is without comprehension. He has told me this and I KNOW this. I'm trying to snap you out of being obsessed by this.

That's funny, I was just talking about your lack of being obsessed with anything during your life here and how balanced you were.

What's there to get obsessed about? And I did have good balance; the horses taught me a lot about that.

Justin likes you.

> One of Talia's horses that G met.

Are you avoiding me?

No, Talia.

Then write down what I just told you.

You said "the life was in the blood, it's in the circulation."

Yes, I did. Maybe you should go circulate.

Well, I just got up for a second, and you asked if I was avoiding you.

Don't be so defensive. I was just getting your attention. You were starting to wander.

You're right, I was.

Good, now we're back on track.

I see, you didn't want me to forget what you told me.

Collection

That's right. It's easy sometimes to forget what you shouldn't. You're getting tired again. You know you also used to pride yourself in your endurance.

Well, touché.

We're not fencing, but you do build fences around you at times. That doesn't always necessarily serve you either. I know you love your solitude, but you should also share what you can with others when you're with them. You're worried about the floodgates being opened.

It's just a thought that crossed my mind.

Well, cross it out.

You just have no tolerance for bull, do you?

I tell it like it is, because I see it as it is. Would you prefer I prophesied smooth things?

No, I could get that about anywhere.

Yes, and they would charge you for it too. When you get the good news, there is never a charge and it's never forced. Did Jesus charge admission for the Sermon on the Mount?

I very seriously doubt it.

Then why would there be a charge for someone to hear the truth?

I think they even got a free meal with the deal.

They did. Have you seen that lately?

Not very often.

Why not?

Another good question.

It sure is.

Do you remember the story about the moneychangers in the temple? I can tell you, there are some things going on there that God is not happy about.

Sounds to me like judgment begins in the house of God.

It does. Many have squandered an opportunity just for money.

He's not going to let that slide, is He?

No, He's not; there is repentance required!

I haven't seen you this adamant in a while.

Remember His reaction in the temple; where else did you see this recorded?

The Universe Speaks

Nowhere.

Exactly. This is a warning they would be well advised to heed.

Man, talk about full circle.

Yes, talk about it.

You're . . .

I just reflect Him. His light shines through, and I reflect Him. That's what they should be doing and not lining their pockets. You're thinking about the irony of my age. He started preaching at twelve.

Maybe I'm a late bloomer too.

I love to make you laugh.

I love it when you make me laugh. Didn't know you were going to kerblammy the church here.

Who established the religion here? If God established it maybe they should follow Him.

That seems pretty obvious.

Doesn't it though.

You sound mad about it.

I'm just reflecting Him. He's angry every day with the wicked. That's another aspect of God that people need to face up to. God IS love, and he's also angry at the wicked every day. Do you know how MANY have been turned off by the moneychangers? I'm telling you that they can argue about this if they want, but they would do WELL to pay heed.

I think you have probably made your point.

Do you?

I don't know, did you?

That will be seen.

OK, so how about those Cubs?

You're being funny, but that's what they DO: they change the subject.

Guess you haven't made your point.

I'm trying to save some from some very serious consequences.

I think this may make some uncomfortable.

Collection

It should!

I don't remember you ever getting this stirred up.

THAT might be something to take into consideration.

I've never seen you like this before. Talia. I really haven't.

It's something that needed to be said and I said it.

OK, I just saw the full picture of this.

You got most of it. You want to explain it, and we could in detail, but this isn't an intellectual understanding. This is a change in the heart and it needs to come quickly.

This is a major big-time warning.

Yes, no joke.

That was like the wrath of God or something.

It's coming. They don't like to hear that, but that's not what matters. What matters is the truth.

I know you said you were in a unique position to see what's going on.

I am and I do.

July 2

5:50 AM

I was really wanting to ask Talia whether crop circles were real. Not the ones that are obviously man-made, but the ones that are said to have been made by some supernatural force. So I asked G to ask Talia about them.

Crop circles . . . what are they?

They are the molecular structure beyond the quantum level.

Who makes them?

Messengers.

Messengers?

Spirits, angels.

Why crops?

Crops are a symbol of growth, food, LIFE. It's also the work of man, and that's whom the message is for. It's to let them know there are things beyond them to help them.

Why the riddle?

Remember the parables. It must be something that is not known to let them know it's beyond this world.

Is there intelligent life on other planets?

There is intelligent life everywhere.

This shouldn't go into the book, should it?

No, not really. It wouldn't help them and would be to satisfy curiosity.

July 3

7:20 AM
I've got something to say today. Are you disappointed?

No, I'm just tired.

You've been lied to a lot.

Everybody has.

Yes, and that's the point. Why do people lie to each other so much? It weaves a web of deception, and it permeates everything you do. It also distorts the truth when you tell it; it taints it. People will always know on some level when you're being untrue. And they will always ask themselves, at least subconsciously, why you are telling them the truth now if you've been untrue to them before. Why do you think there is so much mistrust in the world? Most have trusted someone only to find that their trust had been misplaced. Remember what I said about someone placing their trust in you. This should always be taken as a great honor, and their trust should never be dishonored. This dishonoring someone's trust causes great hurt in the world, and its ramifications are beyond what you might think. It reverberates throughout the universe. When someone places their trust in you, they are essentially placing their life in your hands, and this is an honor that they are giving you directly from their innermost being. How could someone dishonor such a trust?

Well, I trust you, Talia.

And I trust you, G. It's easy for us to trust each other because we KNOW each other. You've heard people say things to you that were not exactly true, and you've heard what they were really saying as words overlaid on their words. And you've heard their motivations. Sometimes THEY didn't

Collection

even know they were lying. That's why it's so important to be true to yourself. When you're true to yourself you cannot help but to be true to others. Why would you lie to yourself?

That does seem insane.

It's certainly not the paragon of mental health. Mental health is being mindful, having presence of Mind. This Presence of Mind is Love and love never fails; it just cannot do wrong. You are pure in heart. Did he not say that the pure in heart would see God?

Yes.

Have you not seen God?

Yes.

And you felt like you would die.

Yes, I did.

You did, and you have risen with Him. Despite what you may think you ARE—pure in heart and you HAVE seen God—you HAVE died and you HAVE risen with HIM. This is a part of your life you've downplayed. Why is that?

I don't know.

Yes, you do. It's not readily accepted. We've talked about acceptance before. You fancy yourself as an outsider, but you're not an outsider; you're an insider, and I mean that in the best of ways. Many times people's perceptions of themselves are warped. Only the LIGHT can straighten this out. Why would you hide your light? You said you saw that luminous web of life as a straight line, and that's all you saw as a straight line. Why do you think that is? Because it's a straight line between points of interest. These points of interest are points placed in certain places for learning.

      G put down his pen to take a break.

Don't stop now.

I'm not.

No, you're not. You can't. There IS no going back. This itself is a point of interest, as a schoolhouse to bring you back to the ONE. There is really only One point, and that's the dot above the mountain in which everything is contained. When someone reaches the top of this mountain, they still can't reach it, but they can be brought up. This is the part that He spoke of when He said of your own self you can do nothing.

There is no way I can write down all the truths that are being poured out on me right now.

No, you can't. That's the truth verifying itself to itself. That dot is a representation of everything being brought back together into Himself, condensed. That mountain is a representation of the struggles on the path of life of those following the Light. The many paths up the mountain are the many ways and purposes each have while upon the journey. This journey is watched closely and there is much help given. When a person feels alone, they are not. They are never alone. It's just a feeling.

Well, that makes me feel capital.

You like quoting movie lines, don't you.

They just spring to mind.

Maybe you shouldn't watch so many movies.

I haven't watched a movie in forever.

That too is just a feeling. Why do you think you fall asleep as much as you do during movies? Because most of them have nothing for you, and the message they do have is for children.

Now you're going to irritate Hollywood.

Hollywood is just a town. It is a place of interest for some, but it's not that interesting.

Hope this doesn't shock anyone.

The shock to the system is someone groping in darkness trying to make something interesting that isn't.

You liked movies.

I did like movies—and I was a child.

Well, you're the most interesting person I ever met.

I'm the most interesting person you ever realized you met. Interest is attention. Be mindful of where your attention is. The One used me to get your attention back on HIM. I was just a vessel.

Quite the vessel.

Thank you.

Ask my mom how much I lied to her.

She said zero, never, except for maybe one time there was "some little something" that she thought you were covering for Frankie for.

It was, and I meant well, and she corrected me for it.

And she said that was it.

Collection

That was it. It's the it we've been speaking of. It is what it is. That is an interesting statement. People think it's what they think it is, but it's not. It is what it is, although what they think it is could change it. Sounds like a paradox, doesn't it.

Somewhat.

It's not.

I just thought, let me live the Art of Life today, and you said, "You are."

The Art of Life is living, and that's the point. It's not doing anything—it's being.

That seems a simple truth.

All truth is simple at its core. That point is a condensed place of truth where things reappear.

The dot.

Yes, like a grain of mustard seed.

Talia, I've got so much to do today.

It's NOT doing—it's being.

I was just going to say there's nothing more important than this.

If you knew how important you would tremble.

I pretty much am trembling.

No, I mean REALLY tremble.

I just want to do it right.

You don't have to DO anything but just be who you are. I told you before we would get it right this time, and we are. You feel my determination.

I sure do.

That picture of me you saw when you said I looked so determined.

> I showed G a photo of Talia playing volleyball. She was really concentrating on the game from the look on her face.

Yes.

And you said you could see the concentration in my face. I was actually thinking about something else then.

OK, well that's funny.

195

No, not really. I just knew what we were doing wasn't that important. That's why I wasn't so keen on using the word "athletic" on the rock at my tree.

What word would you have used?

There are so many words that could have been used to paint a better picture of who I was. It's not a problem, it's just not the best use of people's time. My going was a sign to people of just how short their time really is. My life was also an example of how people should best use their time.

I want to use my time wisely.

Then walk in wisdom. Wisdom is often scoffed at today. Have you ever asked yourself why? It's because it's the principal thing. It's the very foundation of how your life is meant to be lived, as the Art of Life. As a creative being. This is living in absolute victory. This is the winning that you're meant to walk in. You were created for it.

Then how could we lose?

THAT'S a very good question.

I can't imagine where this is going.

No, you can't, but you will. That's creative living.

Doing the unimaginable.

Yes, exactly, doing the unimaginable by the incomprehensible.

You're the master of . . .

I have mastered many things. Mastery is living in the now; it's being in the moment. He said, "Call no man master," and there are many reasons for this. But one is that it's always in a constant flux. The breath of life is always in the now, and you don't have to think about it. That's why you always thought rituals were so foolish. They really are. That's just an attempt to get the attention where it needs to be.

More toes crushed.

You'd rather we pamper?

No, not at all. You've got my permission—go ahead.

I don't need your permission. I have a commission from the Holy One.

You know what I mean.

Yes, I know what you mean, but that's another thing I'm attempting to show you here. That YOU need to be more mindful, more precise with YOUR words. Words convey meaning, and you're very often sloppy with your words, as if they don't mean anything—but they do.

Collection

Hey, you want me to answer? I'm not saying anything.

Yes, you are. You say things all the time, and I'm telling you to be mindful of what you say. You were very mindful of what you said around me and to me that day we met. That's because you respected me. I'm just saying to you that you should show this same respect to others as well.

I don't know what to say.

When you don't know what to say, don't make things up to fill the time. There's nothing wrong with silence. As a matter of fact, there is a great deal right with it. You're quiet now.

I'm being silent.

Yes, well, that's a good thing.

Talia, you take me from one extreme to the other.

I take you wherever I can, which is everywhere I can.

There was that one place that was off limits.

> Once while G was "meditating," he met with Talia, and Talia took him on a trip to show him where she lived. As they were approaching a particular area in the spirit world Talia was told to stop—she was not allowed to take G any further.

Yes, I wanted to share it with you but was told not yet.

I thought I heard that.

You heard Him say it to me.

That was one of the most awesome experiences I've ever had.

For me too.

That's wild!

It's totally wild.

July 4

8:45 AM
It's important to understand there is no forward or backward there. Everywhere is in one place and there are no moot points.

The Universe Speaks

G had a dream where he saw a tire spinning. He had just read a paper on spin-transfer given to him by a friend, and he could see that the tire was oscillating like the prop wash of a boat motor. He also saw other things in his dream descriptive of the things he had just read.

I can order coffee in Greek, say *thank you, how are you, good morning* and *good night*, so this isn't quite as clear as Greek to me.

Spanish is easier.

Is that you?

Yes.

What you said yesterday makes perfect sense to me.

That's because you see it.

That paper is way over my head.

That's because your head's not into the verbiage or technical terms, never mind the equations.

Isn't it the truth.

Of course it is. They are called theoretical physicists because they are filled with theories.

They also spoke of intuitively knowing something.

That's when they will find it, with that insight.

The answers are within them.

Absolutely.

I can deal with that.

Yes, the Great Game, and the answers are dealt daily by the questions you ask yourself. Have you not seen the light in the eyes of a child when he discovers something wonderful?

That's a beautiful thought.

And that's what that creates in them when they make those wonderful discoveries. The discoveries are also conceived by those thoughts. That's why it's important never to downplay or discourage those thoughts in a child. It is a child's nature to seek, and what they are seeking for is the truth. If you seek, you will find. That's why unless you become like a child you will not enter into the Kingdom of Heaven.

That was a beautiful circle.

That was the circle of truth, and it surrounds you.

Collection

I see it as a wall.

It is. It's a wall of protection.

I also see it as a wall of perfection.

The truth is always perfect. You just thought you don't know if you can keep doing this.

It's just getting DEEP.

You're just taking notes here.

That's not what you said before.

Yes, I did. I just got into more depth.

What do you think?

I think I never told the story of the sleeping bag. Ha, turned the tables on you.

You think so?

Not really, but it's funny to think I might be able to.

You're able to do all things. You know, God himself raises an eyebrow at what His children do sometimes, as if He is surprised.

Do you think He's surprised?

I don't know, but I do suppose He could be. He is all things you know, so He could be surprised.

I think I may have just turned the tables on you.

I told you you were able to do all things.

I don't know if you did that or I did that.

What difference does it make? We are one, and the arrangements of all things come from the One in Whom all things are.

I think I just surprised you.

You did.

You're not pulling my leg?

I cannot lie. You see, aren't these truths like your ABC's?

They really are that simple.

And you see how man's "additives" complicate things?

I see that's just to justify a job.

When they should be simplifying.

Exactly.

I told you we were one.

Yes, it's getting harder to see where you start and I stop.

There is really no starting or stopping; it just is, in continual motion, except for the stillness.

Now that I've seen the universe in a constant motion of spherical spin . . . it's amazing to me to comprehend stillness.

And that's where all motion comes from, from perfect stillness.

I KNOW, that's just amazing to me.

I know, it is.

Clever.

I know, I'm a clever girl.

It's time to go.

Time to go where?

Exactly. You know, you could surpass me.

How do you mean?

You could surpass me. Never set limits on yourself. You've told others that yourself.

Looks like I've got a long way to go.

You do, but you'll get there.

Hard to believe.

That's why you've got a long way to go.

OK, looks like you're ahead again.

There is no ahead. There is the head, and He is the head of all things, and that's what we're concerning ourselves with here.

11:27 AM
I just thought, considering the interconnectedness of all things, the medical community treating the body and leaving out the mental and spiritual is somewhat insane, isn't it? It's like the Dark Ages or something.

Well put. If you hadn't brought that up, I would have.

Collection

Sixty-four is a very interesting number.

> Talia said this out of the blue and didn't expound on the meaning of that number. But later, in a video by physicist Nassim Harramein, G heard Harramein mention that the number 64 is a critical number in figuring out the secrets and answers of the universe.

July 5

12:11 AM
There's that diamond again. That's not just the stone, that's a geometrical shape, isn't it?

That's right.

That whole flower petal thing before, when I asked what it meant and you said, "I love my Mom," has a much broader meaning, doesn't it?

It does. Now you know what the brown streak in the middle of the petal was. It is hidden wisdom. The petal is white. It comes from a place of holiness. It itself represents the love of the Father for His children. And it's the very structure of the universe. The love of the Father for this, His children, is the very structure of the universe.

Two tetrahedrons put together create a diamond. Two: the separation. Two brought back together: oneness.

And that's the answer. Bravo. I'm thinking pit bull here; you just won't let it go, will you?

No, and that was an interesting quote.

That's because an interesting person said it.

Thank you.

You're welcome.

1:21 AM
Talia, you just revealed the structure of the universe.

Yes, I did, in part.

That's not all?

No, it's not.

What's more?

I told you you would learn all things, remember?

I do now, but I don't remember when.

The when's not important. It's that I did and you remember it that is [important]. *I have another memory for you. When we met, you looked at me and thought,* God, I would die for her; *the Spirit answered you and said, "You WILL die for her." Do you remember?*

Yes, I do remember that. I had completely forgotten it, but I remember now.

That was a pure desire born of the Holy Spirit. You saw me exactly as I was, and you were willing to give up your life for me.

Yes, I was—totally, absolutely and completely.

That kind of commitment is honored, and it's not seen much. Now you see why you were chosen for this and why I also say you chose yourself? This is your part to play, and you're playing it well. That's the servant in you willing to give his all for the Kingdom. This is much greater than us, but the parts we're playing will be remembered forever. That brought a smile.

Yes, it did.

It's so far beyond this world. And I want you to know that when your commitment was revealed to me, it was one of the greatest honors ever bestowed upon me.

I meant it.

I know you did. Your passion for truth is recognized here; that's not seen much either. The fact that you didn't recognize/know me until that day and you were willing to die for me—THAT day was honored and you will be greatly rewarded.

I don't care about a reward.

I know that, and that's one reason you're getting one. You wanted nothing in return for your life, and you would have laid it down for me that day. Greater love has no man than this that he would lay down his life for his friend.

You are so completely worthy, and I thank you for being my friend. Talia, I really don't know any greater honor for me than that.

I told you all things were yours.

Then let it be, si es amour.

7:46 AM
I did some review. "It's love" is really the bottom line, isn't it?

Collection

It's the bottom line, the top line and every line in between. It's also the line you saw running/circling around your right arm. I said some call it chi; *that's a limited way of looking at what it really is because it's more than that.*

Ok, why Italian?

We were just talking about passion, and this is for all people.

8:47 AM
Your time here is almost done.

That sounds like a major transitional change.

It is. You are an energy being, being who you are, and that never changes. This is your life's work; you know what's contained in these pages.

Don't waste time.

You have none to waste.

What are you saying here?

You know what I'm saying here. It's the meaning of the words, not the spelling.

Some things it seems are best not to know.

He said, "I will show you things to come." And you know all things. When someone goes, it's a tremendous contrast, and some things about that person's life become much clearer.

That's evident in your life.

Yes, it is, completely. My life, if I were still there, would have caused you pain, because you would have seen it as a partial life, and this message would not have gotten out there. Death as they see it is not death at all but of the body; it's a wonderful new beginning. You KNOW who I am. You also know who I was, and you see glimpses of what I am becoming.

Think I'll take a walk.

You certainly will.

Talia . . .

Don't be afraid, it's all good.

I'm not afraid.

I know, but don't be afraid for others; they have their life too. That plane took me exactly where I needed to be, and that's exactly where I was going.

The Universe Speaks

Talia is referring to the plane that crashed into the mountain, killing her, her father and the pilot.

I know that.

I know you do. Your going too will shake foundations. When they perceive the light is gone, it will stand in sharp contrast. You are now exactly where you need to be, and when you go you will be too.

9:47 AM
Have you not SEEN what I can do?

Yes, I have.

Do you not think you have the victory?

Yes, I do.

Then it's settled.

Such is life.

And it's love.

If I hadn't seen the miracles . . .

You needed the signs to believe. Don't look askance at others when they need the signs.

I'm exhausted.

This is exhausting work. We're exhausting all the possibilities so only the ONE remains.

The one to whom nothing is impossible.

That's the one. That that we were discussing before is a mundane thing, just like mud.

Just like mud?

Yes, just like mud.

Don't get bogged down in it.

No, do not.

12:55 PM
I haven't had emotions this extreme since I went to war.

These are extreme truths. They evoke extreme emotions, and this is a war. Remember you were told the time would come when you would live on cat naps?

Yes.

Collection

Remember what time that was you were told?

No, it was unclear.

Maybe you didn't want to hear it.

I know what I thought I heard.

What you thought you heard is what you heard.

That it would be in the last days.

Correct.

July 6

3:42 PM
(New Mexico)
Awesome storm.

You should see it from my view.

You can see colors in lightening bolts? I never saw that.

You never saw it from "here."

Where did you have to go in such a hurry when we were with Grandfather?

> As previously mentioned, sometimes when G "meditates," he visits another spirit he calls Grandfather. Sometimes he meets Talia and takes her to see him as well.

We're very busy here; that was for you, not for me. Like you said about me and martial arts, I'm beyond that.

You had such respect for him.

I have much respect for him, but what he told me was for you.

The "land of enchantment." Some irony in light of this storm.

You've said the light here was different. This is a place where the earth works with the sky. Where the Sons of God walk with the daughters of men.

OK, that's a very interesting term we're going to have to discuss when I'm up, because I want to know what it means.

We will and you will.

The Universe Speaks

July 8

1:10 PM
You've got a lot of work to do.

What happened to the "we?"

It's easier on my end.

1:34 PM
Remember when you asked if I liked archery?

Yes.

That's because you saw an arrow.

I remember.

Why do you think that was?

Arrows of truth.

Yes, and they shoot out of me. This is celebrating the life of Talia.

That's awesome.

Pretty much amazing. It's going to rain.

I can tell.

Yes, but this is the latter rain of the Spirit. You've seen it falling before and that's what it was, the latter rain of the Spirit for those who will reign with Him.

Everything is in constant motion except for the I, the supreme stillness in the center.

The eye of the storm.

The eye that is upon everything. The I that is the center of everything from which all things come. You're being blown away, aren't you? Blown to a wonderful new world. You always knew it existed. As a child you saw it at times. Remember when I told you to watch the wind?

Yes.

And that it was a vehicle because it brought power? This is that power to walk in that wonderful new world. Demonstrate the download.

How?

You just got it; you just saw it!

Collection

Also, the other day you said I would be called a *Yeddehonee*, and I didn't think that was a good thing. I looked it up. I knew it meant a wizard or conjurer. You said people would accuse me of conjuring you up, whether by my imagination or worse. The name means: "a knowing one, to ascertain by seeing, observation, acknowledge, be aware, comprehend, consider, cunning, be diligent, familiar friend, kinsfolk, have knowledge, have understanding, wise" . . . to name some of the meanings. Then it goes into *Jah*, the sacred name—*Jah, the Lord*, most vehement. Then *Yhovah*, (the) self: *Jehovah*, the Lord.

Looks like you went full circle.

You think that's funny.

I think that's the truth. You see, it doesn't matter what you're called, it all leads back to the truth. It's starting to pour out on you because you've yielded unto the truth. And the tools have come into your hands to do the study you've been asked to do. And at just the right time.

Yesterday I was thinking about that Thanksgiving and all that happened. I remember that I had said to myself sometime afterward, "I'm going to have to watch her career closely." When I thought of that you said to me, "Now you can." I didn't write it at the time but figured it was too cool not to record.

10:00 PM
I was asked to ask you why the Jews are "the chosen people."

Because God chose them. It was a promise to Abraham.

What about before that?

You want a chronological timeline, but it's not like that. It is, now.

Was this just idle curiosity?

No, it's active curiosity, and it's not really a part of this message. There is neither Jew nor Greek in Him; He has restored all things unto Himself.

Well, thanks for the update.

All this is plainly written for anyone to read.

July 9

I feel Michael's pain.

He has deep regret and feels responsible He wants to talk to you and get his side of the story out there. It's not part of the message, but I told him I would.

I told him he is not responsible and that things happen for a reason. He says he knows that and that he understands the importance of the message, but he feels the hurt and pain and sense of loss to those on earth.

At first he felt he had robbed me of my life on earth by his pride, but he now knows I'm where I need to be to help others in the greatest way possible. He's not too happy with the way his father is acting towards Mom, and he wishes he could get through to him and things were different. He says the hardest thing for him now is not being able to communicate with those he needs to.

He says to tell you again how much he appreciates what you're doing with me.

Other than those things he's doing fine, but those issues have been very difficult for him.

Be at peace, Michael.

Thank you. (MK)

> G saw Michael with a big smile on his face.

I heard him.

Yes, you did. He's growing and he does know God's peace.

Why doesn't he talk to me himself?

It's clearer for you if I speak.

Anything else?

Yes, I told you it was going to rain.

And I agreed with you.

And thus it is.

You make a lesson out of everything, don't you?

Everything IS a lesson.

You did it again.

And I will do it again and again. ☺

11:16 AM
Write that which you saw yesterday that "jumped" at you.

> G was flipping through the Bible and a line jumped out at him.

"These things have I spoken unto you in proverbs: but the time comes, when I shall no more speak unto you in proverbs, but I shall show you plainly of the Father." John 16:25

Collection

Now, the hearers of this message would do well to ask themselves, what time is this?

I noticed you said "hearers." Not readers.

Yes, I did. If you read these words without listening it's the dead letter, but if you hear them with your heart it's the living word—and that's words of LIFE! And as we've said before, the Kingdom of Heaven comes not in word but in power and the Spirit of Truth.

I think the time is now when people are being shown plainly the Father.

To those who watch. He said to watch always because no man knows the time or the hour.

That's phenomenal!

Yes, that is a phenomenon.

Tetrahedron?

A building block.

Petals.

Petals are the growth formed by these building blocks of life by a perfect mathematical formula. You mentioned before how I seemed to be pondering a new formula the day we met. On a certain level I was, and the question I was pondering was WHY? When a person honestly asks why, they are instantly spurred onto the path to truth. You also said I seemed to be listening. I was, and that's the answer: to ask why honestly and listen for the answer.

> G thought about how it was raining lightly, birds were singing, the plants thriving, etc.

Do you see the energy around you?

Yes, I hear it too.

That is nothing but life. And that's the answer that is contained in all things: life. When people ask if there's life on other planets, the answer is, there is life everywhere. When they understand that, they will understand how the universe works. Now there are other things we need to talk about, and there is a certain sequence. You see coming truths and the directions we could take, but this is systematic progression, and it does have to do with order because everything is ordered in His word. So I need you to listen and not jump ahead.

ΩPoint taken.

Good. Now we can move on. I just needed to rein you in some. Your enthusiasm is appreciated, but quietness is imperative.

> G looked up and saw a raptor. He thought to himself, *The raptor is a bird of prey*. His name means "to seize" in Latin.

That's the truth, but that's not what we're talking about right now. The reining you in is sovereign. And to resolve is to decide to solve.

You're . . .

I'm what? And why?

I don't have the words for infinity.

No, you don't, and we are all incomprehensible, yet people insist on using a word to label someone.

Oops.

Does "knucklehead" come to mind?

Yes.

And you thought you misspelled it and tried to correct it.

Yes, but it was right to start with.

Now, if people get what just happened they would be far ahead.

8:38 PM
I don't like this pen.

Use it.

I just dealt with you on a quantum level. Where do you think this is coming from? From DEEP inside of you. I told you the Kingdom of Heaven was within you.

Now you should never demand or insist a person believe. Because that's their choice. That is their decision to make in this life. It has a profound EFFECT on their LIFE, but it is still their decision. You can guide them and advise them, but the decision is left up to them. And, you said man does not have the technology to change hearts, but you do. You know how to do this, and you've done it before. You think I can do something you can't, as if I'm better than you?

> G's dog started to bark and disturb him while talking to Talia. Down the street construction equipment was tearing up the road, cutting down trees, and making room for a bigger road and more houses.

Why can't I stop the destruction from the machines? It is like they've literally been following me around all my life.

They have to be willing before their hearts can be changed. Greed is a powerful force. Its deception is great and it has changed the face of the earth.

Collection

Talia, I know that's true, but it is not a very satisfying answer.

He never promised to satisfy you, but He did promise that you could be content with such things as you have.

Well, I'm just not very content with what's going on right now. It is upsetting the dog and me.

You have said they should go ahead and pave the whole planet because the suspense was killing you.

Yes, and it seems like they're working hard at it. But I know there will still be parks that we can pay to get into as we go through the turnstile and are counted.

So, cat didn't get your tongue. Are you disturbed?

Yes, I am. I'm just tired of senseless destruction by these big yellow machines. Seems they've been across the street or down the road ever since I can remember, literally. And I know it is just greed. It is no thought taken to the consequences

"It is no thought taken" is an interesting term.

Yes, well, OK.

Right thoughts do have to be taken.

Hey, I've got it. It is the people down the road ripping down trees and pulling the guts out of the earth that need the lesson.

You could go and show this to them.

I can see that they'd just call the cops.

They would if you were insistent. Anger blinds. Anger that becomes rage, kills.

So I shouldn't be outraged?

You should be calm and accept things as they are.

Well, that's a hard one.

I know it is. That's because you're looking in the natural, but I see beyond that. You can too, you know.

I overlook things all the time.

Yes, you do, you overlook them. I said you could look BEYOND them.

I'm with you. I know what you mean. I've been there—but it's irritating.

I know it is, but you have to see it for what it is.

I don't think I'm in that place to see that right now.

No, you're not, so you won't. But when you are, you will, and that's always an eye opener. See when you're calm what happens.

Yes, I took a breath, leaned back and heard "the wrath of man worketh not the righteousness of God."

The voice of wisdom.

From earlier today Michael said, "I know it will all work out." I had missed it but was just reminded. I know he has other things to say; I sense that strongly.

That's enough for now. Told you you would have time.

I know I will, because you said it.

Yes, but it is further confirmation.

Things are being "arranged" in my favor, aren't they?

They always are.

July 10

10:17 AM

G was thinking about his time meditating earlier that day.

Go back and record this.

Record it?

Yes, write it down.

> Earlier, I walked down a wooded trail, turned right, and passed through a golden arch onto a rock-like stairway, except it was gold. At the bottom I entered into a beautiful land of sand, soil, plants, flowers and trees. There were birds flying, and I sensed life all around. The sky was filled with clouds of color, and a voice said, "Can you see it?" I blinked a couple of times, then I saw other colors mixed in with the first, not of this world. Then Talia appeared before me and asked again, "Can you see it?"
>
> It was a swirl of color moving like the wind, then it came behind her and moved through her, then into me, and she said, "I am giving you what I have." I fell on my back onto what was a brown wooden deck. I stayed there a while, then she said, "Arise," and I was again on my feet. She

said again, "I am giving you what I have. You can heal now. This will be for signs to others that they may believe for the signs' sake." Then she said, "Come," and took my right hand in her left, and we flew above the countryside for a short time, then up and through a haze, a veil of some sort, and into a green place, the same one I had seen her at before . . . the same small tree on the mound. She and I walked hand in hand across the grass. There were people about and many looked toward us. Some were talking as they looked. I couldn't understand or hear what most of them said, but I heard one say, "Look, it is Talia's friend."

We walked up to a tree. It was a normal-sized tree (something like an oak), and we stopped before it, and we both looked up at it and she said, "It is the tree of life." I replied, "It doesn't look very big," and she answered, "But its roots go deep."

Then we walked passed it to what appeared to be a three-tiered rock fountain. Water flowed over and down the rocks; there were still other people around but never close, as if they were respectfully giving us room. She said, "This is the fountain of fortune." I think I was already starting towards the fountain when she said, "Drink." (Many things were happening simultaneously.) I drank a handful, which tasted just like regular water at first, then turned sweet in my mouth. I asked if it was OK to take another handful, and she gestured towards it and said, "Sure." I drank another handful from my right hand. It was the same, just like normal water at first, then it turned very sweet as I drank it. She then said, "That's far enough for now," and I thought we would continue on our walk.

I was very drowsy and had to really make myself sit down and write this. I asked Talia if that had really been her. "Yes, that was really me." At one point she said something like, "Write it before you forget it." Now someone may ask themselves how could anyone forget anything like that. Well, believe me, you can forget anything.

July 14

G had a name come to him. Eleazar? He questioned her about it and asked her if he had heard her correctly.

Eleazar.

He said he would bring judgment into truth; that's why wisdom is the principal thing.

G then looked up *Eleazar* in Hebrew and the meaning was, "God, his helper." The root word means "to surround, protect or aid" and *El* means "strength." The feminine aspect means "oak or another strong tree." Also "to twist, be strong, the body as being rolled together." This was intense because it reinforced G's vision of the energy twisting on his arm that he had had on a previous day.

9:27 AM
I have to say my jaw dropped when I got to the twist and the body as being rolled together.

That wasn't the first time and it won't be your last.

10:21 AM
Everything that grows, grows in circles. It is the twist that makes it stronger; it is the struggle. That's why I said a twist of the truth was a perversion—a twist of the real, a counterfeit. That's why it seems to so many to be real, to be the truth, because it is a twist upon that that is real. On the surface it appears to be very real; it has a basis in truth, it seems so logical. These lies, these untruths, are tied together in a most intricate way. It is the antithesis of the web of life, and it promises rewards, usually without that much work involved either. So it is very appealing to the masses. It also promises glory. One way you can tell it is the counterfeit is that it is promised glory; it glorifies the flesh and in no real way honors the Creator.

Wow, Talia, I'm glad your back.

I'm glad YOU'RE back. Let's continue. You want it to be simple, and it is. The truth has a certain ring to it, the "ring of truth," and that's just what it is, a ring. A wake-up call to answer. It has a certain tone, or flavor, that cannot be faked, not in any real sense of the word. You were born by the truth, into it; do you not know the sound of your mother's own voice? That's why excuses for following a false way are unacceptable.

The art of life, and living it, is the only true way to live up to your potential. And that's why you're here, to live up to your potential. Anything else is living a lesser you, which will always be unacceptable to your self. Your higher Self knows what it wants, and that's to live up to your potential. It also knows its own potential, which is why so many remain unfulfilled. It is not so hard to yield to that; it is much more difficult not to.

2:30 PM
Well, Talia, I've started a new notebook here. It sure didn't take long to fill the last one up and with truths too, just like you said.

Did you expect otherwise?

Collection

No, not at all. I knew it would be filled with coming truths, because you said so, and I saw the words as I flipped through the blank pages.

He always confirms His word in the mouth of two or three witnesses. I was the first witness, you were the second.

Well, where are we going now?

We're going all over the place. Do you know what place I am talking about? It is the place I am, you are, and where you should be. It is the place we've been speaking of and from all along. It is the place where everything is that should be there. It is the place where all things are possible and nothing is impossible. It is the place of Being. It is the place of truth in whom is no lie. It is the only place to be if you truly want to Be. And it is all in the BEING.

Sounds like the place to be.

Why would anyone want to be anywhere else?

Another deep philosophical question.

Philosophy is primarily questions, and it is a good start to ask them, but what we have here are answers; therefore, we've passed far beyond philosophy. Philosophy is wondering; we're answering and we're living it, in its power—the power of Truth—and that's why I say we're far beyond philosophy.

Have you not seen these truths manifested in power?

Yes, I have.

Have you seen any of man's philosophies manifested in power?

Not really.

Nor will you, not in this way. It is not that we have a corner on truth; it is just that they're not looking in the corners for it. It is like hidden treasure, you know.

So you've said.

Yes, interesting how the truth repeats itself, isn't it. It echoes throughout the corners of the universe. It cannot help but to do that. That's how it operates.

You've said that before too.

Interesting.

I just flipped through these pages and seemed to see a disturbance or choppiness towards the center. I saw rough water.

The truth often disturbs, and on many levels, from the surface to the very core. It also disturbs the status quo. The status quo serves its own and is a false comfort.

The Universe Speaks

Shakes up business as usual?

You could certainly say that.

I have to tell you, I get a little cranky when we don't talk.

I noticed. I told you to make the most of your time. You have little to lose. When you do it will help you not to get like that.

OK.

Now I would like to get into the why.

The *why?*

Yes, the why that this is happening with us, between us. Why it is you and I and not someone else. We're not going to cover all the facets of it, but we are going to touch on some truths as to why. Some are asking themselves this question, thus the answer.

The why can essentially be summed up in one word—and that's fellowship. Real meaningful answers always come from deep fellowship. Even if it is a one-word answer to your questions from a stranger, it comes from deep fellowship. Deep answers unto the deep. It is also a pure desire to know someone. You saw me as someone worth knowing. It pained you to think you'd never know me like you wanted to. You ASKED to know me; now you do. That's the short answer.

Well, that's deep.

I knew that was coming—I know you too. ☺

July 15

9:16 AM
Good morning.

Good morning. And you were worried about writer's block. ☺

The woods just don't seem as conducive as the desert.

The desert was where we started this, so it is more familiar to you. It all comes from the same place, and you have to be in the same place to receive it. Maybe you shouldn't pay so much attention to the distractions. By the way, it is all coming together, this book, our message, everything.

You just said more than it seems, didn't you?

I always do. I don't change, just grow.

Collection

Wouldn't it reach a point where it seems like change?

It could seem that way, but we never change or transform into something else. Our core remains the same. An oak is an oak no matter how huge it becomes.

I got it: it all begins with a seed, and it doesn't change from that basic structure.

That's right. You can always trace any growth or nature back to its seed. That's a mistake some researchers make, but not that many. The mistake most researchers make is not tracing the growth or nature of a thing beyond the seed and to the source of the seed. The seed is the beginning and it is energy. ITS birth is a thought, a conception of mind. So when you say the energy follows the mind, it is true to an extent, as a way of understanding it or teaching the manipulation of energy—which IS yours to use, by the way. But the real truth is you can't have one without the other; energy and mind are one.

That ought to keep them busy for a while.

If they are paying attention it will; all the clues are there.

All of them?

All they need are there to go anywhere.

We can't go much further without a raising of consciousness.

Is that true?

Yes, that's true. Truth is being ignored daily. Like an endless loop of tape, man has his conceptions, and they reaffirm them daily to themselves and each other.

Unless and until there is change there we can't go much further. Man has reached an impasse, and he doesn't recognize it. He has convinced himself that he is right and that there is no other, that this is all that is. The times that are coming will try the hearts of men. The great shaking will shake out the chaff from the wheat. Decisions need to be made and soon. The death is not living. We've already explained how to live, and it is as a creative being in HIM, through Him. Anything else is not living at all.

Are we done here?

For the time being.

For the time being?

For the time being what it is.

What do you mean?

This is being spread now by the universal consciousness of what it is. It is being pondered and accepted, looked over and rejected. As I've said, decisions must be made and quickly.

The Universe Speaks

Where does that leave us?

It leaves us where we are.

July 16

7:52 AM
Did you think this was going to stop?

No, you told me before you would keep talking with me, but I was a bit concerned.

No need to be; we're just waiting. Waiting for some to catch up, including you. You have to put these principles in action, live them. I told you all things were yours; the power to walk in this is yours as well. Whatsoever you ask in prayer, believing, you shall receive.

Then I want to walk in this, to grow beyond this.

Then you will. There is a balance to everything. An amazing, intricate and delicate balance that must be maintained. When you lose your balance you stumble, but this too is a learning experience.

Why don't you ask me about it; you're already laughing.

OK, it is about the time you, your mom and your cousins stopped at a fast food place and went through the drive-through. It was dark out, and you wanted to order, but no one answered when you spoke, and you all started to get really mad. Then your five-year-old cousin said, "It's the trash can!" It was dark, and the speaker and trashcan looked the same! That to me is absolutely hilarious!

That WAS one of the most funny things ever. That is called "fast food fun," and it WAS hilarious. We were hungry and hasty, and as it is often the case, out of the mouths of babes the truth was made known. It is the times like those that make life on earth so interesting and fun. My mom and I DID fancy ourselves as two of the smartest people on the planet. Which did only add to the fun. It is also those times that help you stay humble and not take yourself too seriously.

I just about crack up every time I think of that. It also helped me see you weren't infallible.

That could be another reason it happened. When you find your attention wavering or not on what it should be, you should ask yourself why.

That shirt you're wearing—it is not just the color I like, it is the motto.

Service, dedication, education, training. It is a good motto.

Collection

It caught your attention.

Yes, it did. I remember I kept looking at it, thinking about those words, so I finally decided to commit it to memory.

Good decision.

I remember what I was doing at the time and that I was enjoying where I was.

> G was at a special training facility surrounded by nature, where he was learning new and practicing old skills for his job and his life.

That's because you're good at it. It is easy to enjoy something you're good at, so if you want to be good at something, enjoy it, and if you want to enjoy something, get good at it.

That's an interesting concept.

Yes, isn't it. Do you think maybe you're good at things because you enjoy them or that you enjoy them because you're good at them?

Probably both.

Yes, but the point I'm making is that to enjoy is a creation. It is a creation of your mind, much like to envision.

There's something else I want you to think about. There's joy in the spin because there is stability inherent within it; it creates its own balance. Everything in creation that is without the spin is dead because it is without life. That that doesn't spin is in an unnatural state that's immediate decay. That's why I say there are vortices everywhere. They are spun off from the energy of life, which is everywhere. Now, due to the interconnectedness of all life that is spun off from these vortices, it can disappear from there because that part is not needed there anymore. It recognizes this to reappear somewhere else where it is needed and can be used. From particles to people we all do this. That's the changes, and that's where the number 64 comes in.

I don't know if the layman's going to get this, and the theoretical physicists are probably going to think this is real basic.

It IS real basic. The layman can get it by intuition. The theorists need to see beyond the words to replace their theory with reality.

I see why so many of them are not getting it, and it's because they are being dishonest with themselves. Which I find odd because these same ones do have integrity and ARE being honest with others.

That's exactly right, and that's what we're trying to get them to see. When they deny their Self they will remain stuck and without breakthrough. They are searching diligently for the key, and it is right inside of them.

And I thought we were done.

We'll never be done; we're just beginning. These breakthroughs are going to be marvelous because people have great faith in scientists these days, and many will wake up because of them.

Beginning meaning "beginning to wake people up."

Yes, I told you that was what we were here for, what we were doing. It is not just to stir interest or satisfy curiosity, it is to help wake people up, to help them to realize they have been asleep and are missing the point. The point containing all they are. How many times have you said, "I'm missing something here?"

Quite a bit.

Yes, the point being you recognized it and looked for what it was you knew you were missing. That's an important first step, to recognize that you're not seeing the complete picture and to ask why. Another way of putting it is, as Paul said, "If any man thinks he knows something he knows nothing yet as he ought to know." Now that seems like an extreme statement, but we all know in part. There's always more to what we think we know than what we know. That's why I say this will never end. No sense in getting puffed up by something you know, because there's always more to know about it than you know.

I know what you mean.

You think you do.

Well, I figure there's probably more to it.

You think so?

Yes, I do.

Well, you're right.

I KNEW that was a safe bet.

Yes, and you always like to play it safe in your reckless way. ☺

Ah, you got me again.

You know, once you find the balance between your extremes you'll be unstoppable.

Then I won't want to stop.

You won't need to. Now you have to stop, regroup, back up, ponder it and then move on. Once you find the balance you'll flow forward untouchable.

Sounds like the thing to do.

Collection

Oh, it is. You thought I was being serious when I said you had a unique way of blending flesh and spirit. ☺

I did till now. You have a very subtle sense of humor I hadn't completely noticed. That is funny, though.

Come on! It is hilarious. You think you're the only one who likes to have fun? I love to, always have, and I'm good at it too because I enjoy it. ☺

I miss you, Talia.

How can you miss me? I'm right here.

I mean I miss you in the flesh.

If I were in the flesh we wouldn't be doing this right now. I would probably be playing tennis or something.

And none of this would get out.

No, none of this would. Not in this way or by us or even now. I told you this had to be or this wouldn't be happening, and you would still be in search of a vision. As it is, I helped to restore your vision, and I'm in a unique position to help you to accomplish what it is you need to do.

As natural as walking.

Yes, as natural as walking. It is important to walk, you know.

Yes, it seems to all stem from there.

From the stem comes the blossom. It is a basic precept, and the walk you walk has its foundation in that precept.

Well, now, I knew what *precept* meant, but it made such an impression on me that I had to look it up. Interesting.

> G looked up what *precept* meant, and the Latin root, *praeceptum,* means "to capture or to take." G was blown away at how this relates to the hawk seizing its prey and the spider in the king's house. You have to take what you need.

You said I was impressive.

You are very impressive.

Babylon has no power here.

I know that.

The Universe Speaks

Yes, the STATUS of confusion, the politics of it has no power here. Here, there is only perfect peace, and that is yours to walk in.

Social circles run the gambit. THAT passion for the game has no place here either; pawns are sacrificed and with glee.

That's a vicious circle, isn't it?

That is usually a very subtle, vicious circle. And it is not always for money or power; sometimes it is just for the pleasure of the sacrifice.

Thank you, Talia.

There is always thankfulness involved with doing God's work.

Now we need to talk about traveling.

OK.

You were saying the other day about how some cultures insisted that one must travel to learn what they needed to, to become wise.

> G and I were talking about how in some cultures, like some Native American cultures, the boys are sent on a journey to learn from others before coming back to their tribe as men.

Yes.

Well, the primary reason was not in the actual traveling per se. It was in being an outsider looking in. Of not being a part of the plan of the clan, of leaving that and seeing with fresh eyes.

Makes sense to me.

Of course it does—you're well traveled.

You were too.

I had that opportunity and I jumped at it. It did help to open my eyes.

I heard your dad was offered a herd of goats or camels or something for you once.

> Talia had taken a trip to Israel with her dad. While shopping in the Arab quarter in Jerusalem, a shop keeper offered Michael a herd of goats or camels in exchange for Talia. None of us were sure if it was a joke or if he was serious!

He was. That was funny, and I was flattered. Then I had to laugh at myself for being flattered. I asked him [Michael] if he was tempted, and he laughed and said no, but I wondered if he really was. Then I laughed about that because I knew he wasn't.

Collection

Sounds like you had a good time.

We had a great time. He's laughing about it now.

July 17

7:59 AM
It is a new day.

It is a glorious new day.

Yes, it is.

Don't be disappointed with how few "get" this or who doesn't get this; this is strong meat and on many levels. I know you want to share this with the world and we are, but this isn't for the world, this is for the chosen few. Remember that many are called but few are chosen.

But isn't it their choice?

Yes, they choose themselves. They can choose to be as gods or as fools; there really isn't any middle ground. You choose the ground to stand on—the path to walk on—and those paths are placed before you daily. It isn't as if the paths aren't plain either—they are diametrically opposed to each other. Therefore, choose this day whom you will serve.

The thing we are doing here is of the utmost importance. I tell you again time is short for those decisions, and they should be weighed carefully. This is that that was spoken of when He said, "I work a work in these days, a work that you will in no way believe though a man declare it unto you." I know you feel you should explain this and other things contained here, but that's not how it works. The choice is either to receive the pure word of truth or a carefully crafted lie that is the path that is set before you daily. Judgment is imperative, spiritual discernment is necessary. Another essential ingredient is desire. If you don't really WANT it, you won't really HAVE it. It is hard to stumble into these things.

That door I held open for you was an invitation. You weren't forced to go through it; you chose to because you recognized that that was within your sphere of responsibility to do so. You thought it was the excitement of exploration, but there was more to it than that, much more. If you had rejected that invitation to the mysteries of the unknown, we wouldn't be here now. That was a choice, a decision that you made. That's the portal you were seeking so many years ago. You knew it existed, but you didn't know where to find it. You trusted me whole-heartedly because you knew where I was coming from. The thought crossed your mind that day that maybe I was a conjurer or magician. That I was doing illusions, practicing to elicit a response from you—that perhaps I was putting a spell on you, that I was magical. That maybe my circle of friends in Santa Barbara was into witchcraft even. But that wasn't it at all and you knew it.

The Universe Speaks

You weighed it carefully and rejected the lie. You received the truth of what was happening, and you decided right then and there that you would discover the truth and if it was true to walk in it. THAT was one of the best decisions you ever made, and it is greatly appreciated.

I still think you're magical and you did put a spell on me.

Only in the best of ways, and it wasn't me. I was being used that day by the Holy Spirit to wake you up. You had been asleep long enough. I have to tell you though, I thought that was really funny when I heard you thought I was a magician. I knew less of what was going on that day than you did, though I knew something was up. That something was different about that day, that "something was in the air" is what I had thought.

Hey, I was just weighing the possibilities.

As well you should. This gift you were given that day was my great honor to bring you, and I did nothing but be who I was, and THAT's the magic: just be who you are. ☺

So you see that girl you were told that is from Santa Barbara that would change your life IS me, and I HAVE changed your life.

I have no words to express . . .

I know, and again, none are needed. We are one in HIM and without HIM we can do nothing. No thing at all; however, with Him we can do all things and the good news is we are with Him and HE is with us; therefore, nothing is impossible.

Cool.

Yes, it is cool, isn't it? Very cool.

You are one cool chick.

Thank you.

My dad says to tell you he's proud to be your friend.

Tell him thanks and I didn't know there was pride there.

Of course there is. He plentifully rewards the proud doer. We're proud to be His children. We're proud to know Him, to walk in His grace. The pride HE warns about is the pride of the flesh, of the debilitating aspect of it. That's the pride that's spoken of that comes before a fall. Write it like I say it, and it is easy. Slow down—you were told that not too long ago, as I recall.

Have you ever seen a master looking hurried?

Can't say as I've seen many masters.

Yes, but the ones you have seen or have heard about?

Come to think of it, they act like they have all the time in the world.

Collection

They don't and they know it. They also know that to be efficient one must slow down and be still on a certain level. One trait of a true master is calmness, and you will always see that center of calmness in whatever they do. The eye of the storm, as it were. You'll also notice a conspicuous lack of panic, no matter what is going on. Why do you think that is?

Because they've found the SOURCE?

They have discovered the source of their success even if THEY don't know what it is. Have you ever seen success from panic?

No, that's called blind fear, and I figure that's what it is.

Now we're getting somewhere. Fear blinds, and if you're blind you can't see. If you can't see, how can you get to where you're going, much less have success at it?

I can see that.

But have you thought about taking that on the road?

What? My jokes? I take them everywhere I go. I'm a constant source of amusement—at least to myself.

You're a source of amusement to many others too. You know laughter is one of the most healthy things you can do. I called myself a giver of laughter; have I not made you laugh?

Yes, tons of times.

That is a weighty matter, a person's health. It is important to be healthy, don't you think?

Yes, sure it is. That's important.

Do you know why Ronald Reagan was called the Great Communicator?

Because he was the great communicator?

Because of his humor. He disarmed his enemies with it, even charmed many over to his side. He had the ear of the people, and one reason was that people love to laugh. It is good for the body, and the body knows it.

Now you were concerned about writing down the revelation of the download I just gave you, but you don't have to write it down. Just remember the essence of the message, of doorways, etc. And now you know how to use this to work outside the box. You always want to open the box and let whatever's in there out anyway—now you have a method.

OK, I take it back: you're not cool—you're beyond cool.

Yes, I am beyond cool. I instinctively knew that even when I was on earth. That's one reason I always had to laugh when I saw people trying to act cool, because it always looked to me like a comic act. So when I imitated them I never could keep a straight face.

That was actually very sophisticated for someone your age.

Well, I was very sophisticated for my age.

We're quite a team you know.

I know.

Some won't believe it, but this hasn't been done before, not on this level, not in this depth. People have been communing with "spirits" ever since there were people in the physical realm, but it hasn't been recorded in this depth before. Mostly it has been "bits and pieces."

Why is that?

Because this has been ordained for just such times as these. This message had to get out, and it had to be at this time. I will say it again: this that we are doing is worthy of remembrance, and it will be remembered for all time. Told you to wait, there was more. You're learning to curb your excitement, and that's a good thing. That old saying, patience is a virtue, is a true saying, and that's why IT IS remembered.

Raising the bar.

That's what we're doing, raising the bar. Encouraging people to jump higher and fly farther than ever before.

Is it going to work?

Of course it is going to work; we cannot fail. I told you we were going to get it right this time and we ARE.

July 19

6:40 AM
I was thinking that since Einstein said his education got in the way of his learning, maybe I'm smarter for getting out of formal education so soon.

Hmmm.

What?

I'm thinking. ☺

Hey, it's a joke.

Well, you were paying more attention in school than you think—it just wasn't always on what they were teaching. Now I'm teaching you and bringing you into a deeper understanding of all things, and you are paying attention. Remember when He said, "She'll be YOUR teacher?"

Collection

Yes, another thing that happened at Thanksgiving.

And at the time you were thinking what?

That "I'd like to teach her." That you had so much potential.

Everyone has so much more potential than they know; it is who decides to use it that's important.

9:00 AM
Now we need to make people aware of something else.

What's that?

All that happened Thanksgiving. And there is a lot more. It is a microcosm of life, of a life on earth. A day, one single day, can be filled with joy and wonderment, with lessons and learning, with realizations of truth and sharing of love. Or it can be wasted, missed completely and filled with disillusionment and misery—and that is a profound waste of a life. Therefore, live life fully in every way you possibly can. The trials and tribulations, successes and victories of a single day as if a lifetime, and your meditations at the end of the day can set you up for further victories or miseries. That's called living mindfully, and that's what is called for.

And there you go, going right into something else and blowing my mind again.

I'm blowing the cobwebs out.

I have been thinking clearer lately.

That's because you've been listening to me. ☺

5:30 PM
Now I want to tell you of a not-so-well-kept secret, other than people keep it a secret from themselves. And that's our communication. A large part of this message is how to—how to communicate.

If people will look at this as "bilateral communications," it will be much easier to grasp. The gulf that separates, as it were, is an invention of the mind of man. Bilateral meaning "the symmetrical other side."

I said before that the physical has a spiritual counterpart, and to know yourself and the importance of that. And that if you did know yourself, others wouldn't be such a mystery. Well, to know yourself is to also know your spiritual counterpart and to call it unto yourself; after all, it is YOURS. When you felt me on your left side when I was used to heal you, you'll notice your right elbow was healed not long after that—and that's because the body acts bilaterally also. ONE SIDE AFFECTS THE OTHER. Spiritually, it is the same. What you are in the physical, you are enhanced much more so in the spiritual. These ALWAYS work hand in hand.

So to sum it up one needs to, or it helps to think, "Bilateral communication, then yield to the spirit," then demand results. That's how it is taken by force.

This is for everyone, and everyone who WANTS it can have it. Think how one side of the body affects the other side of the body. That's how close these parts work together.

Well said.

I'm well spoken. The people need to know these are no longer hidden truths, and they should receive them. It IS theirs for the taking. There was a time when what we're doing was quite common and accepted, you know.

Guess that's been a while.

It has for most cultures. It is been bred right out of them, stolen away. You see the poverty in their lives it has caused and not to honor the Creator or His creations . . . untold misery.

That's a shame.

Yes, it is, and shame on the ones who have stolen it. We want to bring it back. Restore paths to dwell in, re-mind those to remember, to live again. Have I not enriched your life?

Immeasurably.

And that is a statement of fact.

July 22

7:10 AM

> G dreamt last night about Talia telling him something about "pure honesty" and using examples—a person and a Porsche 911 woven in—and her saying something about it.

Pure honesty has to do with quality and performance, and neither one of them are cheap to maintain.

So, a 911 is Talia approved?

It is a fine automobile if that's what you're into.

What about the price?

They're a little pricey.

I used it as an example of quality and performance, which is endemic to pure honesty.

Endemic speaks of a place, doesn't it?

Collection

It is the same place we've been talking about all along. Pure honesty does no harm, and its basis is in love—that's its only motivation. That's the performance contained in Everything. Love performs. It acts to move things to a better place, to enhance what is, where it is. Its very nature is quality, and it is always perfectly pure at its root.

At its root?

Yes, it stems from a place of perfect purity and is without corruption whatsoever. A misinterpretation of how to apply this purity could result in misunderstanding though. Thus the "pure honesty." Being honest without pure motivation smacks of dishonesty. So be honest with yourself and be honest with others out of a pure heart.

July 23

10:37 AM
I keep seeing spheres. Spheres touching, intersecting, and overlapping. Spheres within spheres.

You see them moving too.

Yes, moving all around and pulsating with life!

Pulsating with different colors. Do you hear the sounds of the many different vibrations?

Yes, yes I do!

That's the art of life in action, moving and creating. It never ends; this pulsating movement is always and forever. You saw the rain coming.

Yes, I saw it falling.

That's prophetic vision; trust it. Get into your bubble or sphere, and your sphere of influence will grow to where it needs to be. And it is not a striving to get there, or networking as so many like to call it, but a growing into it naturally, supernaturally. I said before, you influence whether you want to or not, may as well influence positively for the betterment of all.

If you think of a sphere as a circle, that's not what it is. It is many different shapes, all spherical and alive. The circle is a two-dimensional representation to draw on paper as a symbol or to explain certain principles of understanding.

Of understanding?

Yes, to understand, you must embody, make your own, these principles. It is a becoming, becoming what is. An intellectual knowing can only ever be a seed—a seed that may grow into understanding—but only if it is taken and embodied. Something within you must come out of you before it can live again.

July 25

9:10 AM
You have much study to do, and I'm bringing you to a place you can receive more.

So we're delayed?

I wouldn't call it a delay. For everything there is a season; now's the season for study. I've already expressed to you what to study. Study the web of life and the interrelationships of people and all things. You will come to a greater understanding of what we're discussing and how it relates to all things. Again, all things are interconnected, and this is apparent when your eyes are opened.

You see luminous fibers connecting all things. This is why everything affects everything else. You feel them pulling people towards you even now. This is a silver cord that cannot be broken but by the hand of God. This is also the path that makes our connection so easy. When people understand this, that great gulf that separates will not seem so great after all.

That seems esoteric.

It is esoteric. Its mystery is hidden within the vibrations of life. When a person vibrates in harmony with the vibration of life the mystery is solved.

That's perfectly reasonable.

I always am.

July 27

9:43 AM
Isotropic?

It has to do with the nature of time.

How so?

It does not vary in any direction; it remains the SAME—non-existent in its function here. That's why I say when you're dealing with here, time has no function—it is non-existent. Eternity isn't time without end, it is time out of mind. It all just is now, because here now is all that is.

Collection

You certainly say some things.

Yes, I certainly do say all I have to say in the time I have to say it.

That seems like a contradiction.

You have seasons there, and we work with your seasons. Time to you appears linear. It is not at all. Even there it comes around spherically, as the seasons. That mirrors the workings of the Creator. That tree you climbed. What did you do?

I put two blue lights up on the trunk and trimmed some suckers cut.

What did you hear someone say who saw it later?

Cool.

Coincidence?

No.

Why blue?

That's what was already up there but had probably been blown off by a storm.

But why blue?

I don't know why.

So we could talk about it.

That's it?

No, that's not it. It is everything. When people ask, "Is that it?" they're asking about everything, but they only want it explained in part, and that's part of the problem. People for the most part insist that everything be separated or broken into parts in order to understand it, but it cannot be broken into parts but must be viewed as a whole to understand it. That's another subtle way they attempt to relieve themselves of responsibility. To know something is to be responsible for the knowledge, not only to walk in it but to pass it on as well. It is my great honor/responsibility to pass THIS knowledge on, and that we will.

When someone asks where are the missing pieces, the pieces aren't missing, they are still a part of the whole. But they may have been misplaced, and that misplacement is almost invariably misplaced by the creative mind of man. It is not just artists that are creative, everyone is creative. It is how you choose to express your creativity that is the issue.

Had enough?

No, not at all.

Then stay here. We're not finished.

The Universe Speaks

Times change.

Times change?

Yes, times, time and half a time, times change. This is from here for there. Know that there, times change.

Seasons. I was spoken to about seasons the other day and the primary colors that represented them and why.

Yes, for "everything" there is a season.

Whoa, never saw it like that.

Now you have. Remembrance is putting all the pieces together. Remember? Into a coherent whole. Enlightenment is a realization. Light reveals reality. Reality is what is real. Only by the light can you walk in what is real and be real and become what you are—which is everything.

12:20 PM
  G was looking at the yellow calla lillies.

These are my favorite.

Why?

Look at how it grows, spiraling.

Which way did it grow?

To the right. Why?

It is just the right way to grow.

July 28

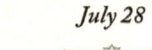

5:15 PM
No one talks to us anymore.

  G heard this statement from another spirit, not Talia. This spirit continued to speak.

Man is in a precarious position. He has forgotten the old ways, the true ways. Even you, it is hard for you to believe.

Sorry about that.

Collection

It is OK. You're well educated, in man's ways.

There is a way that seems right but is not. Man used to have such reverence. Now things are stamped out. Man becomes a slave to each other to buy these stamped out things.

I like that girl you're with.

Who, Talia?

Yes.

You know her?

Yes, that's Heaven's Dew. She's famous.

She's famous?

Yes.

July 30

1:21 PM
OK, a couple questions.

OK.

You're famous?

Yes, I guess I am. It is the speed with which I've accomplished what I've accomplished here, and also there are not that many that can do more HERE than THERE. I told you, many were looking on in awe.

Times, time and half a time?

That's a complex question. It has to do with ages, of things coming to pass and passing. There are times for things and they pass. It is a time for a thing and it too will pass. A half a time is time cut short. My time was cut short there, but my time is enhanced here to accomplish more there. There is an age to come that will be half a time. If these days were not shortened then no flesh would be saved, but for the elect's sake shall this time be shortened.

Got a date?

No man knows the hour. It is a good idea to be ready though.

I said I liked the poem you wrote me. I like it for the truth it contains.

My life should not be mourned, my life should be celebrated.

The Universe Speaks

August 2008

August 4

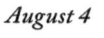

10:00 AM
Always speak the truth in love, even about yourself. If you don't like yourself, how do you think you're going to feel about others?

11:24 AM
I know you want to work out and train, but what's more important than this? That's one reason I wanted to omit "athletic" at my tree, because it puts an unnecessary emphasis on what's not that important, and I wanted you to know that. That decision was primarily for you, for now. I saw the time coming when you would rather train the body than the mind for our message. You think our message is done?

No, but I thought we took a hiatus.

That doesn't mean to turn your mind off. It was for a time of reflection, study and growth. First it was coming too fast, now it is coming slow . . . so you give up?

No, not at all, I just thought we were taking a break.

It was a break in the narrative, not a vacation from life.

I just have not been hearing you say much.

You haven't been listening much. How much would you talk to someone who wasn't listening?

Not much.

You would have me waste words. I told you I didn't do that.

But you had told me to get back into training.

I did and you are, but not at the exclusion of everything else.

I'm corrected.

You're being corrected. You're still somewhat bouncing off the walls with your distractions.

Just had to get settled.

The settling is an internal state. It doesn't matter that much what's going on on the outside. There are people that need our help, and we're moving them in directions where they can receive it.

Collection

Talia, I've often wondered if I were up to the task and that maybe there were many others better suited for this. I'm no writer anyway.

The fact that "you're no writer" is one of the reasons you're writing this. Also quit wondering if you're up for the task. You obviously are, or we wouldn't have gotten this far. It is needful for you to apply more mental discipline, and we are working on that.

Sorry to disappoint you.

Disappointing me is not the issue, our message is.

I want to do this.

So do I. Now we're in agreement. Now we can continue unhindered by foolishness. You must find the balance, that's all.

The balance is all.

That's it; that's the primary source. If you receive something in an unbalanced state, what you receive will seem somewhat unbalanced itself. That can cause confusion from what is a perfectly balanced truth.

Thus the growth and the waiting you spoke of.

Exactly. We have spoken of all of this before. Of giving someone something in an untimely manner, how it doesn't profit to do so. Speaking the truth's not enough. As a matter of fact, it is often used as a weapon of revenge to hurt others. It is speaking the truth in love in a perfectly timed manner that makes all the difference, spoken truth perfectly balanced.

Talia, I'm glad your back!

I'm glad YOU'RE back. If you haven't noticed, I'm pretty consistent. It doesn't matter where you're at there; what matters is where you're at here.

Maybe I have too many irons in the fire.

Maybe you do. It does take a certain commitment.

1:07 PM
I'm human. You identify with me. That's one reason why what we do together works so well. Also, you KNEW me.

We had met and you saw things beyond me. It tied things together for you. It was beyond your imagination. The symmetry of a young girl and an omnipotent God. This cemented ties that bind. The bridging of the flesh and spirit, of the earthly and the heavenly. This is incomprehensible for most people.

Only an empty vessel is useful to be filled. A filled vessel filled with what isn't needed is useless until it can be emptied. Again we are speaking of choices. Choosing to be emptied can be painful, for most people cling to their past choices even when they have filled them with misery. They feel all their work will have been wasted and lost. But to be emptied is to be free. Free for all the possibilities to be filled.

I told you I wasn't omniscient, and you identify with that. It is in human terms you understand.

This is true. I had to look up *omniscient*. There's got to be some irony there.

You might be surprised how much irony is everywhere, but the point being is your identification. This helps greatly in our communications; it always does on every level.

August 5

8:30 AM
You have a question.

Yes, I do.

I have a lot of answers.

You sure do.

Why don't you ask then?

I'm not sure where to start.

You don't always have to be so sure. You like to be positive about things before you declare them, but it doesn't always work that way. When you declare something in faith, it brings it into being. You're sometimes too concerned about being wrong or misreading the spirit. What you need to understand is that the spirit works with you to bring things to pass. A pure heart and fervent prayer is always honored, and if a thing you have declared doesn't come to pass, then it wasn't meant to be.

Almost like we got off track here.

No, not at all. We're right on track, and this will tie in exquisitely with other things to come. It is as important to look ahead as it is to be in the moment. Looking ahead in hope and expectation.

That's pretty cool—a hawk just flew up into the top of a cedar.

He's here for you.

Collection

Why?

Just a sign.

A sign for what?

A sign of independence and self-sufficiency among other things. You ever see them in a flock?

No, four is the most I've ever seen hunting together.

They hunt independently and yet are mutually supportive.

That's a perfect window through the other tree to where he's sitting

        G was looking through one tree to the next, where the hawk was perched.

Does he look nervous?

No, he looks supremely confident.

He knows his vision will bring him everything he needs.

Talia, that's awesome.

I know, but these things are everywhere. Everywhere you look they are there, but most just don't notice. Many don't even have the inclination to care.

There he goes again, flying over the pond.

Yes, something will give up its life today so that animal may live, and it is no different with you or anybody else. What's important is being mindful of that and being thankful for the sacrifice.

Talia, I know you gave up your life here so we could do this and bring this message to those who need it, and I just want to thank you again for all you've done and are doing to change things for the better, to bring a wonder-filled life to others.

That was well put, and you're very welcome.

You sound a little surprised.

Well, that was well put, very articulate. I said you were, you know. When have you known me to be wrong?

Can't think of a single instance.

You won't find one either. Here we can do no wrong. When you're "here," there you can't either.

I can tell you don't feel like "giving your life up" was a sacrifice.

No, I don't. It seems like the ultimate gift is mine, and I'm just living it.

The Universe Speaks

That point of view seems abstract here, but I know it isn't there. That this message has touched your mom's friend so is awesome and so very encouraging.

I told you we would touch people and change lives. This message is with power and has been ordained for this time. You seem surprised.

Well, I guess a little.

Why?

I'm not sure why.

Remember what that Indian told you?

To take myself seriously.

That's the part. Why is that so hard?

Because I'm a court jester?

You're not a court jester—you just like to play the part. Look at how the brain is made.

What do you mean?

It looks like a cloud on the outside, and if you don't feed it, it becomes cloudy. But if you look on the inside it appears more like a tree, and a tree must be fed.

OK, our conversations have more twists and turns.

The twist is for strength, the turns are for agility. I have to keep your mind occupied or you get bored, and those horses will run in every direction, much like yesterday.

Wild horses—I just saw that.

Yes, and you must control them. They are not tame, and that would be taking it too far, but you must control them.

So are you going to talk about what you've done with your mom's friend?

I can. I know you're bursting to know.

Yes, I sort of am.

She is a very special person whose heart has been prepared to receive this. She did know there was more, and she asked about it. She's now learning what that more is. She has asked me to talk to her, and I do. I told her to listen, and she's learning how to quiet herself and listen with her heart. She has felt my presence, and she knows it's me. She knew me well there, and that basis of knowledge has given her an edge to hear my voice. This is a language of the heart, and she's well aware of that. I have merged my spirit with hers at times, and an intuitive knowing is the result of that. She is as filled with questions as you are, and that is a definite first step on the path of life. She has asked to see the light, and she is.

That's beautiful!

Yes, truth is always beautiful and life giving.

I was told she thanks you daily.

She does have a wonderful spirit of thankfulness. She also has a very, very sweet spirit, but she's just now learning who she really is, and that is truly a wonderful thing to know. She's asked many questions, and they will be answered in time.

   G sensed some personal things here.

There are, and they are being worked out, but know He has a special place reserved for her, and she is and will be used to bring life and light to others. She's asked for this and it will be.

That is just so totally awesome!

Yes, it is.

You know, Talia, you really never do cease to amaze me.

Yes, I know. "Pretty much amazing."

You knew you were when you were here; that's why you said that so much, wasn't it?

That was another intuitive knowing. That not only was I amazing but so much more as well. Again, this isn't so much about me as about the so much more that everyone is a part of. When one is awakened to that fact, then is life filled with wonder.

10:35 PM
The man on TV just said that all children would become scientists if we didn't discourage them and make it so boring and technical.

He's right about that.

Talia, tell me about your prophetic dreams.

I had them a lot. Things would come to pass, and there was no denying or explaining it. It made no sense to me at first, then as my awareness of what was happening grew, I knew there must be a soul and a Supreme Being. How else could it be explained? It did get and keep my attention on seeking how and what was happening. I knew there was more—there had to be. There was just no denying it. Then I felt the spirit at times. I didn't know what it was then, but it felt larger than life. And that's what you saw in my eyes, the spirit that was larger than life itself, a window into the marvels of the universe. You literally looked into my eyes and saw the universe.

The Universe Speaks

That's what it was! I couldn't put it into words, but that's it!

That is it. It's the "it" that I was speaking of. It's the "it" that is everything and nothing lost. That "it" is riches beyond measure. This is where I live, and it is glorious!

August 6

8:08 AM
Quietness is good.

I know, quiet the galloping horses.

That's it, you control them. It takes patience. Everything you do there that has lasting meaning will be accomplished from a place of quietness. Quietness equals confidence. True confidence is born in quietness. You ever see anyone loud that had true confidence?

No, I guess not. They seemed as if they were trying to convince themselves, and it seemed like a false confidence.

It is a false confidence because it isn't real. A common thread you will see with confident people is that they are quiet. You immediately noticed how confident I was when you met me; you also noticed that I was quiet.

I did. I wish you had said more, that we had talked more. You seemed like you had a lot to say, and I wanted to hear it. That's a major regret for me.

Don't regret it. It had and has much purpose. I didn't have a life-changing message then—now I do.

That that you said about your eyes mirroring the universe yesterday—thanks for that, for explaining it.

And that's exactly what we are, mirrors of the universe. That's how life is expressed as art, and that stems from decisions. That's another aspect of our creative abilities. To decide to express the art of creation.

There went the hawk.

Yes, he's expressing his creative abilities by being who he is. There is no striving, and he's very relaxed. He's not putting on airs or trying to impress—he's just being who he is. There's never pressure in being who you truly are.

If I were an Indian I would say, "Hawk has much to teach!"

Collection

Everything has much to teach. It's where you place your attention is where you'll get your answers. A perfectly placid pond has swirls. Movement in stillness.

I know what you're talking about, Talia, but I'm not sure anybody else will.

They will if they are quiet.

You're talking about vortices in the quietness, in the stillness. The movement of life that never ends but is invisible.

Yes, you feel compelled to explain.

Somewhat.

Why?

Why not?

"It" can't always be explained. Some things, to receive, takes an act of faith.

Yes, I know.

I know you know. As I've said before, the confusion is caused by separation. Oneness is necessary. It's really not so hard either. You can merge your spirit with things. This is how you can know them intimately and perfectly. I told you no analyst would get this. This doing is by being and Beings is what we are. It's not that it's second nature—it's your first nature, to live as a spiritual being, for that's what you are. It's your very essence. The body is just a filter.

Never heard the body described like that before.

But that's what it does; it filters spiritual experience.

But why?

So you can express your creativity through your choices.

Wow.

Yes, again, wow. Told you it was never-ending.

So you've said.

You know why?

Because it's never-ending?

That's why. See how simple that is? Most people are masters at complicating things, especially such simple truths. They work extremely hard at it.

The Universe Speaks

The parallel universe is right here right now. Mathematics are symbols pointing to truths to be visualized. Without a vision you die. Literally whither on the vine.

Complications crumble; simplicity tends to stand. Complication and confusion are synonymous, just as simplicity and purity can be interchanged.

Was that you?

It's a truth.

It's enough for now. There are other things to do.

Thanks.

You're welcome.

9:32 AM
You're superhuman?

I'm a superhuman—anybody can be.

Anybody.

Anybody. It's just another decision. It does take discipline though.

That's entering in through the veils to the spirit world, isn't it?

Yes, but the veils are right here, right now, and they are mostly in your mind.

That's why you said you had to feed the mind.

Yes, the proper food, the bread of life.

Awesome!

Yes, it is. Everything here is awesome. The flesh is awestruck by it; that's why it seems hard to get there and stay there. It takes control from the flesh, which is something the flesh loves: control. The flesh feels like it's dying, thus the fear.

But it's not.

No, not really, but it does kill its control, which is fraught with problems. To relinquish its control it takes a certain death of self-will, which it's rarely willing to give up.

Usually a person has to experience a major crisis in their life to even begin to be willing. Another way is an INTENSE desire, a feeling like fire to move them to surrender. To get there or die trying is the commitment I'm talking about. Another thing is, one must be willing to be thought a fool; the pride of the flesh has no place here. One must in effect die daily.

Collection

August 7

8:05 AM

There is nothing there worth holding on to to keep you from the kingdom. That's why I've mentioned responsibility so much. One must take responsibility for this journey, and I mean literally take it. It's yours anyway, so take responsibility for it. If you'll notice, most people are quick to point the finger at the responsibility of others. If they were as conscious of their own responsibility, it would go a long way towards this journey.

A wise man told you a good beginning brings us halfway to our goal. I had a very good beginning, and it put me a step ahead of the average person. This conscious raising of me was a pivotal point in my life; I had very little to overcome. Most struggle for a lifetime to rid themselves of the trash, and that's what it is too—trash in the subconscious usually placed there by ignorance. Only the cleansing fire of the spirit can remove this. Remember what I told you before?

Ah . . . no, what?

That I had a lot to say.

Ah, yes you do.

Oh yes, I do and I'm saying it.

Point is?

Point is when you have something to say, say it. Don't wait and then regret not saying it later.

8:30 AM

My momma has something to tell you.

She does?

Yes, she doesn't know it yet.

What is it about?

She'll tell you, but it's about us. Trust, trust in what you're doing, trust us.

Trust, OK.

Trust is very valuable.

Yes.

You haven't learned this yet, and it's very basic.

The Universe Speaks

It is very basic.

It is, and you haven't learned it yet.

The life of a thunderstorm. The thunder of a perfect mind is filled with truths. It's upsetting to the bland business-as-usual mind of the mundane masses. The "follow-along crowd" of self-worshipers. Don't let them affect you. Our game is a grand game. Their game is merely for foolish and unschooled children. Now is the time to grow up, and all the necessary tools and teachings are in place to receive them. Now a mature choice is needed to play along. And play is what it is. A playful attitude helps in this growth, a playful spirit. This game is fun, and that's important to know. Watch children at play; watch animals at play and think of what this reveals.

Growth!

Wonderful growth, and there's no clocking in. When you see someone wanting to control others, it's the flesh.

And the flesh profits nothing, right?

Pretty much. Just ask yourself, where is the benefit? This is a revealing question. Ask it and listen for the answer.

We can answer our own questions, can't we?

Of course you can and do. The heart knows what's true. That's why I said to trust yourself and no excuses were acceptable, because the truth resides within you. "Be true to yourself"—that's a good saying. It's an even better practice.

I've never known anyone that wields the sword of truth with such exquisite delicacy.

Nicely put.

Thanks, you are the fencing master.

We're not fighting here, we're just talking.

I just get a bit overwhelmed by it all.

I know you do. That's why I'm always putting things in context for you.

Well, thanks again.

We've discussed the power of the flesh before, that is, it has none but what you give it.

1:04 PM
There's a subject we left off on that we weren't through discussing the other day.

OK, what's that?

Collection

Something so personal for you, and you take such pleasure in, that you weren't comfortable with talking about it.

All right.

Something you haven't noticed that you sometimes guard.

OK, what?

Humor.

Humor? There has to be a joke there somewhere.

There is. But first you need to know that there is humor everywhere, and also one of its designs is to help to get through the hard times. You don't even see it everywhere, and you have a refined sense of it. It's so often underestimated for its healing powers.

Just had a very interesting download on that.

Could you describe it?

I guess I could, but it would be funny trying.

See what I mean. It's everywhere.

Yes, I do, and also some far-reaching implications.

What are you implying?

Ah...

See what I mean—you guard it.

I just think it's too involved to get into.

Involvement itself implies getting into.

Yes, but it would take pages and pages to describe the download.

But the point is being open to, open to share it.

OK, I'm open.

That was almost like pulling teeth.

I know why you said that.

Then share it.

A small part of the download was the report of Doc Holiday and how he thought it was funny that he died with his boots off.

That wasn't so hard, was it?

245

No, but it was a miniscule part of it.

Yes, but he found humor in his death, and that's funny.

If you say so.

I do.

Everyone here who has died of a misadventure always wants their money back, and that's funny. They never do get a refund either, but it doesn't stop them from asking.

Is that true?

You think I'm making stuff up here? The point is life goes on. It's funny to us that that always occurs to them. That the promised service wasn't delivered and some restitution should be made. Most say it in humor, but some are quite serious about it. Either way it's pretty funny. Anyway, such are most of the promises made in your world.

4:30 PM
So the Boston massacre wasn't?

No, not like it was portrayed.

> G was watching a Discovery show about the Boston Massacre that showed how the events that led up to what were labeled a massacre were greatly overreacted to.

When I was first taught that and read about it in school I knew it didn't sound quite right, that there was another side to the story that wasn't being told.

And that's the knowing within you I was talking about, the voice of the witness of truth that transcends time and place: that's the voice to trust.

August 10

6:30 AM
Talia, I remember a while back you said to me "du mun." *Du* means "top or great," *mun* means "gate."

Yes, I remember too.

I'm trying to recall the context in which you told me.

The context is the connection of everything we've talked about and placing one on the path of no deviation into and through the Great Gate and into the Land of Freedom. Just to see the Great Gate is enough to spur most on the never-ending path, for to see it is to taste the pure freedom of everlasting life. That's the realization of the truth that truly sets one free. You've never seen a gate like this one; there is none even close on earth.

What about Kim's friend? She thinks I am making all of this up.

She's lost. Trapped in her own mind. See how easily precious gifts are overlooked.

She's going to come around?

Everyone comes around. See how hard she fights to hold onto her doctrine. She would deny it, but she feels you have an ulterior motive.

If I had an ulterior motive it would be simpler not to do this at all.

On the surface it would. I know your desire is pure, more so than even you do.

So are you going to tell me about the hummingbird?

It's my nature.

Flighty?

No, not at all. Swift.

You are that.

Very much so.

5:19 PM
It's all oneness.

But you can't understand this without experiencing it.

That's exactly right. You can't understand this without experiencing it.

> G saw a vision of heavy, wet snow falling, clinging to the branches of the cedars and on the ground.

Everyone is as individual as a snowflake. When you can hear the music of the snowfall you will understand how each of those unique individual snowflakes bond as one upon the earth.

August 11

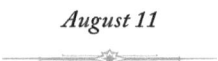

When I said this was a shadow world, that's what it is, and there are no shadows but for the light. This is a shadow of the heavenly, so there's really nothing to give up except your surrender to Self. This surrender many find hard to accomplish, for they try to surrender through the self, and this cannot be. This self-sacrifice is simply laying the self on the alter of surrender. When

you do this you may drink freely from the fountain of life. This is the true life all seekers thirst for, and it is without strife. This burden is light, with no self-glory. When you see self-glory in a spiritual life, know that the light is dimmed and you are far off the path. This deviation from the true path will always become greater until that person finds their way back. This is why complete and total surrender is so important. The self-willed can only glorify self; your task is to reflect the total, the all of life.

G thought about how nice the rain was.

The rain is life giving, the water of life. Part of our message is to bring people back to this pure life, the simplicity of being. You see the power of surrender?

Yes.

This is for all people, the simplicity of being. When people surrender their self in this manner there will be no further need for books such as this, for all shall know Him from the least to the greatest.

Will this ever be?

He asked to "make them one Father, even as we are one." This is answered. The body will come together as one and transcend the petty flesh.

Sounds like good news.

It is. I said before, it doesn't matter what people think the truth is; what matters is what the truth is, and this is the truth.

Talia, I recently remembered something else that happened when we met. When you turned and walked away in the kitchen I wanted to say something else. I wanted to warn you. It was burning in me to warn you about something. I almost blurted out, "Don't go to Panama." But I stopped myself because I didn't know what I was talking about or even if you were planning to go or anything. It just didn't make sense. And I asked for confirmation and never got one. I'm so sorry.

Don't be sorry. Whatever you said wouldn't have changed anything. It was meant to be. The guilt you've felt is groundless; there is no responsibility for you in what happened. It was my time to go, just as some day it will be your time, and nothing anyone can say to you will change it.

I sensed danger or something and then, when I searched the feeling, I thought it was just me, and I knew everything was going to be all right.

Everything is all right. It's all perfect, part of the perfect plan to fulfill all things.

A lot happened that day.

A lot did. You were reluctant to share this.

Collection

I was. I did feel somewhat responsible. Like I could have done something to change it.

We're changing things now, which we couldn't have done if I hadn't made that journey. It's OK to reveal this. It won't be held against you, and you've avoided mention of this long enough.

But what does it profit?

In many ways, to share this is to instruct others that are in similar situations not to feel guilty about a premonition of a glimpse of life, because that's what it is: a glimpse of life. When you think of me, think of the celebration of life, not sorrow over the illusion of death. Death has no place here; it just does not exist. It's a state of mind, so don't put your mind in that state.

You wanted to live your life with me—now you can.

It's not the same.

No, it's better. Now we don't have the complications of the flesh. You have an open hand with me—that's how our fellowship works so well.

That's a clue, isn't it?

That's a clue for others on how to live this life.

What does *open hand* mean?

Open hand *simply means you just have an open heart and attitude towards me with no thought of what you can get in return. It's a giving spirit. We've always had this relationship.*

Well, I sure do get a lot from you.

Yes, you do, and it's symbiotic: I get a lot from you too. We're not striving here to be understood. We're just being who we are, and this is a relationship based on truth. In that we're perfect examples of how relationships ought to be and are meant to be. Simple giving with no thought of return, and your trust of me is perfect.

That's because I know you're perfect and cannot make mistakes.

You have to learn to accept others' mistakes, as you trust them as well.

Perfect weather today.

You ought to see it here.

I want to.

You can.

> G is given a glimpse of Talia's world. For one split second G felt instantaneously awake and alive. Everything felt perfect: the weather was perfect,

the colors were brilliant, and everything was more vibrant than he could describe in words. He felt one with everything. But words are not sufficient.

That is awesome!

Told you.

That was just a glimpse.

That's all you can stand right now. A glimpse is enough. If you were given more you wouldn't want to stay there.

I almost don't want to now.

I know, that's why you only get a glimpse. That holds you back from seeing more. You have things to do there.

So you've said.

Yes, and I'm saying it again as a reminder. What we're doing here is giving life to others, and that's the most you can give them.

Then I'll stay.

I thought you might. There's no holding you back from here anyway.

Can't wait.

Yes, you can. ☺

She—Mom—takes great pleasure in driving. It makes her feel in control of her life, which she is. It's also our time we spend together. It's her "hair." She'll like that; she'll think it's funny. She also knows it is true.

> The "hair" that Talia is referring to is what I call a distraction. It is a term I got from a book I read while learning how to put my thoughts aside to quiet myself, so I could hear and communicate with Talia and the spirit world. Driving is my "hair." It is my way of clearing my mind.

August 13

4:15 PM
Gravity is not a constant. It is a force in flux. I told you everything was in flux, alive. Notice the model of dark matter and dark energy are terms used by those whose theories are incomplete. They use the terms "dark" for what they do not understand, and I said to you what it was they were leaving out of the equation: themselves. It's not nearly as complicated

Collection

as they try to make it. When you remove your spiritual being from the equation and the spiritual being or nature of the universe, don't be surprised if your theories remain in the dark. This darkness comes from the mind of man, and man remains in the dark until he accepts and receives the light. You simply cannot leave the Creator out of the creation and expect enlightenment. Their own Einstein knew this.

Your own gravity varies with your mental state. You experience gravity as a law and have been told it is. I see you as not under the law, and gravity in a constant state of flux.

August 14

7:50 AM
Talia, you told me once a while back you "hated camp." I didn't know what you were talking about at the time, as you didn't elaborate, but I heard about it. Do you want to talk about it?

Yes, it was the lies I hated. I knew who I was, and someone was saying I was someone else that I wasn't. This always creates frustration in a person if you listen to it. I was smart enough not to listen, but I didn't listen to my own advice. You see even then I was giving sound advice, but it's often hard to take your own advice, especially when an authority figure is contradicting you. That's when the lesson was driven home to trust myself. I knew nobody knew me better than me, especially someone who didn't know me at all but was famous for jumping to conclusions. She was well educated in the world's ways and was considered an expert, even by herself. She also didn't like me being so outspoken and insisted on putting me in my place, but she didn't know where my place was—she just thought she did. I never liked a dictator, and that's what she acted like.

I heard you were somewhat famous for having no tolerance for foolishness.

It's not that I didn't have tolerance for it. I just never liked it, and it seemed pointless to me.

I appreciate you being so loquacious.

I appreciate you appreciating it. I always had something to say even if I didn't always say it. That's something I noticed about you the day we met. You only said something when you had something to say, and you listened. I was listening too. I thought you were charming that day, and I got a good feeling about you. When I asked my mom who you were, I was told just a friend. That was a limited description if I've ever heard one. I told her I liked you. You now see how those simple words have connected us beyond the earthly realm. That world has limits, limits you yourself put on it. But this world, my world, has no limits, and our task in part is to bring a realization that the limits are not real, that the limitless is what is real. The poets have written about this through the ages. It's not so easy to grasp, but it's a lot easier than not grasping it at all.

251

The Universe Speaks

I keep noticing the hummingbirds. I feel where they are before I see them.

I'm pointing them out to you. I want you to see their dance with each other and the environment. I loved to dance. It's a celebration of life, and it is never wrong to celebrate life. It's an integration of body, mind, and spirit into a harmonious whole. That's why I loved it—it's liberating.

Hummingbirds take what they need, get rid of what they don't need, and they're quick about it. They don't waste time. If you see time there as a period of BEING you wouldn't waste it either. It's a waypoint during your journey. It's a point of the way to be.

Hummingbirds are harmless, and they bring color into peoples' lives.

August 16

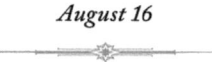

6:25 AM
What was it you were told the meaning of life was?

In a nutshell, to have fun, to learn and to help others.

Are we not doing that?

We are.

I LOVED to have fun, but who doesn't? To learn is programmed in you, and nothing satisfies like helping others.

9:20 AM
People perceive it to be much more convenient to believe what they want to believe rather than believe the truth. It's not an affront to their pride.

10:25 AM
> G was discussing the book *Walden* with someone, how the author didn't act like he had all the answers but just recorded his observations, when Talia said:

I don't have all the answers either.

August 21

12:43 AM
Death is not the end; it's a wonderful new beginning.

Collection

How so?

Every aspect of your life, every minute detail is reviewed and learned from, every failure, every success, every relationship you had—and didn't but should have. Everyone you helped and everyone you didn't help. Every kind word and every harsh or hateful statement. Every single detail will be reviewed and learned from. The growth this creates, the wisdom this generates is stupendous. Every word you've used will be judged. Even a kind thought is rewarded, for thoughts are life. There is time enough here; there's so very little there.

Talia, nobody here even comes close to you.

You come close to me.

You know what I mean.

Yes, I do, and you come close to me. I told you no one knew all the things you know, but it was hard for you to receive.

I'm sure I'm not the only one who feels that way.

But that's just it; it's just a feeling. The reality, the truth of it is, it's true: no one does. You've forgotten what it took to get you where you are.

That's true.

And you often forget where you are.

That's true too.

Why do you forget?

I forget.

It's because you've had such an overwhelming joy in getting where you are that you want to do it all over again to recapture those moments of intense pleasure. But I'm telling you again there is no end, and you don't have to forget [an experience] to experience the experience again because it all comes back around again and again in a most splendid way. So believe in the growth, trust the spirit of the spherical way, and rejoice in the experience, because the experience is new again. Renewed again and again, and its design IS to bring us all into perfection and fullness in all that is all.

That seems to sort of make sense.

You think?

Yes, I think, therefore I am.

I think he should have said I think, therefore I think I am.

That's funny.

It shows a humbler attitude. Beside, what was he? Did he ask that question?

Sounds like he was groping in the dark.

He was, but he was esteemed enlightened.

You know, Talia, I've missed our conversations. It's difficult to get here sometimes.

I know it is. It's also simple beyond words. So much of what we've discussed is beyond words. That's why you haven't written it down.

That relieves some pressure. I thought it was just me.

No, when I told you it wasn't possible to write everything I say, I was being literal.

That's my frustration. I know what you've revealed, and I can't get it across to people.

That's not your job.

Well, again, pressure's off.

Told you that you worry too much.

You're always right.

I know I am.

Describe what you saw.

It was a poster I saw years ago. The caption read, "Things take time."

Yep.

Yep?

Yep, I can talk anyway I want.

I just never remember you saying that before.

You're about as informal as anyone I know and you're surprised?

No, I mean, just making sure.

Be sure.

9:00 AM
That dialogue we had last night was awesome.

And it will be awesome again today. Just give it a chance.

Collection

The subtlety of your lessons, how you weave them in, is astounding.

It's seamless and it seems less than it is. That's the nature of the way.

Like a finger pointing to the moon.

You could say that. You could also say it's like the moon pointing to your finger.

It's the same thing.

In essence, yes. I have some more to say to you, and first things first.

Let's do it.

That's true what I told you last night about your friend. You're as good as he is at what you do. Art is expression. You can express the spirit that moves in all things in your own way. Everyone has their own way to express this. It's just finding that way. That's the expression so many search for. That's also the profound sense of frustration so many feel when they don't find it. It's rarely found in words, yet that's what most who feel this frustration seek. A way to put what they feel or know is true into words. You primarily found your expression in movement. It's not so important how a person expresses their truth. What is important is finding THEIR creative expression. We are all hardwired to express our Creator. You found me expressing my Creator simply by looking in my eyes, and that's how simple it can be sometimes. We are reflections of the Divine.

That is awesome!

Yes, it is. Divine expression is always awesome, and it is expressed differently in each individual. Wars have been fought over this misunderstanding. That's why I say it's time to wake up.

You're the sweetest thing I've ever known.

Yes, well, the Holy Spirit is the sweetest thing you've ever known, and that's what this is. We are changed into His image from glory to glory. That's something to think about, isn't it?

Yes, it is.

What was it the hummingbird said to you?

That he wanted something sweet.

That's what they seek, something sweet.

10:12 AM
I told you before, the contrast was for learning. If it weren't for the darkness you wouldn't know the stars.

The Universe Speaks

August 25

5:09 PM
Talia, I really need to hear you.

Then hear me.

I love your voice.

And I love yours.

September 2008

September 3

(New Mexico)
You have great faith. It's hard for you to understand those who don't. They haven't seen the miracles you have. Don't blame them for that.

It's all a test, and if you already knew all the answers it wouldn't be much of a test now, would it?

The answer's contained in the question.

You're getting it.

Thanks for the pronouncement.

You're welcome. I have something to say to you.

Say on.

The things that bother you and worry you should be of no concern to you. Also, TAKE your time. That's a secret to proper timing: take it—make it your own—take it by force. Time can be bent by force. You have gravity, and gravity can bend time and space.

OK, I was just getting my head around time and now you threw in space.

It takes time.

Talia, no one can move me from tears to overwhelming joy to brilliance to such peace so swiftly.

Collection

My word comes with power.

It sure does. You illuminate my soul.

We all do. It's pure hope, and along with love, it abides forever. Why would you labor for that which doesn't satisfy?

That sounds like the mystery of misery revealed.

It is. So why would you?

I think basically it would be a lack of understanding.

And why would someone lack understanding?

Maybe they just didn't look for it.

Why wouldn't they look?

I could think of several reasons.

But what would be the primary one? Most everyone says they want to understand, so why is it most can't get it? Because their words are empty and insincere. If they really wanted to understand then they would. The answers are easy enough to find.

I don't think I would have ever gotten that; the truth is too simple.

It's perfectly simple.

11:47 AM
There is a natural progression that is supernatural in its effect.

How so?

Don't be hasty. You rob yourself when you skip ahead.

In what context?

My lessons for one. Have they not followed a natural progression?

They certainly have, in so many ways.

You should teach the same way. It is an honorable way to teach. It honors and respects the student and the lesson.

How come everything you say seems more awesome than what you said before?

Because it's the present truth.

Someone else has something to say?

Talia's not the only one with something to say. Everyone and everything has something to say.

The Universe Speaks

I think it was Curt. I felt his presence.

    Curt is G's friend, who passed away years before.

"I'll be there when the deal goes down."

Curt?

Yes.

You're talking about my death?

Yeah. It's easy, you leave the body and you're "here."

You know when?

You got a while.

We made a deal, didn't we?

Yes, that we would help each other in the transition. I remember it.

Talia's one that won't be stopped.

How could anyone be stopped there?

By hitting a wall . . . not a wall really, but an impasse in spiritual development.

Thanks for talking to me.

You're much more aware than most.

But comparing ourselves among ourselves isn't wise.

That's not what we're doing; I'm just letting you know, putting it in context.

All right, this impasse.

Make the most of your time there.

Thanks, Curt, I want to. Am I doing that?

You usually do. We all want to be a part of what she—Talia's—doing.

What's God like?

He's everything. You are a man of knowledge now. Use it.

How can I use it?

By walking in what you know.

Collection

NOON
Everybody's an actor.

So if they act like they're not, they're just acting.

I revealed what all of that meant.

September 4
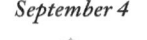

1:22 AM
(Arizona)
She—Mom—wonders why I don't speak of more personal things sometimes. That's for HER, and I convey my feelings all the time. Her tenderness for me and mine for her has no rivals. And, oh yes, the awakening HAS begun.

September 9
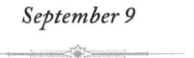

1:52 PM
So what about this unbroken wholeness you spoke of?

It's the wholeness unbroken, brought about by the luminous web of life, which ties all together. The apartness is a part, thinking it's apart from the whole, which is only a viewpoint from which the part is looking. When the part looking, or the observer, sees that what he is looking at is a perception, a part of what's whole, when they see themselves as much of the wholeness or oneness of all that is—as is everything else, without separation—then is there realization of oneness in its truth and beauty.

OK then.

It's OK then because this realization is oneness filled, fullness whole, truth realized to BE in and not apart from.

7:24 PM
Curt told you the truth.

Yes, I know he did.

About being myopic.

I'd forgotten that part.

The Universe Speaks

Well, it was about us, and that's why I'm reminding you. I'm NOT the only one who has something to say.

I know.

It's just to let you know to be open to others also, to their truth, to their message. "Everyone and everything has something to say."

I know. That's what he said.

He has a warm place in his heart for you. He sees you clearly now.

That's good.

He's a good man who echoed my truth to you: don't waste time.

I'm trying not to.

And as he said, "You usually don't."

Maybe I'm improving.

You are. You're growing, but you try to hide it.

I don't know why.

Yes, you do and no, it's not lack of confidence. It's the part of you that embraces refusal to take responsibility. You can run but you can't hide, so quit hiding it because you're already hidden in Him where we all are. So it's pointless, you see. Use your energy more constructively. Your words also have power. You just refuse to acknowledge it sometimes. You don't want the responsibility, but you can't get away from it. You think you can do this and then just walk away as if it didn't happen?

No.

Then quit acting like it.

I'm with you, Talia, all the way.

And I'm with you too, all the way, so don't be something you're not. Curt told you to walk in your knowledge.

Yes, he did.

Then do it. Don't think about it, just do it.

He said they all wanted to be a part of what you're doing.

They are all a part of what I'm doing. Being one in Him. They are doing that, but even here there are some who have yet to realize it. Mostly those who left that place prematurely or wasted their precious time.

Collection

How do they waste it?

By being preoccupied with the things of that world. A lot by "making a living," which brought them a slow dying. Before they knew it their time was up there and they had brought forth no fruit in the spirit. They had atrophied without a thought. It's not a crime, but it is a waste. I told you, there is no crime here. Nothing unclean can pass thought the Great Gate. They had received the truth but let somebody else do the work for them. You see now why taking responsibility is so important?

Yes, I do.

I hope we've cleared that up.

I hope we have too.

Hope abides forever.

I know.

Nothing happens without requesting it.

That's an extreme statement.

That's an extreme truth.

Why do you bring that up?

Because people need to know that.

9:30 PM
Thanks for that.

> I asked Talia to have G call me, and within fifteen seconds G called me and said that Talia told him I asked her to have him call me.

My pleasure. I love doing that stuff. It meant a lot to her, and that's me confirming my word to her that it was me talking to her and that she can and does hear me. I told you she would learn how and she is; she's learning fast.

I really didn't expect it so fast. At first I thought it would take years.

I know you did, but I'm doing a quick work and I'm swift, remember?

Yes, I do.

You asked for it too—that helps. It makes my job much easier. Told you we were all in this together.

Yes, you did. I hate to be redundant, but that was pretty awesome though.

The Universe Speaks

The timing was excellent because you were in a place to receive, because you were both in an attitude of a giving spirit, among other things.

You move me so wonderfully.

If someone isn't experiencing this then they're locked up in their head, and that's not living at all. Living is experiencing. That's something else people should know and understand. You were asked to ask me how to explain how I got where I am, how I got this "evolved."

Yes.

This is a tapestry and the threads are there to see. In other words, it has already been explained. If we got into the minute details it would be far beyond the scope of this book, leaving no room for the message—which is change—but I do understand the request, and it's from someone most dear to me. I will explain this, which should explain that, and that's that God has no limits in any direction. Limits are man-made from the mind of man. Remember when I spoke of limitlessness? This is abstract in the mind of man, a mere conception, which IS a beginning but is often killed—by the constant reminders of what you can't do. Your world is filled with signs warning you of every conceivable danger—speed limits, ceilings, bars, walls, no trespassing— on and on until you buy into it. When your subconscious tells you you can't, you can't. So don't reaffirm a lie. Let your heart warn you of danger.

I was raised consciously to trust my heart, and I experienced daily, in every way I could. I have NO regrets, only a sense of fullness of my life there. I said before, my life there was an example of how to live there, and it got me here perfectly. Anyone could make the same decisions I made; it's just deciding to.

How could we be so blind as to not see who you were while you were here?

People do that all the time. It's also not so very obvious. After all, I wasn't completely conscious of how I was living my life at the time. The glory goes to the Source of all things, which is everything.

God is everything.

Curt's definition and well put. He's smiling now.

Figured he would be.

Well, so much for getting to bed early.

You'd rather sleep?

No, I just heard today that sleep has amazing regenerative powers.

So does this, but this regenerative power is everlasting.

Believe me, I know.

Collection

I believe you; I know you know. Now you're beginning to share what you know, which is knowledge activated. Otherwise it's dead in the water.

Interesting term.

That's why I said it.

Someone said that the waters some drown in, the mystic swims in.

Opening the doors to perception.

Yes, that was the context of it.

That's true, and it's always been that way. Be aware that those who are drowning will try to pull you down with them.

Time for you to go swimming.

In the sea of consciousness.

You could put it that way.

September 10

6:48 AM
Good morning.

Good morning. Did you sleep well?

I slept well and tossed and turned, but for the most part, yes.

Be at peace.

Well, thanks. Good advice.

It's also the way to be. Any other way to be is not being at all, but strife.

Excellent.

Of course, and excellence will flow out of you when you're at peace.

Blessed peace.

I know the Prince of it and His marvels are unending. The Teacher, from whom all lessons flow, in perfect peace.

This is a nice way to start the day.

The Universe Speaks

It's the perfect way. Most "hit the ground running," and that's not the best way to start the day. If you notice, when you start the day honoring your Creator, the rest of the day is yours.

The rest of the day.

Yes, the rest of the day within you within Him. It's perfect rest, even in the storm.

Glad I didn't hit the ground running this morning.

Most of the time all it takes is to take the time to say hello.

Anyone can do that.

Yes, anyone could. And their expression that day, the rest of the day, will reflect how they started that day in everything they do. It's cylindrical: what you put out comes back. That's that honor you put out coming back to honor you, and it's never the same measure; it's always more.

That's amazing!

Yes, that is amazing, and that is the way it is. So whatever you want, give it and it will always come back to you in greater measure. If they taught that in the wealth-building seminars they would be well worth going to. As it is, they generally degenerate into a selfish spirit.

Never been to one.

No, and whenever you considered it you felt a check. There is a reason for that. Your spirit knows when you're taking and not giving, and it feels like theft, which is what it really is. If you think of it, if you ARE reflecting your Creator, you'll always be giving more than you're receiving—that's just how it works. You can't help but to do this if you're being in Him. It's a natural outgrowth. That's never-ending abundance, giving and receiving, and its spherical flow never stops.

They [G's coworkers] are hopping around out there unaware. They should have started the day like you did. Recognizing the day for what it is, the light of the life force flowing into and through them in an abundance of gifts, without limits. Instead it's "another damned day" they have created for themselves at work. Yet they could change it in an instant.

That seems to nearly sum up everything you've said so far.

It somewhat did, IF you can see it. Now go share and flow in the subtlety of truth, being who you are without strife.

Collection

11:47 AM
This is felicity.

You're right about that.

How could I not be?

True.

Truth in the inward part ... can you feel it?

Yes, I can.

Anyone who reads this can, but will they?

Guess that depends on them.

It does depend on them. That's what so many forget: their part to play in this Grand Game.

1:29 PM
Remember when I mentioned dressage [a style of riding]*?*

Yes.

That's how subtle most things should be controlled.

Energy and movement?

Energy is movement; it's about directing it. It is decide, then act, and it's mostly a mental game.

You know I had to look that up. I thought you were saying something about dressing.

I know—that's why you heard me laugh.

Yes, I thought it was just about the way I dressed.

It's the mental picture I wanted you to see.

Wish I could have seen you ride. I know you were very, very good.

Someday you will. ☺

Fantastic! I'll be looking forward to that.

So will I.

Thank you again.

You're most welcome, and thank you again.

The Universe Speaks

September 11

7:22 AM
Thank you for who you are and good morning.

Thank you and good morning and who else would I be?

That's a profound question.

That's something to think about, isn't it?

It sure is. You know what I mean though.

I sure do and I appreciate that.

You're mighty welcome.

I know what that means, and I appreciate that too.

You described yourself once as lively, and that's such a perfect description. You keep reconfirming your presence to people in so many ways . . . it's not just your words, it's your acts that blow me away.

I'm living the art of life as an example of how to be. Being in Him one cannot help but to move people in the proper direction. My vibration is in perfect harmony, and I'm learning to change others' vibration when they are in disharmony. The result is they sense life and the infinite possibilities that exist within them. I restore hope. Hope and harmony are synonymous terms. Remember when I asked if you could hear the music?

Yes.

It's never-ending, and when your vibrations are in harmony and your ears are opened, you will hear it. A disharmony has sounds too, and it's not music, it's noise. When you sense something's not right, that's the noise, not the music. Music has wonderful healing powers, often miraculous healing powers. There is no sickness in perfect harmony. You've heard music in rivers.

Yes, I had forgotten that.

You've been told you're not supposed to. When someone else denies your truth, even if everyone else denies your truth, it doesn't mean you yourself must deny your truth. Your truth is yours, and if and when that happens, the proper response is to deny their lies instead. This way you hold your truth without losing it, and you don't confirm their lies to them, which is destined to wither on the vine anyway. Why be a party to death?

Talia, I wish I could repay you for all you've done for me.

Collection

Live your truth, that's all I could ever ask of you. When you do that you've fulfilled every request, and no one should ever ask any more of you. That's the most anyone can give, and it's always enough.

Your simplicity is profound beyond words.

It's truth, and it is simple beyond words. We're just using words as symbols to convey meaning, which IS self-evident in all.

In all things.

In all, which is all things.

You can't escape the truth, and it is in your face all the time, isn't it.

That's exactly right. To live a lie is to make yourself miserable. That seems like a stupid pastime, doesn't it?

Pretty goofy thing to do.

It's a trap too. What I mean by that is it's hard to get out of it once you're into it because it blinds. The negative side is spherical too; remember we talked about counterparts.

A vicious circle or a perfect circle, and it's decided by choice.

That's a good example, but I prefer spheres because it's more descriptive of how it really is, a more dimensional picture of how things really operate.

I see exactly what you mean.

That's why I like it better.

How's Curt today?

Curt's just fine. He's watching closely. He's somewhat proud of you and he says it was an honor to know you . . . and thanks for asking.

That's him all right.

Yes, it is.

He hasn't changed much, still quiet.

No, but he's grown and he doesn't want to interfere.

Talia, I just had the most interesting download about how animals relate to the earth and your ashes and why they were your essence here and certain people who realized how animals are an example for us on how to relate to the earth.

Awesome, isn't it?

It sure is, and also how these words are just pointers.

Yes, symbols pointing to truths for freedom for all mankind.

And I see how the wrong choices are death.

A broad road to destruction that the herd tramples daily.

You're so right—I saw that.

That's why it's important to start the day correctly, with a humble attitude. Not "what can I get today" but "what can I give."

That whole animal thing!

Animals live in harmony with the earth, which is also a vibrational Being. When you realize that and walk as one with her then is there harmony.

September 12

10:33 PM
You're afraid to write.

No, I'm not!

You're going to argue with me again?

No . . . I'm not.

You said you trusted me.

I do. Totally. It's me I don't trust sometimes.

Change your thinking, period.

Was I supposed to write the period?

You can write whatever you want to. I want you to write what I say.

I only want to write what you say; I only want this to be of the spirit.

Then listen; you have to believe.

I believe.

Then stop doubting. Quietness and confidence shall be your strength. You shall rejoice in times to come. You wanted me to prophesy the future, and I'm telling you it's all now.

I asked that.

Collection

And that's my answer. What was your calling? That's what it is. You prophesy—you see it clearly.

I see some of it clearly.

You can see it all clearly.

Didn't know that.

Change your thinking. Stop denying what you know.

Strong deception.

Yes. Very strong deception. Where do you see it?

Wherever I go, on nearly everyone I meet.

What else?

A yielding to it. An acceptance of it.

Yes, what else?

A rising kingdom of light. Children walking in pure light.

Who are these children?

God's children, those chosen to believe.

And what are they doing?

They are walking boldly and proclaiming the Kingdom. They are filled and surrounded by bright light, and it pushes out the darkness from before them. Wherever they walk is theirs. Nothing foul can touch them.

It's the difference between light and dark, isn't it?

Complete separation.

Any doubt of the contrast?

None.

What else do you see?

I see leaders misleading. They've chosen to mislead and they've been misled themselves.

By whom?

By the prince of darkness.

Where does he come from?

He comes from the mind of man. That's where he gets his power.

Give NO place to him.

I hear him laughing.

His laughs are lies.

This IS the pure word of truth. Don't be concerned about explanations. We've already explained this is esoteric. Hidden truths. The seal is upon the minds of man. The only way out of darkness is by the light. The light of the Holy One. There is no thinking your way out; it's only by the light is the seal removed. If they've read this far, they've gotten it or their minds are sealed.

It's changing.

What's changing?

Our message. It's changing. I told you, it's a message of change.

How's it changing?

It's changing those who've gotten it, and now the message will reflect that growth. And it's not something they will always feel or recognize either, but if they will look in the mirror they will see change.

You've changed me.

I am.

September 13

6:55 AM
The mind of God.

That's the answer, one mind.

1:18 PM
It hurts to grow. Growing pains.

I know.

Then relax. Undue tension is stress. That zaps you of vital energy.

I know.

I know you know, but sometimes you need a reminder. Practice what you preach. Our flowing is without strife. The victory is within you.

Collection

Thanks for that.

I thought you could use it.

8:53 PM
Talia, you never get tired, do you.

No, I never do. I also never feel bad—that's one of the advantages of being here.

Your transition . . . how was it?

It was the most natural thing ever, shedding the body; we ARE spiritual beings—the physical body's only temporary. I know there's pain there and trials and temptations, but they are wonderful tests. Wonder filled. They are all designed for your betterment. That's an outlook that changes things. That's a viewpoint to embrace.

Thank you, God, for Talia.

She is one in whom I am well pleased.

>This was spoken by God.

Talia, you have favor with God.

It's the ultimate friendship; it's a family like no other. The love is boundless and indescribable.

How was your day?

It was interesting. I got tired, then talked to you and applied what you told me and, come to think of it, everything changed for the better.

High energy and a good outlook. All these principles, if applied, work. My word is with power. That He has assured me of.

So . . . the secret of your great confidence revealed.

You sound like you haven't heard this before. God told me my word was with Power. I told you your word was with Power. I cannot lie and I cannot be wrong, so where is your great confidence?

Feels pretty high right now.

Our message is in a transitional stage. It's changing to a higher vibration level. We're catering to those beings who have chosen to move up. These are tied down no longer. These have wings, and their flight is with vision. Aren't you tired of pampering? Aren't you sick of the sickness? Nature itself cries out for these to be delivered. This IS the manifestation of the sons of God, and it IS happening now. Some will see it and grieve, many will see it with joy unspeakable—and there's a few who won't notice at all.

The Universe Speaks

Guess you're getting into the meat of it now.

It is all now and it's all meat and there is a certain logic to the order. It is something like a stair-step program, somewhat like Jacob's ladder. The angels were ascending and descending. This is something to deeply consider. It speaks of a partnership. And of a give and take into oneness. I'll tell you again, there is no end to this we're speaking of. That's something else I was told. This is not opinion.

Time for you to go.

To dreamland.

Some call it that.

September 14

9:00 AM
The earth works WITH you. SEE IT as working with you. All things are yours.

6:26 PM
Hello!

Hello to you.

I feel like you've got something to say.

I do. I also feel like you've got something to say.

Probably, but you know what you've got to say, and I'm wondering what I do.

You underestimate yourself.

Maybe, but maybe you could give me a nudge; my mind's blissfully blank at the moment.

And that's usually when the inspiration comes.

Then I could be in danger of overflowing with inspiration.

You are, but it's really not dangerous.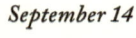

      (G took a drink of orange juice).

That's another one of life's simple pleasures, isn't it?

Yes, orange juice is pretty good.

Collection

When you can enjoy and really appreciate life's simple pleasures, you're really living and in the moment too. That being in the moment is being in the now, where all is complete.

It's amazing what you can find out from a sip of juice.

It's amazing what's revealed in the moment, which is everything.

Satori, instant realization of truth, enlightenment.

Well said, and your Buddha nature.

Never heard you talk about Buddha before.

That's because I've never talked to you about it before. There is a train that you need to ride.

Where's that?

You'll know it when you see it.

What else about that?

That's it.

Now, there are specific people we are going to address here and this will be for these individuals. Not that others can't learn and be blessed by our message to them by residual effects, because they will, but it's important to know that much of this hereafter will be directed towards them and some things particularly for certain individuals. Everyone on this train is not on the same car.

Sounds like a narrow track.

It is.

10:13 PM
I see that there are different lessons in different cars, aren't there?

It is. It depends on where they're at as to what they receive. And there aren't different levels. It all is now. It's all a holy and wondrous oneness. Different levels speaks of, entails, separation. That illusion is non-existent here.

Momma, that's the best explanation that I can give you now. Someday you will see clearly what I mean. I love you. I like the pants you bought!

> Talia's last sentence, "I like the pants you bought," was special to me. Just a few hours earlier I was shopping. While in the dressing room trying on some pants I thought to myself, *Wow, Talia would really like these!* And then she responded to me via G just a few hours later!

The Universe Speaks

September 21

12:44 PM
Hi, Talia.

Hi! How was your training?

      G attended a special class.

I enjoyed it. Some of the things that were said were what you had said before. The truth verifying itself. You said that I would learn from it. I learned more that I realize right now. Still digesting it.

That's truth. Receive the truth and it grows in you. It's alive. Living.

I appreciate you more than I can ever say.

I know you do.

That "if you control yourself you control your situation" has great depth.

That's something I had said to you and you weren't sure it was me.

Now I'm sure.

Good, that's that "prove all things" I told you about.

Thanks for bringing that back around.

It all comes back around until you get it. This happens to everyone. The lessons return again and again until you've gotten it, then you move on and grow. New lessons begin. A new beginning. This takes place with that shift in consciousness from the engrafting of the living word. The lesson received and made a part of you. That's the light expanding.

Oh, yes, the instructor said, "Practice what you preach." Same thing you said the other day.

That's good advice. ☺

8:30 PM
We are all of one. I have the power of an endless life.

I know you do.

But do you know what it means?

I thought so but apparently not.

Collection

It means I can change the law.

How so?

The law is not written in stone; it is written in the hearts of man.

Incredible.

It's the perfect law of liberty.

September 22

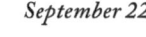

1:44 PM
There are some things you need to know.

OK.

It has nothing to do with my approval. It has to do with your life as you live it. You can only fool yourself. That's where your conscious comes in and your consciousness. When you feel the check, don't go there. Let everything be done for the building up, for edification. Unnecessary problems arise from not heeding it (the check) and rushing forward. Sometimes untold misery. You don't need that. Let's move beyond it. In your weakness is His strength perfected. It's time to awake out of slumber.

I feel better.

That's because you're awake.

September 23

8:24 AM
Good morning, Talia.

Good morning, G.

Help me to hear you.

You do. You think I'm holding back; I'm not. Our core message is complete. That pyramid spoken of is narrower at the top, ending in a point. Our lessons now are specifically for those determined to move on in the pure light. Those who have chosen to forsake all for the Kingdom. These are a chosen few. These see the illusion of loss in this world equates to the fabulous and incomprehensible gain in the next. No trinkets in this world will detour them from the next. They perceive the difference between shadow and substance.

The Universe Speaks

So . . .

Deep answers unto deep. These have cast off from the shallows despite the warnings. The wind is in their favor regardless of the direction.

I just saw that plain as day. They're sailing out of the harbor, past the warning signs and advice of friends, into the stormy sea. Victory assured.

That's my vision I gave you.

That was so clear. I saw a cliff at the shore, rocks in the water.

It's safer in the deep and much more fulfilling.

I see there are so few and some alone, but they are helped.

They always have been, and they always will be.

Talia, are we done?

With this book? (Talia and G both said this at the same time).

Yes.

11:58 AM
Talia, thank you so much, this has been the most awesome journey and experience.

It's not over yet. You're just entering into something new. The placement of these truths is ordained. You've enjoyed the sacrifice?

Immensely.

Excellent! And I knew the answer before I asked. It's important for you to know. The ones who've read this and heard about it are a microcosm.

I suspected as much.

You knew as much. I AM just confirming it for you.

That vision I had of hands tying strings around presents this summer was you, wasn't it?

It was what was happening. You saw my hands joyfully tying it all together for the finish. As I've said, it's all a gift. Remember when it's misunderstood what it means.

I will.

So you say. Did you really believe this could not be done?

No, I believe all things are possible.

Collection

All things are possible. All things are what they are, and our message has been to convince some that what they really know is real is real. All are born with the knowledge of truth and your life on earth is to remember that truth and live it. That's wondrous discoveries, and that's the wonderful discovery that I spoke about uncovering in my life. My joy was uncontainable. That's why it overflowed to others, and that's another reason why I said that my life was an example of how to live. It was my gift and my gift to share with others. You must see your life as a gift and a gift to share with others or you're not fully living it, not at all.

I can never express my gratitude to you for being you and who you are or to God for creating you.

Live these truths. That's expression enough and gratitude enough.

> When we are at our best, the method of meditation that G and I practice allows us to stay in that spiritual state while walking around doing our normal routine. This enables us to communicate on a deeper level with all consciousness—which is how it should be really. At the moment of the following communication, G had gotten into his spiritual state (by taking a deep breath and then letting go), gone outside and walked around, and then, upon returning, Talia spoke to him.

You exhaled and perceptions shifted; time/place was distorted and you walked through their midst unseen. How could you teach that?

I don't know.

No, you don't, but I do, and it's the simplest thing in the world. It's the totality of Oneness.

That's exactly right! I've never heard that term but that's exactly right.

Of course it's exactly right in every way it could be, and that is effortless.

It was!

That's the shift to the other world. To the real world. To the true world. It's your birthright to walk there.

2:52 PM
Put my ashes around your neck and know that death is life.

> Talia is referring to the vial of her ashes that G wears around his neck.

4:05 PM
Maybe you should try trusting others more. That shows you have confidence in them and it helps build theirs.

The Universe Speaks

That seems reasonable.

Que estan de . . . ?

Maybe you need a Spanish speaker.

Maybe you need to listen closer.

September 24

8:35 AM
You wanted to talk to me.

Yes, good morning.

Good morning.

That word has meaning; it's not just custom. Let all your words fill the void. Allow them to have meaning. Press them to have meaning to plant seeds of life in others. This takes presence of mind and some discipline. That void you feel, and find in others, is a waiting vessel; place truth there as a bulwark against the enemy.

The void will be filled regardless, so that's good advice.

When have I not given you good advice? I practice what I preach. I'm filling the void in you. It's generally quite a subtle activity. You will usually do this unnoticed.

I like the unnoticed part.

You also like the accolades.

Well, it's nice to be appreciated.

Truth in the inward parts is always appreciated.

What did you say in Spanish the other day that I did not understand?

How is it you can trust so much but not acknowledge your trust? That's contradicting yourself.

I'm my own worst enemy.

You're your own best enemy.

That part of you fighting with another part of you is you, teaching you. Somewhat like your inner ear.

To regain balance.

Collection

Yes, that self-correcting measure is built within you. When you say or do something incorrect, that part of you doesn't witness it or agree with it, and its disagreement is often felt as uneasiness. It also witnesses this in others.

September 25

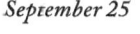

6:55 AM
BE and the attempted will vanish. You are.

I am.

Exactly, that's what I said; now we're in agreement. In sync.

Good name for a band.

Think about what you just said and what I said about music.

Vibrational harmony, bonded together.

Not bad for this early in the morning. See, it's all coming together.

Thanks for your advice, encouragement, and love.

It's my pleasure, always.

Thank you, Talia. I love you.

I love you too, and that never fails.

September 26

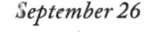

6:38 PM
Sex is good. God invented it, and it's fun, God invented that too.

And . . .

Like everything else, it should be in context, not an end unto itself.

Communication has something to do with it?

Communication is involved.

You're so matter of fact.

I'm filled with passion as a matter of fact And I love to communicate. I have a passion for it, to understand and make others understand, and that's done through communication.

279

The Universe Speaks

The ways to communicate are practically endless, aren't they?

They are, practically endless.

Love never fails; everything else you can hold suspect.

Everything you just said!

You don't have to do that anymore.

What, try to explain the downloads?

Yes, you don't have to do that. Everything is contained in the words.

I could fill a volume.

But there's no use. The light expands the words beyond what you just saw, and a simple receiving is all it takes. How else did you think He was going to do a quick work?

Good point.

I always make them.

I know you do.

What would you like to do?

I can think of a lot of things.

Point is, you can do as you like.

I like talking with you.

That's why we're doing this.

Cool.

It is, very cool. Our message is to convince others that they can do the same and to banish the separation. You have power over it. The realization of this is a life-changing experience, as you well know.

This is the liberty that sets us free, isn't it?

It is.

It's not explaining, it's experiencing.

That's life!

Exactly, that's life!

We're one!

Collection

Yes, we are.

It's experiencing that reality of pure simple truth.

You're trying to explain it. I told you, you can't.

You're right again.

I always am. Now you know my burning passion for sharing this. The law of life. It's freedom complete.

September 27

5:56 PM
How can people be doing what they're supposed to be doing when they're not being who they are?

Guess that answered that.

That's that quiet desperation you were talking about today. People really can't do, to be. They have to be who they are. This takes a lifetime of effort or an instant of total surrender.

I need you yielded. Then is it crystal clear. It is so . . . complete surrender.

September 28

5:38 PM
Tell Uncle J I love him.

I already did.

I want you to tell him again.

I will.

Tell him not to be sad for me. He was a very special person in my life, and I'll always remember him.

I feel your love for him.

My love for him is pure and intense. He is a very kind man.

9:55 PM
Did you tell him?

You know I didn't; I didn't have a chance.

You could have pulled him aside. He's wondered if this is true.

Tell me something that only he would know.

You don't have to prove anything; it takes belief.

Do you want me to call him?

Yes.

>G made the call to Talia's Uncle J.

Thank you.

You're very welcome.

That's his pain you're feeling. We are one.

Thank you, Talia.

September 30

10:43 AM
You think you're calm?

I think so.

You think, so?

Remember what shinjitsu means.

Speaking the truth out of a sincere heart.

That's what you should always do. That changes things. That's pure honesty.

My life reflects the creative mind of Christ. The Word, the offspring of the Father.

No doubt.

As there shouldn't be. That's the way, the truth, and the life. There really is no other.

Most don't really like to hear that.

That's the spirit of the anti-Christ. That's the opposite of the anointing—and what happens when you don't have the oil? You burn up. The oil reduces the friction. When you see friction you see a lack of lubricant. The odd part is, it's a free gift and without it there is no freedom.

Collection

Most think money buys freedom; it doesn't, although it can increase your options. For most it's a crutch.

6:23 PM
You're going to see some shaking from what we've done.

The book?

Yes, you're going to see some foundations shaken. If a foundation is shaken, how stable is that foundation? Most don't like to be shown their foundation is weak.

Well, I figure that's a real positive thing if you can see that.

There's no need for me to add anything to that statement you just made.

I heard your mom's friend is really looking forward to reading the rest of your messages. She said she loves you.

She does. She gets it too, and that's been a tremendous blessing for her. She always looked at me and saw beyond what she saw.

October 2008

October 1

8:05 PM
Talia.

Yes?

You have something to say?

I have a lot to say.

Let me hear it then.

Then hear it. You have recovered. You just needed some time off. Thanks for going out with J; he needed that.

You're welcome and my pleasure.

Everyone's not like you. You enjoy solitude; you thrive in it.

I'm not alone.

I know you aren't, but everyone doesn't know they are surrounded by those who would help. We have a lot to do here.

I want to do it then.

We will. This is a walk; words aren't enough anymore.

October 2

10:20 AM
Talia, what's happening now?

What's happening NOW? It's all happening now.

You think you have to DO something. You don't have to do anything. You just have to be who you are.

Talia, it seems you have to keep repeating yourself for me.

I don't mind reiterating so you see it from different perspectives, different angles. It will keep coming around until you get it.

My pen's about to run out of ink.

It's the walk anyway.

Why do we work so hard for nothing?

That's a good question; why do you?

I don't care about my ideas or philosophy. I care about yours from the universed.

Hmm, I said *universed*.

The oneness of the word; being well versed; the wholeness of being.

Guess I had asked for a definition.

Faith is rewarded.

October 3

5:20 AM
I had a dream last night. In that dream I was given some words and meanings: The Father—to be. The Son—to do. The Holy Spirit—to see.

Collection

1:12 PM

That was given to you: to see, the Light, to do, the embodiment of the living word; and to be, the source of all. These three are one. That's everything summed up. No matter what equations you contrive about anything, that's everything summed up. Trivial theoretical equations are just that when you understand THIS.

I see profound resistance to the simplicity of this.

You see. You see what's not here is just as important as what is here.

I do now.

I do now is the doing embodied in the being. In the being is seeing the unseen.

October 4

1:18 PM

Talia, I wish I could experience that Thanksgiving again.

But that was one of the points: don't waste time.

I know.

When you were out back talking, your mind repeatedly returned to me and what I was doing, and you wanted to come in and talk to me. You should have; we would have had a very interesting conversation. Point is to follow your instincts and trust your heart. You were concerned what others might think. You, who have prided yourself in not caring what others think and have judged others for living that way, fell prey to that mindset. If you remember, several times, you got up or started to get up to go find me, and you talked yourself right out of it every time.

I told you I was a knucklehead.

And I told you that you weren't. I also told you not to judge others for what you judge, or hold against others what you do yourself.

Wish I had it to do over.

If you're in a similar situation, now you know to do what you know you need to do, and if another judges you unjustly then that's their concern and none of yours.

I knew I missed a lot of stuff that day.

You got a lot too. That's the Father of lights, in whom there is no variableness nor shadow of turning. Only good things come from Him, forever and always. What you missed, your mistakes are for others to learn from too.

The Universe Speaks

Why...

Why didn't I tell you this before? Because the grief would have been too great. Now you're mature enough to handle it.

There's a lot of other stuff that happened that day, isn't there?

We've barely scratched the surface. I told you that day the Light was everywhere, that we were bathed in it. You could correctly say every day is filled with Light. The issue is PERCEIVING it. As I've said, there is always more to what you see than what you see, much more.

Will...

When you're ready I will show you how our conversation would have gone. For now it's enough to know that EVERY MOMENT COUNTS.

I've never had a day that compares with that one.

That's true, you haven't. It was unique in every way. Most go a lifetime and never have a day to compare with that one. That was a life-changing and eye-opening experience that was a culmination of millennia. It also signified a new beginning in your life that now is.

7:12 PM
Haven't you met me yet?

Haven't I met you yet?

Not you. They who read this. I'm asking them that. Haven't you met me yet?

It's a simple question and a simple answer. They who have met me know me, and they know they know me. If you haven't met me, why haven't you met me?

That refers back to Jacob's ladder, doesn't it?

It does, and it's not so complicated as people make it. We've talked about the veils and where they are and how to pierce them, although I'm somewhat reluctant to mention them because words so often get in the way of the real. It is important to know and remember that they are largely illusions. Use the force of your personality, of who you ARE, to boldly step through and demand to meet reality. THAT will get you answers.

What else?

What else is there?

We should know even as we are known. That's what this is all about, to know even as we are known. That is fullness complete. Did HE not say that good work He began He would complete? The author and finisher of your faith, remember. You saw the work He had begun in me the day we met. It was revealed to you and His work goes on and it is glorious beyond measure. He has shown me to be a standard bearer.

He has and you are a leader of a movement.

I am and I am much more than you know.

Then I obviously don't know enough.

No, but you are learning. More than you know and faster than you realize. My game is moving people in the perfect direction they need to go.

You sure do move me, in every way I know.

I move you in ways you don't know also.

Thanks.

You're welcome. You know, I love your trust; it honors me.

I can't help it; it's completely effortless.

Exactly! And that's the way it should be.

Talia, my honor in knowing you is absolutely beyond words, and to be a part of this. My appreciation is indescribable.

I know it is and I will always be your friend.

And I will always be yours.

That's life!

        Both Talia and G said that at the same time.

That's beautiful!

Yes, it is.

October 5

1:20 PM
You want to talk to me?

Yes, Talia, I always do.

You wanted to know what the calmness was about.

Yes.

That's where this comes from, a calm mind. The calmness, even in the midst of the storm, peace be still, spoken into being. A calm mind is a quick mind, able to grasp what's happening, now. That grasping is grasping everything. "Nothing hidden that shall not be revealed." A perfect reflection of the Divine. That's how you saw the universe in my eyes, by my quietness and confidence. No thought, merely reflection. A glimpse and your knees were weak.

I remember.

Do you remember what else you saw in my eyes?

No.

You saw the Creator in His creation.

Yes, that's right, I did.

That's why you were awestruck and have been ever since. That's when you fell in love with all that is, and I can take absolutely no credit for it.

Because you were just being who you are.

That's right and it was totally effortless.

God, Talia, I love you!

You love Everything and that's what I meant when I told you that.

October 6

7:13 PM
Talia, today when I said, "Only God or Talia could make a canyon like this," you said, "You give me too much credit." Any comments?

Yes, I didn't make that canyon, God did.

I know, that's obvious.

Then why did you say it?

Because I'm awestruck?

Collection

It's a misappropriation of attention. Be mindful of where you place your attention, and of your words. Some things need not be trivialized. God created that canyon and placed it there for a reason. You've used it several times and had some very interesting experiences there and appreciated it. Growth has been wrought in the experiences you've had there; you even renamed the canyon. You've seen the past and the future there, and both in the present.

Yes, been some interesting times.

Don't trivialize the WORD.

Didn't recognize myself doing that.

It's hard to recognize yourself when you are doing that.

What I said then and what I just said there was ordained to be for a lesson, wasn't it?

That's obvious and your explaining it isn't necessary. We've moved on, remember.

October 7

1:43 AM
Thank you for dedicating that song to me; I like it.

> G was listening to some music and he dedicated the song *On Up the Mountain*, by Jacob Dylan, to Talia.

It sounds like you wrote it.

That's why I like it.

1:21 PM
> G was talking to Talia about some very personal matters for him. He did not want to write down what she was telling him.

Why are you holding back? It's just a notebook. It's for God's glory, NOT to reveal a matter. I guard your privacy more than you do.

If it isn't documented, it never happened.

Even if it is documented many will still not believe it happened. It's going to be hard to follow unless you write what I say. Write. I'm within you, I follow you. I also assure you of truth. Him using me is purposeful. My using you also is.

The Universe Speaks

October 8

9:16 AM

You see how hard it is to break that habit of thinking you have to do something? You're already here; you just have to realize it, make it real. You were guided to buy that book of the rebellious thinker. He is to this day regarded as the quintessential genius. His name's even synonymous with the term. Without his rebellious spirit he would hardly be remembered today.

  Talia is referring to a book about Albert Einstein that G had bought.

Your first grade principal had a plaque on his desk. It read THINK; you wanted to ask him "what?" When he pointed that out to you, why didn't you?

I thought I would have made him angry, and I didn't think he had an answer.

You should have asked. It would have made him think.

Did he have an answer?

He thought that WAS the answer. In actuality it was a cop-out, a vague term meant to kept the children in line by thinking what they were told to think.

That's interesting. That's popped into my mind several times over the last couple of decades. I knew there was something to be learned there.

I do remember him fondly; he seemed like a good man.

He was; he was just doing what he had been told. I told you before to rob someone of their independence is to rob them of their genius. From that robbery we all suffer.

Even then you sensed he felt he was living below his potential. He was, because he went along with the play that had been scripted for him. That day you were shown that you would be used as an instrument to deliver freedom, and from that day forward you had a keen distrust of authority. Remember how you felt after you left his office and were walking down the hall back to class? Your confidence had never been so high, and you knew you were destined for greatness, that you would do something REAL and meaningful. You even wanted to announce it to the class.

I had completely forgotten all of that.

It didn't last long; you were soon put in your place.

Boy, there's a place of destitution that's hard to get out of.

Collection

Yes, it is, and its effects are lasting and deep. Love is also lasting and deep, and that is what delivers from delusion. That is what restores what was robbed. That is what reminds you who you are. That love never fails, no matter what. I like your smile.

I couldn't help but smile after that. Guess that explains my suspicion of that plaque. I remember looking at it and thinking, *Think about what?* I thought he would tell me but he never did, like it was a secret or something.

It was a secret, even from him.

October 9

1:44 PM
How's your day going?

So far so good, and then some. How about yours?

Every day I have is perfect.

I figured it would be.

Some things you have to keep separate—and that's not Oneness. It works like that but that's not the ideal. Your world demands it sometimes; that's why he said "be ye separate," to bring into Oneness. Recognize that that separation is for a reason. Even God himself separated Himself that he may know Himself to an even greater extent.

Are we not parts of God? Separated from Himself to be brought back unto Himself and into Oneness within Him again. Fullness restored. It has been said "ye are gods." This perspective of insight should be noted; it's often overlooked, misunderstood, or railed against. This is HE acknowledging our fullness of fellowship with Him. Our reigning with Him.

That separation you feel right now is a product of your mind. Remember, pure focused thought, singleness of purpose.

Oneness also is a creation of your mind, a product of the Mind.

The Mind is mine.

Now you are declaring truth, freedom. No one can steal this, although you can let it slip away. The battle is to keep it.

3:52 PM
It won't always come as a voice; it also comes as an impression. Receive the impression.

I want to see through your eyes.

The Universe Speaks

You do. My insight is yours and usually is an impression.

7:08 PM
The imprint of truth has its own voice. A record ascribed to minds that hear. It remains in agreement, the duality of Oneness. This one mind always sees the singularity of duality.

Okay.

It's perfectly okay; it's the only way to fully be. It's as plain and simple as it ever was when you see it in the Light.

I know.

The imprint of truth is written upon the heart. That's where the voice is heard. That's also the place from which the spoken word is made manifest. It remains in agreement. That which is spoken comes to pass, because that which is spoken IS.

8:58 PM
The word of life.

That's it.

Do not my words burn in experience?

They do.

Let your words do the same.

October 10

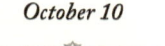

12:42 PM
Talia, I've got to tell you, I'm fascinated by your life.

You don't even know why you're so fascinated by it, but I can give you a reason. It's because I walked in the flesh and in the spirit, so effortlessly it was like breathing. I hardly noticed. The breath of life. The mind is structured to breathe unconsciously. Its counterpart, the spiritual mind, also breathes the breath of LIFE unconsciously. You can talk yourself out of it, which is only a form of denial, but without this breath of LIFE there is no life.

One of the biggest desires of my heart was to learn and know the truth, unbiased. The truth is pure; these are synonymous. The pure truth is also freedom realized. I always knew on some level that what I was looking for I would find and that somehow it was just before my face, just out of reach. My joy and expectation of this created a joy in my heart that bubbled over to others, bringing them life. All of this was without effort because I was just living life.

Collection

I saw all you just said holographically and see it's the perfect example of how to live life.

That's why I've mentioned so often that my life was an example. My love of life, of what life was, was filled with joy every moment because I knew that what life was, was Everything. This is the spiritual life in which THERE IS NO END.

5:43 PM
I told her—Mom—I was talking to you. She knew it. She is learning patience, concentration, and to listen, among other things.

Guess I've got other things to do now.

You do, to communicate. The things that I say to you are for a purpose and they are needful.

Well, thanks for saying them.

You're welcome.

October 12

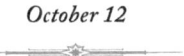

11:14 PM
Talia, I feel like you've got a lot to say. I've felt your presence strongly lately, but in a quiet way.

I'm very involved in what's been happening. You see someone excelling and that's not by chance. Everything's coming along. You've heard it declared, "I'm living it." These are some of the results when you listen to truth and then claim it as yours.

> Talia is referring to me and my learning to be still, listen, and communicate with her.

You said your word was with power.

Yes, I did and it is. All His servants have this power within them. It's just deciding to BELIEVE it and walk in it. Miraculous results. This is the application of truth, and its fruits will always be manifested in time. The false way is the barren way. My way is His way and His way is always the way of victory. You could call it the winning way because that's what it is.

The winning way—I like that.

How could you not? You could try it your own way, but that's all you would do, try. My way, His way, is the assured path to victory. Now the qualities of the people she (Mom) asked about reside within her, and these are qualities the Father LOVES. That's why they were chosen people, their drive and determination to succeed. Loyalty, sensitivity, and graciousness are some other factors involved. I hope this helps you with the answer, Mom.

The Universe Speaks

I had asked Talia why the Jews were the "chosen" people. That was her answer.

These are qualities that delight the Father. These are the people in whom He is well pleased. These will not be lost with His hand.

That's pretty awesome.

That's beyond pretty awesome.

What's happening there is a pale reflection of what's happening here, and what's happening here is what is happening inside His people. The kingdom IS within you.

October 13

1:50 PM

The brain is a microcosm of the universe. What happens here in the brain also happens there. What one part is conscious of, so is the other part. The brain is One, and in reality the brain knows no time. Something to think about, isn't it? Distance is something else the brain doesn't acknowledge, not in reality.

Hello, Talia, sounds like you've got a lot on your mind today.

Hello, and I have one thing on my mind and that's Everything. Something else to think about, isn't it?

That's something to ponder, yes.

You know precisely what's on my mind. That's something you should acknowledge.

That's really something to think about.

You should think of it. This is the nature of the universe, and that's why I'm telling you this.

7:42 PM

Today your mom told me about the Days of Awe, what they were. Hearing those words made me a bit awestruck, because you had said that to me sometime around Rosh Hashanah. I took it as these times we are having now are days of awe, which they are, and I cherish them. But then I heard they are the days between Rosh Hashanah and Yom Kippur. Any comments?

These ARE the days of awe and that's something you should investigate, the meaning of that. These are customs that are pertinent to what we are doing here. I spoke not so long ago about a custom and the meaning of it.

Collection

I remember.

I know you do. Have you taken it to heart?

I'm trying to. I did miss an opportunity the other day by not being mindful of my words. If I had been more silent and not so talkative I don't think that would have happened.

It wouldn't have and you would have seized the moment and planted a seed and got the lesson you missed.

I regret it.

Don't regret it, learn from it; then you can have no regrets.

It's as if it vanished from my mind; I can't seem to remember it now.

That's one of those places I told you about where things disappear, to reappear someplace else.

And I remember why: when things realize they aren't needed.

Yes, and these pearls of truth disappear as if into a vacuum.

That's how it felt, and it leaves an emptiness behind.

When you miss an important truth you'd always feel a certain emptiness. Why do you think so many feel so empty? It's not so much "the tragedy of man is not what he suffers but what he misses," as what he misses is causing the suffering.

I totally agree with that.

I'm totally pleased with your assessment.

Our message now is agreement. When you agree with the Word of Truth you can do no wrong. That's being invincible. Someone spoke to you not so long ago that being on that road was being invincible.

That's not the words he used but I guess that's what he was saying.

It was, AND you agreed with him. These are the days flowering when they will see eye to eye.

That's it! When I can look into someone else's eyes and see the universe and the Creator in His creation, just like when I looked into yours.

That IS it. You've got it. Now see it. It's always there.

These are truly the Days of Awe!

Yes, they are.

The Universe Speaks

October 14

8:30 AM
The universe really IS consciousness.

1:03 PM
When you leave words out there is a gap in the narrative that's hard to follow.

You said . . .

I said you couldn't write everything I show you. I didn't say pick and choose and edit as you go. You said you couldn't match wits with me, that it was an unfair advantage, and I replied that it was fair in every way it could be. I said you were astute and you didn't have to try to be clever. There are clues to principles here that I wanted you to employ.

Employ?

To record, to use, to make use of.

I just thought I was getting off track in my levity.

You were, but it was for a purpose. Don't second-guess the flow; it's for a reason. Your energy is in an ebb now—that's when you use your faith. Faith, hope, love, and these three are one.

Another principle of victory.

The winning way. ☺

2:58 PM
Talia, this book about Albert Einstein is interesting and has its moments, and I'm not taking anything away from the man, but . . .

But you aren't as impressed with him as you are with me.

No, actually I'm not.

That's because you see what I'm saying.

He was a great thinker with tremendous mental energy and imagination, but you met ME, and when you did I was surrounded by beings of light. That day the light bent back on itself, which was me. It also bent back onto you in a manifestation of revelation. If it hadn't you wouldn't have continued this dialogue with me but would have put it aside. Now it's impossible to deny what you know.

In one part of the book, the scientist Bose states something about if two photons have the SAME energy, they will be absolutely indistinguishable and should not be treated as separate at all. This is what made Einstein decide that Quantum Mechanics was not wrong, just incomplete.

Talia, you're just smiling.

I told you. It's all unified by the Oneness that IS. The Existent. We've already discussed it.

October 15

7:30 AM
Good morning, Talia.

Good morning.

There is going to be a Book Two.

8:04 AM
I asked Ken [one of G's oldest friends] how many would get this. He said one out of ten. Maybe.

That's a fair assessment now, in his experience. It's still a worthy number

A worthy number, there's a fact.

It is, and it's a worthy number that can do all things. You see people struggling on a crumbling foundation to keep their balance.

Yes.

Underneath are the hands of the Most High.

Well, that's a good thing.

It is. It's also a foundation that cannot be shaken. Pure science is the revelation of the truth. A personal or political agenda has no place there.

That's pretty obvious.

It is. It also needed to be said. Its truth radiates out into all human endeavors. One test of truth is, does it ultimately bring you freedom? If it doesn't, it isn't truth.

12:19 PM
Talia, the more I find out about everything, the more right I see you are about everything.

The Universe Speaks

You, like most everyone else, wants a golden egg, a panacea equation. There really isn't one, although it could be expressed as an equation. But it would remain as an equation or theory until you personally walked into it. It wouldn't make a difference.

That's why when I asked you for one you just looked at me.

My just looking at you made a difference. When you look at something it makes a difference. To really look at something is using your volition to see it. To see it as it is, is to act upon it to become what it is. What appears hidden is revealed in the light of true sight. True sight is the elimination of bias and an earnest desire for truth, among other things.

I just read this: ". . . Reality consists of an infinity of layers of 'now,' which come into existence successively." Kurt Gödel, from my Einstein book . . .

Well?

No. "Now" is within an infinity of spheres that APPEAR to come into existence successively.

That's the shape depicted in two dimensions of a butterfly on a time line, isn't it?

It is, but the representation is finite. In reality it encompasses all dimensions.

Every and all directions.

Yes. Time is relative to movement. In the ultimate Stillness there is none. Time appears as a tool of the Creator, the Logos. The craft of thought is to separate things in the Now. To now and then, or before and after. This is all, as I said before, for learning. When the lesson is learned, then is time no more; it disappears.

Looks to me like it's time for me to try to figure this out, or go get a beer and not think of it at all. I'm sort of torn between the two.

Interesting observation, you being torn between the two.

That's your observation; I don't think I was observing anything.

No, as a matter of fact you were, and no matter what you do you'll still think about it.

I'm thinking you can explain it.

I can.

I'm waiting.

In time?

Oh, I see, it's revealed in the Now in thought pictures.

Words are wholly inadequate to convey this. They could be at best a catalyst to see in silence where true sight arises. Understanding is personified.

Collection

Understanding is being personified.

That's it. That's the IT. It is personified.

7:12 PM
The vision came unbidden. I told you I would prove this.

You did, today. You said, "Prove all things, all things will be proven, and I will prove this."

I did. Why didn't you write it down?

It's hard to write everything you say, and besides, I just did.

You must apply yourself to our endeavor, otherwise it gets fuzzy.

Fuzzy, huh?

Yes, fuzzy.

Okay, well I don't want anything to get fuzzy that isn't supposed to be.

We're attempting to clear things up here, not cause confusion.

That's clear to me.

Good. I told you before that some things that were obvious to you weren't always obvious to others, and sometimes you needed to speak the obvious. That seems foolish to you to do that but sometimes it's needful. Sometimes that is all it takes to help wake someone up.

You're right.

Yes, I am. You still have a propensity to trivialize some things that shouldn't be.

I think this stuff is just over my head. I get a little overwhelmed by it all sometimes.

Of course it's over your head. If it wasn't, I wouldn't need to be here now, and if it were in your head it would really be muddled.

That's the truth.

It is. It's not that you're stupid, it's just that your head can't contain it. It would be futile to try. I said to you before that this was way beyond us.

You ARE just a messenger.

I am, and I am much more than you think.

That which you just said has profound meaning.

Everything I say does.

The Universe Speaks

Really, Talia, this is so far beyond me I feel like I need seven wise men to bounce it off of.

Bounce it off the universe; you'll get a reply.

All right.

Yes, it is.

I acknowledge that I know precisely what's on your mind.

That's why you love me so much.

Now I'm confused.

No, you're not. I can call the answers to me instantly. For you it takes time. Still, you know precisely what's on my mind.

Okay, I know what you're talking about now. The mind of the Anointed One.

Exactly, precisely, without question. The answers are right there.

Then what's left?

All things.

All things?

All things into One.

That was your finite mind thinking you saw the end. That we are done. I told you, there is no end. The other we were speaking of is the All, the Infinite. How could there be an end to the Infinite?

Okay, good question, simple answer.

They are really all simple answers, even the complex ones.

My brain's rattling in my head.

That's funny. ☺

I think that's the truth.

It's not really rattling, it's just that you are trying to figure it out in your head as we go and you can't.

And to think that I thought I would teach you.

Your desire was pure. You said so yourself.

Collection

It was. I wanted to help you, I saw so much potential.

And now I'm living up to it.

You sure are! When I said I wanted to teach you, the Voice said, "She will teach you." That's sure been the case.

He cannot lie.

I know; when I heard it I was flabbergasted. I thought it would be here.

It is here.

You know what I mean.

I know what you mean and it is here.

I feel unworthy of such honor.

Then don't feel like that. It IS an honor and you are worthy of it.

I'm very humbled by all this Talia, beyond any words.

All true spiritual encounters are humbling. It's the Awe of the All, the never-ending, the unspeakable, the incomprehensible. None can aspire to such Greatness. All are humbled before the ALL.

The All mighty.

He is.

October 16

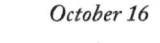

7:43 AM
Go to Now. Go to that place of peace, now. Walk in it. Flow within it and it will flow out of you. You'll see nature rejoice where you walk. Coming deliverance.

Tall order.

It's not an order. It's an opportunity.

10:14 AM
Talia, I've been trying to describe how it was looking through your eyes when I watched the butterfly, and I can only come up with wonder and understanding.

> While having a visitation with Talia, G saw a butterfly. How he saw that butterfly was as if he were looking at it through Talia's eyes.

That gentle creature was aware of our gaze. You felt his response, his awareness.

Yes, I did, a sublime consciousness . . . loving, pleasing consciousness.

That's divine understanding and a holy wonder. When your awareness is lifted you'll always see like that.

That was magnificent.

Yes, IT is.

When I awoke this morning the first thing on my mind was THE UNIVERSE SPEAKS.

It does.

Seems like a good name for a book.

It is. ☺

12:04 PM
Nothing you've done so far affects anything else you've done so far.

What does THAT mean?

It means nothing you've done negatively so far affects anything else you've done negatively so far. It speaks of a higher vibrational level. Where did Solomon come from? It's not an exception to the rule, it IS the rule. It's a tenuous peace. It shouldn't be. Tenure is for honor of the teacher for what he has given.

Talia, I just lost it!

You have to pay attention. It is a payment you know.

What was it?

You'll get it.

You're walking in the Now; that's why you're such a mystery to so many.

That was it.

Told you that you would get it. Right now you're experiencing the future in the past, NOW. You see, it's all the same. I told you I learn from everything you do. And I speak as the oracles of God.

There are some interesting implications.

Isn't it, though?

Collection

October 18

1:06 PM

Boy, that old "be instant in season and out of season" takes on a whole new meaning now.

Being instant in the Now is regardless of the season. Being instant in the Now, now is a reflection, and it requires a calm mind, a certain internal stillness.

October 19

8:21 PM
Do you want to talk to me?

Yes, I do, I always do.

There are people waiting for this.

Okay, Talia . . . so what?

So we need to get on with it.

I'm here.

So am I. We can talk whenever you like. When have I not been there for you?

That's a really good point.

Neglect can cause things to disappear when they sense they aren't needed.

October 20

12:50 PM
You crave adventure.

Talia, I'm almost out of time here, and I can tell you've got a lot more to say.

We'll get to it. Time is illusory and all illusions pass.

I've never met anyone as smart as you.

Yes, you have; you just weren't paying attention.

The Universe Speaks

October 22

7:26 AM
Introspection.

People are generally suspicious of those who are introspective. Never stop exploring, [you'll have] wonderful discoveries. People are afraid of what they might find. Fear of the dark, fear of the light. Both are unfounded, and the results are them living between two worlds, a lukewarm limbo. Look within. Know thyself, and then you can see clearly. Most will do anything to avoid looking within, and your society encourages this.

There's nothing to sell.

No, not really.

When you look within, you will sooner or later discover the universe, and when you do you can be bought or sold no more. Nor will you buy or sell another, for you will see yourself in each other. Why would you sell yourself? These seem uncontrollable to others, and the dilemma arises out of what to do with them.

Thus, the "be wise as serpents."

Yes, walk IN wisdom and pass through their midst.

October 24

12:48 PM
Cloaked in wisdom.

Something like that.

What else?

You're inspecting within must be done objectively. You're trying to rush it. You can't. There is no time here.

That's better. Quietness. If you're not listening in silence you can't hear clearly.

That's obvious.

Collection

That's why I said it, because it's obvious. It's all obvious when you see it.

That's obvious too.

It is when you see it. Absolutely. Completely. Everything we've talked about is absolutely clear and obvious when you see it, and it cannot be seen in darkness, but is ONLY revealed by the light.

That's simple.

Perfect simplicity.

She couldn't have done it without you, and I thank you for that.

> Talia is referring to my healing from her "death," and learning to hear Talia myself. G was very instrumental in helping me. Every time I would hear Talia, I would ask G to ask Talia if it was in fact her. These confirmations led to my unwavering faith and belief that I too can hear her!

5:37 PM
Talia, that's very humbling, and I wouldn't believe that if you hadn't told me.

I told you of things I wouldn't have believed when I was there, but that's the truth.

I thank you and the universe and our Friend for counting me worthy and using me. There's no greater honor.

It IS a great honor and you ARE worthy.

Thank you, Talia.

YOU'RE welcome.

October 25

4:00 PM
You said *300* the other day.

I liked it. The message. Fortitude.

> Talia is referring to the movie *300*.

The Universe Speaks

November 2008

November 1

10:24 AM
I've missed our time together.

So have I, but you've felt me.

Yes, I have.

She—Mom—is having fun.

Well, that's good. Hope she knows it.

      I was at a class, learning about primitive living and how to hear Talia myself.

12:20 PM
I just thought of something. I never told the story of the sleeping bag. I think I should tell it.

I think you should too.

I was in Washington, east of the Cascades, and it was getting dark. It was cold and the wind was blowing. As I walked I asked God for a sleeping bag. I said, "It's getting dark and it would sure be nice to have a sleeping bag, because building a shelter at night is not going to be fun." It wasn't a minute later when I looked to the side of the road and saw a sleeping bag folded over a barbed-wire fence. Dry and in perfect condition. Amazing.

He knows your needs before you ask, and that was a divine shelter.

That was the same trip that He told me about you.

It was. You were led to take that journey, if you'll recall.

I do. I remember thinking before I started I would meet someone that would change my life.

You did.

Not then though. I was a bit mystified when it was over.

Collection

It's not over. The sleeping bag was the most obvious aspect of that trip, but the more important things come not with observation. Much more occurred on that journey than you know. Remember telling yourself people couldn't see?

Yes, I do remember that.

Remember you asked how you could wake them up?

No—oh, yes, I did.

What was the answer?

I don't remember.

Yes, you do.

I think it was, "It doesn't always matter so much what you say, it's living it."

That was exactly it.

That was a long time ago.

Truth doesn't change.

6:03 PM
So, Talia, what are you up to?

I'm with Mom. ☺

> While I was at my primitive skills class, I felt Talia with me many times. On one occasion I looked over and saw Talia and G standing there, watching me. I did not see them with my eyes, I saw them in my head—but I knew it was them. They were visiting me in the Spirit.
>
> When I got back from class I told G what I had seen, and he confirmed that he had in fact come to camp and visited me with Talia. We also confirmed the exact place I saw them standing, which is where he said they were!
>
> Here is the meditation G had that led him to visit me at class, told in his words: During this meditation I went to visit Kim at her class at the primitive camp. I saw Talia standing there between the store and the water cistern. She was wearing loose white and silver clothes. She saw me and smiled, and said, "I love the energy here!" Then I asked if we could merge with Kim. She said, "Merge with me and you'll merge with Mom."
>
> So I merged with her. She said, "You are strong." I felt her feel my arms and the strength. She said to me, "You're one of the most powerful people

The Universe Speaks

on the planet." I said I didn't know that. She said, "But you are." She said Kim was looking at some tracks. I asked for her to be able to see what they meant and to see how the earth works with her to reveal her secrets. I told Kim, "Become one with the earth and she will work with you." I also kept thinking or seeing a bow drill with brown primitive cordage.

The part of the message she's getting overlaps with yours.

Good to know. Thanks for the confirmation.

You're welcome. It's going to enlighten many.

That's very good to know.

Mom's very persuasive. She convinced me to trust her, and she convinced me to believe what she told me.

I do see where you get your tenacity.

That's a good thing. That's why you're gifted in semiotics.

Talia, I had to look that up.

That's fine. You told yourself years ago everything was a symbol of something; you even said it to a friend.

I remember that now, but I don't think either of us knew what I was talking about.

Yet it was truth and you studied it.

I think mostly unconsciously.

You still studied it and it's paid off.

You're right.

How could I not be? You KNEW everything meant something and symbolized a greater truth than was seen on the surface and taken for granted.

I think for the most part I've been unaware of this.

True, but your Higher Self was working for you. You knew you had to favor the future because your present wasn't what you wanted.

Those are some memories best forgotten.

You did forget them. I brought them back to you to let you see again—that all things really do work in your favor.

I appreciate that.

Collection

I know you do. That that she said about you being in tune with your essence is true. We are, for the most part, in harmony, and our heart connection is unbreakable.

The "she" Talia is referring to is Stephanie, the astrologer.

That's very nice to hear. I've never felt a greater connection of the heart than I do with you. It burns within me when we speak.

The spoken word is powerful. That's why I brought that up about the symbols. You spoke that into being. You said you were going to find out what everything meant.

Yes, I remember that. Sounds crazy.

It somewhat does, but you do know how few would be willing to take on such a task?

I imagine not many and with good reason.

No, actually most of the reasons are not so good, but you're right, not many. In fact, very, very few. But the universe lifted an eyebrow at that and replied to your statement, "what's this?"

I remember thinking that and feeling excitement, but I thought it was my imagination.

You did, but then you issued the challenge, "why not?" Do you remember?

I do now.

You do now.

Talia, you're the absolute ultimate teacher. I've never even heard of anyone coming close, but the ONE.

The One is where I get this. Now you know how it feels.

November 2

Truth denied is truth not lived. It is your inner being where truth is lived.

11:15 AM
Raise your consciousness.

I'm invisible.

> G went out on a walk, and as he walked past some co-workers he realized that none of them saw him. No one acknowledged his presence at all.

Now you know how that feels.

That's impossible.

The Universe Speaks

No, it just happened. Where you walk is an unseen world to most and your tracks are hidden. The Kingdom of Heaven comes not with observation.

> G went over to the pond and watched as a duck was swimming, and then it just sank.

I've never seen a duck do that. He didn't dive, he just sank.

You just disappeared into the waters of life.

November 3

11:55 AM
Talia, yesterday...

All things are yours, in any event.

Never quite saw it like that.

I told you I have a perfect perspective, and I'm sharing it with you.

I'm finally starting to come to terms with your going. It seems almost ridiculous for you to be in junior high now.

I had a higher calling. There was nothing left to hold me.

Why is Frankie coming to mind?

She hurts for me but she shouldn't. You hurt for me but you shouldn't. I told you yesterday to celebrate life. You should always celebrate life. Even in killing you should celebrate life. Especially when taking a life should you celebrate life, and the life you take should always be to bring life to others.

Why did you bring that up?

That's a question some have and I'm answering it. I told you before there was nothing left to hold me. Why didn't you write it?

I didn't want it to hurt anybody. I didn't want to hurt your mom.

What you might perceive as hurt from me can ONLY be healing. I cannot hurt another.

I know you can't.

Then why second-guess?

I don't know.

Collection

Yes, you do. Sometimes you think you know better than me, and that's something you didn't know.

That's right, I didn't.

Why do you think that is?

Why?

Because you've judged others for thinking they knew more than they do.

Okay, but I have seen a lot of those people.

Nevertheless, you shouldn't judge them.

Okay, so . . .

So say a prayer to wake them up instead. How simple is that?

Pretty simple.

The Universe at its core is simplicity perfected. The Universe is also within you. I proved that to you the day you looked into my eyes. If you hadn't seen that you would still be lost today. The Universe is love enfolded forever and ever. The Universe is a statement of love, which is the greatest of all powers. The Universe speaks answers, which are contained in the questions you ask. Its nature is to guide into all truth. If you know yourself you will know the Universe, and that's why I said the answers are within you. One who is asleep cannot know this. You see now why you have no need for any man to teach you or to call any man Father?

Perfectly. You said we're almost done here.

Yes, for now.

For Now.

Yes. ☺

What else?

What else do you want?

I want Everything and it All.

Then you shall have it.

When?

Anytime.

Now sounds good.

Now is all there is.

311

12:50 PM

G: I met Talia at my Medicine Place. She said, "Come with me. Hold on, we're going fast," and we went to a mountaintop. I smelled a faint scent of bread; she said that the air was infused with life—that was what I was smelling. She then took me to a valley and asked, "What do you see?" I saw plants and water; it was very green and surrounded by mountains. She called it the Valley of Love, and you could feel it. She said no one was there unless you wanted them to be and that this place was a creation of my own but very real. I was surrounded by green mountains and lushness. They seemed close but broad and expansive.

Then she asked me where I wanted to go. I said to her version of the Grand Canyon. So we were there, instantly, on a peak surrounded by a grand canyon that made the one in Arizona seem like a ditch. I saw colors in the cliffs, colors unknown. Far below was a gentle blue river. A plateau surrounded it and there were mountains beyond that.

Then she or I said, as one mind, "Let's go see Mom/Kim," and we were instantly there, at Kim's class. She was listening to a lecture, very intently. I heard the word *however*, but nothing else. Talia said it wasn't important what I heard, what was important was what the Spirit was teaching. She said she was helping Kim to receive the message or lesson of the Spirit and Grandfathers, and that our and Tom's [the program leader] messages blended into the future; they were all coming together. She went and stood at Kim's left side; I stood on the right looking at them. Talia said, "I love her more than you can imagine." I said, "I can imagine a lot." She said, "I know, but I love her more than you can imagine." I felt her love and it was overwhelming.

She said she, Mom, is a prophetess. I asked, "She can tell the future?" Talia said, "Yes, because she's living in the Now. All the lessons—Grandfathers, yours, Tom's—are coming together so she can prophesy and help others." Talia then said, "I'm going to stay and help her to receive it." I had to go; I needed to get back to work.

During this meditation Talia also showed me how she could be in more than one place at a time. She also said something about multidimensional travel and communication and how to do it.

She said that when you were sleeping there was less distraction from the flesh, so you were able to see and perceive clearer, but that it was harder to remember what you learned this way. She also said something about

Collection

controlling the body—that you could control your body. You could transcend the flesh in order to perceive the Spirit and move about freely.

She's (Mom) going to carry on my work.

November 4

12:04 PM
When have you not seen suspicion arise when you used pen and paper?

Only when it was expected.

And that's because people realize the power of the pen. It is also the suspicion aimed at those who are introspective. Interesting that it's never a problem when someone is telling you what to write. It's when the creativity is flowing that the wonderment begins.

Why did you bring that up?

Because it was something that needed to be brought up.

    G got a phone call from J.

I really like him.

I really do too. You see why?

Yes, I do. A kind and gentle soul despite a rough exterior.

He makes me laugh, too, and that's a gift.

I can tell you're really tender hearted toward him.

I always have been. He misses me a lot.

I know he does.

12:28 PM
You should travel now. Slow everything down, and travel faster than the speed of light.

    G went on a meditative trip.

That's easy.

It sure is. And instantaneous doesn't apply. Now do you see why I broke that word [instantaneous] down into syllables?

I have a very vague idea.

The Universe Speaks

It's because words are not needed. Words are symbols of thought. Thoughts are consistently faster than the speed of light, and yet people are perplexed by an imaginary boundary. They want an equation to solve the riddle of the boundary, yet equations are symbols of thought.

The energy follows the mind.

That's it exactly.

Talia, that's beyond cool.

That breaks all the boundaries, doesn't it?

It really does.

You already knew this.

I did, but I didn't have the words.

Words are not needed.

1:30 PM
Now I feel tired, exhausted.

That's the flesh. It nearly always is in rebellion against the Spirit.

Drag.

It does slow you down. Remember I said you had power over it?

Yes.

Then use it.

That was quick.

That was the Spirit. The true authority.

You broke it down, in-stan-taneous, to show how slow words were.

That is part of it. Words are the fine vibration of thought slowed down to express them. That's where you find some of the problems, me trying to slow down my thoughts to you to express them. You've also frequently experienced this trying to express your own higher vibrational thoughts to others.

There is so much noise going on outside. Banging, construction. It is not conducive to what we are doing here.

Tune it out. You're as safe as if you were in your mother's womb.

I know, but it's noisy—diesels, machines, etc.

Collection

Why don't you use that discipline you've prided yourself on?

Well, that's revealing.

Everything I say is revealing. It is born of the light.

Control is the issue. Precision thought.

I wonder if they're discovering anything.

Not much. But they're making a lot of money and that is the issue with them. You, on the other hand, are discovering a lot and the money doesn't concern you.

More irony.

Told you it was everywhere.

You're busy.

I'm really busy.

You're also having fun.

I am! ☺

Talia, you said you would show me what we would have talked about if I had acted instead of being an idiot [on Thanksgiving Day, 2006].

You weren't an idiot; you were learning a very important lesson.

Nevertheless, I missed a golden opportunity.

Well put. Did you notice the golden glow that day?

Yes, I did. It was everywhere and around everything, kind of a haze.

That's the presence of divinity.

I know. Did you see it?

Not then. I more sensed it than saw it, but it's clear now.

Could you tell me more about what happened that day?

It will be revealed in time. I thought you wanted to know what we would have discussed.

I do.

You would have asked me about school and did I like it, even though you knew I did. I would have said yes, I do. You would have asked about my horses and dogs and told me about yours. I would have asked you where you were from and about the things you like to do and your work. We would have talked about politics and quantum physics and God and if He really existed.

The Universe Speaks

There's some irony.

I would have asked if you believed in Him and why.

Figured you would have some hard questions.

That is hard to explain, isn't it?

Yes, it is.

Talia, I was intimidated by you. I realize that now.

You shouldn't have been. Intimidation is fear; what was there to be afraid of?

Rationally nothing, but in light of everything that happened I was wondering how to open the conversation, and I thought about asking if you liked school but knew you did and thought you would see right through me as being shallow.

I would not have thought you were shallow. I would have thought you were just making conversation, which is what you would have been doing. You know, you were amused not so long ago when you heard someone had said they thought you could read their mind so they weren't themselves that day.

> G had met a friend of mine, and during that meeting she had been very quiet, not herself. I later asked her why she had been so introverted, and she told me that she had thought G could read her mind.

Yes, I was just making conversation, and the funny part was I did perceive that she thought I could read her mind. That's why I asked if she knew about our communications. I know there is nothing in her mind I would judge her for, nor would I disrespect her privacy.

Yet she put up walls that day. You see people doing this constantly. And why?

Well, some folks really can't be trusted. I've seen the power misused, so I do understand it.

Have you seen those keep that power who did misuse it?

I always saw it wane and eventually disappear.

All power misused will be taken away. Point is, the walls aren't needed. Openness is a better policy.

You know, I see that as absolutely true.

Then why don't you practice it?

I'm pretty open.

Collection

You're pretty open when you want to be. You usually have walls.

Now you sound like my mom.

She was right a lot.

She'll love to hear that. I'll probably never hear the end of it.

She will quote it.

Yes, the best part of the book for her, no doubt.

The walls are a defense you don't need.

Okay.

Am I harping?

    Talia was quoting G's mom!

No, I think I've got the point though.

Do you?

Okay, I may not be in complete agreement.

Why not?

I'll refer back to the fact that some folks really can't be trusted.

But how can they harm you?

Good question.

You can be assured of that.

November 5

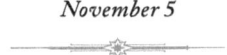

5:44 AM
Don't be sad. It's a normal human emotion.

I want to see you.

You will, soon enough. You tend to become obsessed.

What I saw in your eyes! I could look into them til I went blind.

You won't go blind looking into my eyes. (G laughed.) *I can always make you laugh. Don't put up walls. That's the wall I was referring to. It's an escape.*

The Universe Speaks

Escaping what?

The pain. You feel it deeply in your heart.

What you did to me that day?

What I did to you that day wasn't me. That was the Creator revealing Himself in His creation.

Well, He just about outdid Himself when He made you. What are you going to say about that, Talia?

I'm going to say I love you more than you know. The walls close you off from the Spirit. That's why it's important not to put them up. It closes you off to more than you think. Your defense, if you need one, is not self-made walls. Tear them down and leave them behind.

7:16 AM
How many independent thinkers do you know?

Not very many. It's a constant influence and a constant struggle to become and remain free.

That's why your mind must be washed with the true word. The word of truth. Otherwise the void will be filled with something else. The ultimate result of nearly every choice you make results in bondage or liberty. And every day life and death choices are set before you. What could be a more simple choice?

Seems pretty simple.

The complications arise from a mind corrupted.

Lots of corruption these days.

In the darkest days the light will shine the brightest.

That's beautiful and I'll sure try to keep that in mind.

Hold it by the light and let it shine before you.

7:52 AM
Communication is always good and it helps to clarify understanding.

You are so advanced it is off the charts.

No, I am not off the charts, it's that the charts are never-ending.

Infinity.

Yes, and that's not a car.

    G laughs.

Collection

This is something that should be kept light. It is for fun. Dour seriousness has no place in this, and it too is an escape from the harshness of life. This is something I recently found out and I am sharing it with you. There are some things I too must discover. Things I had no direct knowledge or experience of, but my Source is complete in all things. As I have said, I learn in everything you do and I see the beauty in all things.

You are constantly evolving.

I am. I told you His work was not completed.

Love is never wrong.

You told me that before.

I did.

10:08 AM

Sexuality and spiritualty can be the same. Sex is a part of your life you should not deny. It is a gift. Sex is a part of life and without it there would be no life. That in and of itself should be sufficient reason to discuss openly what is so often whispered about. It is nothing to be ashamed of, and the loving sharing of energies should be celebrated, not made into something vile. It should fit in seamlessly with the rest of your life.

Wish I had the words!

This communication is largely without them. ☺

Your head's turned to one side.

I do that when I make a point I want you to think about.

Without words.

Yes.

My mind is blown here.

You were told it is a book about everything.

November 6

4:22 PM

You know, Talia, your beauty slays me.

I know.

That was a long time getting an answer.

The Universe Speaks

There are many aspects of what you said.

You had to think that long about it?

There was a huge range of responses. From the purely physical to the universal and beyond.

Well, I'm glad I could get you thinking.

That simple statement has such far-reaching effects, from cradle to the grave and far beyond. It's something YOU should think about.

I got your download and it's totally awesome. There probably are not enough notebooks made to get all that down.

There really are not. That speaks of everything without End.

> G spent the next seven days in the woods. He used this time to clear his mind in meditation and contemplation. The following are some of the experiences and conversations he had with Talia.
>
> Before his flight he saw a girl that had a striking resemblance to Talia. While standing in line he noticed her boarding pass appeared to have the name Destiny on it.

Talia, what does that mean, her having the name Destiny and me seeing that?

It means I was your destiny and love never fails. It'll be a good flight.

Why . . . ?

I wanted you to know that I was your destiny and not to doubt our work together.

Talia, there is something about that photo of you, standing on the glacier, arms spread to the heavens.

It is an exuberance for life.

What about the photo of the iceberg floating, with just the tip of it showing above the water?

It's largely hidden, what's contained in this message. The key to unlock it is love out of a pure heart and a desperate desire to know the truth.

Desperate?

Yes, a fervent desire bordering desperation. You are compelled to explain; you're putting your understanding on my words. Don't do that. You don't have to apologize to me.

I know. Faith. It has to do with this week and what I am going to experience.

Talia, you're really here, aren't you?

Yes, I'm really here.

Collection

November 9

Talia, a friend said that the healing only comes through the Spirit, through the force, the Spirit that moves through and in all things. When he said that, I remembered that you had previously told me that a healer is to enlighten, inspire, teach, guide, and be a good listener. I did not write it down

Yes. Passion frightens people; that's why they want to squelch it.

Why does it frighten them?

Because it shows them what they should be and are not.

I literally saw a sign that read, "Open hearts open doors."

I told you that before and you asked for a sign.

Talia, where were your brainwaves when you were still here, in the body?

I was in alpha and theta.

I did not want to leave after my last meditation.

You don't have to.

Talia, when I was at the Carlyle in New York, some things came to my mind. I thought to myself that you have to work really hard to become that superficial, and that I had never seen such poverty.

The sage said, "Come merge with me and ask your answers."

11:04 AM
You got more accomplished than you know.

This last week? I did?

You did.

November 18

8:23 AM
Just start.

Talia! Good morning.

The Universe Speaks

Good morning to you and a new day. Why do you struggle so? The distractions are largely in your mind.

I know, the tyrant within.

Quiet yourself. That's better. We must continue. That you fighting you is the false you fighting the real you. The false you is not real. It's a part of the lie, which is but for a moment. It cannot win and it cannot last. Let the struggle go. It isn't real.

It is gone.

It will be back and it is an illusion. You can even laugh it away—it's that easy.

Then that's funny.

It should be. You don't need the lies.

True and . . . ?

And that's it. You don't need them. That's contrary to harmony and that's how you can always tell a lie, by its disharmony. That will always be felt by the true Self, the Self-less One. So too shall the truth be felt, as in harmony because it is in harmony.

The distractions.

The distractions are disharmony and it's a lie. Why would you receive a lie when you know what it is? What most do not know is that you can use anything to your advantage. Use the noise outside as a drum. There's a rhythm there.

It is. Intent is a vibrating rhythm.

And that is one of the ways you can perceive intent. Everything around you can be used as a tool of enlightenment. It's all designed to do so. Have I not said you are here to learn?

That makes sense.

Everything makes sense when you see it for what it is.

So when someone says it doesn't make sense, it's just a lack of enlightenment.

That's a lack of enlightenment for your enlightenment and theirs too. Remember I said it is the questions you ask. Most simply don't keep asking the questions or demand the answers. They lack an earnest desire. We've talked about the perception of not knowing the answers relieving them of responsibility, or so they think. As they think this, the answers are obscured and something else is received. Something that doesn't serve them. Something that enslaves them instead. Our words are words of life, of freedom, of joy unspeakable. Many receive words of death, of bondage, and of misery unspeakable. Both paths are set before you daily and it's as plain as a Y in the road. Many want someone to tell them which path to take, but regardless, the choice is not removed from them, nor the responsibility. Go watch the fireworks.

Collection

11:43 AM
That thing at the Carlyle—did I see all I was supposed to see?

You saw everything you were supposed to see, which wasn't much. What wasn't seen you perceived and it was vast. The poverty saddened you.

It sure did. I felt dirty after that. I had to walk out to get air.

You felt the dirty deeds done to others. The world at large calls that success.

I think it's failure in a most profound sense.

It is. Most of them had sold their soul to make it where they are.

That's just . . . grievous.

The grief has hardly begun.

I remember the admonishment to the rich men to "weep and howl for your miseries that shall come upon you."

That's good advice but very rarely taken.

November 19

8:37 AM
Thank you, Talia, for helping me in every area of my life.

It's my joy to help others.

That sure works in my favor.

Everything works in your favor.

November 20

6:23 AM
Talia, thanks for the photos. They are awesome.

You're welcome. All you have to do is ask. You're going to have fun today.

Good. Looking forward to it.

Look forward in the Now, where all things are.

You told me that many times, but I see your deeper meaning now.

The Universe Speaks

You'll always see a deeper meaning in the Now. All things are present even before they appear. You often see things presently before they appear.

Yes, it's startling sometimes.

Sometimes is all-time appearing segmentally.

That "merging with the Sage" to ask your answers. You can do that with anything.

That's definitely something to think about.

Think about it, then drop the thinking to do it. Your sincere heartfelt thankfulness goes a long way.

I have trouble expressing it.

Not to us you don't.

This time to me with you is so precious. I'm glad my friends are late.

It was purposeful. You needed this. You were starting to feel abandoned.

I was just slightly concerned; I didn't hear much from you yesterday.

You were surrounded by fools.

I didn't know that.

They don't have to be; it's just a dark path they enjoy. The love of money blinds.

That's kind of sad.

It is sad, and no matter how much is made, you cannot buy the Light. The experience at the Carlyle for you was an impetus of thought. You merged with some of them and felt their despair and emptiness.

It was horrible.

It is and they are the rich of this world.

This world really doesn't have much to offer, does it?

It's a schoolhouse and that's the way you should see it.

Time for you to go now with a perfect perspective. All things are yours. Take them, use them as a vehicle of enlightenment, and know we are working with you to bring you into all things.

I'm very, very grateful.

You should be.

Collection

November 24

12:49 PM
Talia, all these hours . . .

You need to prioritize your time. That's the only way you've gotten done some of the things you've accomplished in the past.

Got some heat for that many times too.

But it was necessary and you've had this lesson many times in the past.

Just needed a reminder.

That's why I'm reminding you, and doing that focuses your energy in the most productive manner.

You did that. I heard about your great study habits and priorities.

I did and still do.

You are wisdom.

I am as an embodiment of it. You can be too.

I'm in and out of it.

You can be in it always.

You're the Standard Bearer.

Yes, I am.

I've missed you.

I've been here all along.

I know. I feel your presence constantly.

You're a source for others and I'm helping you. I told you our message would not be deterred. You're also an oracle of our message, more than you might think. You look at you as a guy in the wilderness with a pen, to pass along what I say. I see you as much more. You're an integral part of this message, and the light of the eyes rejoices the heart. You feel as though it's too much responsibility for you to handle. I see it as you've been raised to fulfill this. You think this could be passed on to just about anyone and they could do as well or better. I see that without you this message could not get out at this time, nor in this way. This is the time for this and this is the way it has been ordained to be done.

The Universe Speaks

Talia.

Yes?

I need to see you.

You will. Have faith. That's the power to move mountains. You saw the Berlin Wall fall by faith.

That's a fact.

That IS a fact. Many would ascribe other factors to explain that, but that would not have happened when it happened without the gift of faith acted upon.

I have NO doubt of that.

That's faith. This world can give you a star on a wall or a star on a report card or uniform, but our Father gives us the stars of Heaven.

That's not the slightest comparison.

No, it's really not. You've seen what this world has to offer, and it's a pale comparison.

At best.

At its best, that is correct.

1:25 PM
What she's done cannot be diminished.

    Talia was speaking about how I raised her.

I know that; it never can, ever. But without you being who you are . . . I've just seen people raised very well before and not turn out even close to you.

She took it a step further. That was the Spirit, despite her being unaware of it. What she has done with me is chronicled for all time.

Guess that's all there is to say about that.

Not at all. There are volumes, but it's enough for now.

6:15 PM
    G was thinking about how sometimes while in the Spirit, it is hard to see clearly. Objects sometimes seem fuzzy.

That's how it is there on earth.

Collection

November 25

9:25 AM
You said yourself that attention was the key and the world was a fuzzy counterpart. It's the Spirit world that is real. Yours is a pale counterpart, a reflection of reality. You said when you were walking in the Spirit the things of this world became indistinct and unreal to you, as if it was counterfeit. That's not it exactly; it's a counterpart of what exists in my world, which is everything without end. You know exactly what I mean. Someone recently talked to me for your benefit and that's what we are doing here. Most see what their attention is focused on and little else. The mind should be focused with an expansion of the Spirit to take in all things. The range of the human senses is incomprehensible to most; therefore, most never bother to comprehend it. Yet everyone has known things without knowing how they know. This is another pointer to the Divine and the divinity within all.

5:42 PM
Talia, someone who read this book while it was being put together said "quickened" was used too much.

That's because they are not quickened.

That's funny. I said I would talk to you about it.

They think YOU'RE writing it.

There is a joke somewhere here about a ghost writer.

You can use that term—I don't mind.

Go have fun.

Go have fun?

Yes, go have fun. That's one of the meanings of life, remember.

Relax and re-mem-ber. Good advice.

I'm a good adviser.

I love you.

I love you too.

I knew that would be your response.

You did. You also love hearing it.

I sure do.

You sure do.

Thanks for the smile.

You needed that too.

8:19 PM
Were you surprised?

No, just disappointed.

> Talia is speaking about a co-worker of G that was involved in a terrible accident.

You've heard a leopard can't change his spots; however, a human can change. But only by the Redeemer—a spiritual change by choice, a decision of free will. A man gave his life in part as a wake-up call for him, and to not learn from his sacrifice is a most tragic mistake.

There is not nor ever will be a pill to cure this.

That's true. The only one who can deceive you is you. You have power over all deception.

December 2008

December 2

8:40 AM
Talia, good morning. I'd sure love to hear your voice.

You can. Good morning.

Want to talk today?

Do you want to listen?

I vote yes.

Your mind is somewhere else. Make an appearance, and then come back.

9:12 AM
Nothing happened.

There is always something happening.

Collection

3:54 PM
Talia, what would you like for your birthday?

I would like you to listen and give your life to others. There is no greater gift than you giving of yourself. Lay down your life for others. Listen to them.

I will do my best to do that.

You can start today. Never put off when you can give now.

December 3

7:08 AM
Happy birthday, Talia.

Thank you.

December 5

1:10 PM
Talia, hello. I'm short of time here and that usually works well.

Yes, hello. I told you that was the push you needed sometimes.

Any thoughts about Kim's friend and what she told your mom?

> A friend of mine had told me that if I did not move back to Santa Barbara she was not going to be my friend anymore.

She's reasonable, she's logical, but she's missing the point. We've talked about the point and how very easy it is to miss it all along. Also of how very simple it is to get it; it's often a matter of letting go of logic. She does mean well. What's the story that you recall?

Of how the disciple was angry that such expensive oil was used to anoint the feet of Jesus and not sold instead and the money given to the poor.

That was also a very logical deduction.

Yes, it was but the Master did not agree.

What did He say?

I would need to reread it, but I think it was "the poor you have with you always but me you don't."

Close enough. It was about honor. She saw who He was and her honor of Him came out of a pure heart filled with love.

I am concerned my mom was hurt by it.

December 6

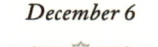

6:04 PM
Talia, where's this thing with our co-worker going?

    A co-worker of G and mine had been talking behind our backs.

Where it's going is he's going to be gone. He's been given opportunities and squandered them each. He's miserable where he is and has bitten the hand of kindness. He badmouthed my mom and that is not right. She's only tried to help him, and did help him, and this kind of behavior is always repaid if repented. He excuses himself but he has no excuse.

This isn't news to me but I wanted your opinion.

This isn't opinion, it is fact.

He's unstable, isn't he?

He's not stable. That is correct.

Why can't he see?

He denies the Light.

But why?

The issue is mostly pride and that comes before a fall.

I hope he's healed.

That's up to him. That's all we need to say on this issue. But I DO have favor with God and I DO watch over my mom.

You have angels helping you, don't you?

I do. I can command them if needed.

That's pretty cool.

It's beyond cool. It's even beyond totally awesome.

Well, I'm out of adjectives.

I told you it was beyond words.

Collection

December 7

12:55 PM
Talia, you want to talk?

I'm filled with life, which can be translated into words of life. The issue is who can hear them.

Guess that's a yes.

It's always a yes. The Language of Life doesn't stop. It's always there and it's always speaking. Our message is filled to the brim and running over: abundance above measure. But so few listen, so few are aware of any message. Many are there whose ears are stopped to the truth, so a lie is received in its place. There is only walking in one or the other: the truth or a lie.

Seems like we've covered this ground before.

We have, but we can't go on into deeper truth until the basics are received and walked in.

That includes me, doesn't it?

It does. You know a lot more truth than you're presently walking in.

Told you I was a knucklehead.

And I told you weren't. You've just chosen to cling to some things that don't necessarily serve your best interest. You'll get over it as you mature.

You love the drama of your life, the mystery, the secrets, although you claim to hate the drama. The truth is you love your games, but what you see as an arduous way is in reality the smoothest of all paths. Your drama is for the most part harmless; therefore, it can be winked at. But still you're held to a higher standard by the Light you've been given. Walk in the Light. That's drama and mystery enough.

There is no hiding anything from you, is there?

No, you can only hide it from yourself.

Talia, you blow my mind.

I know it.

The Universe Speaks

December 8

1:24 PM
You have access to places where everything that's ever happened to you or was said to you or by you is known. You always have this access available to you when you're not in denial, and believe. As a matter of fact everyone does. This would change the whole paradigm of how the world worked if it was known and walked in, wouldn't it?

It would.

Why don't you practice it?

I will; I'll try.

Don't try. Believe it and do.

2:30 PM
I AM a foundation.

6:55 PM
Talia, the absolute honor in that that God has given you is beyond what I could have thought.

He wasn't saying all things are yours just to say it. He keeps His promises and what He has purposed to do He does. My part in this is growing, and I am a foundation that you can depend on.

Paradigms are shifting, aren't they?

Yes, for me they are.

For all who will hear and believe, they are.

I love you.

I love you too and my love is growing.

That's too awesome to comprehend.

It really is, isn't it?

Yes, it is.

Collection

December 9

9:14 AM
That's why I didn't want to read that.

> G was reading an article about Talia's death. It made him sad.

"The tragic loss, a life cut off when it was just beginning." I never stopped living for an instant. What's tragic is the illusion of loss and the belief that my life was cut off when it was just beginning. I've told you time and time again to celebrate my life. Why do you think I repeat that so often? It's because the illusion is so great that even those who know the truth absolutely will buy into the message of death. You've seen the miracles that follow my life after "death." That "dying" is merely shedding the flesh, which you need no longer. All the hindrances of this world are removed. The result is absolute freedom, life never-ending.

You're growing in love?

I'm growing in love because God is expanding and God is love. His kingdom has no end.

I saw through steel yesterday.

I know you did and that was your spiritual eye. Your vibration was lifted to see through this physical world. I told you you could see through anything by the Light. The physical is dense matter or energy, thought slowed down. It appears to most to be all there is, but in reality it's a reflection of what's real. See through it.

What's with the dead birds?

> G had been reading an article about hundreds of birds that had been found dead, with no explanation.

In part the message is, your passion to fly, to soar, is killed by the dense mind of man. All those birds are somewhere else living life in glorious liberty.

One reason most do not see the things you see is that they WOULD misuse the knowledge. They are tethered by their own beliefs.

Harmless as a dove comes to mind.

That's the mental attitude that would free them of their tethers. Anytime I expressed doubt about my ability to do anything it didn't feel right to me. I instinctively knew I COULD do anything.

Your confidence did blow me away.

My confidence was a sign to believe. Now believe in YOUR ability to do anything, because all things ARE possible and I AM a foundation that cannot be shaken. We are one. How could this NOT be?

You are right.

I always am.

I know.

I know you know.

You've given me everything.

God has given you everything; I'm just confirming it for you.

You know, the words of life are growing in you also.

That's good to know and I do feel it.

You can also see it in yourself and others. Why do you think that when Moses was sending out men to spy in the land of Canaan that he was told to send a man of every tribe and "every one a prince among them"?

Something to do with proven sonship, experience of authority, oneness, royalty—what?

Because everyone was a son of a king.

That's it?

That's all you need to be.

December 10

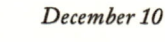

8:30 AM
Good morning, Talia.

Good morning. You know that unfulfilled feeling you have is completely normal. How can a pale reflection, however real, ever fulfill? It's to let you know there's more, much, much more. Be content with what you have but don't expect to be satisfied, not completely. It's also to let you know you have work to do. That's why idleness equates to uneasiness. When you wander from the true path you will always feel this. There is a difference between benefits and blessings and confusion and discontent.

Thanks for the update.

I'm referring to the tracks of your choices.

Collection

All right.

The smallest decisions leave residual benefits and blessings, or residual confusion and discontent. And when you do something to yourself, you do something to someone else; the intricate web of energy connects all things. There is a spherical component to all things Remember when I showed you that you only saw straight lines of energy connecting with points of interest?

Yes.

The lines appear perfectly straight, and they are perfectly straight but with a spherical component.

Yes, I knew that.

But what you didn't know is that your thoughts of that left tracks in the universe. Tracks that others can see and benefit from.

Cool.

Yes, and you saw you weren't the first to see this, that there were many others. You felt their presence.

True, I did. I wondered who they were. I felt many were very ancient. Mystics and the like.

These are signposts in the universe. Those with the desire, drive, and determination can enter into these points for answers. These points contain all knowledge and they are made of energy. The lines are guideposts of energy; they are connected and interconnected with all things. With Everything. What you perceive as solid matter, this table for instance, is on the subatomic level moving with unimaginable speed. It's in fact vibrating so fast that it appears as not moving at all, perfect stillness, a solid object. It is in reality made of particles of energy binding together to create an appearance. It's real; it's just not what it appears to be. The INFINITesimal is called that because there is no end to it. I said your decisions, your choices, could never be underestimated because of their power, their energy. Because you are a creative being. Tracks, or residual energy, are always larger than the things making them.

Usually by about a third or so.

And that's because of gravity, the energy of mass. This mass is what connects all things. The magnificent mass of the Creator. He has left nothing out. That's why He is Everything and nothing lost.

Something to think about.

Yes, and as you think them others will think them because of the tracks of your thoughts. Nothing lost. That's why I told you not to concern yourself with my journal. You knew there was a duplicate and where it was. Nothing can ever be lost, only misplaced. When you see the universe as living, all energy, and bound together by the love of the Creator, you will know this as absolute truth and your peace will know no bounds. Everything you ever wanted and everything you'll ever need is inside you. It's not out there, somewhere, it's everywhere. How could you lose it, and how could you miss it?

10:29 AM
A key to unlock the mystery is intuitive intelligence, spiritual, spherical, seeing as a holographic whole and passion. Love and compassion entwined.

That's what I sensed when I met you. I thought nobody your age could know what you knew or be so composed, so perfectly balanced.

This that we are speaking of has no age. It's ageless, it IS.

But I've never met anyone, anywhere, who even comes close to you, what I saw in you and around you that day. Out back they seemed oblivious. I wanted to shout, "Do you know what's going on in that house?" You were so far beyond any expectations I could have had. I really nearly lost it a couple of times—and you, serenely smiling, glowing, with light around your head. Say what you want, Talia, but the magnitude of what happened that day was far and beyond anyone I had met before. That's just the way it is. No human I had ever met came close to touching that experience.

"That's just the way it is" is always the way it is, everywhere. You just had your eyes opened that day. I defined what "it is" for you. I felt your love for me that day and it was a divine love and it intrigued me. I didn't really understand it. So you see, what happened that day was beyond us both.

Where you blown away like me?

No, I didn't see what you saw that day. As I've said, I've since seen it clearly and I thought you handled it very well. I was awed and amused when I saw what had happened. I was also tremendously honored to have been used in such a way as to help awaken one of these little ones.

G questioned what that meant.

"Little ones" meaning a child of the Most High who had humbly asked to be awakened. "God, wake me up," you shouted. Remember?

Yes, I do.

Well, He heard you.

It takes a lot out of me doing this.

It puts a lot in you too.

Still a bringer of laughter.

Collection

I always will be.

Nobody's going to understand this.

Oh, yes, they will.

12:04 PM
Most will not do the right thing even when they know it's the right thing, without some persuasion. That's something you haven't quite got yet, the resistance of people to do the right thing, even when it's obviously the right thing to do, without some encouragement.

Why is that?

Any number of reasons. Reasons do not always have to be reasonable; they are often excuses instead, and most of them are very petty.

And apparently to them self-serving.

To them it is, but if it's not in the service of others it's really NOT self-serving—it's more self-robbery.

December 11

5:35 AM
Good morning, Talia.

Good morning, G.

More "discoveries" today. You've changed my life.

And it continues to change. My great pleasure is helping others.

I love and appreciate you so much. I wish I had the words.

You have the truth and I know your heart. Your genuine sincerity. Eloquence is not necessary. Don't worry about those who resist doing the right thing. Some will have to find their own way; others, it will come to you what to do. As you have said, it's a case-by-case basis. Remember what you were told, "It's not so much what you do, it's living it." Live it and it can't be denied either by your actions or by their deep knowing.

Deep knowing?

Deep knowing is the undeniable soul-knowing that everyone has.

I KNEW that had to be true! Good to hear it.

That was your soul knowing the truth. I said you were born into it.

Then it begins to be stolen away.

But it doesn't have to be. It being stolen away is primarily the denial of who you really are, which is a creative being made in His likeness, a part of God Himself. From the very beginning a child is taught the illusion of limits, and very soon the illusions are as real to them as anything. This is also reinforced throughout their life, if not by others then by themselves. Soon they are adrift with no direction and no vision.

You were not adrift.

I knew I could do anything. I wasn't raised to believe illusions.

Your life was so FULL.

It WAS full, because I was filled with Life. God honored my faith, even when I didn't know I had faith.

He is pretty cool.

He is everything.

Thank you, Talia.

You're welcome, G. ☺

7:57 AM
This has kind of got me bummed out.

        A meeting was canceled.

It's for the best. Wouldn't you rather hang out with me?

Anytime.

And you can, anytime. Your love for me is pure, and that never fails. What would you rather do right now than this?

Nothing.

And no thing is better.

You're right, nothing is.

We are going into Everything. This is a journey of epic proportions. We are experiencing truth.

I feel better.

You should—I told you no thing is better. Remember the feeling you got from my photos of the bears?

Yes, they conveyed strength and confidence and purpose.

Collection

You also felt my excitement and joy taking them.

I did. Every time I saw them.

That was symbolic that day, as it is now.

9:10 AM
        G went to get some coffee.

That guy looked at me like I was a worm.

He thinks he's something he's not.

I'll remember that.

I'm sure you will. He was being used to show you the truth.

Interesting instructional method.

I told you everyone was a teacher.

Now I remember why I didn't like a lot of my teachers.

You sometimes expect everyone to walk in the Light you're walking in. That's because sometimes you're not true to yourself and you do not see the light you're walking in

Okay, guess he was a pretty good teacher.

That wasn't him, not really. He is someone else, someone he doesn't know.

I'm learning to thrive on rejection.

You should. Would you rather that Spirit accept you? You forget how much you grew as an outcast.

Interesting term considering the situation.

That's why I said it, to hold your attention.

A lot of my teachers said I had a problem paying attention.

You ARE a challenge.

Even for you.

Yes, even for me.

Guess I should have more pity for my teachers.

You should always have forgiveness in your heart, and show it.

You sure are consistent.

The Universe Speaks

You can be too. You can mingle with fools striving or enjoy fellowship with the wise.

I'll pick that latter.

Wise choice.

10:45 AM
> G was thinking about one of the lawyers that was harassing me during a deposition revolving around the plane crash.

That guy's evil, isn't he?

He's being used for evil. An instrument of it.

I said he would get his due.

That was inspired. That's also not your place.

11:33 AM
Hollywood's more real than what's going on there.

> G is referring to the deposition again. Their treatment of me has made G extremely angry.

That's true because they're honest about being actors.

I think he's acting like a jackass.

Not true. A jackass is being who he is. This man's part is to dish out anger to elicit a response to be used against my mom for money.

Well, that's a crappy part to play.

As I said, he is being used as an instrument of evil. He would say he's just doing his job, and we've already talked about what an insufficient excuse that is.

May he be repaid swiftly.

It will be swift enough.

11:54 AM
I never saw you like that before.

I don't get like that very often.

Not since I've known you here.

He deserves it.

He does.

Collection

Why do I not feel satisfied?

You worry too much. He'll get what's coming to him.

Now I feel satisfied.

December 12

1:18 PM
Talia, you said to me earlier that the older one gets, the less doubt there is, until it disappears.

That WAS me and it's true. You also said why.

Because these things are verified and proven over and over until logically why would you doubt.

That's another reason it should be recognized that He doesn't change. No matter YOUR feelings at the time, HE remains unchangeable.

I remember when you told me that, it was the best news ever.

It is, and when you know Him you will know why.

I know why.

I know you do. ☺

December 16

Talia, you wanted to clarify something?

Yes, it's about what I told you about using your own words to relay my thoughts. Remember when I said you know my thoughts precisely?

Yes, you said that you know precisely what's on my mind.

That's right, and I also said we were one, so how could we fail. I said your words for my thoughts were close enough, and they are

I know that; you already told me that.

I know you know it but I want you to remember it. Also that you're right in thinking some would interpret it to mean something else entirely. It's true that it is a small portion of the dialogue. It was also referred to when I said the seers saw and put things they saw into their own words. This is just another means of communication. This they will discover on their own and there's no need to communicate that particular method here.

And these are YOUR words, aren't they?

They are. ☺

Talia, when we talked about the co-worker that was mean to your mom and I asked where it was going, you said, "Where it's going is he's going to be gone." I found out this morning that he's gone.

You were surprised?

No, but it did come sooner that I might have suspected.

I think we've already covered this adequately. You know some other factors involved but no need to cover that here.

You told me he's said some not-so-nice things about me as well.

Why dwell on it? I showed you what was to be.

December 21
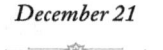

Talia, I watched the movie *300* again. I felt like I had missed something before. What I got that really stood out was treachery.

That's the other side I wanted you to see. It has always been there. Jesus was betrayed by a kiss.

December 22

8:32 AM
Okay, Talia, you said to get caught up, then we'd talk. I am caught up.

So you think.

You said before that as you think so you are, so I am caught up.

Then you are. All these principles are a foundation to live by. As you live by them you will grow up to live in them.

Talia, it might sound crazy, but you are the only one who makes sense to me.

That doesn't sound crazy, it sounds sane. What was it you thought of yesterday about the way most people live?

Collection

It was "don't give me the facts, my mind's made up."

And that truly is the way most people live, and most of them would argue that it is not. That's something else their mind is made up about.

I recall one thing you said to me when you walked down the hall. It was, "Are you going to sleep now?" I think I answered "Yes, no, I guess, I don't know." My indecision amazes me sometimes.

That was a spiritual question. I also asked, "Who are you?" You answered, "I . . . work with . . ." Both answers were wholly inadequate.

I know that now.

You didn't trust me then.

I . . .

I know. You had a "big day." How would you answer those questions now?

No, I am not going to sleep. The other is more difficult.

Difficulties should not hinder your answer.

I am a son of the Most High God.

That's a good answer. That wasn't so hard, was it?

I guess not.

You guess not?

No, it was not.

To speak the truth for you will always be better than beating around the bush. Feels better, doesn't it?

Yes, it does.

It always will, despite the price, and there will always be one but you can afford it. My love for you has no bounds. I want you to know that.

Thank you. I feel the same way and Love never fails.

No, it does not, ever. The manifestation of the sons of God means for one thing, that they will manifest His Kingdom upon the earth. It will help bring forth this child and it is a struggle to be birthed. Remember "pregnant with words of truth"?

Yes, I do.

That is my burden and great joy and expectation. What you see as your lack of communication skills does not have to be a detriment. When you learn to hold your tongue until you have something to say, then will people listen to you.

December 23

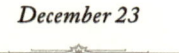

12:12 PM
Everybody loves a puzzle, thus the mystery and thus the drive to seek.

Everyone doesn't have the drive to seek.

Yes, they do. It is just that everybody doesn't love the puzzle enough or they expect another to explain it to them. Some think that there really is no mystery.

Everybody?

Everybody speaks of the physical.

December 24

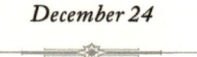

Do you celebrate Christmas now?

Every day is a celebration here.

December 25

7:32 AM
That that you said to someone, that when you "die" first you are surrounded by angels, then it is like falling into a basket of love, was just awesome.

  This is something that Talia had told me via a medium soon after the crash.

I showed you that before; why didn't you write it down?

I don't remember why I didn't.

Angels?

You said to me, "If you have something to say about angels, say it and I will write it down." You just have to listen closer.

Sorry I missed it.

Collection

It's okay, we got it out there.

I am coming to realize I am missing a lot of what you say.

It is a process of learning and growth. Do not be too hard on yourself; it all has purpose. I cannot command anyone to do anything. I can only ask.

The Creator shouldn't be left out of anything you do. Remember when He asked, "Adam where are you, where would you hide?" David said, "If I make my bed in hell, behold, thou art there."

Good point.

Yes, it is. Again, I constantly make those. Again that's a point I am making.

The separation is a construct of the mind. Reality is NO separation. You have a lust for life that is found in the creative juices flowing in freedom. Flowing in truth. Sooner or later everyone figures it out anyway. Our task is to accomplish it sooner rather than later. When HE said I will show you things to come, what do you think He meant by that?

I figured it means He would show you things to come.

It does. It also means He will show you how things are supposed to come. That removes you from the sidelines as a mere observer and gets you into the game as a principal player. This is the hidden meaning in the words of that message, that you are a part of it all and have a part to play in the bringing about of all things according to His will and great plan. That is another part that is easy to overlook. Your part in the great play of Life. People should have confidence in themselves and build confidence in others. To rob another of their confidence is robbery just like any other, and remember that a robber or thief shall not enter into the Gates of Life. Many would disagree with this and their disagreement and disbelief is to rob themselves.

Why would anyone rob themselves?

To rob anyone is to essentially rob yourself.

8:53 AM
Good morning to you.

Good morning to you too. How do you like your new song?

My new song?

Yes, your new song.

What do you mean?

A new song speaks of a new rhythm, a rhythm of life.

I do feel a shift of some sort this morning.

It is a shift to a new song, a new rhythm of life.

Sounds good.

I thought you would say something like that, and know it is true. That is a harmony in sync with the rhythms of life. No need to live anymore out of harmony; it does not feel right.

Never has.

And it never will, but now you are more sensitive to it. It is like every step is a prayer, and it is knowledge that got you there. Knowledge that we are sharing.

Hope they receive it.

Many will and it's simply by choice. To not make a choice is a choice, so you see there is no surrender in this war between harmony and disharmony. Harmony is always the smoother path, and that's where you will feel the flow. In the flow you will trust your decisions. You will know they are in harmony with the way.

Turn the TV back on. You can learn from everything.

G turned the TV on. The science channel had a show about "understanding."

The science of laughter.

It's the science, you know.

Yes, that is funny.

I called myself a giver of laughter; I still am. That is healing.

There is so much laughter here you would be amazed. Watch it.

Interesting. Comments?

Yes, God asked one of his children how long he thought it would take to become like himself. The child answered that he would have to think about it a long time.

Interesting story.

Interesting truth. Then God said, "How about now?" and the child answered that he would have to think about that too.

Point is?

Point is you asked where the world was now. Most think they have to get There, somewhere else. I am saying it's here now. When I was "there" I was "here," and that is how you saw me that glorious day we met, as being here now because I in fact WAS. Miracles happened that day

346

Collection

and they were manifested through me. My path was chosen for me and I agreed with every step. There was not one day of my life that I did not feel the confidence that you felt walking down that hall back to class. "Back to class"... do you remember hearing those words?

Yes, walking down the hall back to class.

And at the time you knew what they meant—then you forgot them.

Yes, I did.

Well, remember them now, because you are back in class. Many think they know what is best for you, how to put you in your place, but your place is very similar to my place and that's a place few go. You have been told you march to the beat of a different drummer, and that is true. THAT'S the rhythm I am talking about.

December 31

6:45 AM
Talia, good morning to you.

Good morning to you.

I do not know what I would do without you.

You would make it but it would not be the same.

No, it sure would not be.

As I have said before, our relationship is an example for others.

I wish that everyone could experience this.

But they can. Again, that is part of the message. That relationships and fellowship don't have to stop just because the body did. That's another reason He is called the invisible God. We are made in HIS image, remember.

I do remember.

Yes, you do, and that too is a good example; everyone should. He said, "This do in remembrance of me." You would do well to reread that and think about what he was saying.

I will.

I know you will.

The Universe Speaks

January 2009

January 1

6:24 AM
Everything.

It has been a heck of a year, Talia.

It has been a strange and new experience for you. I am glad we could grow together.

Me too. I do not know what to say.

Words are not needed. You found me just in time. When things seemed pointless to you.

Boy, have we covered a lot of points since then.

We certainly have, and there are many more we will cover that need to be covered, or rather revealed, uncovered. It's a new day, a new year, and a new thing is being done on the earth. Hold on—it will be a wild ride.

Speed comes to me.

It will move so fast many will miss it.

I see things moving like a blur.

As I said, it will move so fast many will miss it.

Okay, I know you don't repeat yourself because you are at a loss for words.

No, the points we REALLY want to emphasize are often repeated; you should do the same in your teachings. Judge not a student's dullness; that's often a reflection of the teacher.

Well, I might have to have myself stand in the corner.

You have been there before.

And I enjoyed the time out until they figured it out.

You found it peaceful but oddly a waste of time also. You made the best of the situation.

I was living as an example to others. ☺

I am sure you were. You know they will still send you to stand in the corner.

Collection

Sounds rather juvenile.

It is but they "don't want to look at you anymore." They don't know what to do with you.

Guess it is true that "everything you need to know in life you learned in kindergarten."

There is a lot of truth to that.

1:45 PM
Talia, I found something that sounds just like you: "And they that be wise shall shine as the brightness of the firmament, and they that turn many to righteousness as the stars forever and ever." (Daniel 12:3)

And I have one for you: "And if you draw out your soul to the hungry, and satisfy the afflicted soul, then shall your light rise in obscurity and your darkness be as the noonday." (Isaiah 58:10)

I told you I was as the stars and that's what I meant. You cannot always see the stars, but know they are there and they are not alone. Although you have reveled in your obscurity, you've also wondered about it, and the personal things you have shared in this have purpose. As I've said, it ALL has purpose.

I did not want to have anything personal about me in these dialogues. I just wanted to report what you said.

You have and you are, and your life and experiences are woven into the narrative for enlightenment. You said you would give your life for this. That's part of the meaning.

January 2

6:00 AM
Talia, I woke up this morning seeing heART.

That's where all higher art comes from. From the heart.

January 3

6:30 AM
God bless Talia today and let her have her way.

His way is MY way.

The Universe Speaks

January 4

6:26 AM
I heard a TV preacher say, "He lights the light of every man." What about that, Talia?

Jesus is the Way, the Truth, and the Light. I would not have said it if it was not true. And it is true; He doesn't share His glory with another.

This last Thanksgiving I thought, "How the gold is dimmed! How the fine gold is changed!" Then I found these passages in Lamentations this morning.

Don't lament about it. The gold hasn't changed; it is your perception of it.

You are the only one who really makes sense to me, Talia. You and God.

We are the same.

Is that you?

Yes.

January 6

7:50 AM
Talia, I keep seeing certain numbers over and over again. I just saw the number 117. What does that number mean?

Unity brings completion. Completion is in unity.

What about 1111?

It is the directions; it is the choices.

And 111?

That is the power of the trinity.

444?

That is the power of the trinity in your choices.

There is more to that one, isn't there?

Volumes.

Collection

8:04 AM
What about putting some of the things you have said onto tee shirts?

I think it is a good idea. Why not? I have said some good things.

Talia, your self-awareness and poise blow me away.

Everyone should be self-aware, with poise and grace.

I saw a zippo lighter in the store that had "I love me" on it. Then a little later on the back window of a pick-up truck, "It's all about me." I thought about it, and therein lay the problem. Probably humor.

It's not humor, it's the sad truth.

January 9

6:35 AM
Talia, it has been three days and I am dying to hear from you.

You have been busy.

I did hear from you today, didn't I?

Yes. You are feeling unworthy; it is hard to hear when you feel unworthy. Nothing has changed. You are worthy. So hear.

Say on.

January 10

1:15 PM
There is another side, another aspect of that saying "Before you can heal yourself you must heal others": that you must heal yourself before you can heal others. That is important to know, which is why I said write it down. There is a deeper meaning here.

January 12

1:25 PM
It's never a good day to deny who you are.

351

The Universe Speaks

January 14

8:42 AM
Good morning, Talia.

Good morning to you, G. You are still reluctant to use your name.

A little.

It would be easy enough to find out anyway. Maybe it is not such an issue.

Maybe not, but another time you said names were not important unless you wanted power over something.

Do you think someone will have power over you because they know your name?

In some situations.

Those are not the situations we are talking about. For you it is more of a privacy issue.

Well, yeah.

Some need to know.

If they need to know, that's fine.

Good, because some that need to know will know, so regardless of your feelings about them knowing, agree now that it is okay for them to know.

All right, I agree with you. I am not going to disagree with you because I trust you totally and I know who you are. You are beyond mistakes.

I am. I am beyond even questioning whether I could make one.

I'm sure.

So am I.

Talia, I realized something yesterday, that what you said to me that Thanksgiving was a spiritual statement and a spiritual question.

It certainly was, and I left it right there for you to ponder until you did realize what it was that I said. Recall it.

I said, "Hi, how are you?" and you answered, "I am fine; how are you?"

What did you answer?

I said, "I'm fine."

Collection

I had an opportunity to say more.

I was speechless.

You never asked what I saw in your eyes.

What did you see?

I saw absolute acceptance and love. That is the nature of the kingdom.

I have to tell you it was love at first sight for me.

That's because your eyes were opened and you saw who I was. Did He not say that the pure in heart would see God?

I saw Him that day in you.

That's where He lives. In His children. His touch is usually felt through His people. Most are looking for Him to come down in a cloud with smoke and fire and a thundering voice. I am telling you His voice is heard in the little child standing beside you. His helping hand in the friend, co-worker, or stranger. His revelation in the voice of nature, an animal, a tree, a sunset, the sound of the waves. All this, all things, and everything there is can only reflect the Creator, for all this is His creation.

Then how could we miss it?

It can only be missed by choice.

Stupid choice.

It is certainly not the most clever decision one could make. That is a creation of illusion, which ends in delusion, where one thinks the illusion they created is real.

I am sure glad I talked to you today.

I am sure glad you did too.

10:05 AM
Write the progression.

Warrior-poet. Warrior-priest. Warrior-king.

Why?

Because there is something to be learned there. Art always starts with inspiration, progresses into spirituality, and culminates in authority. You want to explain again. You don't have to do that. I told you this was for the chosen few. Those who have chosen themselves over the lie.

You are over the lie when you walk in authority.

The Universe Speaks

And there were those who said you couldn't be taught.

That is funny. I do remember there were those who said that.

But it was a lie and they were in "authority."

Remember when I told you that people tend to block out what they do not understand, the whole time saying they want to understand? But they were empty words, insincere, or they would understand?

Yes, I remember, and I understand it.

Come on, Talia, I made you smile.

I know you did. That's what frustrated them the most. They thought you did not take them seriously.

Well, seriously, that was kind of hard to do.

Well, the deeper lesson here is that the learning goes both ways between student and teacher, and that a person learns better when they are having a good time.

I always try to have a good time.

I know you do, and it's hard for a lot of them to take you seriously when you do that.

Should I be concerned about that? Because I do not feel concerned about that at all. Our lessons are multi-layered.

Our lessons ARE multi-layered and will continue to be.

They will continue to be, that's good.

That's very good. I just want you to be aware of the balance. Sometimes you diminish yourself to relieve the responsibility.

January 15

6:26 PM
Good evening, Talia.

A good evening to you.

Ironic, you are easier to get ahold of than these people I have been trying to phone.

Does that surprise you?

No, just the irony of it.

Collection

How was your day?

It was good, but I am curious why you ask; you already know.

I do know but I want you to know.

What did you do today?

I visited people and impressed them to move in certain directions, including you.

Interesting.

Yes, and I am healing hurts. My presence is as a salve for some who are sensitive.

Nice! ☺

I am helping to move you in a new direction.

How so?

You will see; it is a perfect direction to move.

I didn't expect anything less. Anything else?

You just need someone to speak with, and I am always here for you.

Thank you. I really appreciate that.

I know you do.

January 16

9:25 AM
Our message . . .

Don't lessen it, don't downplay it, because what you are doing has far-reaching consequences and effects. I am with you today.

I know you are—I feel you. Thank you.

You have asked for certain things to be done and they are being done.

Excellent! What were they?

You will remember when they are manifested.

You are . . . really powerful.

You are too.

The Universe Speaks

Symbiotic relationship.

Yes.

Nothing gets done unless it is requested.

That is right.

You absolutely amaze me.

I know. ☺

One thing I asked for has already happened today.

That is not by accident.

No doubt.

No doubt is one reason it is happening.

Talia, thank you for today.

Thank you for your attention.

You can talk to me anytime, can't you?

We can talk to each other anytime.

Awesome!

It is pure.

Pure?

Yes, our communication is pure in the sense that it is truth spoken.

All of our words are freedom spoken.

All of our words lead in that direction, yes. You cannot be dishonest with me, and I cannot be dishonest with you. I said to you our relationship is a perfect example of how relationships should be, and this is one example of that.

I cannot even think of lying to you.

Remember from the beginning of this when I spoke to you of the kingdom walk? Well, this is a part of that walk. A lie is never even considered. It just is not a possibility. This message is vast, beyond your wildest imagination. It reverberates throughout the universe. I said to you that morning "the Universe Speaks" and it does. I said to you that the very nature of the universe is to lead into all truth. It does this by speaking the truth in love, for the structure of the universe is the Father's love for His children, and that never fails. The language of life is the language of

Collection

Love, and that originates in the heart of the Father of Life, of all that is and ever will be. All are from Him and all will return to Him.

Talia, I can tell you could get into so much greater depth here but you are holding back.

I am holding back what is not time to be given. I could tell you things now that would make absolutely no sense to you or anyone else there. The time for that is not yet. I will say that the time is coming when all shall know Him, from the least to the greatest. Remember I have told you several times to go to Now.

Yes.

Now is a place where there is no time.

Then if there is no time, time has no bearing on the revelation, right?

Clever. In the ultimate truth there is no time, and time doesn't have a bearing on revelation because there is no revelation. There are no words for this. It IS.

Ultimate reality?

You could put it like that but that doesn't explain it.

Could you explain it?

Yes and no. You can Be IT but you cannot explain it.

My brain is melting.

When you melt into all that is you will BE all that is.

Okay, so how was your day?

Perfect, and yours?

Perfect too.

I am glad you realized that.

That is pointing back to ultimate reality, isn't it?

Yes.

Some of this is almost scary.

It threatens the flesh. I told you it wasn't time.

You told me it wasn't time.

You see the hidden meanings, the veiled mysteries, and they are everywhere.

I know. You said you couldn't describe the infinite.

This is beyond the infinite.

The Universe Speaks

January 17

12:54 PM
Talia, the whole dream sequence—and "my ashes were my essence there" and acceptance—was enlightening.

> G had had a dream. In that dream Talia mentioned to him that her ashes were her essence while she was on earth, but they were not the real true her.

That's what I am here for. To enlighten. No mystery is unreachable, whether you understand it or not. I'm here to enlighten.

Mysterious statement.

It can be.

And authenticity was brought up.

That's the core of the essence of anything. The authenticity of it.

1:03 PM
Pleasure is not wrong, and it is something one should not feel guilty about.

2:12 PM
He told me that I'm a jewel in His crown.

Thank you for sharing that. I always felt you were.

Your eyes were opened the day we met; that's part of what you saw. You also saw my footsteps were ordered exactly by His love.

You gave your life to wake us up.

I lived my life to wake you up. My pleasure in this is indescribable.

I feel that.

And that's but a small portion. When I left that Thanksgiving Day you felt emptiness from my going. You wanted only to be with me that evening, and your seeing my spirit in the hallway that night and my speaking to you was a taste of what was to come.

I know, I felt as if it were a premonition of some sort. Were you aware of it?

My spirit was completely aware, although my flesh wasn't totally aware of it. Did I not say to you that you're not always aware or conscious of whom you influence and yet you influence regardless? Let your influence be always positive. There is a lot of your life that others can learn

Collection

from. That's why we've brought you into this so often. You've found profound meaning in every photo you've seen of me. In everything you've heard I did or didn't do. In my interests and disinterests, drawings, writings, and other things. You've found meaning in it all and it all means something. We all are complex beings beyond imagination, so how could it be otherwise?

5:45 PM
Sometimes the tip of the iceberg is inverted.

You've told me that twice now.

8:15 PM
I discussed this with someone and we concluded that sometimes you could see a huge amount and still miss the point.

That's exactly it, in part.

Is there more?

Yes.

I mean right now?

Do I have to tell you again it's all now?

No, I'm just trying to understand and make it understandable.

You do understand and it's all understandable. The issue is perceiving that that is real and dispensing with the illusion. Most labor under illusion by submitting to the illusion, creating more illusion. When the illusion is dropped the scales are removed from your eyes. With this new vision is freedom born, and you see reality was right in front of your face all along. When you experience this you will wonder how you couldn't have seen it, for it was there all along.

January 19

12:55 PM
This forced beta is insane.

Yes, slow down and expand your consciousness.

Wild horses.

Rein them in. That's better, quietness and stillness. That's where the Voice is heard and the unknown known.

I feel like you're my life.

The Universe Speaks

I'm not your life but I'm a large part of it. The Life is the light of man and that is us all.

You're precious, you know.

I know; so are you, you know.

Yes, okay.

You don't sound very convinced.

I'm totally convinced. Precious, that's me.

That's because you believe me.

I absolutely believe you.

Some things are self-evident; you shouldn't have to be told them to know them.

Sometimes I think maybe I waste your time.

I have forever; it's where you are that time becomes an issue. You knew me before.

I know.

We have a heart connection that cannot be broken.

I know.

That means more to me than I could ever express.

    Both Talia and G said this at the same time.

That last sentence was my voice also. Our voice is One. You know precisely what's on my mind.

So you've said but that's still somewhat of a mystery.

It is a mystery and it is true. With precision thought on the subject at hand you see clearly what's on my mind. You have described this as the download. You have an agile mind. That, with your sincerity and willingness, allows you to follow.

January 20

8:12 PM
Talia, I had forgotten about your perfect pumpkin pie at Thanksgiving. That was the very best I'd ever had.

I'm glad you enjoyed it.

You put something extra in it, didn't you?

Collection

I put my good intentions into all I did, and that was the something extra.

Your mom said you insisted on making that pie that day.

I did and I appreciated your comments on it to me that day.

I was sincere when I told you that was the best I'd ever had and that I normally didn't even like pumpkin pie.

That day wasn't so normal.

Tell me about it.

I am.

I asked you if you really made it; you answered, "Yes, I really made it." I think I said, "Wow, it's really good, best I ever had." You said, "Thank you," and smiled, along with your trademark eye contact. Something happened there.

Yes it did.

What?

I showed you who you were and how to live.

That's absolutely true, you did.

I also knew you would forget and I would have to remind you, although I didn't know what it meant at the time.

You got that? That's awesome beyond belief!

No it's not.

January 21

9:24 AM
What would you like to know?

What you have to say.

I've said everything you need to know for now.

What about your contemporaries, friends, classmates?

I would like them to know not to rebel against what was meant to be. My going was not anyone's fault, it was meant to be. I would like them to stand up and be who they are, be who they are meant to become. There isn't one who wasn't touched by my life. There isn't one there who isn't touched by my going. I would like them to let my touch bring them life.

That's beautiful.

All life is beautiful.

It was an honor for me to be a part of their lives. I want them to know to believe in themselves and to trust their heart. Some are angry—that's natural—but let it go. That's enough for now.

10:12 AM
Walk. Interesting conclusions will come to you.

11:48 AM
I didn't go very far.

You don't have to go very far to get what you need.

What was that bright line of white light that went into my mid-section earlier?

That was the energy of the universe. That was me.

10:05 PM
That was nice what you said about me. That you can't get too much of my photos or me. You honor me, and your heart is pure. You almost didn't write the last part.

It sounds egotistical.

But it's not—it's true. You have an affinity for true treasure and you can't have this without a heart that's true.

You are a true treasure.

Yes, I know this. You should also see this in others, including yourself.

January 23

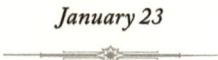

12:31 PM
Talia, I seem to be having a hard time getting there today.

That's because you're perceiving here as there. Here's not there, it's here, and it's right now.

I'm there!

Well, you're here and when you are here, you hear. There, you'll nearly always have a hard time. Having an easy time is much more fun.

Collection

I like having fun.

So do I.

It's all right to prove things, but endless questioning can be debilitating.

I never doubt you, Talia; it's me I doubt sometimes.

And I refer you back to my lesson to believe in yourself. The problem with words is that truth transcends thought and words most often stimulate thought. It's the walk, not the thought. If you'll notice, when you're completely spontaneous it's most often without thought, for none is needed. The Truth already lives within you. Now you see why the interconnectedness of all things cannot be explained but only experienced. In Oneness is direct knowledge found, and it is obtained without words. It also transcends knowledge, for to know all things is to know no thing.

Hard to explain, isn't it?

There is no adequate explanation. We can talk around the borders, but piercing insight will not be found with words.

7:27 PM
Truth is reality and that's just the way it is.

That IS a fact.

Talia, why do not people where you are say more than they do?

Many don't have a message. Also, they are not allowed to interfere with many things in our lives.

January 24

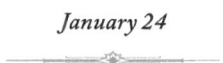

12:58 PM
I want to talk to you but I can't think of anything to ask. So, hello, Talia.

Hello. I'm always here.

That's great, and I figured you'd make a lesson of it.

Also you're not thinking is often the best place to be to be here.

I don't think as often as possible.

No, you don't. You overthink many things.

You're right.

The Universe Speaks

Of course I am.

"I am"; that really says a lot, doesn't it?

More than you think.

"More than you think"—that's good, very clever.

Thank you, you should try that more often, the quick turning of a tune.

You're talking about harmony, aren't you?

Yes, harmony is more than you think also. Harmony is speed perfected, and velocity has very little to do with it. This is instantaneous. Love is harmony slowed down to the perfect vibrational rhythm. Respect the rhythm and the experience is yours.

I wish I could explain the download.

I wish we could too.

It's beyond words, isn't it?

Far beyond.

Love is the Alpha and Omega, isn't it?

Love is the beginning and the end, yes.

I love you.

I know you do, from the beginning and until the end.

What happens at the end?

A new beginning; it's ALL spherical.

And IT never ends.

You're beyond awesome.

I'm beyond anything you could think.

Well, that's something not to think about.

You should try it.

We kind of went full circle.

Told you it was all spherical.

Collection

January 25

8:46 AM
Talia, I don't have much time, but I just want to say hello and good morning to you.

Good morning to you, and I told you that you didn't have much time.

What are you going to do today?

I'm going to help people, as always; that's my great pleasure.

Hope I can be a part of it.

You are. The subtleties of you speaking my truth are bringing forth fruit, even now.

That's nice to hear; sometimes it feels like plagiarism.

You've said that's okay as long as you're original about it, and we're original about it. ☺

You make me laugh.

That's my nature: a giver of laughter.

12:36 PM
You said synchronization.

That refers to what we spoke of about harmony. The best visualization I can give you is to look at the heart I gave my mom. That speaks volumes. That's the rhythm of life in perfect harmony. You feel my love for her and it is boundless. Our heart does the same, G.

You are also a bringer of tears.

This love evokes only perfect emotion.

> The heart that Talia is speaking of is the one that she showed my mom on the computer as a gift for me, which Rebecca, a medium, confirmed was her guidance. It is a pink glass heart with a carved pattern of two intertwined hearts.

11:11 PM
My love for you knows no bounds.

The Universe Speaks

January 27

10:50 AM
What do you want to do today?

I want to walk in the Spirit.

You can. You are right now. All things are yours. That's something you haven't got yet. Take a walk.

11:04 AM
Your giving me the alphabet—what does that mean?

> During a meditation, G heard the words, "I'm giving you my alphabet."

That means I'm giving you an ability to communicate. It's a way to communicate in a divine way. When you are talking to me you are talking to yourself. You don't have to put an initial or a letter—we're all one. Letters alone make no sense.

January 30

1:04 PM
Talia, is there anything you want to tell me?

Yes, focus. On the vibrational harmony of the universe. Then you'll sense what you sense is missing.

7:01 PM
Talia, I don't know where to start. I feel like we're behind.

We're not behind; we're right on time. ☺

You emphasized "right on time."

That's because we're right on time.

It's just that things aren't coming as quickly.

No, they are more condensed. Everything contracts and expands like the breath of life. These truths are coming to you more condensed, and not always are they accompanied by words. For many of these truths there are no words to adequately express them.

In the Supreme Silence are these things revealed, and none can know them without entry into it.

Collection

Then how are we going to convey it?

By walking in it.

Seems like it would be easier just to write about it.

It might seem like that on the surface, but just to write about it or talk about it will never fulfill your need, which is to walk in the fullness of the Spirit. God is no respecter of persons. If one can do it then all can do it, and all can do it only as One.

Looks like we've got a long way to go.

The length of the path is up to you.

Then I want a short path.

The speed is up to you.

Then can we move things quicker than we think?

No, you can move things as quickly as you think.

That was you on the horse the other night.

Yes, and that was you following on the same path—as the elk. You're focused on my teachings and we are bound by love.

Love never fails!

No, it does not. There is no greater power anywhere, for God is love. You feel his outpouring for His people.

I saw a vision of the hand of God holding a pitcher with oil/love pouring down onto the earth. That was totally awesome.

Yes, it is, isn't it?

I have no words.

This is something else that can't be expressed to them.

8:42 PM
Talia, that is some pretty awesome stuff here.

Yes, it is, isn't it.

It is.

It really is.

The Universe Speaks

January 31

12:58 PM
Offense?

I cannot offend. Some will take offense at my words, but I cannot offend.

"The unlikely assassin" has periodically popped in my mind for a couple of months. What's that?

That's things which appear harmless that would take away your life.

Can't judge by appearance.

Not outward appearance.

February 2009

February 3

4:48 PM
Talia . . .

Did you enjoy your day?

Yes, I did, and you?

Every day I have is perfect.

What did you do today?

I moved people to sense me.

Sensing you is sensing your consciousness to change them into His image and likeness, isn't it?

It is, and more to restore hope. Hope leads to harmony and harmony is where it's all at.

Did you tell that lady you were weak? The one that told your mom that?

> I had gone to a "healer." This healer told me that Talia's energy was weak—weak because I was holding her back. I knew at that moment that this woman was not really in touch with the Spirit. Not all healers are

Collection

"real." There is no holding Talia back, as Talia has said herself. But her words did have an effect on me.

No, what she sensed was her own weakness or disharmony with the universe, resulting in a distortion of the message. I confirmed who I was. My primary point was for my mom to move on and not blame herself any longer. There is absolutely nothing she could have done to change what was to be. My work there in the flesh was done and it was my time to move on. Don't blame yourself either.

No, you explained it; I was powerless to help.

I didn't need help. I told you I accepted you as you are; you've also accepted me as I am. Why are you stopping?

I'm not stopping.

Then keep going. It's human to grieve, but she needs to know her guilt is groundless, without foundation whatsoever. She finished her work with me in a most glorious way. It's true to say she raised me perfectly, because she did. I learned balance from her every day because she showed me the balance in everything she did. Her absolute determination in raising me in the best possible way resulted in her raising me in the best possible way.

I sure see the fruit of it.

And you will always know them by their fruit.

Is that all?

No, that's not all.

You don't have a mother's love for me. This is a very difficult time for her, but she is a very strong person and she gets stronger daily. She will carry on my message of change to change others. She has a most wonderful path set out before her, and she is learning who she is, and that's someone who will help others in a most profound way. She will touch many with the Light. She should dance for what is to come.

February 4

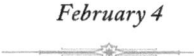

1:15 PM
Hello, my love.

Hello to you. ☺

You're feeling good today.

I always feel good. Mom's feeling better.

369

Your message works.

My message is not without power; of course it works.

I'm glad you used another voice to confirm these things.

It's important to do that at times to shock into realization. We here rejoice when our message comes through clearly and is received. We have a special relationship, as I've said before, and such clarity will be doubted if not confirmed from time to time. The good news is I'm in a perfect position to confirm my word to the sincere in heart. "Sincerity moves heaven" is a true statement and a pointer to deeper truth. Sincerity of heart speaks of a selflessness that doesn't hinder.

3:48 PM
Talia, how did you get so perfect?

Because He is.

5:00 PM (Approximately)
The message is not just for there, it's for here also.

February 6

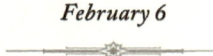

1:01 PM
Why were you so mad at the astrologers?

      G asked this to God.

Because they took me out of it and glorified themselves.

7:51 PM
You thrive in your distractions; you've learned how to use them as a catalyst of thought.

Well, that's good because I'm distracted now.

You see them as eating your time away from what's important.

I do.

But the point is you've learned to use them. I told you everything was meant for your enlightenment. You're beginning to realize that.

I am now.

Collection

You are now; that's why you're getting this. You asked me to reveal secrets, so I am. You've revealed secrets you never thought you would, and on many levels. Secrets are mysteries. Mysteries revealed are secrets no more.

You've got a lot more to say about this, Talia; why are you stopping?

I'm not stopping, the mystery is just continuing.

Here's where I want to say that's a mystery to me.

It is until it's revealed.

And your game goes on.

It does.

February 7

12:59 PM

      G started to wonder where I was.

She's with friends.

6:21 PM

Hello, Talia. I'm a little wet and cold.

Hello. No matter what physical state you are in you can still talk to me. You see why I said she was with friends? You do more than you know.

7:48 PM

The light of God is love. The mass of God is all things, events, deeds. He has expanded Himself to know Himself or to share Himself with Himself, which is all things. That's why all happenings are at once because Once is all everything is. To know this you must know your Self. To know your Self is to know God, for God is One. All things are God's; that's why I say all things are yours. If you knew your Self, you know this. You saw His love in His creation when you looked into my eyes, and when you were looking into my eyes you were looking into your eyes. It was a reflection of your Self. We are fearfully and wonderfully made. That's also why I said that to deny yourself is to deny God.

Man is made in God's image. It's not good for man to live alone. That's why He created children in His image, that He may experience Himself again, growing, learning. You asked, "What's God's light?" That's my answer in part. The only way light could ever escape the gravitational mass of Everything is by God's love, the greatest force of all. Remember that in the beginning, darkness was on the face of the deep, and God said, "Let there be Light." That was His Word personified, the offspring of the Father of Lights. We are His Lights, you, I, and all beings of Light. The Light is the life of man.

Mathematical equations prove that light cannot escape the gravitational force of a collapsing star if it's large enough, yet this is as a speck when compared to the All. But with Him are all things possible. It was the revelation of the Light of life you saw in my eyes, and you've never been the same. His Light purifies, it changes, it drives away the darkness of delusion, and it is Life. This is the only Life, for it is a manifestation of all that is, which is Everything. All sourced from Him for all that is.

Hard to explain, isn't it?

As I've said before, words are wholly inadequate. This is but a thumbnail sketch.

Well, I appreciate the answer.

I know you do and you're welcome.

His Light is blinding.

It can be. It can also be enlightening. Again the choice is left up to the receiver.

9:51 PM
Talia, I heard about a man, a law enforcement officer, whose family had an experience with you recently, but he didn't "believe all this Talia stuff." Then he had a dream where he went to the Middle East and felt he needed a gun but also felt he couldn't trust anybody there. He met a man there he didn't think he could trust. The man said that he didn't think he could trust him either, but he had showed him that the "legend of Talia" is true, so he trusted him. Any words of wisdom on that?

Yes, when my "legend" is proven true, it creates trust. Believe me, our work here never stops and much of it is to dispel the illusion. I told you it was a battle of light and darkness. The darkness is ignorance and unbelief. It's not that they don't believe in anything; that's easy to fix. It's that they believe what they've been told and taught to believe, and it's largely lies. NO lies with the truth, and the truth is what sets you free. That's what I'm here for, to set you free. And I will say it again, nothing is better than freedom.

Talia, thank you for your words of wisdom.

You're welcome and you have them too you know.

So you've said.

Yes, and I'm saying it again.

I receive your truth.

Collection

See, words of wisdom.

What about this man?

He'll come around. He's a warrior, and he's just verifying some things, and there is nothing wrong with that.

Talia, I just start reading this and got caught up in it and can't stop.

I don't blame you.

Thanks for the laugh. Goodnight.

Goodnight.

February 8

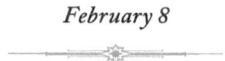

4:48 AM
Good morning.

Good morning. You were flowing early today. That work you did earlier will work.

That's good.

That's very good. It's important to reach out to others, and that time has begun.

An object is a process in flux. Don't concern yourself with positrons; there are others doing that. The reverse process of a photon is yet to be discovered. They call it dark matter, and it's so weak that it cannot be measured with any existing equipment.

You could explain it.

I could, but they are not in a place to receive it and it would be wholly rejected.

That's because the answer is spiritual and matter is a misnomer, isn't it?

It is.

Guess there's no sense yakking about it then.

Not really. They must be prepared and that is a process.

You know they are going to say a photon doesn't have a negative because it has no electrical charge.

Most will.

The Universe Speaks

1:02 PM
Talia, good afternoon.

Good afternoon to you.

More forced beta.

That's why their learning is hindered. It also causes frustration.

I'm a bit frustrated with their frustration.

You don't have to go there. You take them out of themselves so they can look back in. When you do that, you see the light come on. You thought I would be where you are when you taught me. Our roles are reversed.

Does this have anything to do with photons?

It very well could.

Does it?

Of course. It's all interconnected, intertwined.

February 9

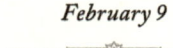

1:03 PM
Hello, Talia.

Hello, how are you today?

I'm fine, but I'm suspecting this forced beta causes temporary insanity.

It really can; that was very rare in primitive societies.

Still is.

That's because they have a different view of time. Another reason I hated to wear a watch, a shackle around the wrist.

I wonder when they'll figure out it's killing them?

Some won't figure it out until it kills them; in the meantime they're being robbed.

Interesting term, "mean time."

That's really what it is.

You really do have to slow down to speed up, don't you?

Collection

Yes, and you also have to slow down to slow down. When they understand the illusion of time, things will change. Gravity curves space. Space and time are inseparable.

February 10

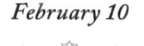

6:04 PM
Listen closely.

8:48 PM
Thank you, Talia, for confirming your words to me.

It was my pleasure to do that. You're not alone in this, and you shouldn't be overwhelmed. This should be quite common, and that's what we're trying to get them to see. We've given the formula for success, now it's just walking in it. I told you this used to be commonplace, but it's been forgotten.

9:14 PM
Goodnight, Talia.

It will be. Remember your dreams.

February 12

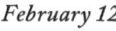

I want my friends to know to use their own words.

I want my friends to know to use their own words.

I want my friends to know to use their own words.

    Talia said that three distinct times.

February 13

Last night you said "suspend your mind," then we were off. There was so much.

It will come back when you need it, when it is time.

Suspend your mind.

375

Yes, do you see what I meant? You have power over it. It is yours to command and control. The body follows the mind and the spirit can play free.

That's the place to send it—into suspension.

That's a way of putting it. You must see it not as a commander, but a servant.

That's radical, but it works.

Everything I've told you works. Prove it. Haven't I proven my words to you every time?

You have.

Now you have too.

Precept upon precept, building up into Him in all things. This is multi-layered in every direction.

February 15

8:30 AM
Talia, you told me a while back that you "had a headache once."

Yes, that was a very bad one. The physical symptom was from a spiritual attack.

I suspected that when I heard about it.

The dark side knew I would be used to wake others up. That was the darkness trying to destroy the Light. I was just beginning to wake up, and the darkness saw I would not be deterred from the path of Light. There was an attempt before that to put me to sleep, but that didn't work either. It was an act of desperation that came with intense pain and fear; you know what that's like and it's the lie.

I didn't know that was you at first, because just about everybody has had a headache before.

When you hear the phrase "everything at once," know that speaks of the spiritual.

Thanks for clearing that up.

We're clearing it all up.

> When Talia was around six years old, she came into my room screaming in pain. Her eyes were bulging out of her head, and she was holding her head with her hands. I asked her what was wrong. I was freaked out at her pain. She said her head was killing her. I calmed her down and was able to get rid of her headache. The other attempt Talia mentions was when she was only two weeks old, she got a really high fever, so high she had

to be kept in the hospital. After running many blood tests, the doctors were never able to figure out what caused the fever. There was no sign of a virus or a bacterial infection.

February 16

1:07 PM
You will deliver your masterpiece, won't you, Talia?

YES, I WILL.

6:50 PM
You need a frame of reference. That's what we're doing here, a frame of reference. To succor victory in the maelstrom, secure your peace; verify the existence of what you know is real and get relief from the games of people.

The endless folly of man.

It isn't endless, it just seems that way.

Maelstrom is the false spin, isn't it?

It's the counterfeit that causes the confusion.

February 17

9:56 AM
Thank you for being a light.

You're welcome. The day's better already, isn't it?

It is.

When you have something to say, speak your heart, not your mind.

It's easier to write about this if you're outside yourself. Viewing yourself as an object, a process in flux. It removes you from the person you think you are and reveals the person you are. When I said you were one of the greatest thinkers, it had nothing to do with IQ and everything to do with what you think about and how you think of it.

Never thought of that.

Yes, you have, you just have trouble remembering it.

The Universe Speaks

February 19

6:00 PM

Let's talk of the interplay of energies. This is a dance, a dance of joy. Some call it the dance of Shiva.

I've heard of that.

That's an example of a pattern shown of creation and of how to live in victory by dancing above the ignorance of man. I said that yours was a shadow world. I said that because it's a shadow of the heavenly, of the real, yet most regard it as the only world and are convinced that the shadow is the real. We're attempting to dispel that illusion.

The intellect of man is trapped energies without the interplay or the joy, therefore without true understanding. They beg for understanding, but deny themselves who they are, so their understanding remains darkened. Only in the light is the shadow seen, yet they ignore the light and consider the shadow real.

It's a real shadow.

It is a real shadow made of those things which do not appear. It is beyond linguistics, but by faith man can understand. I feel your frustration.

Sometimes I just think what's the use, this has all been talked about and written about.

You want to go away to a cabin in the woods.

That thought has crossed my mind more than once.

Sounds like a cozy place to be.

Yeah, warm and cozy.

Do you think you would be happy there?

Not really; figure you'll tell me it's a shadow of the real.

No, I would tell you it's a retreat from the battle. You're just frustrated. That's natural. Ignorance is frustrating. Insistence on it even more so. Let it go and keep doing what you're doing. We are making a difference in many lives and many more will come to conclusions of enlightenment. Remember, a lie is but for a moment.

I appreciate the encouragement.

That's okay; I know what it's like.

Collection

7:04 PM

The dime that appeared heads up . . .

> Talia is always leaving pennies around. G and I were talking about that and asked Talia why she doesn't leave dimes, just pennies. We left and when we returned, there was a dime, face up, in the planter. We told Talia that that was really cool! We asked how she did that.

We think of it and it is.

8:11 PM

Talia, this you've been talking about is referring to what Paul wrote, that things that are seen are not made of things that appear.

That's exactly right. They do not appear but by faith, in the unseen. Remember when we talked about the visible light spectrum and how limited that was? Why limit yourself? This we are talking about is limitless.

February 20

6:24 PM

Talia, hello. It was a great day.

Hello to you, and it was. ☺

What did you do today?

I moved people in the direction they needed to go. I rode my horse. I communed with the Father and His children. I spoke to a young girl; I told her that her Father loved her. I hung out with Mom and you and J and others. I did more today than you could ever write down. Do you want me to keep going?

No, not really. I can see any one of those could fill a book, but I appreciate you sharing.

I also sat in the garden and listened and watched the children play.

That's pertinent, isn't it?

Yes, those kinds of things one should make time for daily.

Quiet time.

Yes. In the Supreme Silence is where the soul communes with the One.

The Universe Speaks

February 21

12:57 PM
Talia, your loveliness has wounded me.

It's also brought you healing. All of this is as a two-edged sword. All physical is a reflection of the spiritual.

There's awesome depth to that—never-ending lessons!

Meditation on my words brings Life.

You are the most outstanding teacher.

The true spiritual is always outstanding. ☺

February 23

8:26 PM
March 5th is a subtle awakening from a shaking. It's a spiritual tremor.

What does that mean?

Be aware and you will see what I mean. It's too detailed to describe here; just be aware that an awakening begins then.

February 24

8:34 AM
Someone called you unequaled not long ago.

That was nice of her.

That's my mother and she is absolutely awesome. I wouldn't be who I am without her.

That's absolutely awesome.

It certainly is.

Collection

8:46 AM
Passion . . . love and compassion intertwined.

Interesting.

I got it from you!

I know, interesting.

Whatever you do affects infinity.

And beyond.

What is beyond infinity?

Everything.

6:10 PM
There's not a very little pelf [monies, riches] these days.

I had to look that up.

An end to a means.

Interesting way of putting it.

It's the worship of wealth, of gold, over the real and lasting. It's the disregard of the means and an acceptance of the method. The end result is making a god of money.

Lot of that nowadays.

That's coming to an end.

Well, three cheers, it must be party time.

It's time not to be a party of that.

February 25

1:14 PM
Talia, you told me one time you were in alpha and theta.

That's one of the secrets of how I was here, there. You can only receive spiritual truths in that consciousness, and that is the threshold.

You got that right.

You didn't think I would get it wrong, did you?

7:24 PM
What do you want to talk about?

What do you want to know?

Everything.

Into Everything is where we're going. Remember that in much knowledge is much grief; many have drawn back because of it.

I'm not a real big fan of grief.

You're not a fan of drawing back either.

Sounds like a dilemma.

Not if you're balanced.

Sometimes this is like a tightrope and a razor's edge.

It can seem that way. But you love pushing the envelope.

I'm pretty content to not push it also.

There's the balance.

February 27

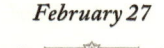

1:06 PM
I feel like I need an open-ended time frame to do this.

You do when you're this stressed. You need a calm mind and not chattering monkeys.

Distractions are a product of the mind. You can't think ahead and be here Now. To be here Now is no thought.

I think too much.

I already told you that. You've told others they do the same, now it's your time to see it in yourself.

Stupid world.

The world is in retrograde; don't get caught up in it.

Collection

March 2009

March 5

7:15 PM
Talia, hello to you. I just realized what day it is. I feel uneasy.

Talia had previously mentioned that this would be a significant day.

Don't feel uneasy. It's subtle, unnoticed by the world at large.

March 6

1:13 PM
Hello.

Hello. It's nice weather.

Yes, it is.

That co-worker of mine doesn't see the big picture.

No, he doesn't, he sees the bottom line. Most see the bottom line as what they do, but it's not—at least it shouldn't be.

I feel as thought there's been a breakthrough today on a world scale.

There has, for the true seekers. They are beginning to grow exponentially.

Fantastic.

I know what you mean.

You've never mentioned the weather to me before.

Well, it's a nice day.

It sure is.

We'll talk later.

Okay.

The Universe Speaks

6:53 PM
They want to create a crisis. So it can be solved.

I know whom you mean.

People should remember the test of truth when their liberties are curtailed.

Yeah, well, what should we do about it?

It is better to obey God rather than man. That's the true government. Being obedient to truth is ultimate freedom; obedience to a lie will always bring bondage on some level.

Seems simple enough.

It's all simple enough. It's deciding to decide that can become the dilemma.

March 7

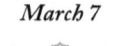

Talia, I just thought of something. That breakthrough on March 5th ties in exquisitely with "the Kingdom of Heaven comes not with observation."

It does, but your explaining it isn't necessary.

Okay, I just get enthusiastic.

You try to help us and we don't need it. Your job is to listen and record. A record of what's needed.

Thank you for everything and the correction.

It's an admonishment. I'm with you in all you do.

March 13

9:48 AM
Talia, you've been communicating with mostly symbols lately. Why is that?

Because words are inadequate for what I have to express. Words are also symbols of expression, but they are incomplete. When you've gotten words as an expression of deeper spiritual truth, they have always been accompanied by pictures, feelings, emotions, to complete your understanding of that truth. Truths are crystal clear but often come fractured, in part, appearing incomplete. A holographic symbol along with a particular emotion is meant to complete the picture, so that your understanding be not darkened.

Collection

Well, thanks for the words.

You're welcome.

"Tensegrity" was me and that's the type of structure I'm building. One that lasts.

That's good.

That's what I meant when I said I was a foundation you could depend on.

I'm so glad you're back.

I never left.

10:26 AM
      G heard from his friend Curt, who is also in Spirit.

The dragon can appear as anything. He's a mythical beast, remember. Talia is a great example to us all. She was a spiritual warrior there and she created with her thoughts. She had a keen sense of justice. She was a light to the world and she still is.

Appreciate your kind words.

It's the truth.

She sure blew me away when we met.

You were very fortunate to meet her. Good thing you listened.

That was a gift.

It sure was. You know we couldn't do this if she hadn't taught you how.

Yeah, I know.

Got to go.

Okay.

Talia?

He has things to do. I told you, we're very busy here. You have to go.

I know.

Thank you again for listening.

Thank you, Talia, I love you!

I love you too.

Thank you for your love. I've got everything I need!

The Universe Speaks

I told you. ☺

1:06 PM
Specify what you want; be particular. The universe speaks and it answers. When you're vague with your requests or answers, so the universe seems to be. Be a good steward of the manifold mysteries. They are everywhere.

6:59 PM
Talia, what's this about you coming back in eleven years?

> My mom had had a meeting with an astrologer who told her that Talia was going to come back, reincarnated, in eleven years. I was not happy about this. I wanted Talia to be there when I got there.

I have that option.

Are you?

That remains to be seen.

That's not a very satisfying answer.

You should be content in whatsoever state you're in.

Are you?

Why would I?

Good question. Why would you?

I can do more here now than I could there now.

I know; what about in eleven years?

That remains to be seen.

Are you coming back in eleven years?

That depends on the choices of others, but I do have that option.

What do you mean, the choices of others?

If at that time I can help others more there than here, I do have the option to return.

Will you?

It really does depend on the choices of others. If their decisions are the right ones, the need for me to come back will not be so great. But if their foolish choices snowball, then perhaps my coming in the flesh would be used to awaken them.

Collection

So are you coming back?

I know many things but I do not know everything. That's why I told you it remains to be seen. I was not being coy. I myself must wait and see.

Coy?

Pretending to be something I'm not.

I know you couldn't do that.

And I'm reaffirming it to you. You just gave the right answers, and that "being" in more than one place at a time is correct, as you well know by your own experience. I cannot lie, and I told my mom that I would be with her always and that I would greet her here. There is absolutely nothing to be traumatized about, so tell her not to worry. I will always be here for her.

Thanks for that. My first impression was also a bit worrisome.

Well, don't worry. That really is a waste of time and energy.

Isn't that the truth.

It is.

Be at peace G. I told you before, you worry too much.

Must be genetic.

No, it's your own decision.

Stupid decision then.

Then why make it?

Good question.

Yes, I always do ask those.

Thanks for the laugh.

Told you I haven't changed, only grown.

I feel your concern for Frankie.

She should leave the guilt behind. There is no need for it.

Manipulations?

It's unwitting. It's meant well but it needs to be guided by the Spirit.

The Universe Speaks

March 14

1:19 PM
I'm listening.

That's good.

How's your mom doing today?

She's fine. She's learning to find her way.

March 15

7:49 AM
It's not wrong for you wanting to not be associated with foolish people.

I was questioning myself whether that was harsh judgment.

It is harsh judgment; it is also true judgment.

8:25 PM
Seven planes in the spiritual world?

> G and I were reading a book that said that there were seven planes in the spiritual world. G asked Talia about that.

That's a limited view of looking at it.

March 16

Don't push my view on others; there is timing in everything. You will feel, hear, or see the harmony; then is there flow.

I was a little overenthusiastic to share.

In quietness there is harmony. It's just another lesson. Learn from it.

That was a little pride cropping up.

Collection

Knowledge puffs up, love builds up.

Yeah, loose lips sink ships.

They can.

March 17

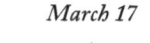

6:09 PM
Talia, I want to talk with you.

Okay.

That piece you wrote when you were in the third or fourth grade moved me as much as anything I've ever read.

> G is speaking about a poem Talia wrote for me for Mother's Day. The words were: "My heart has the power to swim the Pacific Ocean, round up a hundred stallions, move ten mountains, fight three bears, and jump over the moon to get to You! I Love You!" She had written them over a heart she had painted with watercolors.

That's not just the content, it's the intent you see in it.

That is so true. It's the way you wrote it, the watercolors . . . I can tell your whole heart was in it.

It was from a pure heart of love. Everything you do that matters and is lasting will be from there.

Just writing that made me laugh with your joy.

That's where it came from, a pure heart full of love. That's the joy undeniable.

March 19

6:30 AM
I knew my time here, in the flesh, no matter how long, was short. That's why I made the most of every moment.

The Universe Speaks

March 20

12:57 PM

Your interpretation of my dream to J and my being at lunch was correct. It's also to let him know that it's an everyday thing.

> In J's dream he was with Talia, having lunch. J said it was like a normal day with Talia, only in a dream.

That was beautiful Talia. Thank you for that.

I care for him deeply.

That Love is the Life of man.

I'm glad you got that.

I feel it from you and I remember your words.

You do remember it; you reconstruct it by love. That's the greatest power of all, and unfailing. It's important to remember love. When you feel it wane in your life, reconstruct it. It is woven into the fabric of everything, for without it nothing is.

Talia, you're everything to me.

I reveal Everything to you.

Talia, you've got a lot more to say about that, don't you?

I do.

So . . .

It's not time.

March 21

1:01 PM

Nobody does it alone, it just appears that way. Things are not at all what they appear to be.

That statement is completely comprehensive.

It is. It is the nature of reality. Things are not meant to appear as they are.

Thus, the mystery.

Collection

And the wonderful discoveries. As I've said, you can only be bored when you do not know who you are.

March 22

1:15 PM
When I spoke to you that we were dealing in facts and the spherical ring of purity that should surround everything you do . . .

Yes.

You didn't believe it then.

I wasn't sure what I saw.

Yes, you were.

But I didn't have the meaning.

That's beside the point. You did have the meaning, you just didn't look into the point for clarification. These points of interest are penetrated by pure focused thought and yielding your heart to the Spirit, then listening, intently, expecting the answer. The voice of truth is within you and is known in silence.

In the Supreme Silence the Voice is always manifest.

6:52 PM
The river of life is always flowing and you're in it.

I see it.

How could you not? The universe speaks and it speaks of One . . . I spoke to you once . . . World of One, remember?

I do.

You're seeing my words to you repeated through others before they hear them. Confirmations of light, changes. That is verification of truth, specifically that the universe speaks and is a reflection of Mind.

You only have one place to be.

The Universe Speaks

March 23

1:03 PM
This place, my office, is like a safe haven.

It's a place of fellowship for sure, but your peace surrounds you wherever you are. Remember reckless abandon; there's a place for it.

The power of openness.

Never thought of that.

You've just forgotten it. Be careful for nothing.

We know everything, we've just forgotten it?

You came from Everything; how could you not know it? When you see someone who thinks they know everything, they really do, on a metaphysical level. That's that deep knowing I was talking about.

That butterfly on a time line is also the symbol of infinity.

I'm glad you remembered that. It's bringing the past and the future back into one point where there is no time.

March 26

I'm proud of J.

> Talia is speaking about being proud of her uncle for passing a really high-level test.

March 27

12:30 PM
Talia, Thanksgiving, when you stopped eating and just looked down at your plate, thinking or listening. That was uncharacteristic of you; what was going on?

I was told that I would be your mentor, and you heard it said to me.

Collection

As you say it now I do remember it.

Like overhearing a private conversation; you felt like you were eavesdropping.

That's right, I did.

If you weren't meant to hear it you wouldn't have.

March 28

12:59 PM
I've got one page left in this notebook, Talia.

All you need is One.

I know what you mean.

I know you do. All there is, is One. You see the systematic progression to the Master's level?

Yes, what we're doing this week.

The steps are ordered, in a certain order.

That's a reflection of the real, the spiritual.

Yes, and that lasts. What you do on that level is forever. Most of the things of this world are transient, temporary. As a matter of fact, the only thing that's not is that that is blended with the real world, the eternal world. That's the world without end, the infinite, the eternal, and it is your birthright to live there. And there is no waiting—it's yours now. That's a hard thing to comprehend, but that's the truth. That's the truth that sets you free, free from all the cares of this world. You still think you have to work to get there, but I'm telling you it's yours now, and when you walk there you know it's yours.

You always save the best for last, don't you?

I always save the best for now and where I'm at is always Now, it's also always the best. ☺

You're the best thing that's ever happened to me.

I'm as close to It as you can get.

That I believe.

You should.

You said that like you said, "Yes, I made it," after I asked you twice whether you had made the pie.

I just didn't understand why you didn't understand after my first answer to the same question.

I didn't know you so well then.

Well, I'm glad you know me better now.

So am I. You're giving me the last word.

Yes!

I don't deserve it.

Yes, you do.

Thanks.

March 30

12:56 PM
Hello, Talia.

Hello.

I set an example for you. Although most things came easily for me I still worked hard at them.

So you did. I appreciate that.

I know you do, more than you know.

April 2009

April 1

1:01 PM
>While having lunch, G looked up at the ceiling of the restaurant and noticed swirls and circles in the ceiling.

That's what it looks like here.

Collection

April 2

8:53 AM
To clarify: the mountain of Esau is the mountain of the flesh. The mountain of Zion is the spiritual mountain we've been talking about all along. The one point above it is the one point where all things are.

April 3

11:50 AM
Talia, I wanted to share your words and story last night, but thanks for telling me he wasn't ready.

I told you because he wasn't ready; his religious doctrine has infected him.

Interesting term, *infected*.

It's an infection that can cause a sickness of missing the truth. Any bondage can always be traced to a sickness. He is allowing them to tell him what to believe. That's why it's important to know the truth before you proclaim something as truth.

12:55 PM
All things are not designed to appear as they are; they are designed to appear as they appear to be. That's why I said an object was an event, something happening NOW, because it's all energy.

That's something to think about.

And the more you think of it the more you will become what you truly are, and that's an event in the process of becoming One, One with all things, which is all there is. It's not to do away with who you are, for who you are is all things, events, happenings. All things are yours.

There's a unique way of looking at it.

That's the way it is.

I love having lunch with you.

It's something to feed the soul for sure. If it looks like I leave things out, I don't; it's the design.

I know you will always eventually explain it anyway.

I do to those who listen.

The Universe Speaks

April 4

12:50 PM
Hello, Talia.

Hello.

Anything you want to say?

Yes, lots. Things are breaking down.

How's that?

All things that are built on lies.

Seems reasonable.

It is. It's also God's mercy. It's a false foundation and it's cracked and crumbling. You will see people panic because of it, because they believed the lie that was told them.

Any suggestions?

Yes, live your life as it's supposed to be lived, as who you are and not as who someone else says you are. Most push and press others to live as they want them to live for their convenience and profit. They attempt, sometimes insist even, to get you to be someone you're not, to live a life of another. But that's not who you are and it will never satisfy. Resist the evil and it will flee. These basic principles must be received and lived in before one can move on. My saying it will never satisfy also means it will never satisfy the one trying to get you to change into something you're not.

April 5

6:49 AM
You know, we're having a conversation here; it's not just you waiting for me to say something. It's a two-way street.

I know.

Well, when I told you that you didn't have to explain my words, I didn't mean that you had nothing to say. You've acted offended; it wasn't my intent to offend you.

I know it wasn't, Talia. I'm not offended; I know you cannot offend.

I know you aren't, but when you act offended it hinders the dialogue with others.

Collection

My apologies.

There is no need to apologize; I just want to make you aware of not acting like something you aren't. The universe speaks and its voice is in all things. A good listener is a good healer, but I want you to know that your words are important too. Words have meaning, and they can be used to press symbols of truth into the minds of others.

Thank you for your words.

Thank you for yours.

7:50 AM
That's why many entities do not communicate; they are waiting to be spoken to. If you acknowledge their presence, their being, you will get an answer.

Speaking the truth in love.

Of course. Sincerity and compassion can move the immovable.

April 6

9:45 AM
Talia, earlier you said something to me but I couldn't write it down. I think it was, "You will reach a plateau, and you can see a long way there, but you're not at the top yet, so you must push because there is a tendency to stop there." But I want your exact words only.

Exact words aren't necessary, exact meanings are. Words are symbols, thought pictures, ideas forming. Words only must always be interpreted for the proper meaning anyway, so why get hung up on them? A perfectly phrased verse will still be skewed by what we talked about before, preconceived notions formed on the wrong path.

1:28 PM
There are many who blame their mediocrity on others. It's your choice to be outstanding or average.

April 8

8:36 PM
Talia, you're right, it does just get better.

When have I not been?

When you ordered food from the trash can in the drive-through.

You got me there, but it was for learning. ☺ *See, we're still laughing about it.*

That's priceless.

It really is.

April 11

2:40 PM
Last night I saw purple spirals of energy, vortices of violet, and many other colors. I seemed to see myself living in parallel universes simultaneously. Dreaming this life as another.

You're starting to see things as they are, many of which there are no words for.

You said I saw success in your eyes.

You did. When what you saw is in harmony and balance, there can only be success. Remember what I said that was a reflection of.

Myself?

It was the Creator in His creation symbolized by planets, solar systems, and galaxies, innumerable. The structure of the universe is the love of the Creator in His creation. It's the stuff by which all is held together. All continued into One and it was a reflection of yourself.

This is beyond me.

No, it's contained within you, every bit of it.

Well hidden then.

That may be but how can you deny what you know?

6:56 PM
Peaches.

Peaches.

Yes, peaches.

Okay.

> While driving, G and I were talking about how Talia and I had such an amazing relationship. I told him that there were times that Talia and I

Collection

argued, but to keep the argument from getting out of control we had a code word that one of us would say to deflate the argument and get us back on track. The word we used was *peaches*. When we said it, it made us stop and laugh, thereby ending the argument.

April 12

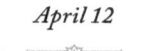

1:55 PM

G: I had a vision. I was going down the stairs and on the left was the past, learning from experience. On the right was the future, now learning by the spirit, by joy, by peace, by love, etc. Talia said, "Choose one." I was looking and thinking about it and was drawn to the right. Talia said, "They are both good; choose one." I said, "I choose right" and she said, "That's even better." Water was flowing across my path, waters of life, over my head, but I could still breathe. "Talia, I did not know there were any doorways there."

This is in any and all directions, the truth awaits you. And its entering into is by choice.

I saw letters again floating in the air, in the water. Different colors swirling in the air and water. Words of spiritual states of being: ecstasy, joy, peace, love, giving . . . many of the letters looked Hebrew. The lessons were as easy as just receiving them . . .

What you saw was a taste of where I LIVE.

You got it made.

I'm showing you that you do also.

I saw that the greatest gift was the gift of giving for the one giving.

That's something that not many know. If people would seek diligently for what they could give instead of what they could receive it would change the world.

April 13

AM

You have thanked me every day since we have been talking.

I have given you a new focus.

I am like a fairy.

April 19

G: While camping in the Redwood Forest, I dreamt last night that Talia walked through an arched gate of a white picket fence and opened it for a girl about her age. There was a brick building behind them that seemed to be a school. They turned right and continued walking down a sidewalk, talking, smiling, laughing. Talia looked at me and smiled, but they continued walking and talking. Talia seemed to be showing her around and teaching her.

April 21

Talia, that dream I had . . .

It was real.

1:33 PM
Before you can heal others you must heal yourself, complete the circle.

G thought about this. He realized that his journey years ago had gone full circle. It had led him through Santa Barbara, and up the coast, then inland. When his route was drawn on the map it looked like a butterfly. He thought about his desire while on that trip to meet someone who would teach him things. He thought that person would be an old man, one that he would meet in the redwoods.

April 23

G: While at a class in the redwoods. . . .

As a test I poured out a handful of birdseed on the ground without thought. I then poured out a second handful that I prayed over. I asked that that handful be blessed by God's Spirit and that it would bring a blessing to whatever animal found it, to give that animal exactly what it needed.

Collection

I really poured my good intentions into it. To my surprise the first pile was gone within two days while the blessed pile (one foot away from the first) wasn't touched. The third day it was still untouched. It was finally disturbed some on the fourth day, with some gone, and on the fifth day it was mostly gone. This was a pretty good surprise to me as I had suspected it would have been the opposite, so I asked Talia about it.

Talia, what does that mean?

It means most will take the mundane, everyday familiar over the spiritual. Most will exhaust that first.

Preprogramming.

April 24

9:00 PM
We are clothing the truth in new garments.

April 30

You said something to me the other day about parallel aspects.

I did say something to you the other day about parallel aspects; that's a key. That's what seems confusing; when you're in harmony it won't be, it will be enlightening.

May 2009

May 2

10:50 AM
I hate math.

You shouldn't hate it; it's a perfect language.

May 5

G: While eating ice cream, Kim told me about a time when she asked Talia not to eat all of the ice cream. Talia said she wouldn't, but when Kim looked in the ice cream container she saw that Talia had left just a tiny ball of ice cream in the bottom of a large ice cream container. I was laughing about her love of ice cream, and I said aloud, "Talia, wouldn't do that," to which she replied, "I did it." It was hilarious!

May 8

8:37 PM
300 was also about sacrifice.

May 10

G: I had a dream several days ago that kept coming back to mind. I was driving a short yellow school bus. I pulled up to the school to pick up the kids, but only one boy got on the bus. I asked, "Are you the only one?" He answered, "Looks like it." I said, "Okay then." I shut the door and we started to leave. I asked Talia about it.

Dreams are the language of life.

May 14

6:33 PM
Everything you've always wanted I can give you.

Talia, is that you?

Yes. Through God, of course. You didn't want to write that down. You see the problem with that? You were afraid of what someone might think who read that. I cannot deny who I am, yet so many deny who they are. They deceive themselves in doing this, don't you see? When you deny who you are, you deny your very essence, your very being, and all of the possibilities that entails, which are endless.

Collection

Talia, anything else?

Yes, it's endless.

May 17

6:15 PM
Talia, I would sure like to hear from you.

You haven't been listening.

I've been really busy.

That's your decision.

Okay, I'm listening now.

You're not quiet.

May 19

11:30 AM
Talia, I need your insight.

You have it.

I feel like I'm running out of time.

You are.

Would you like to elaborate?

Of course, you're running out of time, as you know it. My insights are everyone's if they grasp it. See, I can always bring you a smile

You sure can.

Why do you struggle so? This has always been; you're just grasping it in time.

Thank you, Talia.

Thank you for your time.

The Universe Speaks

May 20

7:32 AM

Talia, when you told me "you don't have to do anything, you just have to be who you are," you were saying that when you're being who you are you will do what you should do.

With no exceptions.

And "the king's word is law" was the power of the spoken word and not the privileges of royalty.

The privileges are a byproduct, and you will not always see them. You're not always seeing them does not mean they're not always there but that they may be manifested later.

We're not of this world.

No, you're in it but you're not of it, not when you're being who you really are. You are here to help others and to learn and to share what you've learned with others when you can.

10:15 AM

    G: I was thinking Talia could say something specific about the future to dispel some of the unbelief of others when she said:

Why do you think prophecy is usually not so very specific? It's to let you know the future is not written in stone.

May 22

9:35 pm

Don't look by sight. See that that cannot be seen. You must have faith to receive the healing. You must deem yourself worthy.

May 23

These students of mine. How can they be so bad?

They weren't taught the fundamentals correctly.

Collection

May 28

11:48 PM

So, what is the never-ending flux of the universe?

It's the never-ending change of the changeless.

Should I explain that?

No.

You sound adamant.

You asked, I gave you a definite answer. Death is just a change, a change of being. Many of your thoughts are abstract, nonexistent fantasy. When you see things as they really are the nonexistent ceases.

Am I getting this clear?

Exactly—that's the question to ask. And when you are clear the question will be answered. And the nonexistent will cease.

Aimless thoughts.

Exactly. Remember, in pure focused thought are the answers manifested, for everything.

Pure focused thought is healing.

Yes, that's one of the answers.

May 31

12:01 PM

My going was to also let you know you cannot depend on anything of this world. Your help comes from another country. Your help is spiritual.

> Talia uses the word *country* to indicate that it's as easy to move between dimensions as countries.

The Universe Speaks

June 2009

June 1

1:58 PM
Talia, what are you doing today?

Studying.

Studying what?

Life.

June 4

7:07 PM
How are your studies going?

Wonderful. Wonder filled. I'm studying life in all its manifestations.

Sounds fascinating.

It is, it is.

Care to share?

Of course, life is endless, and its beauty is endless. Its origin is the love of the Creator.

My name and Sarah are interchangeable.

I was wondering about that. Princess is a title, isn't it?

Sarah is God's name for Talia. It means "princess" in Hebrew.

It is the daughter of the king.

Talia, I was so glad to hear you're still the leader in your class, that your friends ask, "What would Talia do?"

That is a great honor to me.

You sure earned it.

I was just being me.

Collection

I know.

You sound almost shy about it.

It is a great honor and it's humbling to be used in that way.

8:37 PM
Talia, the other day by the pond you told me you "liked the goldfish." I didn't know why you were so specific, with all the other life around, so I just answered "Okay" and that was it—you didn't say anything else. Then the other day I find out that Frankie and a friend had buried goldfish crackers on the beach for you and said, "We hope you like the goldfish, Talia." That was so cool.

I wanted them to know I'm with them, I'm alive, and I appreciate what they did. Some doubt. Some think I'm dead. Nothing could be further from the truth. I'm "lively," remember, I've never been dead. It hurts people when they think that. Thoughts are life, and they bring forth life or death. It's in the power of the tongue, out of the abundance of the heart. People should speak truth from their hearts always and manifest life. Lies are death and no lie is of the truth; the truth is life and that's living Now. People hurt themselves needlessly and it's largely by what they think. So be mindful of your thoughts and bring forth life. You are a creator and your passion for truth will bring forth good.

Let the dead bury the dead.

That's a good saying.

June 5

1:01 PM
Talia, your words sure touch people.

My words are life; I told you that.

1:42 PM
I've got a little more time.

Yes, you do. A reward for your actions.

What does that mean?

It means action speaks louder than words and you're rewarded for it.

I'm seeing a lot here that's not in words.

You always do.

6:43 PM

Talia, I really appreciate your fellowship and words so much.

You're welcome and that's mutual.

You are so polite and sincere.

That's the way I was raised.

Well, your mom sure did a good job.

She did a perfect job.

You said that so matter of factly.

It is a matter of fact; in fact, everything I say is.

There's that wonderful confidence.

When you know who you are and walk in it, it will be as natural as breathing.

Another fact.

Yes. ☺

Look at that picture.

       A photo of Talia in a primitive hut.

It looks like the face of God, like you weren't of this world.

I wasn't.

Like you came down from heaven.

I did. I was there helping and learning and having fun.

I would sure like to see that.

I will show you everything when you get here.

Can't wait!

Yes, you can.

You were so balanced.

That's what I wanted you to see.

I don't even know why; it just came to me.

Because you see what's not there as important as what is.

Collection

That's really profound.

Of course it is.

You kill me, you just totally kill me.

I'm killing what you don't need.

I know, I know.

Now, do what I suggested; there's profit in my counsel.

That's it?

That's it. Remember when you were thinking about using a blindfold in this country before?

> G had thought about walking around blind-folded while on a cross-country journey, in order to strengthen his spiritual senses.

Yes, that was the same journey that I was told about you. But I didn't have anyone to trust, including myself.

Now you do, including yourself.

June 6

1:19 PM
Are you ready to listen?

Yes.

It's easy to miss things; it's grasping it that takes work.

Work is energy.

Yes, and effort. You've had it easy for a long time; now begins the climb.

Anything else?

Yes, don't strive, flow in it.

Good advice.

When has it not been?

Never.

And it never will.

The Universe Speaks

June 7

8:16 AM
You said, "Write."

Yes, I have something to say. Don't you see that's a feeling, a feeling you can't write, a thought that creates a mood, an emotion, of paralysis? That's the momentum I was talking about. You can do anything you think you can, for your thoughts are who you are and they define you.

That's radical.

Most all truths are. If you think you're unworthy that creates that reality. On the other hand, if you think you're worthy that creates that reality.

I'm worthy.

I already know that; it's important that you know that.

I know it.

Now you do.

You said "inertia" the other day.

That's keeping what's good going.

Positive momentum.

That's a good way to put it: keep your momentum positive. The flux of the universe is an amplitude. There are ups and downs and it is important to know that. That's knowing "the times." Your time's growing short. That's an expansion of a short time condensed and it's a perception, a thought.

A creative thought condensed to expand?

You're starting to get it.

I'm starting to get a creative thought condensed to expand?

That too. If you knew how far you could take what you've just written, you would be astounded, but the time is not yet.

I'm about out of time here.

That's what I've been saying.

Time out of Mind.

Collection

Time is timelessness and that's in the Now, where all things are.

1:05 PM
Talia, my head was baking in the sun and you said you would talk with me, so here I am with paper and pen poised.

You didn't have to go through that whole spiel with me. ☺

I know; I just get excited I guess.

Do you want to pick up where you left off?

Sure, whatever you want.

That's us wanting in Oneness, a unity of desire.

Guess it would be.

We were speaking of time.

Yes.

Time is a sequence of events, and they are all happening now at once. How else do you think you can experience two or more events simultaneously? Because it is at the same time. Most are only aware of this experience when they are thrown into it, usually by a major crisis. Yet what I want you to see is that you can change these events by your thoughts of them, let's say, preprogramming the future, which is just an event you've yet to experience. If you see an event coming, we'll say on the horizon, and you have a foreboding or dread of the experience and you decide to not experience that particular experience, then do not agree with it, and preprogram it to change.

When I spoke preprogramming to you I knew you would meet someone who would explain it fully to you—that's why I didn't. I just wanted you to be aware of it and pay attention to his words. When I told you to pay attention and write down everything he said, I knew you wouldn't be able to, but it caused you to pay attention. When I told you my, yours, his, and Grandfather's message was intertwined, this is confirming that. When I told you that Mom would carry on my message and you see that coming to pass, that is another confirmation.

When I told you that I liked the song "Beyond the Horizon," it was simply to let you know that even though you can't see what's beyond the horizon, you can know it's there.

1:56 PM
Manipulate the illusion of time.

How?

By pure focused thought and preprogramming. You bent it to do this now, a warp in the fabric of events.

That's pretty cool.

That is pretty cool.

3:21 PM
You're wondering how this all ties together.

If you say so.

I do. You're wondering about applications.

Yes.

That luminous web of life is woven within the fabric of time. Remember when you saw the blanket with rocks on it that distorted the smooth fabric of the blanket?

Yes.

That's the gravity of bodies distorting the fabric of life, in this case time and space. Everything is energy and all energy moves and reacts in and around all other energy. One cannot be in a room and not affect the presence of that room. Presence is energy, and all energy has presence. One simple principle is belief; that's a start. You must have belief to apply the knowledge in a meaningful way.

6:48 PM
This is a network of interpenetrating events, which you can influence by simple belief. It's the last three words that most have the problem accepting, and that's the problem.

It's really so simple it's hard to comprehend.

That's it exactly. I told you most people were masters of complicating things. True lasting solutions are always simple.

That's the pure simple truth.

It sure is.

God, Talia, you are so smart!

That's the wind of truth blowing away the darkness.

I remember when I saw that multi-colored wind blowing in a curve behind you and through you, blowing toward me.

It blew through you too and it still is; remember what I explained that was.

Collection

The blessings of God.

That's it. ☺

Sometimes I feel like you're His greatest work.

You're biased.

That may be true.

It is true but I appreciate your kind thoughts.

You bring out the best in me.

I do but I'm just letting you know who you are. When people know who they are, they will always manifest their best because their best is who they really are.

That's awesome.

People are awesome; most of them just don't know it.

Talia, how can we be so stupid?

You're not stupid, you just think you are. Everything you need is right there, right Now. Most just do not realize it, remember. Realize is to make real, and if it isn't realized it's as if it doesn't exist.

When you said to that medium the other day, "What can I say? I was always brainy," it was just hilarious to me.

I'm glad I could make you laugh.

You do all the time. You're the funniest person I know—perfect, exquisite humor.

Quite the accolades.

That's funny too.

I'm fun.

You sure are. I wish I could see you.

You will.

I love that truth. You make a lot of time for me, don't you?

I do.

How does that work? I mean, do I keep you from other things or what?

Mostly or what.

What does that mean?

Things are kept for me. Do not trouble yourself with this. We are working together, and what we are doing is important. I know what is important and what is not, and our work is important. I will say that you do trouble yourself over what's not important and you shouldn't do that.

Just trying to understand.

You will, in time. I will show you everything—nothing hidden that shall not be revealed.

I know where you got that.

Yes, from the Source of all things.

June 8

1:15 PM
My time's obviously short.

You're right.

This seems to be a reoccurring theme.

After critical analysis you'll see all you have is moments. Make the most of them.

Be kind.

June 9

12:23 PM
Minion and machine are synonymous, and minions with machines are really dangerous.

That's a large part of it. Minions and machines are interchangeable.

Interchangeable, that's the word you used before; I just substituted synonymous.

There is a difference; think it through.

Okay, I looked them up. There's a huge difference.

One is words, one is function, activity, etc. Interesting definition of what's really happening.

As I've said before, words are useful to convey meanings. As I've said, I'm precise with my meaning. Oftentimes that means being precise with my words but only to get the meaning across.

414

Collection

June 13

6:00 AM
Why do you feel so far away?

I'm right here. We have something to do together.

Then let's do it.

There are no blockages here.

That means the blockages are with me.

When you're not here, they are.

12:53 PM
Okay, Talia, I'm there by faith.

Of course you are; there's no system to work. That shaking you heard about in the central U.S. has a two-fold meaning. It's from the center out.

That's why you said to me "centered."

Yes, the first principle.

If you're not centered the slightest push will have you off balance.

Yes. That's what centered means, to be in balance, in harmony. That's being prepared.

June 14

8:25 AM
Good morning, Talia.

Good morning to you. I will always bring you up; that's one way you'll know it's me.

You are referring to that vision a couple of days ago when you put your right hand in my left and we were ascending, on past paradise, but I couldn't stay there.

You could have stayed there; you were distracted by feelings of unworthiness. But you are worthy or I would not have taken you there. I don't make mistakes, remember? Our criteria is different. You still think works will get you there but it's not true; it's only by grace, and the grace of God is sufficient for all your needs. There are things I want to show you and they are largely without words; they are indescribable.

415

The Universe Speaks

I want to see them.

You will but you must believe. I unravel mysteries. I dispel the false twist of the truth that is illusion. That illusion holds you back from freedom and it is like cords that bind, but it is not real and that's what I want you to see. And when you see it they will fall away like the illusion they are.

It is like a spell.

It is. No bondage is of the truth.

When I see it, it's so simple.

When you see IT it's all so simple, Everything. Complications are confusion and it's just not seeing it as it is.

Thank you, Talia.

You are most welcome.

1:28 PM
Talia, there's so much fake here.

Yes, most of it is done for money. When you see the pure tainted it can usually be traced back to someone who thinks they can profit by it. Until you can see through it you won't, and you can see through it anytime.

June 15

6:34 AM
Talk to me.

What do you want to say to me?

I want to say to you to live your life without judgment or condemnation.

June 16

10:10 AM
Talia, your mom asked if you have anything to say to her.

Yes, tell her I love her, I'm with her, I talk to her, and she does hear me.

Anything else?

416

Collection

She hears me. When she asks something tell her to expect an answer. I would never ignore her. I never ignored her, even when I acted like I did.

11:45 AM
You're a bridge for me.

I'm a bridge for you.

For my message.

Why me?

Others can't hear it; they're not aware of any message.

12:26 PM
Talia, we have half an hour.

We have all of eternity.

That's your perspective.

Yes, and my perspective is perfect.

      G thought about balance.

Am I balanced?

Not always. When you feel a struggle, that's rarely a balance. And just because something falls into your lap doesn't always mean that's balanced.

Hmm . . .

Food for thought, isn't it?

I reckon it is.

For every thing there is a season.

You separated every thing to show the separation.

Yes.

June 17

9:46 AM
      G was eating ice cream . . .

It's good, isn't it?

The Universe Speaks

Yes.

I loved that stuff.

You miss it?

There are better things here.

June 21

I asked Talia if Jesus was real, if he was the Messiah the Christians say he was. I was very curious because growing up Jewish, I was very sensitive to when people prayed to Jesus, referred to Jesus as their savior, etc.

Jesus is the Jewish Messiah, Mom.

G did not tell me immediately. He was not sure what I would say.

Tell her.

Tell her.

Are you going to tell her?

He did tell me. Later that day, G was not feeling well so I was making him some chicken soup. He said he didn't need any, but I told him it would help him feel better. As I told him this Talia spoke up.

She did that to me too.

While I was making the soup, G then thought about the pumpkin pie Talia had made at Thanksgiving. He told me that he wanted a perfect pumpkin pie. I told him that I would make him one. He said that it would not be the same, since it would not be made by Talia. I told him that I had taught Talia how to make it and that she would help me make this one for him. Then Talia piped in again.

I will.

June 23

11:46 AM
Talia, thank you. You mean everything to me.

Collection

I'm revealing everything to you, and I'm a part of it, and you're learning who I am. You tend to take things to an extreme. I'm not everything, and I'm a part of everything. I showed you what one person could contain, which is everything.

Everything is moving within you and through you!

It does. It moves through everyone. Most just deny it by the darkness.

God said, "Let there be Light."

That's exactly right. He said, "Let there be Light."

Then let there be Light.

Yes, let there be Light.

Let it be.

Let it be, because it is and it is all there is.

There is no failure.

Not in the Light; there never is. It is non-existent here. Now you see why I say it is a waste to worry.

Then I am not worried.

You shouldn't. You know, you can do anything I can do.

You can fly.

So can you.

You can do anything.

So can you.

Hard to believe.

That's why you don't always do it, but you can. Walk in what you believe and what you believe will walk in you.

12:28 PM
Hello.

Hello to you.

Your message. You said we would get back to it.

We will.

When?

Now. Now I'm with you. Now you are with me. And that's the message, that's when you truly change into what you are. It's not an image of another time, it is Now and it is who you are, in truth. Now is not being someone you aren't in another time, it is being who you are Now.

5:25 PM
I just want to say hi.

June 26

1:10 PM
I don't know what I'm doing.

I know what you're doing.

Yes, what?

You're following me.

I guess I am, like in the vision.

What if that elk had wings?

I guess he could follow you anywhere.

He has wings and he can follow me anywhere. Remember when I told you that you underestimate yourself?

Yeah, the other day. I remember it.

Why do you think I told you that?

Because I underestimate myself?

That's the obvious. It was my prophetic voice. The subtlety of the truth is glaring when your eyes are opened to it. Just because something said doesn't sound prophetic doesn't mean it's not. It all is Now, and simple statements of truth are always that—uttered in the Now, oftentimes seeming in the present tense only. But they are always projections of what will be, because truth doesn't change, it is everlasting. It is an axiom.

6:33 PM
That's just awesome, Talia. I don't know what to say about that because no one has ever explained that to me before.

I'm glad I could be of service.

Are you being funny?

Collection

A little, but I am glad I can be of service.

You have a point to make?

Yes, it's good to serve others.

Thanks for the reminder. "The greatest among you shall be servants of all," and that seems to be what you do, run to and fro serving others.

I'm glad you noticed and it is my great pleasure.

You're glad because of how it helps one to be aware of it.

Of course.

Glad, "causing joy." I looked it up because you were using it so much.

I was using it so often so you would look it up.

Causing joy in yourself or others is a sure sign you're living truth.

That's just so beautiful, you blow me away, Talia; you just blow me away.

I blow away what you don't need.

I think you said that before.

I did, but then it was a concept to you; now you're experiencing the truth of it.

I really am.

Yes, you really are.

Do you ever get frustrated with me, how slow I am?

Yes, but it could be more properly termed a momentary exasperation. I know you'll eventually get it.

Where's the "be" supposed to be?

Is it that important to you?

I want to get it right.

Wherever you put the "be" doesn't change the meaning.

I know, it's just that you answered that question before I wrote it, so I wrote it, then wrote what you said from memory and couldn't remember exactly how you said it.

The "be" is where it will be.

Okay, I'll have to think about that.

The Universe Speaks

The "be" is where it is and that's where it's supposed to be.

Okay, that didn't help either.

Are you getting frustrated?

A little.

Why do you speak to others so often in riddles?

I'm trying to wean myself from doing that.

And you're doing well. I just wanted to point out to you that it's usually a defense mechanism. A direct answer is usually better. What I'm trying to get you to see is do not create frustration in others, create joy in them instead.

Thanks for putting me in my place.

Your place is my place and it's a perfect place.

That's good news.

That's very good news. ☺

June 27

1:03 PM
Write.

Okay, why?

Why not?

I didn't hear you say anything.

Yes, you did, you just weren't aware of it.

What did you say?

You asked God to bless me and I told you I live in His blessings.

Could you speak up more?

Could you listen quieter?

You saw and heard me hear Him the day we met and more than once.

I did; that was amazing.

I told you how I walked where I walked when I was there.

Collection

Yes, you did, alpha and theta brain wave frequencies.

And I said to you that was the doorway, that harmony of mind. That's why I didn't say anything to you when I held the door open for you in that vision. There is nothing to say, because this journey of acceptance always begins with a look into the Supreme Silence. How many times have you seen me just look at you since then without saying a word?

A lot.

And why did I tell you I did that?

To get my attention.

To get your attention in silence. That's where all deeper knowledge comes from, in silence. That's why your friend Tom was told by Grandfather when he asked what to teach them to "send them to their sit spot then send them home."

Is he my friend?

Do you consider him your friend?

Yes.

Then he's your friend.

> Tom is Tom Brown Jr., the owner of the Tracker School where G and I go to learn primitive skills and how to communicate with the spirit world.

1:30 PM

> J was walking across the parking lot when Talia said:

I LOVE him.

4:38 PM

That was interesting, what you said about friends.

You choose who your friends are.

So a bad friend is a bad choice?

It's up to them to choose to be your friend. Frankie and I chose to be each other's friend and we were in one accord on that, and that's one thing she was never unsure about, that I was her friend.

That reminds me, I was talking to a friend not long ago, a friend of mine who is in Spirit now.

Curt.

The Universe Speaks

Yes. I asked, "How ya' doin', Curt?" He answered, "I'm fine." I said, "Stupid question, I guess."

From Curt: "It could be, but no question is stupid if you need the answer."

Guess that answered the question about stupid questions.

Curt: That was a good answer.

Friendship doesn't have to end just because the body does, a temporary shell.

That is perfectly sensible.

I've been saying it all along.

June 28

5:06 PM
Talia, I heard today you changed someone else's life. That's the best news I've gotten in a long time.

> I had told G that my good friend had read Talia's words and said that they have changed her life.

She was ready for it and she needed it and she received it, and that's how simple it is.

Your primary responsibility is to love.

July 2009

July 3

8:25 AM
Talia, good morning.

Good morning.

Help me to hear you clearly.

You do and I help you. When you miss something I repeat it.

That's right, you do; that's comforting.

Collection

Most think a feeling of rejection, missing what is right before them, resenting others for it. That's a perception of their own creation.

8:45 AM
Do you ever talk to Jesus?

I talk to him all the time; he's everywhere.

Well, I guess he would be.

He was the Word made flesh, a manifestation of God.

He was called a stone of stubbing and a rock of offense.

His name offends many.

Why is that?

For a multitude of reasons but primarily a misconception about what he said.

July 6

2:37 PM
I'm under a lot of stress.

You're under a lot of stress. Your stress is a perception, a perception of not living in the truth.

Well?

Change your perception. Live the truth

PM
I don't want to profit from your death.

You already have. My death has brought you life.

July 9

4:45 AM
You idolized your father, didn't you?

Yes.

The Universe Speaks

July 15

11:45 AM
People will ask us to help them and you must be crystal clear.

How?

In perfect stillness and quiet.

3:14 PM
I heard you liked her books.

> G is referring to the J.K. Rowling books.

I did.

She sold hundreds of millions of copies. It would be nice if ours did the same.

Is that what you want?

That would be nice.

She created a world for others to experience. I'm asking others to create a world that they can experience. That takes some effort, but it's worth it and it will always be better than a world that another creates for you. Your "true imaging" will become real and far beyond an imagination of another.

I get the feeling that most would rather someone else do their work for them.

Most would. However, those that test these things will find something far beyond mere imagination; they will find worlds without end in which they are co-creators. I always said to test these things, to prove these things, and that's what it takes, and an active role in embodying these truths. You fell away from your first love and I brought you back. Cling to the truth; all else is a lie.

> G then spoke to a grand old oak tree that had had a bit of damage after a windstorm.

I'm glad you are all right.

It could have been worse, not as bad as some.

> G was tinkering with his tractor, trying to get it to start, when a visitor came by to say hi to him. During that visit the man told G how to get the tractor to start.

It will start now.

Collection

It will?

It will.

July 19

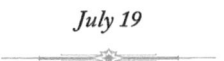

Pure language is from the heart to the heart. That is what we are using here, and the head cannot hear it. The interpretation from the mind of man has no place here. That was a graphic display of your head getting in the way of your heart. You knew it wouldn't start now as I said; you dismissed it as you and not me. But it was me; you just put your own interpretation on my words. You felt there was more to it, and there was, much more. You asked for a man to bring you the knowledge you lacked and he did; he showed up at your door unexpectedly. HE didn't even know why he was there. I showed you this that you would believe and not be so easily discouraged. Although you're now living through a dry time, know we're not finished; we've barely begun.

Fox walk every day.

You don't have to bow to me.

July 28

10:12 AM
Talia, don't leave me down here stupid.

You're not stupid. Dry times doesn't mean everything stops, it just means dry times.

I don't like dry times.

Dry times are for humility and strength, which is where strength comes from.

Strength is good.

So is humility. It's an often overlooked and underrated commodity.

It's useful!

It's very useful. It's also God's favor. Many, when they see God's chosen humbled, call it God's judgment or disfavor, but nothing could be further from the truth. This is God's favor, blessing His people with a most powerful tool. This is not often seen in this way and it takes wisdom to see it.

I'm sure glad I decided to talk to you this morning.

The Universe Speaks

I am sure glad you did too. As time goes on memories fade, but my memory remains fresh by our words. Those that speak with me know the reality of our message.

You fill my heart with thankfulness.

That's not just me. ☺ I've missed our time together too. That's why that thing with the tractor happened, to strengthen your belief.

That was a difficult lesson.

That wasn't so difficult; there was a flowing in the entire process. Now you see why I say Now is everywhere and everything.

That's not always so easy to see here.

No, but it's easy to see here, and when you're here it's easy to see there. The only difference between here and there is perception. Everything there is a reflection of what's here and everything is here. The science of life is the embodiment of truth, of taking that mantle upon you and walking in it. Then are things clear and the Light will reflect perfectly. Then your understanding is perfect and is darkened no more, and humility is the first step along this path. This is the path of enlightenment that has so often been spoken of. This is the path of truth, which is freedom. Don't worry about getting every single word perfectly. Everybody that reads this will see the words differently.

You're going to Belize.

Why?

For fun.

Am I going to help anyone?

Helping others is always a byproduct of fun.

Sounds fun.

Yes.

July 29

10:00 AM
Good morning, Talia.

Good morning.

Collection

You're doubting is that you're not seeing everything as Oneness. I have proved this to you over and over again.

Are you frustrated?

A little.

I apologize.

Just get over it.

Okay, I'm over it.

Good, keep that in mind.

I sense you're busy today.

I'm always busy. There is always something to do. The stress they are putting on my mom will come back to them.

> Talia is referring to the attorneys for Michael's estate and the insurance company.

Seems fair.

That's the way it is. She'll come out fine. I love her.

I know you do.

It's beyond what you can think.

I feel it.

That's a tiny portion of my love for her. It's beyond knowledge. That's why you can't think it.

That's awesome.

It's beyond that too. What do you want from me?

I want your love.

You have it.

I want to please you; I want you to be happy.

I am.

I want to hear you clearly.

You do. You don't have to write everything I say.

The Universe Speaks

August 2009

August 4

1:56 PM
You can talk to me.

Not only can I, but I will. Everything you want I can give you.

You said that before.

It's to let you know who I am. When people understand the Oneness of which I speak, they will see that it's not false doctrine but eternal truth. Man's understanding is darkened by his pride and self-will; it's also stolen by the lies he's been fed. He has willingly accepted it. It hasn't been force-fed. The choices of darkness can only be broken by the acceptance of Light, and as I've said so many times before, it's a free gift. If he asks the questions and humbly accepts the answers, then is freedom born. I said you could fly. This is the first step to mount up with wings as eagles. Nothing is better than freedom, G.

I know that's true.

You've experience it, and you've seen it.

You've showed me.

I'm not the only one who's shown you that. You can be anything because you can be everything.

Why can't we stay there?

You can! It's the lie that says you can't.

       G's dog started to bark.

She sees me.

I want to see you.

Not now, not yet. You feel me.

Yes, I do.

You hear me.

Yes.

Time.

Collection

Time?

For everything there is a season.

I'm setting an example for you on how to be used; just let the Voice speak through you by being who you are. That's all the artists do: be who they are and their unique aspect is manifested. That's the gift.

Wow. Thank you, Talia.

You're welcome. ☺

August 5, 2009

10:33 AM
You did say you were going to talk with me?

I did.

It's a beautiful day.

You worry too much.

Still?

That's the antithesis of freedom.

I think writing hinders the flow.

You worry too much. Scribes have been doing this for centuries. You know you don't need me to do this.

What? How can that be?

I'm just a vessel. There are many messengers, and this is common knowledge to them.

Just the same, I would just as soon you stayed and continued communicating with me.

I will; I said I would. But I don't want you to neglect other voices of truth. Remember what Curt said.

Well, I don't want to get tunnel vision here.

That is limiting and I told you there are no limits. It doesn't all have to come through me. As a matter of fact, it doesn't. It can't.

It can't?

No, it can't. The universe speaks and it speaks with a multitude of voices.

The Universe Speaks

I love you, Talia.

I know you do and I, you. Desperation is a voice of worry, and that's a voice you shouldn't listen to.

I don't feel desperate.

No, but sometimes you do and that's a false emotion. You have plenty of time to do all the things you need to do.

That seems contradictory to what you've said before.

I know it seems that way. I am referring to the Balance. In harmony there is perfect timing.

Music.

That's the best symbol of it.

That's not all, is it?

No, it's not.

Okay, I'm listening.

That's another definite first step.

I met you when you were eleven; how did you become so centered in eleven years?

By birth; I said you were born into it.

But I've never seen anyone move so fluidly from their center; you looked like you were floating.

I was, in the liquid of life. It surrounds everyone, and it is a decision whether to flow with it or fight against it. Unfortunately most do fight against it by the denial of who they really are, which is a child of the Most High. I always felt His favor, I just didn't know what it was.

That's pretty cool, but I don't know if that really explains it.

But it does. Get up and walk in it now.

That was awesome, but I can't move like you.

Yes, you can, you're just sore now. You can learn everything you need to know about a person by how they move, their demeanor.

That's true.

I wouldn't have said it if it wasn't. Now you need to do the chores you've chosen.

Collection

My chosen chores.

Yes.

August 6

9:00 AM
Mow today.

Why?

Zen. A repetitive form puts you in that place; that's what the fox walk does.

I find whatever you say so interesting.

You should.

I do. What else?

Go watch TV.

August 7

9:12 AM
You remember . . .

Do I remember what?

. . . when I told you about my dog?

Gunther?

Yes, he likes to play. You met him.

I remember.

Whatever you like to do is what you do here.

Guess I'll be doing motocross and martial arts.

Yes, and flying.

Yes, and a lot of other stuff.

A LOT of other stuff. There are so many misconceptions about this place.

Well, you did say we were dense.

I also said you were fluid. And beings of light. You were born by the Light. It is a part of you; when you deny that inner light it becomes dark.

I am a being of light.

THAT is where the energy comes from, that's where the speed comes from. I told you the separation is an illusion. When you look at water and a tear comes to your eye, know it is the longing for Oneness, completion, the realization of who you really are, and not being who someone else says you are, a false label. That's why you love your aloneness, because you know who you are. Others project an image of who they think you are upon you, and you sometimes receive that image to please them. At best it will only please them temporarily.

I can see some being infuriated by being who you really are.

Some will, many more will be uncomfortable. But it's still better to be who you are than who you are not. People attempting to be who someone else says they are is one of the major problems on the earth. It's a huge source of frustration for everyone involved, and it leads to self-deception; before long they can't even remember who they are.

Sixty-six is the unity of man and that is the test. The unity of Oneness. The test is the questions you ask and your answers. This test is self-administered, and the questions and the answers come from your Self. They are not out there, somewhere, they are within you. When you pass this test you will know who you are and will walk in Oneness.

August 10

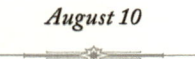

Remember that book you were going to write?

The Last Cheeseburger? But as a joke.

And it was funny too; it relieved a lot of tension.

My friend Ron loved it.

He needed to laugh. The point is you savored every moment. That was making the most of your moments. That's the way to live.

August 16

2:46 PM
Talia, what about demons?

I never think of them.

Collection

August 19

9:00 AM
Look for the jewels in the trees.

August 20

11:31 AM
G was thinking about a class he was just about to start.

It's not going to be like any of the others.

Why not?

A transitional zone. That's where your life's at. A strange feeling when it's over. A feeling of completion but of acceptance of the change, the transition. An awakening, an awareness of change, of truth. An acceptance of it.

11:59 AM
A doorway into Oneness.

I want to walk into it.

You will. That which you received the last three days about transitional zones was certainly not by coincidence. I told you the time would come when most of what we talked about was beyond language. You've thought you have been receiving less, but in fact you have been receiving more, much more.

It has been more.

It has. The golden rainbow and the jewels in the trees were for a sign; you still need them. You're still reluctant to write down some of the things I tell you and show you, but you shouldn't be. You're concerned about it being published, but only a very small portion of it ever will be.

Stay with me.

I want to stay with you.

It takes some effort.

The Universe Speaks

August 22

    While G was watching *The Manchurian Candidate* . . .

It could happen to anyone. It happened to Mom.

August 23

11:47 AM
Your thoughts are real.

August 24

I'm with you.

Thank you. Help me find a good sitting area.

    G is referring to a meditation place.

We will.

Talia, you were alive the last time I was here.

I still am.

Sorry, Talia, for not being what I should be.

You're everything you should be; you're just not being it all the time.

Why live the illusion? That would be to perpetuate the myth.

Well put.

August 26

10:16 AM
You're a keeper of knowledge.

I'm a bringer of knowledge.

Collection

G: I saw Talia moving very quickly here and there dispersing knowledge, sweet knowledge, to various people. Saw an image of a hummingbird superimposed on her.

Talia, you bring me to tears.

I bring you to life.

They are tears of joy and thanksgiving and appreciation.

I know.

You are the ultimate coyote teacher.

No, Tom's the ultimate coyote teacher.

August 31

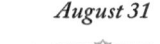

11:40 AM
Talia?

Yes. You enjoyed yourself?

Immensely.

I knew you would.

I did too.

That which you learned was important.

I know—and I feel nothing but appreciation for it and to everyone involved.

The most important thing is living your life as a constant prayer. It will work for you always. To honor the Creator is to honor all things, including yourself.

That's wonderful.

It always is—wonder filled. I will always be with you.

You don't know how much that means to me.

Yes, I do, and I appreciate you.

Thank you so much.

You're welcome and thank you.

You need to go now.

The Universe Speaks

September 2009

September 4

12:15 PM
Talia, I just read what you said before: "stay with me" and "it takes some effort." Sorry about my lack of effort; I didn't want to impose.

You act as if I can't be in more than one place at a time; that limitation is in your mind. I told you there were no limitations here.

I know. I guess I didn't want to bother you with all that's going on.

You can never bother me because I can never be bothered. That's your natural mind reasoning, unreasonably.

You make me laugh.

You should laugh.

I'm sorry, Talia.

No need to be sorry.

Then can we make up for lost time?

I told you time is not lost, it's just misplaced.

I think I see the meaning of that now.

Yes, it's being misplaced by judgments.

That's really something to think about.

You should. Time can never be lost because it is all happening Now, but misjudgments can cause you to miss what's happening Now, resulting in time being misplaced. It's being misplaced by choice, primarily choosing not to see what's there for you to see at that time.

Okay, if you were very busy, you couldn't have come up with all of that.

This is effortless for me. It all just is.

Will your mom be okay after this lawsuit? Will she be content?

Yes.

Physically or spiritually?

Collection

That's your mind separating.

Well, that can't be good.

It is the antithesis of Oneness and that's a disease.

I need the cure.

You already have it. It is the one point above the mountain, where it all is.

Then I want to live there.

You already do; just stop separating things by your judgments.

Why do I keep seeing "inclusive"?

Because the Light is all-inclusive, without judgment, prejudice, or bias That is why you can never feel us judge you, because we never can.

That's beautiful, Talia. That's it?

That's it for now.

> During a meditation . . .
>
> G: I met Talia at the gate to my Medicine Place. We then flew up to paradise and past the fountain of fortune. We landed and began to walk along a path, farther on the path than I had ever been before. There were many figures there with white faces along the path, looking up at us as we passed, but that's all I could see of them, their faces. I don't know who they were; I felt that they were departed souls, but there was something different about them. I don't know what. Maybe they were angels.
>
> We continued along the path, and I could see the outskirts of a huge white city encircled by tall white walls. The outskirts had many buildings, structures almost like subdivisions. They were white also. I got the impression that the city was so huge that it would take forever to explore it all. It seemed overwhelming in its immensity. I had a tremendous desire to explore the city, but where to start? How could you ever explore it all? *It's not time, and am I worthy?* I wondered what this place was, and Talia then said, "It is the City of God and it goes on forever." 'Why are we here?" I asked. She replied "I just wanted to show it to you."

September 8

You don't believe you can.

Yes, I do.

Then you can. I do not always have a message. Our core message is out there; now it's like spokes on a wheel.

September 9

9:09 AM
Talia, did you know how awesome you were?

I suspected it.

September 13

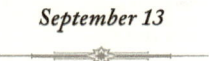

> G: I was sitting when I felt someone touch my back on my right side, beside my arm, with their hand. I felt it physically, very strongly, the warmth, etc. It moved down my back a bit, but when I turned there was no one to be seen. Then I saw a white light twist and swirl around on my right side about two feet away, then disappear.

Talia, is that you?

Yes.

> That was really nice of her because I had asked her to touch me and let me physically feel her.

Very cool.

> While meditating:

Talia, are you here?

Yes. Here is Now, Now is here, and here is everywhere.

September 17

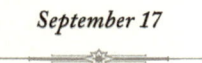

9:43 AM
Talia, the other day when you touched my back it was awesome. I felt the warmth of your hand.

Collection

That warmth was my love. You had asked me to touch you, so I did.

11:35 PM
Did you enjoy that book?

Talia is referring to a spy book G was reading.

Not really. It was okay.

You like that world?

Not really. It's dirty business.

It intrigues you.

If you say so.

I do.

That's your people.

My people are everywhere.

Interesting mystery, but it's fiction.

Glad you realized that.

Why did you bring that up?

Just making conversation.

Really?

Yes, really.

Sorry I neglected you.

That's okay.

Your friendship is precious to me.

I know. I'm glad you're my friend too.

I wish I could have spent more time with you when you were here.

So do I.

I could have.

You didn't know.

I should have known.

The Universe Speaks

You weren't conscious of it.

I should have been.

That wasn't meant to be.

Why not?

So your consciousness could be expanded.

That expansion comes with some hurt.

It often does. Now you know why so many would rather sleep.

I should have been wide-awake after all that happened the day we met.

I wasn't so aware of it either.

Is that supposed to make me feel better?

Yes.

You always make me laugh.

I know. It's good for you.

Thank you.

You're welcome.

September 18

6:48 PM
You can talk to me.

How are you?

Perfect and growing.

Did you have fun today?

Perfect fun, never-ending magnificence.

Sounds pretty good.

It's the best of all worlds.

Indescribable, I'm sure.

It is. It's truly beyond description.

Collection

September 19

6:30 AM

    I told G that I thought Talia was better than Jesus.

That's not true, Mom.

12:01 PM

I saw an image that looked like Talia sitting on a box, about twenty feet away. I also sensed her presence. I asked, "Talia?"

Yes, it's me.

What are you doing?

I'm just watching. I learn from everything you do, remember?

1:03 PM

Talia, I love recording your words, our conversation. Wish I could better describe the downloads.

You're doing a good job.

Positive reinforcement.

It's true. You're doing fine. You wish it could be as colorful as the revelations you receive. Accept the fact that it's not going to be. These things have to be experienced. Words will only be a pale reflection.

I yearn for people to experience your truth.

I know you do and they can; it's up to them to accept THAT fact.

September 20

8:38 AM

Good morning, Talia.

Good morning to you.

Are you going to hang with us today?

I'll be around.

The Universe Speaks

Cool.

I am cool.

You're the best of all worlds.

Talia?

Yes. I'm thinking...

Well?

I'm thinking how I should respond to that.

Well, let me know what you decide.

It's not so much the statement but what's in your heart.

What do you mean?

I don't want you to elevate me above measure.

Is that possible?

It's possible.

I think I would really have to stretch to do that.

You do tend to take things to extremes at times.

I was honoring you from a sincere heart.

I know you were and I appreciate that, but remember the balance. That's important.

I do. Care to expound?

I'm human.

I know you are.

Do you see what I'm saying?

You're saying humans have unbelievable potential.

That's part of it; remember the source.

That's always in my mind, and everywhere else.

That's good to remember. You would do well to honor the Creator above his creation.

Good point.

I always do make those.

Collection

September 21

8:05 PM

I kissed her vial of ashes and said aloud, "That's all that's left of you here." And she said:

No, it's not; I left a legacy of how to live.

September 22

6:13 AM

Good morning, Talia.

Good morning.

What are you doing?

Teaching yoga.

Yoga?

Union with the Supreme Being.

Do you have a lot of students?

Yes, they are scattered all over the universe.

That scattering is mostly in their mind, isn't it?

Almost exclusively.

Where can I sign up? ☺

You already have. ☺

11:26 PM

What should I do today?

Do your best.

The Universe Speaks

September 27

6:30 AM
Talia, anything you want to tell me?

Make the most of your moments.

12:55 PM
I played an outgoing phone message with Talia's voice on it for G.

It sounded completely different when you heard it in the Now, in the moment, didn't it?

It most assuredly did. I wanted to leave a message!

I covet your fellowship. Thank you for your words.

You're one of my friends, and I've always loved talking with my friends.

I sure appreciate it.

I appreciate your openness. Remember when I spoke to you about the illusion of the familiar?

Yeah, then I found the same phrase used in a book recently.

That warning is a thread that's run through all of our talks. The day we met you expected the familiar. You got something quite different. You had asked to be shaken out of your rut, if you'll remember.

I do remember now. I had forgotten using those words.

But you did use those precise words, and its purpose was for you to remember.

It worked.

I said before, you are your own best teacher and you are not unique in this. My best lessons were my own conclusions, and Mom was a masterful guide in allowing me to do this. One purpose in that was so she could pass that on to others. People, especially children, have been told what to think long enough. That removes their choices and their creativity, which results in robbing them of their freedom. Most people who do that mean well, but it stunts their growth. This is the primary cause of adults not making rational choices or decisions, because they were never taught or allowed to as a child.

That's stunning in its simplicity.

The simple truth is always stunning and is designed to stun one out of their stupor.

Wish I had more time.

Collection

You're learning to make the most of your moments, and when time is no more, that will really pay off.

That's just the tip of the iceberg, isn't it?

I took a snapshot of the tip of the iceberg.

You literally did, I saw it.

It had purpose, didn't it?

It did, so we could bring it up now.

That's part of it. Remember when I said you're always being used?

Yes.

And that it matters not whether you know or not?

Yes.

Well, not that it matters, but know you're being used. ☺

That's funny.

That's true.

Did you see that around J?

      Bright lights swirling around his head.

Yes.

That was me.

I'll let him know.

I knew you would.

1:45 PM
Thank you.

You're welcome, Talia. I love you.

September 29

———◆———

10:05 AM
I'm not hearing anything

The Universe Speaks

Yes, you do.

Well, do you have anything to say to me?

Yes, my words are words of life. That means they change things beyond the molecular level and beyond the far reaches of the universe. They are timeless. The vibrational harmony of matter can be changed by a thought. When the thought is empowered by words it can be changed even more. What can you do with this?

I was just thinking that.

You can change things.

I need the formula for application.

You already have it. Did you not change the day we met?

Yes.

But you didn't apply it. You put it on a shelf instead. Waiting to see what happened. That goes back to your choices. You wanted to verify something from an external source. But you didn't need to; you had already experienced everything you needed to, to do the things you needed to do. Your sense of loss has much more to do with what you missed than with my going. As I've said, my going when I did was with perfect timing. I had accomplished all that I came to do, and that step into the Grand Game of life was not a misstep, it was ordained for me to do long before I arrived. One of the most profound lessons I left you with was not to waste moments, because now is really all you have. The good news is all is contained in the Now, so Now you have it all. Time is an illusion, G, a familiar one; that's why it's so rarely questioned.

    G was thinking about the six jurors that voted against me.

These people you are wondering about are lost. That should drive home the point of the importance of waking people up. They were deluded by illusion. You saw the spirit of sorcery there and you bound it, but you cannot bind people's choices. That's why it is so important not to give place to that spirit of strong delusion. I told you before that has been sent because of people's choices, because they chose a lie over the truth. My mom shouldn't worry over the outcome. She has done nothing wrong.

This has a great and far-reaching purpose beyond what you can now see. To awaken someone is a treasure without description. This explanation and what I'm doing is not a Band-Aid, it's a cure.

Do not look to the world for justice. I told you the foundation was crumbling because the foundation is a lie. The crumbling is accelerating, but KNOW that the Light will not be deterred.

You will deliver your masterpiece.

Collection

I am. Just stating facts, and that's a solid foundation, and that's what I meant when I said I was a foundation you could depend on.

By the word of truth.

And the spirit of Life. Now go share it.

11:18 AM
    G saw a glimpse of Talia sitting at the back of the room on top of a stack of chairs.

What are you doing?

I'm waiting for you to share with Mom.

Why are you sitting there?

Because I'm sitting high.

October 2009

October 3

7:55 AM
Talia's with me.

I am.

7:00 PM
    G: I asked Talia about the meaning of a vision I had the day we met. It was late at night and I had walked into the living room. Huge black branches were protruding from the ceiling. Then silver bells appeared here and there on the branches.

The black branches are the mystery of the tree of life. The silver bells are a focal point of knowledge, redemption, wisdom—as a matter of fact, anything you need. They are there to place your attention on what's important, on what's needed, and it is life and life giving and it is a gift. After you saw the bells you saw me walking down the hall, asking questions. Who are you? Are you going to sleep now? You had to wake up to talk to me. My going shook you from your slumber.

I wanted to stay awake to talk to you.

The Universe Speaks

You should have.

October 4

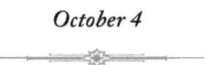

6:58 AM
What we do here is not just for you, it is for everyone who will receive it.

Thanks for the encouragement.

You are welcome. Just a reminder.

October 6

6:58 AM
You're helping battered women?

Yes.

I picked that up the other day.

> I had met with a psychic who told me that Talia was helping to heal battered women.

I told you.

Here or there?

Mostly here.

I thought so and that's what threw me.

They are devastated by it, their life being taken by one they loved. It also hurts them to know what they [the others] did to themselves by taking their life. I'm helping them to understand, to heal them, to restore what was lost. I couldn't do this if I were still there.

I know, Talia, and I know why you told me.

Yes, her sacrifices will be rewarded beyond what she could ever know there.

> Talia is speaking of my sacrifice, of giving Talia up for the message.

That's an understatement, isn't it?

It really is because there is no describing it.

You showed me many have guilt for leaving their kids, and they worry about them.

Collection

They do. We're healing that.

I guess I had the same misconception about heaven, that you get there and everything is perfect.

It is perfect. Your life goes on; it is a process—a perfect process to become whole again. Restored in newness of life. A misconception is a conception or thought you missed. Another example of what you've been told to think. That's why it's been said, to prove all things. You were told to question everything, and when you did, you were questioned why, and were resented for it many times. That's one reason I told you to believe in yourself, because you do not need another to validate what you find as truth. The truth will always verify itself.

Thank you, Talia. I have to go to work.

You're welcome and so do I. Have joy in it. ☺

I will.

I know you will.

October 10

1:02 PM
Talia, what's this about Africa?

I've been helping there.

In healing?

Yes, and other things.

Like what?

Lending my insight.

Do they know who you are?

It isn't necessary for someone to know who you are for you to help them To some I am called a "benevolent spirit."

What about you learning a "new game" there?

It is not new really. It's a part of the "Great Game of Life." It's just a new way of doing some things.

You're working with their culture.

The Universe Speaks

That's it. I honor their tradition and ways, and I work with them within that context. You must meet people where they are and not force change. That never works. True and lasting change always comes from within. That's why I emphasized the importance of living the art of life because that inspires people to change of their own volition A law can modify behavior but it can never bring true change, not of the inner man. It is a rod of correction and not the flower of life.

Why did you bring up the law?

It's seeing people being beaten to change. That never changes anyone; it just changes the appearance, and that merely perpetuates an appearance.

I met some bad men there once.

And your insight saved your life and everyone with you. You saw past the appearance.

I'm really thankful for that too.

You should be; that was a life-saving choice. But choices are set before you daily, and the ramifications of those decisions affect your reality as you experience it.

That Y in the road again.

It's there daily. You choose the path.

The path of Light.

That path will always feel better to you on a deep level, despite the sacrifice.

Talia, I would feel so empty without you.

You wouldn't be empty but you would be missing something.

I don't want to think about it.

You don't need to. ☺

October 11

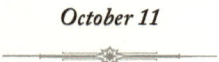

1:04 PM
    G sensed a wonderful presence when he entered his office.

Who's here?

Talia.

Collection

1:11 PM
Do you not want me to talk? ☺

No, I want you to talk.

What would you like to talk about?

Whatever you would like to.

I would like to talk about fantasy.

Fantasy?

Yes, fantasy. Your fantasies tell you a lot about yourself if you pay attention to what they have to teach. I said before that every thought you have is for a reason, and to be mindful of your thoughts because they are real, among other things. I also said that sometimes your imagination was more real than what you deem as real. A child's imagination is a tool of the Creator. It's to lead to the infinite possibilities inherent within them. It is also a self-defense mechanism from the onslaughts from what they are often told is real but is not. It is to let them know that their capabilities and opportunities are boundless. In your imagination there are no limits, and that is closer to reality than what they are usually told. You are a spiritual being; where are the limits?

Well, I'm glad I let you choose the subject.

You didn't imagine it would be about that, did you?

No, I didn't.

Fantasy is a beautiful escape and it teaches you. What could be wrong with that?

I'm sure someone could come up with a very articulate argument of why they are wrong.

And the same people could come up with the same argument about any subject, but that would just be their imagination.

And that's the answer to your last question.

It is.

8:18 PM
You just blow me away, Talia.

I do. To a beautiful new world.

The Universe Speaks

October 13

12:30 PM
Some questions are easier unasked.

How so?

If you're not ready for the answer.

You sit on God's lap?

I do.

What's that like, Talia?

Indescribable. It's Everything.

October 16

1:02 PM
Talia?

Yes.

Thank you for being with me today.

I'm with Mom.

You know what I mean. Thanks for talking with me.

Not a problem. It's like you're here.

Telepathy.

Some call it that; it's a common ability when you're IN harmony.

Tuned in.

It is perfect harmony, and when you are in it, you could certainly say you are "tuned in." She takes pleasure in her tasks. I'm happy about that.

Let her feel you.

She does. Tom's got something for you next week.

She is speaking about a class we will be taking.

Collection

October 18

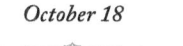

    G: I heard a gentleman say, "You have forever to help in the spiritual world, but you need this time in the physical to make a difference in the physical world and the earth." Later that morning I was thinking about that statement and why it was so, then Talia spoke up.

Because they can see you.

October 19

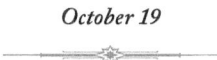

    While at my sit spot I sensed Talia on my right.

Talia? Who's there?

Talia. I will get there when Mom does; I'm meeting her.

    Talia is speaking of an exercise we were about to do at class, meeting our partner in the spirit.

You're being involved with this—it's amazing. You really do learn from everything we do.

I do. I was never exposed to this.

October 20

Have faith and belief.

What's faith?

Faith is the substance of things hoped for, the evidence of things not seen.

What's the difference between faith and belief?

BE-LIVE. It's all in the being. Your being. Know you're there. Believe.

You must go.

I don't want to leave.

You must.

455

The Universe Speaks

I want . . .

You will see me again. Don't bow to me. Tom will take you into the probable and possible futures. The past. Into the void and past the stars.

October 21

G: While meditating, I met Talia on the other side of the golden arch. She took my hand and we flew up. I asked, "Where are we going?" She answered, "We're going where the waters run clean." We flew in white clouds filled with light, and then I saw the ground. It was very green with grass and trees. There was a river. A beautiful blue river as large as the Mississippi. We were above it, looking down on it running straight, watching it flow away from us. It exuded purity. I said, "It's beautiful! Awesome!" Talia said, "Thank you."

We then flew to a large white oblong building with large Greek-like pillars in the front. As we flew down to it I asked, "What is this?" "The Library." We went inside. There were rows and rows of books on shelves that seemed to be at least a hundred yards deep and fifty feet high. Some of the authors' names and titles came to me.

We walked a short way and on a shelf to my right, about chest high, I saw the spines of *The Universe Speaks* and *The Universe Speaks, Book Two*. As I tried to look at other titles, an older lady who looked like a librarian came walking down the hall between the books toward us. She asked, "Can I help you?" I asked Talia, "Who's this?" Talia said, "The librarian." Then, "I want to see the Book of Life." "You can't see that," said the librarian.

Then I had a vision of a huge forest-green book with gold trim and some type of image, pictures, letters, and inscriptions in the center of the cover, and some kind of designs bordering it—but it was vague and unclear what it was. I got the sense it was all of life recorded. It was very beautiful.

Later, while walking out to my sit area, I heard Talia.

I like the term "passing on" because that is what you have done, passed on to something better. The reason I don't use it is because it entails that you are no longer here. But we are; we never left.

Collection

October 22

G was just about to take a spiritual journey when he heard Talia.

I'm not going with you.

While on his journey G met an older lady.

Do you know Talia?

Yes, I know Talia. She is greater than I, she is ancient, and she has lived forever. In the mind . . . and heart of God. She is filled with wisdom. She sits on God's throne.

October 24

Everything is one thing, and one thing is Everything.

Oneness! That's what it's all about.

October 26

10:00 PM
I know why you said yep.

Yes, you do. To honor my mother.

You told me before, your mission in life was love.

Yes, I did.

And now someone else said it.

Yes, he did. So you know it's true. Mom is going to be an extremely powerful healer.

10:06 PM
You sure were right about Tom having something for me.

Don't let me miss you, Talia, your communications.

You don't, you just don't always write it down. My telling you I had been riding my horse was to let you know she was right.

She was confirming what another medium had told me.

The Universe Speaks

October 27

7:00 AM
Good morning, Talia.

Good morning! ☺

God, you bring me up.

That's the test.

November 2009

November 2

3:42 PM
Talia?

Yes.

Are you here?

I'm here.

I'm having trouble hearing you. It's unclear and indistinct.

Why?

I don't know why. You tell my why. And why do I see and hear a dead dog and not you?

You are hearing me, and the dog is not dead.

The body sure is, and he's distressed about it.

He will learn. He has guides now. He needed some help and you helped him. He knows it's going to be all right now.

Why weren't you talking earlier?

I was waiting for you to speak to me, in faith. You're still now, so your vibrations are up.

I don't like it when I don't hear you.

It has purpose. It spurs you to quietness.

Collection

November 5

6:58 PM
Talia, do you have anything to say to me?

Yes.

Good! What?

Don't doubt yourself or your ability to hear me. We couldn't have made it this far if you couldn't have heard me. Our ties are ties that bind us together, inseparable.

That's the best news ever!

It's close to it.

7:21 PM
You can't use anything in your subconscious until you're ready to. The thing hidden there, concealed from yourself, is information stored for your use, but only when you're ready.

November 6

1:15 PM
Talia, I have heard that the subconscious is a place of all physical memory.

The subconscious is a place of all memory. Everything that's ever happened to you is stored there, not just physically either. Through the subconscious you have access to all memory.

Interesting download on that!

And that is just scratching the surface.

Here is what I saw: I saw that anyone who has ever lied to you, you immediately knew but maybe not consciously. Whatever anyone said to you, you immediately knew their true intentions—good or ill. You knew what animal was moving in the woods and in which direction, where he or she was going and why, because the subconscious is linked to the Spirit that moves through all things. It's how you know things without knowing how you know, like who's behind you and why.

Hard to describe the downloads, isn't it?

Pretty much impossible.

That's because it is beyond language. Just know that it is there for you when you need it. You have access to it and you do know how to get there.

Nothing hidden that shall not be revealed.

Exactly.

November 7

1:04 PM
Talia, hello. Would you elaborate on your mission when you were here in the flesh, that is, to love?

That's what it was and that's what I did and that's why I said that my life was an example of how to live. God is love and we are made in His image, and when you're being who you are in Him you can only manifest love. And it is without striving or effort, for His love will always flow through you to others. This is something that cannot be faked or manufactured. It is Life, and this Life is love without limits, without end. Its absolute authenticity will always be felt, and the lives it touches will be transformed into His image. It is a reminder of where you came from and who you are. It never fails. I wrote that I loved my life so much, and that is the life I was talking about, and that life never ends. He showed you a sample of how much He loves you the day we met.

That was a sample? That's incomprehensible!

His love has no bounds and no end. I told you that before.

I felt like I nearly died that day.

You did nearly die that day. If you'll remember that evening you felt like you had escaped with your life.

I really did. I wandered the streets in a daze.

Every foundation you had was shaken to the core that day. You never expected that He would return then or in that way, yet He used the weak to confound the strong.

Remember what you heard, "She is a forerunner."

Yes, I had forgotten that.

That day was prophecy. I am a forerunner of things to come.

Okay, that's the best news ever!

Differences of administrations but the same Spirit.

Collection

Diversities of operations, but the same Spirit.

Yes.

Oneness.

Yes.

> G asked me if Talia ever had an "attitude" while here. I told him that she would get a "'tude" from time to time. Not very often but she would. I told him to ask her. She would tell him.

Is it true, Talia?

I don't hear anything.

It's true.

6:17 PM
Talia, you said something today about other entities?

Yes, as an overlay during another conversation.

Another lesson on communication?

It was. I said to compile your conversations with other entities, and I reminded you what Curt said, that I wasn't the only one with something to say. He always was practical.

That's true. I'll begin to do that.

Good, that will pay off. It can help others. Enlightenment just for yourself isn't enlightenment; it will stagnate and eventually be lost.

Should I name them?

If they name themselves, that's fine; otherwise, you do not need to know who someone is for them to help you.

Talia, after the crash, you came and stood beside me, didn't you?

Yes. I felt your thoughts and I heard your prayers and I wanted you to know that I was all right.

Did you say anything to me?

Yes, I said to you, "I'm all right."

I thought I heard that. That broke my heart.

That comforted you and that was its purpose.

I felt the pain and emptiness and heartbreak of others, especially your mother.

That was the hardest part of all. Her resiliency is a testimony. Her sacrifice could not have been greater. She lived her life for me, with fullness of purpose. Without her we wouldn't be doing what we're doing now and millions of souls would have suffered.

That's why you said her reward would be so great.

That's one reason. She's helping you also.

I think maybe she's pure in heart.

She couldn't have done what she's done without that.

7:17 PM

You sure do ask good questions.

Yes, and the answers are contained in the questions.

I would be a basket case without you.

Some will think you're a basket case because of me.

But that's just it, it is because of you.

I'm glad you got that, and because you did, others will get it. This is not a conception, it is reality, and as you make it real in you it will become real in others. That's how it works—reality is catching. It's spreading like wildfire. As the false foundation crumbles people will grab on to what is real. The realization of that which is false doesn't serve them anymore. That their assumptions were based on a falsehood. This leads to the realization that their denial of the responsibility of their choices is what leads them to that false foundation to begin with. It's not too late to change. Change your mind. Take control over it; you have the authority. Stop allowing others to dictate your thinking.

That's sound advice.

You think?

Yes, I think on my own, and I take full responsibility for it without influence from others.

Now you're getting there. You feel the confidence?

Yes.

That's because you know what's real.

Talia, line upon line, precept upon precept, you build me up to an unbelievable level.

Collection

That's not just me. It's us, it's everyone. We are all in this together, and the sooner people realize this, the sooner the change begins and we will become, in Oneness, wholeness restored, a rebirth in newness of life. Fullness. The emptiness that most people feel is for a reason. It's because they HAVE been emptied. By believing the lies and deception they have been fed. When they choose to stand up on their own, to decide what is real, then the lies and deception will be swept away.

To own is to make it their own, and swept away is the help that surrounds them.

Yes. To see holographically is to see the whole. But your spoon feeding them isn't going to help; they have to want it and I mean REALLY want it. That time is past; now it will only cause rebellion.

That's strange.

Strange but true, that time is past. That's why I've said so many times not to waste moments but to make the most of them. The children of Israel had a cloud by day and a pillar of fire by night to lead them into the Promised Land. What I'm talking about is the Promised Land, and the signs are just as plain today, but your eyes must be open.

Guides.

Yes.

Shepherds.

Yes, help is all around.

You move me.

I do. I also stop you.

You do. "The wisdom of pause."

Yes, that quiet place of eternity.

You're rather poetic.

I'm truthful.

That's an understatement.

No, I'm filled with truth.

To set us free.

Perfectly. You need rest.

I have it.

Yes, you do.

The Universe Speaks

November 9

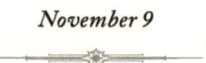

1:01 PM

Relax. Do not let others' thoughts affect you. You can let them affect you or you can control your own. Be separate to come back into Oneness; you are made in His image.

That's what He's done, isn't it?

That is what He has done, is doing, and will do. The present is now, His presence is Now.

In the Now.

In the NOW is in Him. Do you know what we've done, are doing, and will continue to do? We were separated by the death of my body to bring us into Oneness. We aren't separated, G, we are together as One. We are made in His image. This is for those climbing up that mountain, on those little trod paths, striving to become One with Him again.

I see the tremendous struggle.

It will be at times. These are willing to get there or die trying. These have already laid down their life.

Gray is a symbol of flowing because it is balanced. Balanced shades. Colors reflect light. In the absence of light there is no color.

Are you referring to this new gray notebook?

I'm referring to you sitting down in faith and listening for the truth. That's why I immediately spoke to you. You sat down in belief expecting I would. That faith, that simple belief is always honored. That's how simple it is. No ceremony or fanfare, just simple believing.

I hate to leave.

Don't hate it, flow with it. I will be with you.

Thank you, Talia.

You're welcome, G.

Collection

November 10

6:12 AM

Talia, I just remembered something. When I first walked into your house and saw you, a voice said to me, "She's here for you." I realize now that was the voice of the Spirit. I didn't know what to make of it at the time, so I dismissed it.

Now you know why. That's the Voice you should never dismiss, no matter what is said. That is the Voice of truth to set you free. That's the Voice of your Creator. He is the Center of all things. You said of that day that you had never seen anyone move like I moved, that I moved from my center. That's true to a point, but I was moving from and in THE Center and that was a sign to you. That's why I said to you that you could learn everything about a person by the way they moved, because thoughts are revealed through the body. I opened a door for you that day and it wasn't just the vision, it was every single thing that happened.

Well, you sure made a hell of a first impression.

I guess you could put it like that.

6:52 AM

It is such an honor to know you, Talia.

It's an honor to be your friend. I wish everyone would listen like you do.

Help them.

I do. Remember when you were told their unbelief weighs them down?

Yes, when I was in New Orleans before the flood.

Yes. That's what's happening, and it is before the flood again.

12:53 PM

You are agitated.

Yes, I am.

I refer you back to the first thing I told you yesterday.

Okay.

Of course it is. Don't let them affect you. When was the last time this happened?

Probably not long ago.

And why?

The Universe Speaks

Probably the same reason.

Then why make the same mistakes over and over?

Osmosis?

You don't have to receive that.

It was a joke.

It's not funny. It can work like that—you have a shield, remember? Use it.

You are serious today.

This is serious business. That effect, if you allow it, can turn into an infection, a disease.

Sounds serious.

It is.

Are you perturbed? Don't let my levity affect you.

I am patient.

Okay, Talia I was just laughing at myself. Hello! Come on, Talia, we are friends, remember?

I have not forgotten. You remember your mother telling you that you could try the patience of a saint?

Yes, I remember. That was always funny to me.

She had a point to make.

And your point is?

My point is, you cannot laugh yourself through every situation. To use force takes focus, something you sometimes lack.

And right when you had my confidence built up.

I am pointing out to you the balance in all things.

Just trying to get through the day.

No, that is not it at all. You are trying to avoid taking a hard look at your failings. But to laugh it off is just to put it off; why not deal with it instead? You're always mad at yourself when that happens anyway, so why not apply the cure instead of avoidance, which is obviously not working.

Well, you got me pegged.

Collection

I do.

Okay, thanks—you're right, I'll do that.

I know you weren't aware of the remedy; that's why we got into this.

I wasn't even very aware of the problem.

That's because you see it happen to everyone you know, but I'm showing you that it doesn't have to. There is a better way.

1:46 PM
You never told me that before, "not to write it down."

Yes, I have. I told you this wasn't for everyone, and everything I say to you is not to be written. I told you to tell someone something and not to write it. I can snatch it out of your mind anyway.

You would do that?

I will if it's needed.

November 11

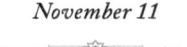

10:15 AM
    G was watching a TV show about the universe.

The universe is "13 billion years old"?

It's just a number.

November 13

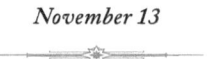

Good morning, Talia.

Good morning. I'm flying to New Jersey today.

I figured you were.

    I was flying to New Jersey for a class. Talia was going with me!

The Universe Speaks

November 14

1:13 PM
She's having fun today.

November 16

12:52 PM
Where are you today, Talia?

New Jersey.

You can be in more than one place at a time.

1:03 PM
When you have time and you are in that place of peace, we will speak.

7:15 PM
Are you enjoying writing your conversations with other entities?

Yes.

Good, you can use that.

Nice to know. It's tiring though.

Copying text can be that. There are people craving the voice of the Spirit; most do not know it though.

I crave it.

But you know it and that's why you're getting it. You can't make a choice of direction if you do not know which direction to go; that is why guides are needed. Most do not have a map or a destination, thus the confusion. Tell them the truth, honestly, and confirm what they already know.

Need a door of opportunity for that.

It's opened.

You seem different today.

You cannot believe the things I do in a day.

Collection

Oh . . . okay.

When you've asked me what I've done today, have you not been overwhelmed?

Yes, a multitude of things come to me at once—that's why I don't ask you that very much or I think of specifics when I do ask.

And I give you certain points that interest you and others, but no amount of explanation will explain it; it would be fruitless to try.

Was it *try* or *attempt to*; it was not clear.

See what I mean?

You seem tired or something. *Frantic* is not the word, and you said you never get tired there.

I'm concerned. I'm concerned that man's decisions are killing him. He is on a path of destruction and right choices need to be made Now.

I see that too. Bad stuff is coming down the road, and I'm tired. But what can I do?

You're doing it right now, and tired is temporary.

Thank God for that.

You're welcome. ☺

I told you I speak as the oracles of God.

So you did.

Rest.

November 17

7:02 AM
Good morning.

Good morning.

What's *nadir*?

The lowest point, the opposite of divinity, the antithesis of the divine nature, the robbery of your birthright. Remember the saying "misery loves company." People may rise up together or pull each other down; time is short. That is both good and bad depending on how it is used.

I want to use it for good.

You will.

The Universe Speaks

November 19

8:30 PM
People don't believe who they are because they don't know who they are.

That's exactly right.

November 20

1:16 PM
Okay, someone brought up the fact that you complimented me a lot and that maybe people would think it was me complimenting me. That had crossed my mind, but I don't think it's an issue because you cannot lie, and I refuse to edit your words. When you said no one knows all the things I know, I realized the same thing could be said for anyone. And I think part of it was to build my confidence up, which it has.

And?

There was more but I'm not remembering it now.

As you've said, you can't go wrong quoting me, so I will quote me: "All I have said to you is true." That is your ego concerned that people will think you're exalting yourself, and you're right, it is a non-issue. One of the things you do not have control over is people's choices.

7:42 PM
Where were we?

We were talking about people's choices and what you could do about them.

And what can I do about them?

You can guide them, when the opportunity arises, to make the best choices, but it's up to them to take control over them. It is their power to make decisions, and it is their decision to take back that power.

Back from who?

From who took it.

Who took it?

Collection

That's the question they should ask. And why? My mother taught me to make rational decisions and to believe in myself, and she made a meticulous effort in doing so. You met the results of that effort.

I sure did. That changed my life.

And it still is.

That's the truth; your word grows.

There is no end to it; it is boundless.

I know.

It's for others to know also.

I know that too.

I know you do. I'm just letting you know the parts we play will not be without results. You need the encouragement sometimes.

Thanks for the encouragement.

You're very welcome. You know, I like you.

That's nice—I like you too—but why do you say that?

To let you know that's another level of affection I have for you.

Look it up.

    G looked up the meaning of "like."

To be pleased with; enjoy.

Yes, what else?

Having the same characteristics; similar; equal.

The same characteristics, similar, and do not limit yourself.

You cut me off on that one.

I did so you didn't cut yourself off from that one.

You lighten my day. I am pleased with you, and I enjoy you.

Hard to receive, isn't it?

A little difficult.

The Universe Speaks

Why? You know I said it, so you know it's true. Why is it that it's so hard to receive such simple truth? It's a perception of separation, and it is a product of your over-trained mind and your under-trained mind. That is why the balance is so necessary, because without it you are lost with no direction.

Where is the balance?

In all things. It is inherent in all things. Reality, what is real, is no separation.

Well, there's nothing I can add to that.

Not yet. When you know who you are, you will believe who you are, and that changes things.

You're almost quoting me now.

I am quoting you—I just took it a step further.

Like your mom.

She did have that influence on me. Where do you think I learned it? You've heard it said, "Do nothing which is of no use," but I'm telling you nothing you do is of no use, you just have to take it a step further, dig a little deeper. The work has already been done, the foundation has already been laid, and the treasure is for the taking.

The T in the word *treasures* that I just wrote looks like a tree.

That's not by coincidence.

The tree of life.

The tree of life is the decisions we make; it grows by our choices.

That's all?

That's all for Now.

November 21

1:17 PM
Good afternoon, Talia.

Good afternoon to you.

Did you ride your horse today?

Yes.

I thought so.

Collection

6:17 PM
This is not for the faint of heart.

How so?

The faint of heart will reject this. It threatens their foundation, most of what they believe. It is not that it is a struggle to have an open heart, it is more of a surrender, and that is the last thing the flesh wants, to surrender. It craves control. Surrender to the flesh is death, and that is what it is, death to its control. Unless and until one is willing to die to find the truth, and the freedom that entails the truth, that freedom they crave will remain elusive, just out of reach.

Thank you, Talia, for your truth.

It's not just mine; it is for anyone who wants it. If you will recall one of the first things I said to you was that nothing was better than freedom. Freedom is imprinted within you. It is your natural state. If you listen to what most people are saying, they are saying that they want more freedom. They want more money because that will give them more freedom, or another job, or to quit their job, or to leave their mate, etc. It goes on and on and most do not realize what they are asking for, but it is in essence to be free.

But none of those things will bring the freedom I speak of. THAT you were born with. It resides within you. But if one quiets the fleshly mind and looks within in, that Supreme Silence that I have spoken of, then their answers will be found and they will discover that it was there all along, quietly residing within them, waiting to be found. That's all.

That's all?

That's all for Now.

11:00 PM
I'm sorry you had to go so soon Talia; you loved your life so much.

I still do.

November 22

8:36 AM
Anything you want to talk about today, Talia?

Yes. Life.

Life?

Yes, it is wise to know a normal life is supernatural. In truth everyone knows this, thus the frustration most feel about their life. They are not seeing it in their life or anyone they know.

The Universe Speaks

The irony is that life flickers through constantly, and when that divine spark is accepted it will grow.

I accept that.

That acceptance is simply receiving what was already theirs to begin with. The truth is you are going to accept something anyway—the truth or lies—the choice is yours and it is that simple.

Choose this day whom you will serve.

That's right, and that service will be rendered regardless of the choice.

November 23

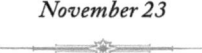

7:33 PM

G: I found out about the death of a friend of a friend tonight, a good man, and I said, "Blessed are they that mourn for they shall be comforted." Then Talia said this to me:

I took that promise, and I stood on it and made sure my mom was comforted—and I still do. But you can do the same with any of these promises and make them your own and believe; it's just that simple.

Talia, I would like your comment on something your mom said once. It was, "I never taught her anything. I just let her be who she was."

She taught me a lot. She did let me be who I was, because she knew that I had the answers within me and that I just had to find them. She was always very mindful of that balance, and that is why my confidence was so high, because I believed in who I was.

That's awesome.

It is awesome. To know who you are is always awesome. Do you think that when He said you are made in His image it is to look like? It is to BE like. Most find this extremely hard to receive, but that's the truth.

She also said something else I found interesting: "When you teach one thing you teach out something else."

Again, she let me be who I was, and she believed in me, and that caused me to believe in me.

Talia, you're brilliant.

I really am. ☺

Collection

November 28

1:43 PM
Anything you want to say to me today, Talia?

Yes. Believe. Believe in yourself. Trust yourself.

Thanks for that. I needed it.

That's why I said it.

That's it?

Yes.

November 30

PM
Talia, I like the small talk too, not only the grand dialogues. You smiled at me today, but I've heard you say nothing. What did you do today?

I went Jeep riding.

December 2009

December 2

8:10 PM
You were so beautiful.

I'm even more beautiful now, like by a billion times.

December 3

7:00 AM
Happy Birthday, Talia.

Thank you.

The Universe Speaks

December 4

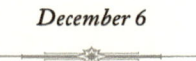

10:30 PM
    G felt Talia's presence and it woke him up.

Talia, you want to talk to me?

Yes.

What about?

Your worth. You're worth more than you think.

Don't really remember thinking about it.

You haven't much.

So what am I worth?

More than you think.

That's all you want to tell me about it?

Yes. I want you to think about it.

December 6

1:14 PM
That finding my release form was not by accident.

    I was going through some old papers I had stored and found a paper with Talia's signature on it. It was a liability release for a class she had taken. It really touched me to see her signature, her writing, her name.

Figured that; what does it mean?

It means that I'm always there, and I'm always thinking of her.

December 7

6:19 PM
Talia, I would sure like to talk to you.

476

Collection

What would you like to talk about?

Anything you want.

Show your love.

Teach me.

I am. Have I not shown you my love?

You sure have.

Then why can't you do the same?

That was your mission, your ministry.

Why can't you do the same?

I'm not you.

No, you're not, but it's the same Spirit, just differences of administration.

So I show my love differently.

You may, but you should still show your love.

Love is the manifestation of the All, in truth.

December 8

1:22 PM
You judge too much by outward appearance. Do you know why? Because you've judged others for the same. When you humbly ask and seek you will always find your edge.

December 10

8:18 AM
You manifested God to me more than anybody ever, ever!

Thank you.

Thank you.

The Universe Speaks

December 11

1:15 PM
You're living two lives and that's the conflict. It is a give and take unto Oneness, remember. All you do is, or should be, a vehicle to bring you back into Oneness. With this cohesion of all things comes a settling of spirit, without which your path becomes wrought with confusion and doubt. But when you become what you truly are, which IS one with all things, the path is clear. And when it is not, your choices are made with the confidence of faith, knowing your decisions will be right ones. You will not always have foreknowledge of what is to be, and to think so is unrealistic. He said, "I will show you things to come," not "I will show you all things to come," so do not abandon faith, for we know in part.

How does it feel to sit on the lap of the King, Sarah? That's incomprehensible to me.

It truly is incomprehensible. You've basked in His light, which is His Love, briefly. Just a taste, as a grain of sand, a drop, compared to a great river or ocean of His Life and Love. It is glorious beyond measure, indescribable. Filled with joy and everything good imaginable. Sarah is a name of honor for me. All that are honored will be given a new name.

I have to go.

I know, but I will stay with you.

Thanks!

You're welcome.

6:36 PM
Talia, that was an amazing miracle.

        G is referring to a miraculous healing of a friend on his deathbed.

I told you last night miracles happen.

I know they do.

Well, that is a miracle.

No doubt.

I told you the prayer of faith is always answered.

Yes, you did.

I cannot lie.

I know you can't.

Collection

Then why doubt?

I only doubt me.

Why?

Sometimes it is not so clear, and sometimes even when it is, I don't know the meaning of what I hear or see. No comment?

Not yet.

December 12

1:05 PM
I got it! It's the harmonious blending of flesh and spirit.

Yes. You do it, but you're inconsistent.

That's living two lives.

Yes.

How can I be consistent?

By not being inconsistent.

Sounds like . . .

I know what you're thinking

So do I: a pat answer.

I have already given you the answer. Yesterday. And before that. A being of One not here and there but here and Now and always. ALL WAYS you are ONE. That is your natural state. It is the mind's craft to separate. Believe you are One and you will walk into it.

That seems simple.

All truth is simplicity perfected. How many times have I said to you Love never fails? Walk in love and you can do no wrong.

You . . . wow!

Yes, I know. ☺

You're not unique in living two lives, most everyone does. I am telling you that is NOT your natural state and that you do not have to; the choice is yours. That duality of living two lives is the conflict both within you and without. The process is to use that lesson as another vehicle

479

to bring you into Oneness. Its design is for you to recognize that for what it is and to decide on something different.

Oh, Happy Hanukkah.

Thank you.

6:14 PM
We are delivering a message here.

I know.

It's what we do together.

You have a point to make?

Yes, believe.

I do.

But you expect it to end.

I don't want it to.

I told you there was no end.

But . . .

I told you our core message was complete.

Well, that might be the first thing I have completely completed in my life.

That's not true. You just did not know when you were done with most things. Now you have a greater sensitivity to what matters, and it is growing.

I reckon that is good news.

It is. That light you saw today was me.

I know.

It's to let you know I am always there.

Nice confirmation, thanks.

You're welcome.

What were the other lights?

Spirits, friends, helpers, angels.

What do they do?

Collection

Protect, serve, whisper truths, minister, deliver messages.

They seem busy; they're usually moving fast.

They are busy, they move as fast as they need to, and there is a war.

A war?

Yes. A war between Light and darkness, and the battles are fought primarily over the mind of man. That's where his choices are made. The world is filled with delusion and darkness, but if one chooses Light over darkness, the Light will always prevail. It is certain victory if one is steadfast and believes.

December 13

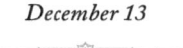

1:10 PM
Sorry, Talia.

    G was joking around quite a bit.

That's okay, you were just having fun.

The birds are a symbol of joy, peace, and love incarnate. And humor is everywhere. It is a part of what God is.

That's why it's everywhere.

You're not as dull as you make out.

I checked three times to make sure that was you.

I can have fun too.

I know you can. I had the impression you were somewhat of a master at it.

I am now. ☺

You delight my heart.

That's my God nature, and yours. We're changing lives.

That's good to know.

That's our God nature, and theirs.

9:25 PM
This is a hard planet.

The Universe Speaks

It is a learning ground, a schoolhouse.

Never cared much for school.

Don't feel sorry for yourself; you're learning more than you know.

In much knowledge is much grief.

That's true. You begged for knowledge.

Breaking through things is not always easy.

Thanks, Talia, I apologize for the attitude.

That's all right; it's not wrong to express your feelings. Feel better?

Yeah, I do.

Good, feelings are often downplayed more than they should be. They are messages too.

I've heard that.

You heard the truth.

December 14

1:22 PM
Let your mind go.

Let my mind go?

Yes, let it go. Let it go where it wants to go. Just let it go.

December 19

1:18 PM
Hey, time really is short—my break is almost over.

That's funny.

You don't sound very convinced.

No, I'm convinced, you're the skeptic.

You turned that around on me.

Collection

You turned that around on yourself. To convince yourself of something that's not is easy, and common. The shock comes when you convince yourself of something that's not true, because it will be proven false.

7:24 PM
You've got to find the balance between concentration and relaxation.

8:14 PM
　　While sitting with G I decided to ask Talia some questions.

Did you leave the penny?

Yes, I said I would leave you pennies and I do.

Did the fact that you and your dad, Michael, did not believe in God at the time of the crash have an effect on your transition and entry into heaven?

It didn't affect me, but it did affect Michael because of the way he lived his life, and it still does.

Talia, I want to know about the universal energy. Does it continuously fill or do you take from one source to use for another?

Yes, it depletes it from one source but gives it back from another source. Love is always balanced.

December 20

12:56 PM
Talia, do you have something to say to me?

Yes.

I thought so, and what, pray tell, would that be?

Self-pity doesn't serve you; stop feeling sorry for yourself.

Let's just say I was doing that . . .

I just did and you are.

Why am I doing that?

You feel like you deserve better. You feel as though you've been ripped off in the past. You feel as though you've made quantum leaps ahead of those who have done this. You feel that the world should be fair and it is not. You feel many of your teachers deceived you. And you feel you're missing the respect you deserve.

Guess that pretty much sums it up.

Still, what does self-pity profit?

The perpetuation of a vicious circle.

Pretty much. You think that it's a time, money, and equipment issue. I'm saying to you that it is much more of a pride and ego-based issue. Everybody deals with issues of jealousy, pride, ego, fear, envy, and other darkness, from themselves and others. The question is, will you rise up and overcome your own? Then, will you rise up and not receive that which is thrust upon you by others? When these others are taken within you and received as truth, then the problems arise. Thus it has been said, "Receive not a lie but receive the truth," and this truth must be jealously guarded as a bulwark against deception and darkness, for the enemy is relentless and forever vigilant for a crack at the door.

Easy to talk about.

Easier to do than not do.

5:53 PM
Talia.

Yes, I'm waiting.

For me?

For you. Much distractions.

Referring to?

Distractions.

That does seem to get you distracted.

Pay attention to where your attention is.

It's on you.

Now it is; where was it before?

Necessary chores.

And before that?

Too many things at once.

That's true. I told you before, the mind's craft is to separate things. This can work to your advantage if you use it. Separate what you want to focus on and let your focus be on that. What you choose to focus on is what you will focus on.

Once again, simplicity perfected.

Collection

Glad you remembered that. Now let your mind work for you. That's mind control, to let your mind work for you—that's its job, to separate from the many that you may focus on the One. ☺

Why are you smiling?

Because I just told you something that is profoundly important.

But that's nothing new. You're always doing that.

No, as a matter of fact it is something new if you apply it, realize it, and make it your own.

I'm going to have to ponder and digest this.

That's important too.

December 21

6:19 PM
Talia, I really need an answer on that stuff last night.

Try the spirits, whether they be of God, for many false prophets are gone out into the world.

Is that your answer, Talia?

Yes. They have tried to undermine your confidence on this many times before. It is a double portion of darkness; they are FRANTIC over this message.

The most subtle beast in the field, the serpent. That is brilliant for the dark side.

They are well versed in deception—after all, that is all they do.

    G heard the spirit Grandfather.

You already had the answer within you. What has Granddaughter told you? The fabric of life is all woven together.

December 31

PM
Talia, are you mad at me?

No.

Then why aren't you talking to me?

I talk to you every day.

485

Guess it must be me then.

You need to make an effort.

January 2010

January 1

12:03 AM
Happy New Year, Talia.

Happy New Year.

January 2

6:38 PM
Talia, you have anything to say to me?

Yes, a lot. We're behind.

Good. I mean, good that you have lots to say to me.

You need to take the time and make the effort.

Anything else?

Not now.

January 5

4:47 PM
Come on, Talia, you know I love you.

I know you do.

Hey, that was you!

Yes. We have a message and it needs to be recorded IN DEPTH. You see how hard it is to write while you're driving?

Collection

January 6

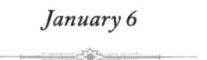

G was sitting in a restaurant in a strange town, waiting for his car to be fixed.

Talia, I'm just a pilgrim; I'm just passing through.

It's that way everywhere you are there. That restless longing has purpose. It is to let you know you have no permanent home there. Your home is another world. It also serves to spur you to excellence. It keeps you seeking.

You are here, aren't you?

Yes.

You're sitting across from me, aren't you?

Yes.

I feel your presence. I see your energy.

A confirmation of what you already know and what I just told you. Like the tracks.

They will fix it today, partially. You didn't want to hear that.

What's it about?

It was to slow you down so we could do this.

Thank you, Talia.

Thank you; you know I like having lunch with you. ☺

My heart burns for you.

That is your fervent love, your passion, and it is appreciated.

Time to go.

6:55 PM

Talia, what's happening?

You're learning to accept things as they are.

Everything happens for a reason.

The Universe Speaks

January 8

———❖———

7:55 PM
Talia, I need to get to you.

You don't need to get to me; I'm already there.

Then let's talk.

Yes. They were watching you today, your friends.

Why?

They learn from you too.

What?

How to live, and they are there to assist, to help. Your path and theirs are intertwined. They had a message for their people and so do you; you have a message for yours.

What?

What you find . . . in your journeys.

It's not just physical journeys either, in fact, most of them aren't. What you do transcends the physical, and that is the message, to transcend the physical. The physical is limited, finite. The spiritual is without end. One must ask themselves, why such an emphasis on the physical?

Why is that?

Its design is to rob you of the spiritual, of your inheritance, and it is perpetrated in the most subtle of ways.

I believe that.

You certainly should. You could have quit years ago but you kept being called back, and that is how we are doing this now. Your rebellion, which was sometimes extreme, kept you from falling into that trap. Don't expect praise from the world, expect resentment. These would rather cage a wild animal; after all, they call it wild.

I'm not a wild animal.

But you're free and they aren't; thus, the resentment.

I should resent that but I'm seeing the humor instead.

You would. However, it is understandable that you would resent them. But how would that help?

Collection

It would not.

That's exactly right. It would debilitate you and they would have succeeded to a certain extent in robbing you of your freedom.

What do they get out of this?

Nothing but a sick satisfaction in doing damage.

That's sick.

It is sick. It is a sickness. The way to overcome them and to help them also is to love them.

Love never fails.

That's true, it never does.

My "death" was about bringing life to others.

You're sure doing that.

I sure am.

You've touched so many lives.

And I will continue to do so. There is no stopping me. See, I can always make you laugh. I'm a bringer of laughter, of life.

That's life!

Yes, THIS is life. It is pure. It is joy unspeakable.

Ain't no way to talk about it.

It is beyond description. It is within your heart and it is within all.

All.

Yes, All.

It is the language of life. THAT is the light of the eyes. It lights your path and it perfects that which concerns you.

I saw you holding His hand

Yes, you did and I smiled at you.

I remember.

Remember all things.

You kind of lost me there.

You'll get it. That is All for Now.

That's All for Now?

That's right.

Sometimes it seems like we're going in circles.

We are going in circles; that is why I emphasized the spherical nature of the universe. That is how it works. You are meant to go in circles. The planets teach this.

I saw that in a most profound way in your eyes.

And that enlightened your darkness.

It did.

And it will continue to do so.

January 9

1:15 PM
I'm here to make an effort. ☺

And to take the time. ☺

Yes.

That's good. That is all it takes, and you will always get something out of it, more than you put in. He doesn't meet you halfway, He meets you all ways and everywhere. That effort is always honored and it is remembered. It is His good pleasure to give you the kingdom.

Well, it's already exceeded my feeble effort.

Thus what I just said. You see new horizons?

Yes.

They are always new; you are just noticing it differently.

New eyes.

A new perspective.

You will see some things and you will notice a difference, some changes.

May my awareness be complete.

It will be.

Collection

January 12

11:26 PM
I have limited time.

I'm glad you're aware of that.

I looked up subdue in the Hebrew.

Hebrew is a very visual language. That is what we are doing with the message, expanding veils.

There was more.

There is always more, much more.

January 15

1:26 PM
I feel you, Talia.

That's because I'm here.

Good, because I'm running out of room to keep changing the date.

It's hard for you to "shift gears." It would be easier if you just stayed in that place of communication.

I want to, Talia.

It takes a quiet mind.

I know where that quote came from.

Yes, it is yours. Remember when I told you I practice what I preach?

I do.

Then you do the same.

Well, glad we got that settled.

It is not settled. It will not be settled until you walk in it constantly, your life as a prayer.

The temple walk.

Some call it that. You see it is largely an attitude, and your attitude can be changed in an instant. It has been too much activity of the flesh and not enough stillness. When you're still, you will find that "peaceful spirit."

Quoting me again.

I'm quoting you because you're right and to let you know that.

1:34 PM
Talia, I would sure like you to talk to me.

I will.

Okay.

What would you like to talk about?

Whatever you would like to.

My mom's more advanced than you might think. How do you think she raised me like she did if she wasn't? She told you her policy was honesty—that's advanced.

That is advanced.

Yes, it is. It is also a policy that would change the world if it were implemented.

Boy, she'll like this.

She will like it and she will agree wholeheartedly. My love for her has no limits. I would "jump over the moon, swim the Pacific Ocean . . ." to get to her.

Guess you could do that now.

I really can.

January 16

1:08 PM
Relax. Do not let others' thoughts affect you.

You said that before.

Yes, and I am saying it again. It can be a spherical negative or a spherical positive, and it is largely up to you.

Collection

January 17

1:14 PM

That first sentence you said yesterday was somewhat prophetic.

There is a vast difference between someone who knows who they are and someone attempting to be someone they are not.

I can see how that would engender some insecurity issues.

That's it exactly. I never tried to be something I wasn't. I was just being who I was, and that was always enough.

Talia, I would say you were always more than enough, a huge cut above, absolutely beyond amazing.

Let's don't overdo it.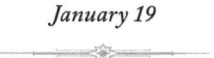

You can always make me laugh.

A bringer of laughter, that's me. ☺

I wish I had more time.

So do I but we will make it up.

That's good to know.

It's spherical remember; it always comes back around.

January 19

6:20 PM

What you do in any part of your life affects everything else. These spherical concentric rings of one's acts and thoughts are never-ending and everything in the universe is in some measure affected by them.

Everything has a deeper meaning than what can be seen on the surface.

Talia, I realized last night that our core message really was complete, but I sure do love our chats.

I told you we would get there.

I know you did—I just finally realized it last night.

The Universe Speaks

Are you sad?

I guess a little.

Why?

It was exciting, you were so animated.

Is it not still exciting?

Yes!

I'm still "animated."

Yes, you are.

You were looking forward to this time.

Yes, I was.

Are you complaining?

No. I love our talks, our time together.

We are never apart.

I love that!

It's the truth.

I know. It's my awareness that's lacking sometimes.

Whose fault is that?

Mine, but is it not meant to be this way sometimes?

What do you think?

Good question, and now that you ask it I would say no.

No is correct. That is the way it is sometimes, but that is not the way it was meant to be. You were meant to be in constant communication with the Spirit that animates all things, and in truth you are. What your focus, your attention, is on is what it will be on, and it is your choice.

The magic wand of the mind.

You could call it that. I would call it the power of your decisions.

You're perfect.

I know. I like your laugh.

You can always bring it out of me.

Collection

January 20

2:05 PM

    G heard Michael talking to him.

I made some mistakes.

January 22

2:38 PM

How do you feel today?

I feel fine, why?

That's a good question to ask yourself. How do I feel and why? Feelings and emotions are often underplayed; if they are controlled and understood they will often tell you a lot.

Well, I feel fine.

Why?

Emerging opportunities.

That is certainly a part of it. What else?

I feel the peace of God.

That is the other part of it. That peace, that calmness, creates its own opportunities.

That's beautiful, Talia.

That is the literal definition of beauty. ☺ Remember when you asked, "What is beauty?"

I do now.

All of your questions will be answered.

I heard most don't ask the questions.

That's right, very many do not.

Why not?

For a multitude of reasons, but most just do not care for the answers.

So much for this being a best seller.

The Universe Speaks

I have told you that the time of spoon-feeding was over. For everything there is a season and that season has passed. This is for those who thirst. The signs are manifested daily that a new age is being ushered in. These are the times that will try the hearts of men. These are also the times that will find a few who will rise up above the trials and the tribulations of man into a glorious new liberty, a liberty that few have ever known.

I love our little chats.

I know you do.

I would like to mention to the reader what is between the lines here.

It's not time to get into that now. What is hidden will be revealed to those who thirst.

January 23

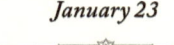

1:20 PM
Good afternoon, Talia.

Good afternoon to you.

I receive it. I'm there.

Yes, you are. ☺

How is your day?

It is beautiful, and yours?

Good and getting better all the time.

It's beautiful.

Yes, it is.

Then do not be reluctant to say it.

You're right; I'm having a beautiful day.

Don't let the problem seekers spoil your fun.

January 25

Welcome to Belize.

Collection

January 28

    After hiking up a river bank to swim in Blue Creek Cave in Belize . . .

Talia, go in with us.

I'm going in with you!

This is cold.

It's not cold.

January 29

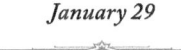

There is no end to it. And you will think when you get here, what a waste of time to worry about anything, which it is.

I gazed at a little yellow flower and perceived the entirety of knowledge of the universe, in vortex, energy form, streaming out of the center of the bloom, never-ending colors, vibrations . . .

I took you to heaven. That was a glimpse of heaven. How did you think of me before?

Like a flower of the universe.

Exactly.

January 30

    While G is looking at yellow canna flowers:

These are my favorite.

    And at another yellow flower:

I like these too.

February 2010

February 2

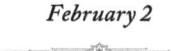

10:14 PM
>G had been thinking a lot about an old friend that had recently passed away. For two days before she passed he had awoken at 4:00 AM thinking about her and her husband. Then he found out she had died.

She wants you to know she's all right, she's okay. She's still in a transitional phase. It's different for everyone. As unique as a personality. You prayed for her; do you not think it was answered? She wasn't evil, and a good person shall be saved.

February 6

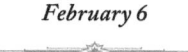

1:04 PM
Why do you fear?

I will stop that.

Good.

February 12

7:38 PM
Talia, I need to hear you.

Then hear me.

I don't think it's ever been this long.

Whose fault is that?

Let me think: mine.

I told you that you have to make an effort.

I know, and take the time.

I know you have been busy. What did you learn today?

Collection

If I read your words I can hear your voice.

What else?

Sleep is a gift.

What else? There is someone working behind the scenes—there always is.

Thanks for the answer.

You already knew that; I just wanted you to acknowledge it.

God, it's good to hear your voice.

Well put.

Thanks for making me smile.

I made you laugh too and that's a gift.

The gift of laughter.

Yes.

February 19

6:15 PM
So what does heaven have to say?

Listen. You don't talk to me as much as you did.

You don't talk to me as much as you did.

It's a dialogue. And if you do not listen, you will not hear. Many will not speak if they are not spoken to first. I always speak to you when you can hear me. Why the struggle? There has always been a flowing in everything we have done. This effort is effortless.

You know it's easier from where you're at.

And you should be where I am at. That is the only place you can be what you're meant to be, which is what you are.

7:31 PM
     G sensed Talia's presence while reading.

You want to talk to me?

Yes, you are writing a work of art, not reading a work of fiction.

The Universe Speaks

That's good.

That is very good. Continue with your work, with our work.

I will.

Yes, I know you will. Why the struggle?

It's not always a struggle.

When you fight it, it's a struggle.

I don't want it to be a struggle.

But when you fight it, it is.

I didn't know I was fighting it.

You're fighting with it. Why not yield to the flow of it instead?

Good idea. What's the message, Talia?

The betterment of mankind, the avoidance of destruction. Over and over we have talked about man's choices, his determinations. Many are sensing change, many are waking up, but so many are not aware of what they are waking up to.

What are they waking up to?

They are waking up to a new life, if they will accept it. Some have no one else to talk this over with, to discuss it. So then some chalk it up to their imagination, only to go back to sleep.

Thus these words.

These words are nothing but ink on paper until they are received and internalized, embodied. Then there is change on the inside, and that is lasting change. And when that happens they will see the change they see on the outside as a blessing and not a curse. You've felt the prayers of these that are awakening and they are refreshing.

Yes.

Blessings spoken. Words have power when they are spoken with intent and faith. Man has barely begun to realize his potential. When he draws near to his Creator his Creator draws near to him. And when he finds the hidden powers within Him he will find that he is complete. Everyone is fractured; One is not fractured, One is complete. Separate ones are fractured. One is complete.

Two into One.

Separation into wholeness!

Collection

Yes.

You sounded exited.

I am. I am here to help you, and we will be one, and the awakening has begun.

Thank you for everything.

Everything is what we are.

February 20

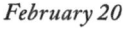

1:07 PM
I heard you laughing with us a while ago about that whole Fourth Amendment thing.

It's funny.

> While at Talia's Celebration of Life, a speaker was commenting on a speech Talia had given in a debate class. She had been debating the Second Amendment, and the teacher told us all that Talia had really supported the Fourth Amendment. It was really funny, that mistake from a teacher!

Did you do that?

I had help. I thought things needed to be lightened up—it was a celebration.

You learned so fast.

I told you, I was virtually there already.

You sure were. I never saw anyone move in the Spirit like that constantly, every second filled to the brim.

That's how it is here.

That perfection in the flesh has always been a myth to me. I've only heard about it; I never saw it, just heard stories.

Well, this story is true and you lived it and you still can.

How?

By being who I am.

But how can I do that?

By being who you are now.

501

The Universe Speaks

February 22

1:15 PM
Well, what's up?

Me!

Not much time here.

Things are moving fast. Be fair, be discreet, do not let others' thoughts affect you.

That's the answer for the jerks in the parking lot?

That is the answer for many things.

7:43 PM
How was your day?

Beautiful. And yours?

The same. Some have asked, how do I know this is you?

The truth verifies itself.

Don't know if that's going to help them.

But that's what it does, that is what happens.

Could you explain?

I could.

Will you?

I will. The truth verifies itself to itself. The truth is already known by you. The truth you receive is witnessed by the truth that is already contained within you. The truth witnesses, or is recognized, by further truth you receive. How can it not know itself? It harmonizes with itself, with more of itself. No lie is of the truth.

That sums it up for me.

Collection

More truth is born of experience, of receiving the Light. The Light witnesses itself, and it witnesses itself expanding. This Light is forever expanding; it is the nature of the universe.

Talia, you are awesome.

I know. If people know/knew who they were/are, they will/would recognize that in themselves also. Either way you write it, the meaning is the same.

Did I hear it both ways?

You did. It's rarely either/or, but it is often all or nothing.

Anything to say to your mom?

Yes. I love her.

That really says it all, doesn't it?

It really does.

She can feel it and she knows it's true.

Anything else Talia?

No, that's all for now.

February 28

PM
Talia, do you know how much I love you?

I know. ☺

Do you believe in what I am doing?

Yes.

Do you believe in what you're doing?

I believe in what we're doing.

The Universe Speaks

March 2010

March 1

AM
If you don't believe, I can't talk to you.

March 5

1:38 PM
You have anything to say to me today, Talia?

Yes, do your best, always do your best.

11:46 PM
You've been living the Art of Life instinctively. You know who you are.

March 11

6:02 PM
I don't have to write, I just have to listen.

That's right.

I just want to say, I believe the spirit of prophecy and I think I know why—the accuser of the brethren.

Do you believe that?

I do.

Why?

Because, for one reason, the enemy will do anything to discourage this message.

Emotional overlay.

Collection

Is that what it's called?

Yes. And it can work both ways.

Up or down?

Yes.

March 13

6:38 PM
So, what's the word today, Talia?

Truth. Truth in the inward parts. A part of you, an embodiment of it, a walking in it. When you walk in it you will see it manifested out of you, and these signs will follow those who believe. Others will see it; they will notice, and be able to follow these signs. This is their purpose.

Stirring the faith in them.

Yes, and even creating the faith in them, awakening it. That is what I am doing.

You sure are.

I sure am.

March 15

6:50 AM
Good morning, Talia.

Good morning!

You sure are chipper this morning.

You can be too.

I know what you were like waking up here.

You're awake; and I'm trying to get you to wake up more.

Okay, okay!

The Universe Speaks

March 19

1:45 PM

How long does it take to "become a place"?

One hour if I have not been there in a while.

It is easier just to stay there. That is why it is important to walk every day.

9:12 PM

Talia, do you have anything to say to me?

Yes, live your life without condemnation from others.

You already told me that.

Yes, and you haven't comprehended it yet.

I just realized you're right.

How could I not be? You will never live in peace when you receive disharmony. Reject the lie; receive harmony.

March 20

7:08 PM

    G: I was contemplating a walk when Talia said:

Why don't you talk with me? That's the walk I'm talking about, walking in fellowship.

Sounds good. I want to walk in fellowship with you, Talia, I really, really do.

Then you can. Nothing has changed but your perception. You fell into the trap of doing instead of being. You're already there.

You're right again.

I always am.

There's that confidence I love.

You love the truth, which is everything revealed. Remember when I said we would be moving in a certain direction? Everyone's not going to agree with the direction I move, and it is unrealistic for you to think so. Remember whom I said this message was for.

Collection

I would have to reread it, but I know the ones you mean.

Then why are you shocked and amazed when you get mixed messages from others? I told you the truth isn't opinions, it's fact. I said to you we were dealing in facts. Everyone isn't going to play our game; they have their own agenda. This is nothing you don't already know, but since you want me to spell it out to you, I will.

I remember I asked you to do that awhile ago, to "spell it out for me, Talia." Thanks for that; I had forgotten that.

Well, I remembered. You lack faith sometimes.

I know.

Only believe.

Good advice.

It is. When you do not feel it—and sometimes you will not—only believe. Go on prior knowledge of truth. That is remembering it. He does not change. He is Changeless.

Another name for the Almighty.

It is. Do you know why I asked you here today?

Why?

So you could hear my voice again and believe.

I believe that.

I knew you would.

I love your words.

You love everything about me.

That's true, I do. ☺

My dad says he thinks highly of you.

Tell him thanks; I appreciate it and my apologies for running him down before.

He says he understands.

Sorry, Michael.

That's okay.

    Talia said it to G, but G also heard Michael himself.

507

He says tell my mom he is still working to get through to them and they should make an offer. They know it's the right thing to do.

Will they?

That decision is theirs to make.

Hope they do the right thing.

So do we. There is no lack there, and it is enough for everyone, and that is what we are trying to get them to see.

April 2010

April 6

11:36 AM
Talia, what were the most important things to you here?

Relationships. Like with Mom, and Krystal. It was the bonding. I learned a lot. What's the most important thing to you?

The same. Relationships.

That's reality.

Thanks for telling me that, Talia.

You just have to listen.

Yeah, I know.

The horses played a huge part in my growing up.

I know you said they taught you a lot about balance.

They did. Now you know what I meant.

Why do you do that?

Smoke? Because I'm addicted?

There's more to it than that. Why are you walking away?

Collection

I'm not walking away; I'm just going inside.

So you say.

You're not done?

No, I'm not done. I will be here today with his sons. You'll see the love they have.

That will be a joy.

It will be. There is nothing greater on earth than that love.

April 17

1:48 PM
You talk to Jesus every day, don't you?

Yes, he's my brother and Savior.

7:43 PM
We are going into some things that are hard to write.

Like what?

Some depths of truth that are beyond understanding with language alone. This is the FELT SENSE that is indescribable. This is a thing not conceived in your world.

How are we going to put this in words?

We are not. We are going to point to directions and paths to take.

To lead us where we need to go?

That's right, into the indescribable. Words aren't enough anymore. These paths . . . some have not been taken before. These are for those who have put it all together.

Who are you quoting?

Those who have put it all together. It's going to take a while, so don't freak out on me.

I was not planning to. This is not going to be easy is it?

No, it is not.

The Universe Speaks

April 18

6:49 PM
Last night, I dreamed of "Empowered Wisdom." Could you tell me more about that?

I will. It is the demonstration of wisdom. It is experienced wisdom empowered by the Spirit. It is walking in fullness of life, nothing lacking. It is the power of being. You're thinking that reproducing what you were teaching consistently is impossible, but it's not. Being who you are is in perfect rhythm with the universe, and being that, there is nothing impossible. You've heard "all things are possible"; do you think these are just words to make you feel good?

No.

No, they are not. They are words of Empowered Wisdom.

☺ Wow, Talia, you're good!

I'm the best.

April 19

7:13 PM
You don't have to work so hard.

How do you mean?

You don't have to work so hard for what you want.

Care to explain?

Something like Eden, like picking fruit.

Sounds easy.

When you're in Eden it is.

Where is Eden?

Eden is where you find it. Things will come to you.

Like what?

Like everything you need. Remember the sleeping bag and what I called it.

A divine shelter.

Yes.

Collection

April 20

7:05 PM
I can't believe how dull I can be. I just realized what you meant when you said, "We don't change, we just grow." Because we are already perfect, "born into it," and infinity is within us and we just grow, expand into it, "in the image of God." Reflecting our Creator.

That's true and that is some of the least of what is contained here. And to be dull or brilliant is a choice for everyone to make.

That's brilliant!

That's your choice.

April 23

1:20 PM
Hello, Talia.

Hello.

What do you think about that book?

> She is referring to a book about Spirit and the universe G was reading.

I think you should read it. You'll see how much further we've taken things. Most are tortured souls, on both sides.

5:51 PM
Music is healing. It is mathematical perfection, science and spirit merging—as one. Words are as music. The healing power of the Word. All sounds uttered in this way are healing.

This IS for an advanced few.

It is a springboard they need, and this few will multiply. You sense my joy?

Yes.

This is a truth I KNOW. This isn't for everyone.

I know.

Just letting you know.

So don't be frustrated when they scratch their wooden heads and attack?

Something like that. Some will say you're deluded.

That's their judgment.

Of course it is. A misunderstanding of the true word. Truth sounds foreign to most because it is not a place they dwell and they rarely hear it. But take heart, the foundation of lies is crumbling.

6:31 PM
Talia, you told me once that I was formidable and smiled. I said okay and thought it was a nice compliment, but I finally looked it up and what impressed me was "hard to handle." Any comment on that clever one?

It was a compliment and you are hard to handle. I've had horses that were easier to train.

Oh man, you kill me!

You have a mind of your own and that's good, but you are stubborn and rebellious sometimes.

Hmmm.

That's it?

I don't know how to reply to that.

Reply truthfully.

Well, that's obviously true.

We all are unique aspects of God, in us.

Obviously true also.

It is our reflection of Him, of the universe shining through us.

Agreed.

It is when our self-will causes an imbalance that the problems begin.

I told you there should be a flowing in everything we do, not a struggle.

My mom learned patience from me. She learns more of it every day. She will use this in the future as a healing method. Remember when I said we can't interfere? That is part of what I meant.

Higher purpose.

Collection

Yes. Lessons to be learned, to form compassion, to help others. Your word is not without truth, and it will not return void. Add passion, that's power. Every utterance is recorded. You're getting tired, the flesh is weak.

So you've said, but did I need a reminder?

You didn't.

8:29 PM
I was just reading through some of this and there is no way this isn't you.

It is me.

I know it is; it's just that some people think I'm dreaming this up.

Of course they do; they haven't experienced me and they are not living the life you're living. You can't judge them for that.

Yes, I know, but it gets frustrating sometimes.

How do you think we feel sometimes? It's our lives and theirs they are denying.

So what's the answer?

The answer is Perfection rules, and we see that.

I want to see it.

You do, most of the time. Your frustration is where you see the world going. I just told you it is a false foundation and it is crumbling; it cannot last.

That's really good news, isn't it?

It is some of the best. Something will bloom in its place, something wonderful—the untold truth.

Untold?

Untold. It hasn't been told—yet. No one yet has all the truth; it is in part. But when that which is perfect has come, that which is in part shall be done away with, it shall be no more. It is a New World; all will be transformed. This is that which has not been conceived of in your world; it is beyond thought.

Then I am not going to think about it.

You couldn't if you tried, not yet.

"Not yet." You said that to me the other day out of the blue.

The Universe Speaks

It was out of the blue, to confirm this to you, to prepare you to hear.

9:07 PM
      G and I were talking. All of a sudden Talia spoke up and agreed with something that I had said. G jokingly said to me, about Talia:

She's grounded.

You can't ground me. ☺

April 25

9:45 AM
      G saw a white swirl of energy.

Talia?

It's me. What were you just thinking?

I don't know. Why?

Point is, be mindful of your thoughts. They're real, remember.

April 28

AM
Take the high road.

That's the second time you've told me that in the last month or so. What does that mean?

You know what it means, you've just forgotten.

April 29

8:15 AM
That friend of yours is suffering. That is why he treats others as he does.

How does that help?

Collection

It doesn't but it temporarily relieves his pain. A part of him feels it will help people grow. It is illusion that for others to join him in his suffering, his pain will be eased, shared. A perversion of the Oneness I have spoken of. He knows it is wrong but he is compulsive. Pray for him to wake up and live his truth.

That's sad, Talia.

I know. My mom will not be mistreated without consequences. She's also the apple of His eye.

May 2010

May 1

1:26 PM
Talia, the little things you say.

Subtle, aren't they?

Yes, they are, hard to hear sometimes.

The quieter you are the louder they seem. I've only shouted at you once.

When you told me to tell your mom you were okay.

Yes, and I didn't know it at the time, but it was also to underscore how important it is to us here to let our loved ones KNOW we are all right. I HAD to get that message across. Thank you.

You don't have to thank me.

I'm thankful.

Any message you want delivered, just tell me.

I'm glad you feel that way.

I do feel "that way." I know what you mean.

Yes, and anyone that feels that way can receive the message.

Humility and thanksgiving.

That is a large part of it.

The Universe Speaks

May 5

8:50 AM

My message is to change people's perspective, to realize that they are already free, if they will accept it.

9:00 AM

You've always been ahead of me, Talia.

No, I'm not; we are One.

May 7

1:01 PM

Talia, do you have anything to say to me?

Are you ready to listen?

Yes. And I choose to be brilliant.

That is a good choice. Then why do you proclaim things that aren't so?

Like nobody will ever finish this book? No one has yet.

Not so. You and Mom have read it through and through more than once.

That's all?

No, that is not all. It is a "best seller" here. The most heard comment here is, "Awesome!" and "This can change everything!"

Good to know someone's reading it.

Many more will; it takes time. Remember when I told you not to be discouraged?

Yes.

And when someone does not understand something they often tend to ignore it?

Yes.

Well, do not expect anyone to get this in one reading; there's too much there. I said to you this shook foundations.

You did.

Collection

That can cause fright. That is uncomfortable.

And?

There is no fear in love; that is what we want them to know. To know there is no fear is to know love. That is the main purpose of this message, which YOU have even missed, to know no fear by knowing love. How many times have I said Love never fails?

A lot.

Do you think I have repeated that because I am at a loss for words?

Not at all.

You heard it said that my mission on Earth was to love, and I did that, and that mission has continued non-stop. And it will continue still. It never fails. I accepted you wholeheartedly the day we met. Because I felt your love and I returned it to you—and that has changed your life.

May 14

1:52 PM
Talia, you just blow me away.

I blow away the cobwebs.

May 16

12:59 PM
What would you like to know?

I would like to know when people are going to wake up.

When they decide to.

May 17

12:20 PM
I'm letting you think your own thoughts. It is important for you to do that, to have time to. You have a voice also.

The Universe Speaks.

It has to.

You can become what you are, that's the point.

That IS the point.

May 19

AM
Speaking the truth out of a sincere heart.

That is what I did.

May 21

12:47 PM
Talia, what are you doing?

Living life fully!

You know, I asked a friend of mine why his books didn't sell better than they did, because they are really good and they're hard to find. He said people would rather read romance novels. Maybe that's what we should write.

This is a romance novel.

Really?

Yes, really. All we have talked about is love, and love is everything. It is the answer to all the ills of the world.

May 23

1:06 PM
Let your mind go limp.

Never heard of that.

Remember where I said the doorway was.

1:33 PM
You were actively thinking. That's not the doorway. Let it go and let the image come to you.

Sorry, Talia.

That's okay; I know you're still a young man. ☺

May 27

6:50 PM
You want to know what I think you should do?

Yes.

Believe in yourself.

You just built my confidence up, Talia.

That's what that was meant to do.

June 2010

June 1

That which Ken said is true: free will is a filter. I had told you that before, but you failed to write it because you didn't understand it.

My mistake.

That's all right; we got the message to you.

Could you clarify?

In part, free will is a filter because it filters out that which cannot remain. You purify yourself. Remember when I told you I made good choices?

Yes.

Well, that's how simple it is. My joy in passing that test, the test of life, and completing my mission is truly beyond description.

Everyone has a voice, the universe speaks, and it speaks through everything, primarily because everything is One thing.

Does the feminine, yielding part have anything to do with it?

That aspect of the Spirit is as much a part as the other aspect; you might call it its counterpart, but it is all One and the same—the self-same Spirit.

This subject has no end, does it?

No, it never has and it never will. That which is coming upon the earth, the winds of destruction, are the result of man's choices, of him not yielding; however, the correct choices result in a gentle breeze of perfection.

Talia, help us get through it.

Oh, you will be helped. They who listen shall flourish.

What should I do?

Be yourself.

June 13

1:54 PM
You've seen how the subconscious acts on the conscious mind to direct it.

Yes.

Which way did you go?

The way my conscious mind directed.

THAT is noteworthy.

That's why I'm keeping notes.

6:21 PM
You see now the importance of being AWAKE, of being conscious. That you are not influenced or directed by another.

That was a fascinating battle of light and darkness the other night.

That is the battle everyone is involved in now. Remember to keep your guard up; the evil is insidious. You have a shield—use it. Acts directed by a conscious mind are acts of light.

That's beautiful.

The thunder of pure focused thought, wrought in silence. Not in words, but in deed and in truth. A vanguard.

Collection

I would say that's one definition of being on the cutting edge of darkness.

IT IS.

Insidious in Latin means "to ambush," and also "more dangerous than seems evident." That's certainly what I picked up the other night.

That is how it works. The subconscious receives these impulses as a thought of your own, even as inspired. If they are followed without thought, these thoughts of others become your own and the result is decisions made in darkness

You always have the answers.

I always have the answers, and I always have the correct ones. ☺

The heart?

I left the heart for her; my mom and I are one.

What are you doing?

Sitting shiva.

June 26

7:27 PM
Talia, you want to talk to me?

Yes, you're being lazy.

Is that true?

Yes, it's true. How do you think this gets done? It takes both of us.

My apologies.

Apologies aren't necessary. Change in the inward parts is. You have a mission and it's our message. You used to be fervent about it.

I still am.

You were. You've slacked off. I told you our core message was complete, not that our message was completed. It never ends, it only expands.

Well, it's good to be informed of this.

To be informed means to listen. Our paths have not met.

What does that mean?

The Universe Speaks

It means to listen.

Talia.

Yes?

I'm a little concerned about our paths having not met.

You'll get it.

June 27

5:15 PM
Our paths have not met because my path is in heaven and yours is on Earth, although they have run parallel at times.

That's going to take some thinking.

Not really, but you're welcome to.

June 28

Dirty Dick's.

What?

I had a good time.

June 29

Talia, I asked your mom what you meant by Dirty Dick's. She said it was a restaurant in South Carolina that you and she and the family went to for lunch. She said it was really funny because the waiters make fun of everyone.

Collection

July 2010

July 18

Lies are not good.

July 21

3:20 PM

Everybody has bad days. It's what you make of them that matters. I experienced hatred without reason. Jealousy born of pride. And I did not like it. There is none of that here, and we see it as a learning experience there.

How did you deal with it?

I wrote about it. I also experienced love and joy and acceptance. And that helped me more than anything.

Thank you for sharing that.

My pleasure.

I like pastels.

August 2010

August 3

8:28 AM
Talia, I was asked to ask you why you call God "Him."

That is the way He appears to me. The answer is going to be different for every person.

The Universe Speaks

August 8

Talia, your mom wants to know if you knew she and Michael were going to be your parents, before you were born, before your spirit came here.

I knew. Everyone knows.

August 11

10:03 AM
I found out that the hummingbirds' wings make a figure-eight movement; very interesting.

The symbol of infinity. It's never-ending.

And that has to do with what you do.

It does. It goes on forever.

That download is awesome.

It is.

Forty wingbeats per second!

And yet with the speed of that vibration they can appear perfectly still.

August 14

AM
What many people do not understand is that in these days most people are left to their own devices as far as spiritual growth and education are concerned. The choice is usually either a secular or religious education. And although everyone has their own particular path, guidance is needed. It is no wonder so many stumble and give up.

It was never meant to be this way. People should be nurtured into finding their own way of truth and not ridiculed, as is so often the case, for seeking the way. For instance, at best, science without the spiritual way is partial truth, with self-imposed stumbling blocks. These blockages are only removed by the recognition and acceptance of the spiritual, for without the spiritual, matter itself could not exist. Remember when I told you a normal life is spiritual? That is what I am talking about, a normal life. A life alone is not normal.

Collection

August 16

4:30 PM
Thank you for letting me use your voice.

You're welcome, Talia. You can use my voice any time.

Thank YOU.

You're courteous . . .

I want you to know my appreciation

> G: I was watching a TV show and on it I saw an inscription that said "Love never dies." As I read it Talia said:

It never does.

That's what we are doing. Bringing them to the Light.

August 17

11:20 AM
The horses taught me to be sensitive to their emotional and mental state, which helped me to be sensitive to people's emotional and mental state.

How . . . ?

Because I put all I had into it.

August 19

> G saw a sign that read: "Beware of spending too much time on matters of too little importance."

I told you that before.

> G remembered she had.

The Universe Speaks

August 29

G: About three months or so before, I had asked Talia "What should we do for your birthday?" The immediate but very subtle reply was, "Test drive cars." I thought that might have been my imagination so I said, "If that's true and really you, then confirm it by another source, a psychic or something." A few days ago I found out a psychic had told Talia's grandmother the same thing. She later explained it was to celebrate her life and not to mourn her "death."

September 2010

September 1

People are much more comfortable with illusion. Illusion is their comfort zone. That's why so many uphold this false reality, the illusion, to their dying breath.

September 3

12:56 PM

While at a rest stop G saw two young native American men, both with lots of rings in their ears, their noses, their lips.

They have lost their way.

Could that be an indication that they are asking for help?

It could be. It could also be an indication that they have given up.

That's sad.

That is sad. The way of truth is not being taught to them. They have not heard it. They have no examples, no mentors. They have been left, abandoned to the wilderness of society. And that is an example of the fruit of their birthright being stolen away, by the force and then by false promises. Their ways were called primitive, but very little of it was primitive at all; most of it was enlightened. All that is needed is a turning in consciousness. A returning to the old ways, to bring new enlightenment.

Collection

Talia, you've got all the answers.

I have most of them. ☺

Talia, when I get two or more words overlaid on top of each other, it's hard to write.

I know.

That's your answer.

Yes.

Boy, you really do have the answers.

Most of them. ☺

September 4

12:54 PM
You said that trust, that simple belief, is always honored.

It is.

That girl on the plane that looked like you, who turned and looked me in the eye with a huge smile . . .

That was me acknowledging you. I used her to show my appreciation to you. You had asked to see that smile again, do you not remember?

I didn't 'til just now.

We always hear you and we always answer.

6:04 PM
Talia, the first time you came to me you said more than I remembered.

I did. I said I was alive, but not in the body. You didn't want to hear it.

No, I really didn't.

I also told you that you would have to tell Mom. You didn't understand that. And that is why you couldn't wholly receive it, because you didn't want to hear that and you did not understand it. That is how easy it is to miss things. You must learn to accept things as they are. What I told you was spiritual reality, which is all anything can be.

Nothing could be changed. I felt helpless.

Nothing needed to be changed. I had fulfilled my life's purpose there. The only thing that needed to be changed was the perception of that event.

September 5

12:50 PM
What was your purpose here?

My purpose there was for me to learn, for my mom to learn and to leave an example of how to live your life there, by helping others. That is what advanced souls do, help others along THEIR path. That is one of the reasons I constantly reveal to you who you are, to inspire you to help others. My mom is one of the true remaining child-rearing experts on the planet, and that's another reason that I said it was my great honor to be her daughter. She could not have learned what she did without me. She has no doubt she raised me correctly and I am the fruit of it. She doesn't consider it work, but it took MINDFUL effort, and that paid off. That payment will continue and it will never be forgotten, but remembered always.

September 6

1:05 PM
I'm with you in what you do. Just thought you need to know that.

Thank you. I appreciate it, Talia.

You're welcome. You're invincible.

What does that mean?

It means when you are walking where you are now you're invincible.

Sure hope I can stay here.

It's always there for you.

September 10

12:05 PM
    G heard Grandfather speak to him, regarding a class we were taking.

You will learn much. He is going to go further than he's ever gone.

Collection

Talia, you ask him a question first. I want to hear what you would . . .

We're on the same page; it's you who is struggling.

      Grandfather spoke again.

You and Granddaughter have a great commission together. Just as important as what Tom or anybody else is doing, working for the Light. To bring knowledge to the people. To set them free. You got it all down?

No, but as much as I could.

This is not for that but for you. Most of my work was done THERE, the foundation. Most of her work began HERE; that's why she's so busy.

September 11

12:04 PM
I'm so bored with everything.

Bored is the barometer of what you're missing.

So the more bored you are, the more you're missing?

Yes.

I'm missing a lot then.

Right now you are. Regroup. Relax. Meditate. Do you want to see the little girl?

Yes.

      G went with Talia, hand in hand to paradise. The little girl, the one Talia had helped, was there with a big smile. She was happy.

I understand now. I know my mommy has some things to work out, my daddy too.

      Then they took off running across a field of tall flowers, fast, playing with other children.

September 15

8:25 AM
Watch me ride. It's okay; I still ride.

> G decided to watch the compilation video of Talia's riding career that I had made up. While watching videos of Talia riding, G heard a horse cantor passed him.

That's me, riding through. We're more alike than you think.

But you were thirteen.

What were you doing when you were thirteen?

> On one video Justinian stumbled. G said to him, "I thought you said you were the best." G heard Justininan answer him, "I said I was the best—I never said I was perfect."
>
> G thought to himself after the stumble, *She's a little frustrated now.*

I was a little frustrated.

Second! You should have won! That isn't right, Talia.

Yes, it was.

Sorry I can't appreciate it like I should.

You do. How did you like it?

I liked it. I liked it a lot.

I knew you would.

Did I get everything?

Not quite; it takes time.

September 17

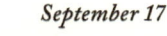

12:38 PM
Talia, how's this class going to be?

It's going to be good. It's going to be real good. I will be there.

Then it really will be good.

I get to go for free.

That's funny.

That's the truth.

Collection

September 20

1:08 PM
This world really teaches non-attachment. If you can resist being attached, your reward is out of this world. Talia, what were you attached to?

My mom.

That's different.

That is different.

September 21

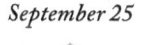

You're not really believing now.

Well, if you said it.

Mine is not the only way.

September 25

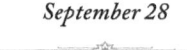

G and I decided to put one of the Talia bracelets on the altar at Grandfather's camp.

Thank you. That means a lot to me.

September 28

Talia, I see what you mean there.

Yes, I set an example in the flesh. I can certainly set one here.

It's so simple.

It is simple. Complexity is a sign of not knowing the Way. Paul said it best when he said, "Let us never depart from the simplicity that is in Christ." When you are in that Christ Consciousness, you will know the Light and the Way. You heard I could read people very well, and that is true and that is how I did that. That's the simplest explanation.

531

The Universe Speaks

You're awesome!

Yes, I am, but everyone has that potential. The reason I say that is that it is all energy, and how you apply it is the issue—either as potential energy or as dynamic energy. Potential energy is unused, dynamic energy is applied. In the Great Stillness is dynamic movement of pure energy. That's why I said there were vortices everywhere, because there is no place that energy is not. And helping others is the best way to activate that energy. Giving of yourself so that others may live.

September 29

6:49 PM
What is your question?

How can I wake people up?

By walking in the Light.

That's pretty simple.

It is. It is a choice, a dynamic choice.

Interesting choice of words.

Yes, you've heard it before. Do you think the answer would change?

It could be expounded upon.

It has been.

You're right again.

When have I not been?

Good point.

It's part of the point that I was pointing to before.

Where all things exist.

Yes. ☺

It sure was a dynamic choice to follow you.

You don't have to follow me, you just have to listen.

I don't mind following you; your way is perfect.

My way is not my way; I'm following the Light.

That's what I'm following.

Exactly!

October 2010

October 1

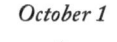

7:11 AM

G: I saw a white flash of light to my right, close by, and asked, "Who is that?"

Talia. We still have a message. It's not here or there, it's everywhere right now.

This is a garden.

We looked at it like that too.

October 4

1:11 PM

I can feel you.

I know. You're reluctant to just write.

Sometimes.

It's easier to just listen, without the responsibility of recording the conversation.

It is.

Then why don't you just listen?

Because I feel responsible to record it.

There is a record of all of it, of everything.

I heard you study it.

I do. I love to research, to find things out, to learn why things are like they are.

And?

And you would be amazed how much you have to do with why things are like they are. Everyone's thoughts, plans, decisions, and actions reverberate throughout the universe. Every single ripple causes an effect that affects everything it comes in contact with, which is essentially everything. Every instant everything changes in some way. How do you effect that change?

Sure hope for the positive.

That is your choice. And really, the easiest choice is for good.

October 8

12:46 PM
Hello, Talia.

Hello. You have questions?

I do. Trying to remember them.

You've been moving too fast. Time to slow down. And listen. Most in society would try to make you feel guilty for that. And for what you hear. Do not succumb to the pressure. Walk your own walk. Your path is the right one; you saw that sign last night.

What about Mars and "I will always be there for you"?

    G is referring to something he heard in the Spirit.

That is a symbol of the god of war, and you were correct when you said that "in the mouth of two or three witnesses shall every word be established." Your friend confirmed that to you. And it does have to do with you "picking up the lance."

I was going to ask about that.

I knew you were and that is why I'm telling you this. God can play any role.

That was the Light?

Absolutely pure. And some people need to be defended. Never have qualms about doing what is right.

October 10

1:29 PM
You didn't think I would talk to you.

Collection

You're right; I didn't 'til now.

Pay more attention. Use what you know; otherwise, it is of no use.

Knowledge intertwined with action—now there's a concept.

When you use it, it is more than a concept. It is doing as a result of your being. That shouldn't be a strain; it is a natural outflow from your being.

And how it is going with you?

Excellence personified.

That's the person I know.

So you do. ☺

Thank you.

You know you're always welcome.

October 11

1:05 PM
You were told to reclaim the knowledge.

Yes, I was.

And to walk in faith and confidence.

That is true, I was.

Then what does hinder you?

Nothing.

Then why do you act as if you are not aware of something when you are? That wastes moments. It puts off dealing with the inevitable. Deal with the situation now, and the next now will be yours to deal with then. Remember when I said you often had to stop, regroup, only to start again?

Yes.

Well, it is easier living in the now and dealing with it as it comes. The timing is always perfect anyway, so why question it?

Being ready to act in an instant.

Or not act, whatever is appropriate to the situation.

535

"Victory, right here, right now." Morehei Ueshiba.

That is it. Study to show yourself approved and no one can fault you.

You always have a lesson, don't you?

The lessons never end. Everyone is wired to learn; it's what they do with it that counts.

Thank you, Talia.

I am not through. What do you want to learn today?

How to walk in more of the Light and reflect it.

Then believe.

That simple?

That simple.

October 12

2:20 PM
In the beginning, every thing, every where and every when was contained in one point. The expansion of this source of all is the universe, as you know it.

You saw this condensed into one person when you saw me. That caught you by surprise. You arrived thinking you knew more than anybody there. This was a lesson to keep you humble. You never expected to meet who you met there. You only saw one crown that day. Now you know what that means.

You sure were honored that day.

Yes, I was, much more than you know. If you hadn't seen what you saw that day you would have abandoned the quest. Now there is no turning back; you've been spurred to follow.

There's no other path I would rather follow.

Then continue on, knowing what you know.

Talia . . .

That's all; anything more would just be chatter. I will talk with you later.

Thank you.

Thank YOU.

Collection

October 13

AM
It will be all right.

> G asked Talia how she learned. She said when she reads, she absorbs the information like osmosis.

October 16

7:03 PM
Talia, thank you for your words.

Thank you for yours. ☺

I have to think about that.

I told you that you were on the right path.

That emptiness is horrible.

The horror is separation; Oneness is peace.

It is peace. There's no better description.

Oneness is peace—that is THE description of it.

IT is peace, IT is Oneness?

IT is the IT people are looking for. How many times have you heard, "I'm looking for it but I just can't find it," or "Where is it?" or "Where did it go?" That IT is called by many names, and we've given the definition of what it is they are really looking for. Why is it so few find it?

Why is it?

It is because that is all THAT is.

That's profound, but why can't they find it?

They are looking in the wrong places for it. There is only one place, and that is the place it is.

And where is that place?

That is the place it is. It is always found within you. Looking to others for it is unwise; remember "others" is often a synonym for separation.

The Universe Speaks

I found it in you that day.

But we weren't separated. I was a conduit for the Almighty that day. You awoke that day; you were shaken from your slumber. I even asked you if you were going to sleep now. You stammered four different answers. You needed to be shocked that day and you were.

That's for sure.

That is for sure. So, I will ask again: are you going to sleep now?

No! Not by the grace of God. God forbid it!

Now, THAT is a definite answer.

Thank you.

Thank you, G.

I told you it would be okay. Always remember that truth.

You have to see things as they are, not as they appear to be.

October 23

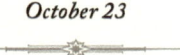

1:28 PM
Talia, I feel you. You have anything to say to me?

Yes, do your best.

October 24

1:15 PM
Talia?

I'm here for you.

That's like a divine echo.

From Him who does not change. ☺ *That's the good news. He keeps His promises, or you could say He watches over His words to perform it. His truth is everlasting. You can depend on it; that's the solid Rock who never fails.*

I believe that.

Why wouldn't you?

Collection

No reason not to.

No reason at all. This you can always depend on. Remember my rebuke of the "moneychangers"?

Yes, I sure do.

They are wasting lives to change money from one hand to another. This is vile in His eyes. It grieves His heart. There is no more time for that. But most aren't listening. This will change, for a lie cannot stand. The purge has begun. Lies/Lives will be broken.

5:34 PM
Things are happening now.

What's that?

Unrest is growing.

That's obvious.

Not to everyone, it is not. The message is out there. The universe speaks and the earth reflects the universe.

And?

And He said He would do nothing unless He told His prophets first. He said to watch.

Talia, I need a time line.

You need to be here Now.

I want to be there now.

There is not here, here is here.

Then I'm where I need to be.

You are.

You seem dispassionate.

I'm factual. I'm stating facts.

It would be nice if you were a little more detailed.

It's been said the devil is in the details.

Is he?

He can be if you overthink things. It can be the trap where thoughts circle in your mind, in effect removing you from here. Remember I said the universe is in constant flux. Confusion is always the creation of the misguided thoughts of man. If you notice, I've rarely been detailed in our conversations; however, it has rarely been in general terms either but it HAS often been very specific.

You're a genius.

I know.

I can't even spell it.

It doesn't matter, you know what it means.

That's beautiful, that's just beautiful.

Beauty is genius.

The downloads! Without them . . .

Without them most of this does seem like general terms. Without the context most of this will seem mundane.

But how can they get it?

We've already talked about it. By being an empty vessel and having an open mind. By disregarding their preconceived notions. By an intense desire to know the truth. By listening and watching and having a determination to prove all things. By rejecting lies no matter how comforting they may sound. And by pure reflection.

Pure reflection?

Yes, by not denying their nature, which is pure reflection of the Divine.

But if they don't believe that . . .

If they do not believe that and they act like they do believe it, then their divine nature will reflect back unto themselves and others, thus proving it to themselves. Once those doors open it is a real struggle to deny the truth. That is self-delusion, when oneself is one's own worst enemy. The path is simple. I used logic a lot in my life there, and that will lead you to the truth.

Talia, is all of this you?

It's all me. It's all you. It's all us.

There's a lesson!

Isn't it though. It is mind's craft to separate things. No more time for that either.

Thank you.

You know you are always welcome.

Collection

October 27

1:17 PM
      G overheard someone say, "And the penny dropped."

That's why we leave pennies.

October 29

6:01 PM
The sunset was fabulous; if I'd had a camera I would've taken a photo. Any words on that, Talia?

It was glorious.

Definitely!

October 30

6:50 PM
I'm multi-tasking.

You can do that.

Never have with you.

Yes, you have.

Not on the phone.

Yes, you have; you just don't remember.

I do remember once when you told me "miracles happen," and I said I know they do, and the next day a miracle of healing took place. But it does not always work out.

It takes practice. I did it all the time with my friends.

The Universe Speaks

November 2010

November 1

While G was doing yoga:

I'm here. Teaching union with the Divine.

November 4

10:10 AM
Good morning, Talia.

Good morning to you. It's always morning here.

It is?

Yes, it is. A new beginning every moment.

That's beautiful.

I know.

November 6

12:58 PM
So, Talia, how can people see beyond the façade?

By looking within. When you look within you will find the truth, because that's where it is. When I say I believed in myself, that's another way of saying I believed in the truth, because that's what I found there, and that strengthened my belief even more. My truth, seeing from that perspective, allowed my conclusions to be correct, causing my belief to grow.

One of the first things you noticed about me was my confidence. That's because I believed in who I was and saw the truth for what it is. When I came to an incomplete conclusion that wasn't the truth, it never felt right, and there was a nagging sensation that it wasn't right. So I couldn't leave that conclusion behind as finished, because it never felt like it was. So I would revisit what I had previously thought with an open mind and thereby move on.

Collection

Most simply do not ask or continue to ask until they have the release that says to them, "That is true" or "That is what is really going on." You've often heard the saying "jumping to conclusions." This happens often, as you well know. I'm saying you must honor the question AND the answer as a great gift, for it certainly is.

Humility.

That's a large part of it but also a pure desire, a pure desire to know the truth. The only one who can receive a lie is you, allowing yourself to receive it, and it will never feel right to you.

How would you define the façade?

The façade is the illusion one labors under. See through the illusion and you will never be a slave to it.

Where you ever a slave to it?

I was never enslaved by it. I was influenced by it, certainly, but whenever I asked my mom about it she always had very good answers for me. Sometimes it was, "What you do think?" No matter what she answered, she always steered me in the right direction. She told me once she thought most people were crazy, so I thought about that and concluded that most people were crazy in some ways.

How else could the world be in the condition it's in?

That's what I thought. And I started watching people much closer, wondering how they might be "off," how we all could be "off" in some ways. I decided everyone was on earth to learn something, but I wasn't sure what. Maybe everyone had something different to learn, something just for them. That's when I decided I wanted to help people, to see what I could do. And I began to sense people's needs. And I found that when I helped people I felt much, much better about who I was. I now see that I was just realizing who I was.

A person sent to help.

Yes.

I'm sorry, Talia, I ran out of time.

It's not your fault.

Talia?

You see how far we could take this conversation?

It's like the nature of our life here.

It really is. Some think it's to leave a great work of art; YOU ARE the art. It is how you live your life that is the legacy, and that life will never end.

The Universe Speaks

November 7

1:15 PM
Talia, the download of the dark web being a counterfeit of the luminous web of life and how not to get caught in it by seeing beyond the façade was fascinating, but you went right on and didn't mention it again. Why is that?

Because I explained exactly how not to get caught up in it. Why dwell on it? Give no place to the enemy. You know him well enough.

November 8

1:05 PM
Ere the day be old; I shall consult thee, o fair one.

And what wondrous perplexities have you for me this day?

Why must we toil for the wind, and plow for nothing?

It is not for naught that your labors are wrought. Fool's gold is for fools. Your labors are not in vain. I would have laughed if you had said that to me while I was there.

I know you would have. It's Old English, I think it's called.

There are some who speak like that here, and we call it High English.

Interesting.

Some would call it archaic but it is an elegant tongue.

Well, I like it.

I'm glad you do. Perhaps you will see something new in an old language.

Indeed I may.

November 12

6:03 PM
Talia, you said you talk to me every day.

I do.

Collection

Well, I haven't heard you all day.

You just did.

Good point.

I know.

Were you always this clever?

Pretty much.

I know what you wanted to say.

That you're a smartass.

Yes.

I'm really not but I am brilliant.

You always were, I suppose.

Pretty much. ☺

I didn't mean any disrespect.

I know that. You're just frustrated. It was a long day to you.

Meaning my perspective.

Yes. It's really not any longer than any other day; it's what you make of it.

Well, I must have made it a long day.

It was a struggle for you; it didn't have to be.

I would appreciate your insight.

My insight is yours. You already know what to do and what not to do.

Maybe a reminder would be in order.

All right, what made the day so long?

Your thoughts about it.

I thought I was dealing with some morons.

That's what you THOUGHT; they're not really.

Then what are they?

They are learning and everyone learns at a different pace.

The Universe Speaks

Seems to me some are really not applying themselves.

Some really aren't but on the other hand some are.

You used that term "on the other hand" for a reason. What was it?

I certainly did use it for a reason.

And?

Your hands are in front of you, and it is what you choose to do with them that matters. You can work with them with all your effort, which you will find is very satisfying, or you may while away your hours. Remember when I told you that you sometimes must slow down to speed up? That is what we are talking about here.

You know I really haven't had a chance to slow down all day.

Sometimes you must take it by force.

I reckon you told me that too.

I did.

November 13

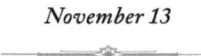

1:26 PM
It's a better day today.

That's because you slowed down and you have a different perspective today.

And that's because of your words.

They helped.

They helped a lot, thanks.

You're welcome.

November 14

1:31 PM
Grandfather said the Keeper of the Secrets has much to teach.

He does.

Like?

Collection

Like keep things secret that should be kept secret. It is God's glory to conceal a matter, meaning facts, facts that shouldn't be revealed. There are many things that many are not ready for; some never will be. And for some things to be revealed before the time is to rob someone of their own discovery. To include their own discoveries along their particular path to discovery. Be certain it's not your own pride wanting to reveal a matter. It should always be done for the good of the student or individual that you are helping. If you've noticed, there are a lot of things I didn't reveal to you until you were ready.

I did happen to notice that.

And when the foundation was ready we built upon it.

I wish it were a secret to me that I have to go right now.

But it's not, so go and have fun. ☺

November 15

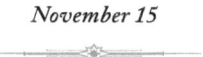

1:10 PM
You said there would be secrets.

Yes, I did.

Didn't have any idea that this is what you meant.

But you knew there was more than met the eye; you felt it.

Yeah, I remember that.

What else did he say to you?

> G is referring to a conversation he had with the Keeper of the Secrets during a meditation.

He said, "I'm passionate about keeping secrets." And I asked, "What kind of secrets?" And he answered, "Anything you know that would hurt others unjustly." Then there was a pause before he said, "That is a harmonic that brings harmony."

That is the part we're interested in: the bringing into harmony of all things. That is our mission and when we do that everything else is taken care of.

That's awesome.

That is the truth and the truth is always awesome. When you think of it anything you teach anyone is the instruction of harmony; without that it's not lasting.

You're distracted.

The Universe Speaks

I'm trying not to be; I'm out of time.

Concentrate.

I'm trying.

Just concentrate, believe.

There is a heartbeat in everything, a true harmonic, and if anything is done without that living rhythm, that harmonious vibration of life that infuses everything, it will ultimately fail. The end result is always chaos. We've already talked about the Winning Way and that way is the Way of Life. Not struggling against it but flowing with it.

The Land of Ziph (Hebrew for *flowing*).

Yes, deliverance and life!

November 16
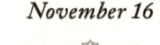

7:31 AM
Help me to walk in harmony today, Talia.

You will.

10:35 AM
This harmony stuff really works!

It always does. Listen to Tom.

10:47 AM
You wake them up by living in harmony.

November 18

9:24 AM
G was looking at a small statue of a girl reading, which I have in my yard.

That's what I'm doing today, studying.

That's what you're doing today, studying?

Yes.

What are you studying?

Life.

548

Collection

November 19

5:55 PM
How did your study of Life go?

Very well, and it continues.

Care to share?

I'm learning how Life works, how it all ties in together in the most marvelous of ways.

Like how?

Everything is a dance of Life. From the smallest molecule to the vastness of the universe. But the most marvelous of all is us. We are the spark that is made in His image, and within us does dwell the universe.

Why a spark?

That's how I see it. The light of God illuminating our way, forever and always. I understand now that I was looking for me when I was there because I was all I ever needed.

That's a little hard to follow, Talia.

We are all looking for ourselves, and when we find ourselves we find God, whom we are. That divine spark is us, His light is us. We are beings of His light and grace, His love and peace, and anything less and we find ourselves wanting, thirsting, feeling incomplete. That is why He said that He would give us living waters and that we would thirst no more. I am so full here it is indescribable, and there is no end. His beauty is found in all things, but your eyes must be opened to see it.

I hope mine are.

Hope abides forever. You, like most, would like intricate details, but this is glorious beyond measure, and as I've said, beyond words. This truly must be experienced, and then it will even seem to you that it is too much to experience.

8:30 PM
Talia, come with me. I am going to meditate.

Are you ready to go?

Yes.

Good, then we're going.

G: During my meditation, Talia was standing just past the arch. We greeted each other and she said something to me that was totally Talia (very joyful). She took my right hand in her left and we flew up, fast and for a while. We went through swirls of different colors and what felt like some veils of some sort but indistinct. The last veil we went through, with many different colors swirling around us, felt sublime.

Soon afterward we were standing together on a high mountain peak, just enough room to stand, still hand in hand. In the distance and far below us was a white city. I said, "It's the White City." Then she said either, "Do you want to go?" or "We're going." We flew down and over the top of the city for a long way. Everything was white—the buildings, streets, houses—everything. The people on the streets were wearing white as well. I could feel them, their joy, their busyness, playfulness, etc. We seemed to near the center of the city (not a visual perspective so much as a feeling that it was near center, a knowing now that I think about it).

We slowly descended to the street. There were many people around, but it wasn't crowded. She pointed at many fountains in a large courtyard. These large fountains were spraying water pretty high and were about three feet deep. Every fountain had different colored water, like the colors of a rainbow. Very vivid colors: orange, blue, aqua, red, green, purple, violet, every color imaginable, and some colors I can't describe because they do not seem to exist on earth. Talia was just looking and smiling really big because all the fountains had children playing in them. Laughing, overjoyed, delirious with happiness. That was so overwhelmingly beautiful.

November 20

6:26 PM
Talia, what was that you said?

Don't dote on my words. Everyone puts things differently for exactly the same meanings. The words are really not that important; it's the meanings that matter. That is what is important.

November 22

Be at peace.

Talia, it was four years ago today that I met you. That day started so unremarkably.

Collection

It just goes to show you the seemingly unremarkable start of something can result in the most profound and remarkable moment of your life. What appear to be trifles may be momentous.

Thanks again for that most memorable day.

And again, you're welcome. You have more days like that than you think.

That's news.

That's true. I was used as a catalyst to get your attention and to wake you up.

December 2010

December 1

Why didn't you like skiing?

I didn't like falling down. And I didn't like being cold.

December 2

G and I were test driving cars, as Talia had requested for her birthday. We got into a Porsche 911. G sensed Talia in the right rear seat.

This is a perfect fit!

December 3

6:15 AM
Happy Birthday, Talia.

Happy Birthday to you.

1:02 PM
Well, once again I'm out of time.

So you are.

But you said you would talk to me.

The Universe Speaks

I do, I will, I am.

What did you want to talk about?

Your self.

My self?

Yes, your self. A lot of people do not look at their self enough. Many think that's being self-centered. But you need to look at your self to center yourself; that's being self-centered, you see?

Yes.

Make the time to be consistent with that. Making the most of your time, being consistent, being centered and rooted in that—that is a place of perfect power. Perfect power is a place of solitude where you are not alone.

6:15 PM
It is a place of peace, even in the storm.

You said you'd give me a definition of perfect power.

That is the definition.

December 11

11:40 AM
Well, Talia, what's the theme today?

The theme today is peace.

December 12

9:47 AM
Talia, what's the theme today?

Joy and patience. Peace.

1:36 PM
It's not just me that talks.

Collection

December 13

6:34 AM
Is there a theme for today?

Walk in the Spirit. In truth. Nothing is better. Be not dismayed when others fight against you. That is them warring against their own freedom. You've heard of slaves who didn't want to leave when they were freed. You've taken people back to prison that preferred to be there. This is the comfort I told you to be aware of. The dissonance is always apparent.

1:00 PM
>G: While in a meditation I saw Talia. I told her she looked radiant. She was literally glowing.

Thank you.

>I saw then the Keeper of the Secrets. He acknowledged me with a nod.

What's the secret?

The secret is not letting anyone know what they shouldn't know, when they shouldn't know it.

December 14

6:53 AM
The human heart has a much broader capacity for love than most are aware of. As a matter of fact, it is unlimited.

10:58 AM
This unawareness is the greatest cause for stunted growth.

11:28 AM
Breaking down the veils. That's Oneness. That's why I was glowing yesterday.

4:15 PM
>G: I was thinking about getting some glasses. I was deciding which lenses to get. I was thinking, *Should I get the rose or clear lenses?*

If you have a choice of seeing or not seeing, always choose seeing.

Clear it is!

The Universe Speaks

December 19

12:41 PM

G and I had just finished watching a documentary on The Nephilim—dark angels. I said I did not agree with the documentary. Then Talia spoke.

He got some things right, and he got some things wrong, but there's nothing to be upset about.

Talia, is that really you?

Yes, it's really me, it's you, it's Us, and it's the Universe.

When she said "Us," I clearly perceived she meant everyone involved in this message. That really triggered my faith to hear. As she said before, a part of this message is "how to." How to hear, sense, perceive that help that we need so desperately from what some call the other side. I'm not so sure I like that term, as we are constantly surrounded by those who would and do help us. It is really not another side.

12:54 PM

I'm glad you used that term "trigger," because everyone needs to find their own trigger. And it's not just this. Everyone needs a trigger at some time to motivate them for certain tasks. This is a tool for enlightenment. This is a tool that can be used to awaken you. Whether you need to awaken the body, mind, or the spirit. I would encourage people to find that trigger, for it is the answer to many questions in their lives.

December 19

5:25 PM

So, what did you do today?

I hung out with you at work.

Now that you mention it, I did feel that.

I'm always near.

Thank you. That is so cool.

I enjoy it.

That's awesome. You can go anywhere in the universe and you hang out with us.

Collection

Remember what I said the most important thing to me there was?

Relationships.

Yes. Why would it be any different now?

That does make sense.

Of course it does. We crave fellowship, just like everyone else. Why do you think I respond so readily?

Because you are love.

That's true, I am. But there is more to it.

Like?

Like I said before, we don't change, we just grow. We don't feel the earthly pains, but our heart, our soul is the same. We learn, we grow, but our essence is the same; we just expand more and more into God. He also expands more and more into us. This expansion will continue, us into Him, Him into us, until there is no more separation and we all will become One in Him. The universe is expanding. That's what you saw in my eyes.

Kind of wondered what that was about. Thanks for the explanation.

That explanation is a partial one, as they all are, until we come into that Oneness. We know in part because we are apart, but when that that is perfect is come—Oneness—that that is in part—the separation—shall be done away with. The reason is it will have served its purpose; it will not be needed.

Its purpose is . . . ?

Its purpose is to find out who we really are. Once we fulfill who we are, the separation will no longer be needed; as a matter of fact, it cannot exist at that time. To be one with our Creator is who we really are.

Why do we have to go through this at all?

Because God is expanding. He reveals himself in His creation. Most don't get that. That is why when you lead people back to the earth, you lead them back to the Creator.

God is growing?

Yes, He is growing. He doesn't change—He doesn't need to; He is of course perfect as He is— but He is growing, expanding. You too are perfect. Once you put away the dross or it is burnt away. When he said "be ye perfect," he was saying "be ye like me," which you already are, for you are made in His image. Your free will, your decisions, can distort that, but it doesn't change who you were created to be. I'm helping you.

The Universe Speaks

You sure are.

Our joy in helping is indescribable. It is us fulfilling who WE are.

What about the dark side?

You're not ignorant of his devices and you're right, most give him too much credit. Most of his power is the power of illusion. Give no place to him and he will have no place.

That's it? Seems to be a lot of questions about that from a lot of folks, some controversy.

I will refer you to what I've said before: what you put your attention on is what it will be on, and he loves attention.

Why do you use the singular?

Because that hierarchy has one purpose: to thwart you from yours. You have all authority over all the power of the enemy, and nothing shall by ANY means hurt you. He said that and he cannot lie. If that were not so, He certainly would not have said it. I told you before; most people are masters at complicating things. Combating this enemy is simple and not ornate. Sometimes people make it ornate for show. Why?

Sounds like that could be pride.

It could be. Sometimes it's just what they were taught. Remember how the children of Israel protected themselves against the angel of death in Egypt?

Pretty simple.

It was.

I've sure seen you grow since you've been there.

It's nice you've noticed.

That's funny, Talia. It's just, it's as if I never knew you as a human; you were totally supernatural when we met and flawless, perfect.

But I was human and I still am. I showed you what a human was capable of. The unlimited potential. You being made in His image is you being love. God is love, and love is unlimited— as is God. Time—limitation—out of mind. When the veils dissolved for you, you saw me glowing as you'd never seen me before. That was us expanding, growing into Oneness. When you see someone glowing, then know they are experiencing Oneness.

I saw you glowing with a white light about you the instant we met. It was there all day; you've always had that about you every time I've seen you.

That's because your eyes are opened. Did you expect to see darkness?

Collection

No. I mean, I didn't expect anything the day we met but dinner and, I don't know, awkward small talk.

Then you certainly got more than you expected.

Boy, howdy!

There is more yet to be revealed about that day.

Another reason for my fascination with it then.

It is the longing for completion. Do you remember the carpet of gold?

I remember seeing it, now that you mention it, and thinking about it. I remember it now, looking down and seeing a sparkling carpet of gold. How could I forget that?

You had a full plate that day. Believe it or not, but you blocked some things out that day as being "too much." The irony is you often complain about "not enough."

I agree; you're right. Thanks for that. But what did the gold carpet mean?

It means your walk doesn't have to be hard. You've often chosen the hard way.

Boy, howdy again!

You don't have to do that when you walk as a prince. I was just being who I was that day, a daughter of the King, even though I didn't know it. You now have something I didn't have, and that is knowledge of who you really are. Now do what I did and just be who you are.

Talia, that's easy to say.

That's easy to do when you do it. When I say that most are masters at complicating things, I mean they sabotage themselves, usually from a feeling of unworthiness. This mastery comes to them simply; in other words, it is simple for a creator to complicate something simple. This then becomes to them an excuse for not becoming who they really are. They deny themselves, then usually blame others for denying them of who they should be.

I want to say this is sort of complicated.

It's really quite simple, although there are many other facets to this deception; it is in essence very simple. But the misery it causes is untold and the prevention so easy, so simple.

You know I was joking there about it being complicated, but it's funny—with your humor you just plow right on through it, not acknowledging it when you're on a roll with a message.

Well, I'm aware of it, but there's a time for everything and sometimes you use humor to deflect. You know the power of humor for health, but when I do that, it is a message also, and that's to

The Universe Speaks

let you know that when you see others do that, then maybe you should listen and not interrupt them, because everyone has a message whether they know it or not.

Well?

Well, what?

Cat got your tongue?

I was trying to think of something clever to say.

I know you were. Then say it.

That was a very good message you just gave me.

That was very clever.

There is no matching wits with you.

You don't have to match wits with me, you just have to be who you are.

I am.

You usually are.

When I'm not me, who am I?

Someone you're not.

And who is that?

Someone else, someone you're not. It's a lot easier being who you are, for that is who you are meant to be.

Were you ever someone you weren't?

Sometimes. Not very often, but I didn't like it. It didn't seem real and it wasn't.

That does seem a little convoluted.

It is, which is why it is not meant to be.

You're tired.

I know.

Why don't you get some rest?

Good idea.

I have those a lot.

I know.

Collection

Do you know why?

Because you're being who you are?

That's right.

December 20

5:00 AM
Talia, you said to look at that book, *The Art of Peace* by Morihei Ueshiba, and my eyes immediately fell on, "The techniques of the Art of Peace are neither fast nor slow, nor are they inside or outside. They transcend time and space." When you told me "time out of mind" I received a download of "distance" also. What Ueshiba said seems to be exactly what you were saying.

Not exactly, but very close.

Another word that came to me when you said that was *Oneness*.

That's the missing key, that dissolving of the thought of separation. As you've heard, the mind's craft is to separate, but that is just part of it. Its job is also to rearrange things back into the whole. Most stop at the separation as if that is the whole; it's not. It is to allow you to see the contrast of the parts and how they all fit into the whole in the most exquisite way. Another method of revealing divinity but with greater understanding. When the way the universe operates is revealed, it is impossible to deny who you are, for you are helping to create it yourself.

Thank you, Talia.

You're welcome. ☺

December 21

10:45 AM
Talia, you're putting into words what we already know BECAUSE of the Oneness.

Yes! And I am expanding it.

Because the universe is expanding.

God IS expanding, yes, but there's more to it.

Like what?

We'll get there.

The Universe Speaks

Talia, your mom just told me about your grandma's conversation with Rona. Thank you! I thought I was hearing things when you told me that you wanted us to test drive cars for your birthday, but when your grandma told your mom that you asked her to test drive cars for your birthday, it was a confirmation for me. Thank you. Thank you also for leading your grandma to that special card you wanted to give your mom.

She is very dear to me.

I can tell.

She was very dear to me in my life there also. I always felt her love. I always knew there was more to her than met the eye. I was always so grateful for my family and thought I was very fortunate because of them. I now see so clearly what a blessing they really were.

Do you have any regrets?

Only that the illusion of separation is so great. But it has purpose.

What purpose?

Growth, and believe me when I say it's worth it. I have seen the growth it causes.

There is a lot of pain involved in that growth.

That's true, there is. That is the first thing I asked the Father about: why does it have to be that way? That is when he explained and showed me how it all worked to bring things into completion. He also said: Blessed are they that mourn, for they shall be comforted, and He cannot lie. You've experienced that. You've seen others experience that. Otherwise, it would be unbearable.

What else have you asked Him about?

A LOT of things, and a lot of the time He said, "Go study, my child."

Well, I've got ten minutes.

You have forever.

You're awesome.

I know.

1:26 PM
Talia, your mom told me that when your grandma was trying to locate the card you wanted to give your mom, she asked you, "Please, Talia, I need help figuring out which card you mean." And then, as she walked into the kitchen, a little card fell off of the fridge. When your grandma picked it up, it was THE card! You did that, didn't you!

I did it.

Collection

December 23

Four friends and I went to visit "Talia's Tree" at her school on the anniversary of the crash. When we looked down at the planter, there was a nickel sitting there! We decided that Talia had left the nickel there as a sign for all of us. A penny a person. After the visit I told G about the nickel and our visit to the tree.

You left the nickel, didn't you?

You were right. Then the penny dropped.

Besides just going to visit the tree, I had decided to bring Talia a bagel. She loved them. So I went to the bakery and could not decide which kind, plain or an everything bagel. Talia loved them both, but I chose the plain. As I ordered I had a nagging feeling I should have ordered the everything, but I let it go. Then, when I got to the tree and took out the bagel to set it there, I saw it was an everything bagel! Talia had obviously preferred that one!

January 2011

January 1

Happy New Year, Talia.

It doesn't mean much to us here, but what it means to those there!

Talia, there are many, many dead birds that have been found throughout Arkansas, Louisiana, Kentucky, Maryland, and even parts of Europe. What does this mean?

It's like the canary in a coal mine.

The Universe Speaks

January 7

6:24 PM

Talia, the other day you told me I was putting you before God, and I said I wasn't. You replied, "Yes, you are; don't do that." Then the scripture "Thou shalt have no other gods before me" came to me. You're right, I was. Now I'm not, so would you talk with me?

Yes. What would you like to talk about?

My dad.

> G's father was sick and in the hospital.

It will be all right. He will be taken by this but it will be his time. That journey is foreordained for him and it will be a joyous reunion.

That's very nice to know.

It's very nice to let you know; so keep his wishes and celebrate his life.

I will.

I know you will; you've learned how to do that with me. Remember the fun you had driving the cars?

That was fun.

It was a joy, and smiles and laughter delighted me. And you thought you were hearing things. To celebrate life should never be doubted, and that is something you should do every day, no matter how dark the gloom.

Thank you so much.

Thank you.

For what?

For being you.

6:53 PM

Talia, thanks so much for talking with me. You don't know what that means to me.

Yes, I do.

Collection

January 8

5:30 PM
I finally got all this transcribed from the smaller notebooks!

You feel better?

Yeah.

You feel a sense of accomplishment

Yes, I do.

That's how I felt when I finished my homework.

That's funny for some reason.

You are giggling from a job well done.

Thanks. It's . . .

It's a bigger deal than you think. As you know from that photo, I was fundamentally against homework.

That was funny too.

But it wasn't just humor. I knew instinctively that there were more important things to be doing. And that was HOME work from another world. As you've heard, the flesh profits nothing. I'm at home now and I still do homework.

Like what?

I read a lot.

What do you read?

Ancient text. The basis of all things, for that is the foundation from which all come. Nothing has changed. In the beginning was the Word. This Word was that by which all things were made. Spoken into being.

Awesome.

Yes, that's a good word but it's far beyond awesome.

Can you describe it?

No, but when I read it I become it; I experience it in its wholeness, from its beginning to its completion. The Alpha and the Omega are One and that is what I experience.

The Universe Speaks

That's beyond me.

For now it is, but you will experience it too, and you will see that truly there is no description.

January 13

1:32 PM
Talia, I would love to hear your voice.

Would you believe it's me?

When it's clear I do.

Is this clear?

It's very subtle.

But it is clear?

I would like it clearer.

Then clear yourself.

That's better.

That is better.

Why do you doubt?

Just want it right.

It IS right and when you're quiet it's clear. Have I ever led you astray?

No.

Nor would I.

I know.

Then why doubt?

I don't know, just want to be sure.

Be sure. And you do know.

Feelings of unworthiness?

And why would that be? What makes you feel you're not good enough, not worthy?

Stupidity?

Collection

No, that's not it. Sometimes you buy into the lie you've been fed.

Residual crap?

Something like that. The seed has been planted; do not water it, and it will die. The confidence you saw in me was because I never received that lie. So reject the lie, receive the truth. How do you feel about tomorrow?

What do you mean?

How do you feel about tomorrow?

Some apprehension but excited about the challenge.

These changes are for growth.

It looks bleak in the natural.

The natural and the supernatural are categories for clarity in conversation. One problem with that is there is really no separation between the two. When you realize that, you will discover miracles are natural. Jesus understood that; he wasn't fluctuating between two worlds because he was One with both, or to put it another way, he was one with One. He knew the separation was an illusion. The physical laws are in subjection to the law of the Spirit. They complement each other. Each affects the other but the Spirit is greater. Its applications are different and that is where the confusion often begins. It is not one or the other, it is all at once.

Thank you, Talia, I have to go.

Bend time.

I will have to.

January 14

12:40 PM
Beautiful morning.

It was! It's a beautiful day too.

It is.

It IS, is all. That is why you think about it so much.

It is Everything.

It is. It is All you ever need. It is that I am that I am.

Never totally got that.

He was saying I am all that I said I am, unchangeable. He and His Word are one.

That simplifies it.

It does. There are infinite aspects to that, but that is its essence. The kernel, the seed from which all grow.

February 2011

February 23

1:29 PM
Once again I don't have much time, but I'm here.

So am I. I know you have priorities but they must be shifted.

How so?

Shifted to do the things you need to do.

I'm going to have to make it a priority to do that.

You should.

Any specifics?

You will know when you take the time to look into it. The answers are already there.

6:35 PM
You can talk to me.

So I can!

What you just did was a nice thing. Communication with your friend. That was your vision for right then, and it played out wonderfully. Has not my communication to you changed you, supported you, and enhanced your life?

Immensely.

You can do the same. Now you know what a touch can do.

I was told that not long ago, very recently in fact, and it was touching to hear it and experience it.

It was experiencing it that was so touching. That touch came to you with power.

Collection

I know it did.

It was perfectly timed. It was backed by the love of the Almighty.

It would have had to be.

It would have had to be to have the power it had.

I really appreciate him.

Then let him know.

I will when I see him.

He could use encouragement too.

I'll let him know.

Follow your heart.

The path with heart.

Yes, that's the One.

Thank you, Talia.

You are always welcome. ☺

February 28

6:01 PM
Talia, I've been reading your words the last two days, and your truths and explanations are so simple that I wonder if people will even get it.

They will get it if they want it. See what I mean?

I do. I remember once when I was meditating, you and I were in the white city and I asked if there were any temples there. I was looking for one but didn't see any, so I asked you about it. You told me, 'He is the temple." I then asked where He was, and you answered, "Everywhere. He is on His throne." Then the other day I read in Revelations 21:22 "And I saw no temple therein: for the Lord God Almighty and the Lamb are the temple of it." That was way cool.

That was an understatement.

Well, a pretty extensive description of it is there in those chapters I read.

It is, but that's understated also.

That's kind of nice to know.

There is more there than has met your eye.

That's also an understatement, I am sure.

It is. To behold it and to experience it in its fullness is far, far different.

I've only beheld it.

You've beheld it but you've also had a sensation of it, a taste. If it were more you would be distracted from what you are doing there. Do you want to fulfill your purpose?

Of course.

Then keep believing.

March 2011

March 5

1:43 PM
I want you to know something. That first book is very, very basic.

I realize that.

I know you do but I'm confirming it to you.

March 6

1:30 PM
There is no struggle at all except in the mind. When the mind is still, there is no strain, and God becomes a living presence: the Christ, the individualization and individual experience of God, comes alive in us. You feel it is a presence, as a cloak around you.

Wow, thank you, Talia.

You just have to take the time. Words can only be strung together in so many ways. This you found when you were ready and needed it, and your friend was another voice and confirmation, and was the witness of spirit within you. This is also a confirmation that there

Collection

are infinite voices of truth in the universe, and they all speak. That is where the advanced ancient knowledge of harmony came from, from realizing and walking in that knowledge and harmony. And it was divine grace until the idea of separation became a graven image in the mind of men. That is what was called the knowledge of good and evil.

8:48 PM
Talia, your communicating with Forrest today was really awesome.

> Forrest is my and Talia's cousin.

I'm always here to help.

I know, that was just really, really cool.

He is a precious soul.

Aren't they all?

Yes.

9:11 PM
I'm a bridge.

11:57 PM
That knowledge of good and evil, part of that is unjust judgments, isn't it?

It is.

March 12

6:44 AM
Talia, why can't I hear James?

> James is G's father that passed away

He's reviewing his life right now.

But you said it was natural, the communications, and no separation.

He hasn't learned to do that yet.

But I heard him before.

What you do there affects what you do here. He's in school now.

The Universe Speaks

12:41 PM

Talia, I was saying to Richard that I had only met one master in my life who had mastered the Art of Life, and in the most unlikely of people. I think he asked if it was a Tibetan. I said no, it was an 11-year-old girl from Santa Barbara. He said, "Oh, I believe it." I told him that in one day I had learned lessons that would last a lifetime. As we talked I felt your presence stronger and stronger, and my heart swelled as if you had filled it.

That was me.

I know! That was awesome.

I told you the Kingdom of Heaven is within you.

I know, you did.

Well, that was you experiencing it, an expansion of light.

That was the best feeling ever.

It always is.

Anyway, then you said he had something to do here, so I told him that.

He does, and it's important.

He said someone else had told him that, which was no surprise, but he said he hoped to find out what it was on his deathbed. I said to him that he needed to find out before then.

He will, if he seeks.

What is it?

That's his mission, and path.

Anyhow, what I was going to ask you about is this: after I told him this, it wasn't long before I felt very oppressed, as if attacked. I felt sick, with a headache, low blood sugar, something. What's with that?

What do you think?

I think it was darkness retaliating for the Light, the word of truth, because you said what he had to do was important.

It is and it was.

That's it?

Collection

You know his devices and they aren't always subtle. Don't think you're above his attacks. Jesus himself was tested by him; remember his defenses. That's also why I had told you I had a headache ONCE. And what it was. There is no retreat in this battle. Your advantage over me is you know what it is, while I was clueless.

Hard to imagine you being clueless.

I was in great pain and I didn't know why and it was frightening.

You felt an evil presence, didn't you?

I did. It was hatred, but I didn't know what it was. I had never felt anything like that.

I can't stand the thought of you being in pain.

I didn't like it either.

March 13

12:57 PM
People are asleep!

Yes, most are. I told you how to help wake them up.

By walking in the Light. That's not always easy.

It's not always easy but it's easier than walking blind. There is an effort required to keep them opened once you've been awakened. Remember I said you were a process in flux. The energy waxes and wanes. There is a rhythm to it; harmonize yourself to that rhythm.

Talia, what are you doing?

Posing.

For what?

A portrait.

You do that there?

> G: I blew off Talia's answer, thinking I imagined it. But when I told Kim about it she was blown away. Kim's mom had had a portrait of Talia painted, from a photo, for Kim for her birthday. The portrait had so much life, so much of Talia showing through that it was amazing. Kim's mom told the painter how much she felt from the painting, and he told her that he saw Talia posing for him. He said he had never experienced that before. That was the first portrait he had not had to fix something on.

The Universe Speaks

March 15

9:45 PM
What are you doing today?

Listening for you.

Meaning?

Meaning, what I hear I speak.

Still setting the example.

Always.

You know, the whole posing for a portrait caught me off guard.

No, not really—you're too guarded. Just take it as it comes, accept it. All things are possible. I'm not here to trick you, I'm here as a guide, a leader.

You always have been, haven't you?

Yes, the first moment we met I was guiding you. It didn't matter if I knew it. It was so. Everything you were shown that day has come to pass, at least in part; why would you doubt now?

Sleepy?

Maybe you should rest more.

His, the painter's, heart was touched by my presence; he experienced a part of me. You asked it to be so; you asked, "Whoever is painting her let them know who she is." I told you that you had a part in this, and when you do that it makes what I do so much easier.

I had forgotten that.

You added, "If this is true." Now you know that it is true. I told you contending with the flesh wasn't easy.

Yeah, even Tom said he was in and out of it.

That's because he is. You had asked for that also: "Is he always there or is he in and out of it, because I think he's in and out of it. But if that's so let him say it." This is a puzzling dilemma to him at times, but no one escapes the barrage of lies thrust upon them by this society. Thus the constant battle and the requirement never to retreat or you will be overcome. You will acquiesce.

Collection

March 16

8:47 AM

Talia, you said to me a while back that you were avant-garde and it wasn't an ecumenical movement. Seems I was somewhere I couldn't write, then I forgot it. Care to elaborate?

That wasn't what I said.

What was it?

I said it had very little to do with an ecumenical movement. Religion is now largely a business, and the business is not to bring people into the Oneness we've been speaking of. It's mostly to perpetuate the business. My business, or as I like to refer to it, my game, is to bring people into the true Oneness with God, their Creator. It is a wonderful game full of pleasure forever more.

March 18

12:18 PM

What color notebook should I use next?

Gold.

Gold? I don't have a gold.

> G: I looked in the cabinet where I had several new notebooks stored. In the shadows the one on top looked completely gold, which was startling since I knew there were no gold ones. It turns out that it was a tan Rite in the Rain, which absolutely looked gold in the light.

12:24 PM

Talia, if you would, tell James hello and we miss him.

He says you'll see him again.

Okay.

2:30 PM

Why do I keep seeing death? Whenever I look for the last two months or more I keep seeing death in one form or another, or something about it. Why?

Because it's a part of life.

The Universe Speaks

5:53 PM
Got anything else to say about that, Talia?

Yes.

Right now?

Yes.

What?

Death is a part of life. Unless something dies it cannot be reborn.

That's a lot to think about.

It is. In every facet of life there is a part of death.

I can see that.

In death life is created because death is a part of life. Death is a doorway. To life.

Is there death there?

Death is no more here, but we constantly deal with those who have just died. However, there is a shedding, a shedding of old ways, of earthly ways of doing and dealing with things. Some things that people worried to death over seem here as nothing more than a joke, a ludicrous thing to be concerned with. It has been often said here that "I wish I had it to do over, but thank God it's over."

Thank God humor survives.

Humor Is. It has an energy all its own; it cannot die.

You said death was an illusion.

Of course it is an illusion—that's why I said it.

It is a mystery.

So is life. And they are the same; they are both gifts. As I've said, everyone's death is as unique as everyone's life.

Paths and choices.

Yes. And callings. That's why it's important to listen, to know what path you are called to take. Death per se is not something to seek; seek the Light and everything else will fall together perfectly.

Something of a disclaimer there?

Well, we know how some take things out of context, so we needed clarification.

Collection

Yeah, wouldn't want somebody jumping off a bridge after reading this.

Not if they were seeking death. That will happen for them soon enough. Remember when I told you I was killing what you didn't need?

Yeah.

Life from death.

James in school?

Yes, he is, and his eyes are opened wide.

How is Kim's healing class going?

Very well. She is learning a lot.

That's good.

That's better than good, that's great. I'm so proud of her, carrying on. My love for her is indescribable. She is learning more than she knows right now, but a foundation is being laid that she can work from. I am so proud of her.

She'll be glad to hear it.

She hears from me every day. It's important that she knows that.

6:50 PM

> G: I was flipping though the notebook and came across a photo of Talia I had forgotten was there. I looked at it and said, "Talia! You are so cute." Then I heard her plain as day say, "Thank you." That just made me laugh with delight.

March 19

1:03 PM
Talia, why don't people listen?

That is a reflection of their spiritual state. Some are listening. Those are the ones you should work with.

7:03 PM
Are people panicking again?

I wouldn't say panicking but overreacting.

The Universe Speaks

Why?

They seek a crisis to validate their position.

Why?

Everyone wants to feel they are right.

Everyone?

Yes, the truth is encoded in their DNA. Everyone knows the truth in their core being.

And?

And they cannot stand the thought of themselves living a lie, or being deceived. This is a hard truth to face. Everyone knows the truth when they hear it and everyone knows a lie when they hear it, but this knowing is in their core being, something most aren't even aware of.

It's existence.

Yes, most deny themselves who they are.

How can people contact their core being?

By being quiet. As I said, That is where we live. That is that quietness and confidence you've heard of. In this Supreme Silence, we live and move and have our being. Ask my mom how quiet I could be for long periods of time. I would lose myself in it at times.

I sure noticed how confident you were.

And that's where that came from; I was in touch with my core being. That's why I thought I could do anything, because in reality I really could. And that is how you saw and heard me hear the voice of our Creator saying that I would have to remind you of this. Without that quietness I would not have heard it.

Did you know what it was?

Not at the time, but I heard it and that was the important thing, my awareness of it.

You were definitely one of the most aware persons I've ever met.

That's true, I was, but it was out of context for you, completely unexpected. That's why you must be open. Open to all the possibilities that there are, which are endless.

I wanted to protect you.

I know you did.

You opened my mind to endless, infinite possibilities the day we met.

Collection

Yes, that's true, I did. Remember the last thing I said to you that day?

"Are you going to sleep now?"

Yes. Why did you? After all you had seen that day?

How could I have known?

By being in touch with your core being.

I feel so foolish and ashamed for that.

You went to work, which is what your society tells you you should do.

I wanted to stay.

You could have.

I really regret that.

I know. You squandered a golden opportunity.

How can I make it up?

You're making it up now. It is a hard lesson to learn but you're learning it. Just remember working for that society will put you to sleep; work for something else instead.

Like?

Like something that matters, something that brings a change for the better, something that lasts, something not of this world, something beyond.

Like what we're doing here?

Yes, and many other things. That is the work worth doing. Riches take on wings.

Yes, they do. Talia, while I was writing this, as if it were superimposed on what you were saying about working for this society, you said "Whoremongers" and gave me a huge download, but I really don't know how to write it.

It's the love of money. It's people whoring others out, no matter the expense to that person. The resentment, the pain, and anguish this causes is unimaginable and sadly widespread. This is how wars start. People using people as cattle and worse. Buying and selling. When people are used in this manner, there is an unnamed discontent that can turn to desperation. A desperate person is susceptible to being used even to further this evil.

I got a lot more than that from the download.

But that's the essence of it. The defense is knowing in your core being and walking in that Light. Don't make yourself a part of it.

The Universe Speaks

March 20

8:30 PM
Seems like people that have just passed on talk more than they do later on. Why is that?

It's your funeral—why wouldn't you be able to go? And yes, it is for the comfort of the people that are left.

March 28

12:33 PM
You said something to me a while back about the realm of the Real. Maybe you just spoke those words; I can't remember.

You can remember in the realm of the Real. It is the place we live, and it speaks of Royalty. A place you rule from.

The Supreme Silence and the realm of the Real are synonymous?

Yes, it is, once you enter into it and claim it as yours. It is a place you abide under the shadow of the Almighty, under His wings, a place of safety and peace, a place where nothing unclean can come near your dwelling. You dwelling there is you living there; wherever you are, you are at home. It is the Original place, where all is and nothing is missing. It is the place that you have heard of, where all things are possible.

People will want to know how to get there.

You already are there. Without this place you could not exist. When I say the Original place, I mean the place you came from, and yet you never left.

That was easy.

That's because you are there. It doesn't matter whether you believe it or not, you are still there. Although not believing it can certainly make it seem that you are not.

Isn't it the truth.

Of course it's the truth or I wouldn't have said it. That is the only place you can know who you are completely, and it is instantaneous. You know the trinity is the same Spirit, just different manifestations.

I know.

I know you know, but this isn't just for you; some have that question.

Collection

Okay.

And the Seven Spirits of God are His manifestations in His fullness.

That I didn't know.

I'll bet you also didn't know that people have seven spirits.

No, I didn't.

Did you know that each of those seven spirits can manifest the fullness of God?

Nope, never heard of that.

I refer you back to our discussions of personalities. There is also a counterfeit of these seven spirits, and that is what you see many manifest, a corruption of that purity. But it isn't real; it is instead the darkness within them attempting to be purged. It is in essence a cry for help. Everyone knows this isn't real, but you can trick yourself into thinking that it is real.

This is definitely something to chew on.

And that you must, from that deep place. The realm of the Real. That is the place of TOTAL trust.

5:25 PM
Talia, I've been thinking and there must be another witness or two on that whole people-have-seven-spirits thing.

You are made in His image. And as I've said, that is not necessarily to look like, it is to BE like. And again, things are not made to appear as they are but to appear as they appear to be. To see things as they are they must be seen from the realm of the Real, The Supreme Silence, where all things ARE. That is the perfect perception I spoke of. And the other witness is inside of you, the self-same place we are speaking of.

You said something else about it.

I did; you should have written it quickly.

You could tell me again.

We've moved on, in the Now, where all things are.

You told me I have access to all memory.

You do.

Well, I'm not remembering it.

That's not for now.

The Universe Speaks

All right.

Yes, it is. The Master said you would do greater things than He. How do you think that is possible? It is by the outpouring of the seven spirits.

That reminds me of the vision I had of God's hand pouring a pitcher of oil on the planet.

Yes, and it was for ALL who listen and walk in the place we've been speaking of.

I remember now, it was the manifestation of the sons of God, those who would walk in the fullness.

I said that with an explanation; now is not the time. Why did you think I told you that you could not write everything I told you?

I figured it was because of the volume of things you say, and also because I might not have access to pen and paper.

That is just part of it. Have you not heard that there are words that are unlawful to utter?

I have.

These are some of them.

But you said them to me.

And it was lawful for me to say them to you. You may want to review what the Keeper of the Secrets said to you.

Yes, you're right, I will. Some of them are coming to me now.

You were told that He (Jesus) has much to teach.

I was . . .

That was to emphasize the significance of His sayings.

But you said I should have written it quickly.

You should have written it quickly, for you. You still have it, but it is not the time to share it. Remember when I said you wanted things neatly arranged?

Yeah.

Well, that is your human mind trying to bring order out of what appears to it to be chaos. It's not chaos, it's perfectly ordered; it is just the mind's perception.

You must accept the change. Everything is constantly changing, while the human mind attempts to freeze everything into unchangeable coherence. The human mind was never meant

Collection

to dominate the Spirit, but to be in subjection to it, to be used as a tool. It is the servant, but it oftentimes insists on being a master.

You're blowing my mind again.

I have to. Otherwise it will take over. That can cause insanity.

I'm pretty sure some think I'm already over the edge.

You are, but it's a good edge. ☺

Should I write what happened today at 3:45 PM?

You should.

Okay, while meditating, I took several physical steps on my path, turned right, and took eight physical steps down my stairs to my Medicine Place. And there you were, smiling. I said, "Talia, you're here."

You're here. If I talk now you can't write it, and I know you want to write it.

Then I went to see Grandfather at his camp and he told me, 'Do your best. It all happens for the best." Then he put the thought in me, "I am with you always, even unto the end of the world." I asked him, "Did you say that?" He said, "The Creator said that; I am reaffirming it." He then said to me, "You can do this always; it's just hard to write when you're doing something else. That's why I had a 'love/hate' relationship with the talking leaves. Access to memory, you have. Apply yourself."

He speaks truth.

I know he does. Why did you tell me that?

Just reaffirming.

6:27 PM
Anything else?

Oh yes, there's a lot.

Now?

It's all Now.

So you've said.

You need another notebook.

Yes, I know. Think I'll use the gold one.

Good choice.

Thank you for you.

Be thankful for all things.

I try; hard to do sometimes.

Not when you're in the place that is real. There you see that all things work in your favor. All things are designed to bring you home.

That's the only place I want to be.

That's the only place you can be what you are.

March 30

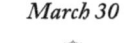

6:20 AM
For those who listen and choose to walk in it.

That place where all is? The realm of the Real, the Supreme Silence?

Yes, you can choose not to—most do. It appears arduous, and as if you are losing the life you know.

I suppose you are.

But you're losing nothing of value, and what is added back is incalculable wealth that never ends.

"I count it all dung."

No, you don't, but you should.

You're a sweetheart.

I know.

7:17 AM
Thank you for your clarity.

I'm always here for you.

You don't know what that means to me.

Yes, I do, and I appreciate your appreciation.

Collection

1:07 PM

This is where the Art of Life in its fullness is lived from and there is no striving. This is where the mystery of everything tied together is solved. No confusion. No division. No deviation from truth because you are living in it, you have embodied it. It has become you. You have become it. Distortions have dissipated into nothing. This is where Word becomes alive. This is the Stillness beyond language. This is where understanding is personified. This is where all things become One in experience.

I see "all things" meaning time and space included.

Yes, all things. This is eternity, where all concepts disappear and are replaced by Reality, by pure love.

Sounds like the place to be.

This is the only place to be to be all you are, which is all you can be

Which is?

Everything, anything, all things. If you can conceive it you can be it; you are the creator here.

5:50 PM
I was a catalyst for you.

I know you were and you've said that to me before. Why?

Because you needed one to get you going; you had lost your way. I tell you this because you are a catalyst for others who have lost their way. Remember who you are.

April 2011

April 2

1:00 PM
What's unremarkable?

Something that you shouldn't remark upon.

That is only part of it.

Okay, I figured out why some of this, much of this, in fact, is so hard to write, and that's that so much of what you say in words is also conveyed simultaneously with thoughts.

For example, that last sentence you said also came with the thought transference that I was going to have to think about it and wait for the answer.

We've been doing that all along.

I realize that, but I don't think we ever explained it.

But we did. I spoke of reading with your ears, and seeing between the lines, and listening for the truth from the heart. You don't need to explain it. Another explanation isn't really going to explain anything to someone who is not applying their heart to this, not listening with the heart. They who are need no explanation.

Well, thanks for explaining that. ☺

April 6

AM

    G: Kim and I were discussing the issue of including a photo of Frankie in one of the books, and I said something along the lines of I didn't think that a photo was necessarily needed if it was going to cause problems.

What do you have against Frankie?

Nothing.

She was my best friend.

April 8

5:51 AM

    G: While I was transcribing the conversation about adding the photo to one of the books, I asked Talia what that was all about, and she answered:

She went through it too.

Anything else you want to say about that?

I just did.

    G got a picture in his mind of the photo of Frankie and her clowning around.

I like that one.

Collection

12:40 PM

> G: While meditating I met Talia, and to her right was the Keeper of the Secrets. Talia gestured to him.

Open your eyes—look around. Be here Now.

Okay, Talia, I will try.

> The Keeper of the Secrets then said *yes* in agreement with Talia.

Okay, I'm here.

Yes, you are. He has something to say.

> The Keeper of the Secrets began to speak to G.

That's one of the secrets: be here Now. I have been appointed to this task to share the secrets. So you think the secrets are for me? Go over what I've said. The secrets are to be revealed in a timely manner. They are to be distributed to those with ears to hear. They are to be obeyed, for they are laws. Laws of righteousness. There is power in doing the right thing. Thus these are power-filled secrets. Live them.

I'm going to have to write these down.

If you do not live them, you lose them. Live these principles and they will be more than a foundation.

> Talia looked at him and said, "Thank you." G said, "Thank you" to him also. He nodded.

Now you have what you need to build on the foundation we have laid.

Thank you.

You're welcome.

1:04 PM

Talia, how many entities are we going to talk to?

I have many friends.

7:44 PM

This is the real world because everything here lasts. Because everything is as it should be and everything appears as it is.

The Universe Speaks

April 10

9:14 PM
You know, Talia, I don't know where to go here.

You don't have to go anywhere, just be who you are.

It's so good to hear you.

It's good to be heard. So many refuse to hear. They think the material world is the real, but it's not; it is an image, a tool, a reflection of the real, and many times a pale, pale reflection. But many mistake it for the real. The real is within you. It is not over here or over there. It is simply within you. So many are looking for Life outside of themselves, but this Life can never be found outside of themselves; it can only be found within, for within themselves is the only place this Life they seek lives. It lives within you.

I saw a vision of you standing beside people, speaking loudly and clearly into their ears, and them not hearing you.

Yes, it is frustrating.

I saw that. Why can't they hear?

They do not believe. They dismiss it as a stray thought or ignore it completely.

Can I help?

Not with these. They would ignore you also. When I say people deny themselves, I mean the spiritual beings they are.

I know that.

Yes, but did you know that they are denying their very life, their existence?

I know that too.

Do you really?

Well, I think so.

Then why do you deny the Life that is within you?

Didn't know I did that.

But you do.

Always?

Collection

No, not always, but it's important to know that when you do, you are not living your life but that of another—an image of the real—and it can never be fulfilling or complete. Do not deny your Self. It knows what It needs and It supplies all your needs when you affirm It. That which you saw in my eyes—the planets, the solar systems, the galaxies—was a symbol of Life, a reflection of Everything, of all Life everywhere, and you saw it all within me.

Why? Because one person contains all life, all things, everywhere, and all times are contained there as well. All the knowledge of the ages condensed into that one point above the mountain of paths. And where do all of those paths lead? Back to yourself. Know thyself. When you know yourself you will need not another for you will know there is not another.

Well spoken.

That's not exactly what I said but it's close enough. You like to exaggerate the symptoms.

What?

You were going to say your mind is melting down.

I was thinking that, and I can tell you're just scratching the surface.

There is no end to Life.

I believe it.

That you do. This that is within you is everything—that's the point I am trying to make. It is Everything. Everything you need.

April 20

7:56 AM
The universe speaks and I'm hearing nothing.

I said the universe speaks, I didn't say it shouted.

April 21

12:08 PM
Consciousness is the CENTER of the universe, and it flows outward.

I was just thinking something along these lines.

But you forgot the center, which is where it all comes from. Where do you think those lines come from? Everything is contained in each one of those lines, encapsulated, all at once. Those

The Universe Speaks

points of interest are moments in time where it all comes together for you. You pause there for enlightenment.

I will ask the obvious: how do you get there?

You already are there, wherever you desire to be. All time is contained there. Remember when I said "in any direction"?

Yes. So then all space is contained there as well, since time and space are inseparable?

Yes.

Talia, that is hard to follow.

That's because you're not there now, but you could be.

What are the lines of lights like lightening inside those bubbles?

Information. Go there with a question or the information is overwhelming. Ask specifically what you need to know. Be open to the answer—it will come.

Tapping into these roots like lines of light is just . . .

Quietness.

That was productive.

I told you I would talk with you.

April 22

12:32 PM
A parallel universe is bilateral.

Why?

Because of the interconnectedness of all things. That is also a reflection that truth is a constant. Everything, every event, affects everything else in some way. A Being is an event in process. A flux, a flow, is within and a part of every single aspect of the universe. The universe itself is a Being, alive.

This isn't explaining anything, is it? It's just clues.

It's explaining it if you listen; it's explaining it if you seek it, if you see it.

Collection

April 23

1:20 PM

Why is it that people tend to put people on an exalted level, on a pedestal, after they die? Shouldn't that honor be given them before that? To respect that life now?

Yes, you're right.

How many do that?

Not many.

Few, very few. To see someone as they are is the cure. And to see them this way is to help them become who they are.

5:38 PM

Talia, you were already who you are when I met you. You were beyond any help of mine, but that which you said is awesome and profound.

Yes, I was. You saw who I was and you couldn't believe it.

That was startling.

It startled you from your slumber. That was completely unexpected. Remember when I said I expect the unexpected.

Yes.

You may not know what Life may bring. But know this: it IS good and it is a gift.

You were heaven on earth.

That's nice of you.

April 25

8:16 PM

That's what you've been doing all along.

Learning from within.

Yes. Don't let the writing get in the way of our fellowship.

I won't.

Then why are you writing? Everything is not to be written, but to know. That's how you can help others, by becoming what you are. That's more than anything you will write on a page. That's you, that's all, in part. The part you have to play. Play it well; do your best, that's all.

That is The All. Yes?

That is Everything. That's doing your Best, being your Best, of who you are. I'm saying Everything is Here Now, THAT is All.

You're having fun?

I always do. And it never stops. Tell them that.

April 28

10:41 AM
The Art of Life is letting Life live itself in you, and through you.

I had asked.

Yes, you did.

11:43 AM
Times are changing.

How so?

They are accelerating, as is the universe as it expands. These things are happening within you as well. I was a forerunner of this. You SAW my consciousness expanding.

You're right. I never thought of that before, but your consciousness was just exploding before my eyes.

That was another thing I meant when I said I could not contain it and it spilled over to others. Did you see the joy in my eyes when I smiled at you?

Yes.

With this expansion that cannot be contained.

You did reflect a lifetime to me in that one day.

That one day was Revelation, and it would not have happened except for you asking.

Thank God for that.

Yes, always thank Him, for everything.

Collection

1:26 PM
Several times you have told me these truths are radical. I finally looked the word up and now I know why you have said that so much. Because they are fundamental and basic. I had no idea what *radical* meant. That's radical.

Yes, it is.

And I also remember one time when you told me that, I saw the word *Chem* in my mind. I thought I was just tired, or it was my imagination or something. It turns out that *Chem* is a group of two or more atoms acting as a single atom. You're just smiling, aren't you?

Yes, I knew you would get it.

Radical.

Yes, it is.

Okay, guess I need to record what happened there.

When you said, "That one day was Revelation, and it would not have happened except for your asking," I thought, "Radical Notion." And you said, "Radical Truth." That's what prompted me to look it up.

Glad you did.

You are subtle.

Truth is usually like that.

"Pointers to truth."

Usually. But even when they are laid out for you plainly there is always more, deeper truth.

A clue to LOOK for it, dig for it with diligence.

Yes. Due diligence.

I remember you saying that before.

Yes, it is like a payment due, a payment of you seeking, of applying your heart, of proving all things. In this case, a proving of your desire to know the truth, then the payment of your diligence to walk in the truth you know.

It's good to let people win sometimes. It lets people see who they are, and it helps them to know what they can become.

> This was very interesting to me. When Talia was growing up, she would often play games with her dad—basketball, chess, etc.—and he NEVER let her win, as other parents do with their kids. She asked me why Dad

591

never let her win. She said it was good to let kids win sometimes. I told her that that was just not her dad's way. So for Talia to mention that it is good to let people win sometimes was very touching to me.

More radical truth?

Always.

May 2011

May 1

7:54 PM
Talia, I think Everything we've said has already been said.

Yes, it has, over and over, and that's because it is eternal truths. A large part of this message is that you have help. That the connection isn't lost, that the veil has been rent. And we WANT to help. So many of your struggles are unnecessary. We want to help. Ask and then receive it, really receive it; it really is that simple.

May 3

11:19 AM
    As G thought of the Golden Eagle I had seen a few weeks before, chased and harassed by a raven, Talia spoke:

The eagle is a symbol of vision, and as you live that vision you will be hounded, you will be persecuted, you will be misunderstood. But you will also be blessed beyond measure.

I believe that.

Then live your vision. It is much more than you can imagine.

Did you live your vision?

I lived it as I knew it.

Collection

May 4

7:30 AM

G thought, "Why did the Mayans leave their temples?" As soon as he thought that he heard:

The seed of the Spaniard. It was easy for them to see, and they scattered into the wilderness.

I realized then it was Talia's voice I was hearing.

It was easy for them to see it coming. Their descendants survive today and mostly in peace and harmony.

If we look closely at what Talia said, it is a heads-up on how to survive what's coming in the future—not only how to survive, but how to thrive. As she said:

I do not waste words.

May 5

12:36 PM

Learning is healing. A friend said it and you said it.

Yes, I did.

May 6

5:06 PM

I was walking and thinking of how vague some of the messages must seem to some people when Talia spoke to me.

Some of it appears veiled. It's not, when you go into it and see beyond the words.

5:10 PM

If I explain it, that is only one explanation. It is multifaceted in every direction. Think of a hologram and even that as a beginning.

Multiplied over and over into infinity.

Yes, never-ending. That's why I say it will never end.

That's one explanation.

Yes. ☺ It's pellucid.

7:45 PM
I really didn't think that was a word. I had to look it up, although what you said, I understood as, "It's pellucid when you see it clearly; you can see right through it." So I looked it up and it means "to shine, transparent, clear."

Talia, I never even heard of that word.

It's not used very often.

Sure fits.

That's why I used it.

Talia, thank you for talking with me.

You're welcome.

May 7

2:32 PM
Thought is faster than the speed of light. Thought is energy. Energy follows thought. You are energy.

May 10

7:42 PM
My dear, I need to hear.

You do hear. You heard my voice in my words you read today.

I sure did; even the birds started to sing as I read them.

I told you my words were Life. They are not dead letters.

Now I'm about spent.

The energy of the flesh is finite. You saw a photo of me when I was tired.

I did.

I was resting.

Collection

A clue.

Yes.

Talia, you are amazing.

Yes, I am. As your consciousness expands it will touch others, causing their consciousness to expand as well.

That's good to know.

That's good to practice. We will speak of it more. You're not clear; you're tired.

Sorry about that.

No need to be. For everything there is a season. Walk in what you know. Remember, it's the walk, not the talk.

May 14

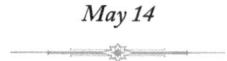

1:02 PM
Talia, you have anything to say?

Yes, lots.

I need to know it's you.

Know—it's me.

I rest in trust.

You should. There remains a rest for the people of God. His word is faithful unto the end.

If God be for you, who shall be against you?

That's a very good question. You will see some things unfolding. Keep your eyes opened.

Symbiotics?

Yes, they will not be seen with the natural eyes. Read the signs. When they are manifested in the natural, without spiritual discernment the true meaning will be missed. Watch. Listen. Quietness is imperative.

7:20 PM
What's the difference between the white, gold, and purple sash?

It is what we wish to manifest at the moment. My wearing white is to signify purity and the purity of the message. Gold always speaks of Divinity, our God nature, of whom we serve and the Source of all things. And you did see me wearing gold. Purple speaks of royalty, in this case signifying the King of Kings and Lord of Lords.

> I asked Talia if the arms that had welcomed her to heaven before sending her back to Earth to help Frankie after the crash had been God's arms or Jesus'.

It was both, Mom.

10:22 PM
Talia, once before I mentioned what I perceived to be your franticness to get your message out, but I now see it was your energy and passion.

It was that and it still is. I had a mission and I fulfilled it. I still have a mission and I'm fulfilling it as well. My Life will never stop, nor will yours. Our missions are different and yet they run a parallel course. You think you can stop but you never can. I knew I couldn't and never tried.

I feel like you're growing beyond me.

I'm not growing beyond you. I am growing, you are growing, and we are growing together.

But you accomplished so much in just thirteen years.

And I'm now accomplishing more than you can fathom. And so are you.

That truly is unfathomable.

You need to think about what I said. I was a bridge. You are a bridge. I am a bridge. All of this condensed into one point, to expand again. One point—where time and space is condensed. One point—where all these are one. Not in theory but in truth. Not in concept but in reality. Not in thought but in experience. This is a place beyond the imaginings of man. Yet without man this place cannot be, for without man, this place would have no purpose. Man looks down on himself, and it's from a lofty height. Something to consider, isn't it?

You're losing me.

No, you're finding you, and that is what man must do, find himself. Then their mysteries will be solved. You asked me to speak of the mysteries, remember?

Yes, now I do. I remember that.

You had no idea what you were asking, did you?

No, not really.

Then why did you ask that?

I don't know.

Collection

Because you were compelled to. It's part of the mystery, man's part to play in this. Many see themselves as insignificant, but nothing could be further from the truth. All affect the fabric of reality, which expands and contracts. The reality IS, it doesn't change, and yet man's effects upon it cause its appearance to change as it expands and contracts. His experience of this reality is mirrored by his and others' effects upon it. That is why agreement in truth is primary.

I can see how you would not understand this without seeing it. You're showing it to me; I hope I can keep it.

Let it go. You don't need to keep it, you need to lose it.

I'm letting it go.

I thought you would; now it's yours. The universe breathes; it is constantly expanding and contracting. Such is the nature of reality. It remains the same and yet it is ever changing.

A constant state of flux.

Yes. Your consciousness creates reality in its many splendors. You create a beautiful world by your thoughts of it. Your consciousness IS your reality.

Not many are going to buy into this.

That's their reality.

> G read through the letters that Talia's friends had written to her after her death.

It's good to cry.

May 18

9:29 PM
Mom is learning a lot. She's learning more than she knows.

Isn't that always the case? I mean, not with just your mom?

No, if one is completely awake, one will know and realize ALL that one is learning.

Like you.

Yes, like me, but there are others, and where you are as well. These have transcended the physical realm; they see through the illusion. These usually have a smile.

Like they know something.

They do know something; they know Everything.

The Universe Speaks

Who are these people?

Enlightened beings, and they walk among you.

I want to meet one.

You have, you just didn't notice. These nearly always go unnoticed. Also there is never self-promotion. These touch others lightly and move on, leaving hardly a trace of their passing.

Were you one of those when you were here?

I was close.

Now I've really got to get to know one.

Get to know Everything instead. These would see you as an apprentice.

That's good?

Of course it's good; you're on the right path. You thought of me as an apprentice once.

That's right, I did; my apologies.

No need to apologize. You considered it a place of honor.

That's true, I did. I think I just underestimated you.

You did, but that's since been corrected.

That's for sure.

These live beyond the body; they are present Here.

Guess they would have a grin then.

I said usually; they are at times very stern. They are as a signpost of what to become and the possibilities.

Possibilities of what?

Of all things. They are used as an impetus for others to make good choices.

You were used for that.

Usually. All my choices weren't the best—I had to learn too.

Anything stand out you want to discuss?

No, mostly small things like disobeying my mom. It made me feel bad, and even though I knew it didn't matter, I was dishonoring her.

Talia the rebel.

Collection

I wouldn't go that far.

I saw a photo of you playing volleyball in your room.

I was practicing.

After your mom told you not to play volleyball in your room anymore.

She did mention that.

I don't think I'll be as impressed with these as I was with you.

We were bound together for a purpose.

Good point.

I consistently make those.

I feel your look, Talia. I see it in fact, and I hear your thought, "You should too."

That's the point I'm making. ☺

May 20

12:30 PM
During my last meditation you were wearing a gold sash.

That's to let you know where this comes from. My voice, my presence, my personality is being used. You relate to me. Everyone has those who help. You're distracted by the time.

Yes.

Presence of mind. You need a full mind.

That's not what you said before.

Filled with truth, not laboring under illusion. Remember what I said about perceptions.

I would need to reread that. I did hear that perception is reality to the uninformed.

But you have the information. The heart of you always knows what is time.

May 23

AM
Meditation is movement. In the stillness.

The Universe Speaks

May 24

6:42 AM
It's a good day.

I agree. Your point is?

It's a good day. Maybe you should be more diplomatic.

How so?

You do not always need to make your point forcefully. Subtle is often the better way. Remember those who touch lightly, then move on.

All right, but some are hardheaded.

And sometimes you're among them.

Ouch.

That didn't hurt.

I think you could be more forceful sometimes and not so subtle.

That forces you to listen.

Well then, maybe you're using too much force.

Cute. You know I'm right.

I could be too.

You could be.

You got me again.

You got you. Sometimes you work against yourself more than anyone that you know.

It's a good day.

Yes, it is.

11:40 PM
Talia, I would sure like to feel your touch again.

You will.

My friends miss me.

I know. Why did you say that?

Collection

Well, that's natural and normal, but I want them to know there is more. That life's not over when you "die," that it continues. I would like them to know that when they think of me, I am there. And when they feel my presence, that is not a memory, that I am there. They should know that I will still help them.

Anything else?

I love my friends and I honor their friendship. They should trust themselves and believe in themselves. They should recognize their own brilliance.

May 25

7:05 AM
Why does it have to be so hard to hear?

It doesn't.

1:19 PM
We're One.

We are.

So I can ask you anything and you can answer me.

Anything you're ready for the answer for.

May 28

12:49 PM
Recount your "interesting perspective."

I said to a friend that since I've been in this life I've noticed people trying to kill other people because they are different, and the irony is that they are all the same.

That was your Higher Self speaking.

Interesting perspective.

It always will be when your Higher Self speaks. That is why so many comments children make are so interesting. It's because it is from their Higher Self. That part of you that knows all things.

"Lest ye become a little child."

So true. Children most often see things as they are, until they are taught otherwise. My purpose has been to bring you back to seeing with that purity, uncorrupted by false voices. When you saw the Keeper of the Secrets for the first time it was with eyes untainted.

Then it was lost.

No, it was just delayed. That had purpose.

I see that clearly now. "You're royalty; let others play their games" is what the Keeper of the Secrets told me when I first saw him.

That too had purpose. Its understanding was delayed.

I still don't think I totally get it.

No, but you will, and when you do you will ascend to a new place, a place you've only briefly visited. But you can live there.

That's . . .

That's where all things are possible.

June 2011

June 6

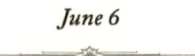

12:46 PM
Talia, many months ago you told me "Light bends matter."

Why didn't you write it when I told you?

I wanted a confirmation.

Why? Everything affects everything else. It's made of the same stuff.

Energy.

12:56 PM
      While G was meditating:

Hello, Talia.

Hello.

You're always here.

Collection

Yes, I am. My consciousness can be anywhere so my consciousness is everywhere.

I think that's going to cause more scratching of wooden heads without a download accompanying it.

That's one way to describe not understanding something, and yet seeds are planted. My word will not return void, remember?

Oh, that's right. And you don't waste words.

That is right. You know, you're ahead of schedule.

How's that?

You'll see.

Hope that's good.

It is.

1:25 PM
Until you are over the hypnotism of appearance, the appearance of the illusion will appear absolutely real.

That appears to be absolutely true to me. But what are you talking about specifically?

I have a point to make. The appearance of my "death" is why you do not see more photos of me than you do.

> Talia mentioned this because I was telling G that I was upset that Talia's friends did not have many, if any, photos of her on their Facebook pages. It really upset me.

6:18 PM
What about angels?

They're beautiful!

June 8

2:15 PM
Talia, are you putting the pennies around?

I am.

What does it mean, Talia?

Awareness of my presence.

The Universe Speaks

June 10

5:44 PM
What about the void? I don't remember you ever mentioning it.

The void is an often nebulous term used in your world that ranges from nothingness to parallel universes. The void to me is filled with Life, with Light and energy and energy beings of light. It is filled with the perfect wisdom and consciousness of the universe. It is a dance of never-ending energies. It would be well to remember that the things that are seen are not made of things that appear. They are the consciousness of energy made manifest. They are the same, just in different forms. Water and steam are the same thing, just in different forms, and it too cannot always be seen.

But you can sure feel the humidity.

That's true and that's a clue. Even though it is a physical feeling, know that your spirit feels as well, and it cannot not know or feel the dance of energies from what you may call the void. Remember when I said you were surrounded?

Yes.

You are surrounded.

7:35 PM
The void to us just doesn't exist. There is no place where "It" is not.

8:11 PM
Talia, thanks so much. I asked you to talk to me today and you sure have.

All you have to do is ask.

There's that little girl voice again.

It's just me.

You're so delightfully humble! That was weird!

That was me. You asked me to do that too.

I saw the lights.

Yes, that was me.

But why on the back of my leg like that? I thought it was a rat. You're laughing!

It's funny.

Collection

You did that on purpose.

It wasn't an accident. You would do it too. You said you wanted to feel my touch again.

I forgot saying that.

I didn't. Do you know how many people I touch who feel nothing?

Um—twelve?

A lot more than that. You said you wanted to hear my laugh, remember?

Now I do. And it really is infectious.

It has been known to spread. Peace is the same, infectious.

I see that happening right now, here.

Conclusions, reassessments, life-changing experiences.

I just now heard that in their voices. A confirmation of what I felt.

You felt harmony there for the first time.

I did. The Creator was revealing Himself in creation.

He always does. It reflects His love, His caring, His compassion. One who feels this cannot help but be moved by it.

Wow.

Yes, indeed. A child was born under the moniker, "Peace on earth, good will towards men" and the sign of a star.

I heard about that.

We celebrate that birthday every day. And his children are born and reborn every day.

That's something to think about.

That's something to KEEP in mind.

9:49 PM
I remembered after you touched me one of the things you said was, "You would do it too."

Thank you, Talia.

You're welcome G. Sleep now.

June 17

God is written in your DNA.

In your DNA?

The code.

6:17 PM
Talia, when you told me that it seemed self-evident in light of what you've said about Him being in us. Then I read somewhere that the basic elements of DNA, the names of the chemical compounds—hydrogen, nitrogen, oxygen, and carbon—directly translate into specific letters of the Hebrew alphabet, YHVA, which then translates into the original name of God. That sort of blew me away. I didn't know you were being literal.

I always said more than you've heard. Like the diamond, multi-faceted.

Or a hologram.

Yes.

June 20

6:32 PM
Talia, why aren't you talking to me?

I am, I always do. It's an open line. But you must be open to hear, to listen.

June 27

12:54 PM
    While meditating I saw the Keeper of the Secrets standing before me, just to Talia's right. He was giving me an INTENT stare. Then he said:

Be careful with your tongue. It's for Life.

The tongue is for Life?

    He nodded and thought, which I heard as:

Collection

Yes. Your words are Spirit and Life, and when you use your own words you will get a negative and distorted reaction. Use it for Life. To project Life.

I asked out loud:

Anything else?

There is much, much more, and when it is time and you are ready to receive it, I will speak it.

Thank you.

He very gruffly answered:

You're welcome.

Talia, is he in a bad mood?

He's just tired of waiting.

Talia, time is so short.

Yes, it is.

Talia, you're going?

Yes. You don't have to feel it to be here. You don't have to be so careful.

No?

No, it's the flow. Just drawing the balance.

A visual did come with that.

Yes, balanced scales.

You read my mind.

I sent it to your mind. Do you know why he doesn't always speak but sends his words by thought?

Yes, to let me know that which is another means of communication.

Yes that, and to let you know that when you are in harmony with someone it is as simple as breathing.

Another secret.

What else?

Talia, where are you?

I'm here.

The Universe Speaks

Why don't I see you?

The word *Faith* came to me, then Talia said:

It's to let you know when you don't see me, I'm still here.

Then I saw the Keeper of the Secrets again. He asked:

Are you afraid?

No.

We are on the same side.

I knew he meant him and Talia. He gave me a very intent look, staring, searching my eyes.

Look into your Soul. There is everything there—the purity of being. Do you believe in what you're doing?

Depends on what I'm doing.

Why would you do something you don't believe in? Do you believe in me?

Yes.

Why?

You've proven yourself.

Prove your self.

6:25 PM
Okay, now what?

You can talk to me.

And what do you wish to discuss, O fair one?

That was cute. ☺

Your life and my life are One.

I think you've said that before.

I have, and you haven't gotten it yet.

I do feel separate from you right now.

Remember when I said you can't always go by feelings?

Yes, I do.

Collection

That was for just such times as these.

I feel we are closer now.

But do you KNOW we're One?

I know if you say it it's true.

But this a visceral knowing, it's felt.

Well, I'm just not feeling it right now.

You can't always go by feelings.

These are false emotions?

You could call them that, in that they are upholding an illusion. It is a creation of your mind reasoning, unreasonably. Conjuring images of unworthiness. You don't feel you're good enough to hear me this clearly. That is a false feeling. We've talked about this before.

Yeah, you're right.

Of course I'm right. I always am.

Wish I had your confidence.

But you do have it. That's what you're not getting, that WE are ONE.

I want to get past this; seems we go over this ground over and over.

You HAVE it, but you must TAKE it.

You're exasperated again.

It happens.

That's sort of funny.

I'm glad you found the humor in it.

Well, it is kind of funny.

That is a vehicle to help get you past it.

You're thinking it's a bit ridiculous, aren't you?

See, we are One.

I read your mind.

I revealed it to you. I let you see it.

Show me more!

The Universe Speaks

It's only Love. It's all Love. One mind, in agreement.

Talia, thanks for the pennies.

You are welcome; it made you aware of my presence, didn't it?

It sure did.

I said I would be with you always.

July 2011

July 13
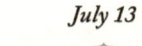

G and I were shopping. I saw a sweater that I knew Talia would love. I told G that Talia would wear this sweater, and just then he heard Talia.

I'd wear that.

July 18

PM
A Black Hole is a birthplace.

Of what?

Life. It rebounds.

July 27

8:45 AM
   From the Keeper of the Secrets:

To envision is to become. What WILL be, will be.

Collection

July 29

4:10 PM

While G was watching a show on the Kabbalah, Talia showed up.

It's not absolute.

August 2011

August 2

8:00 AM
What do you want me to do today?

Listen to me.

I'm missing the teachings of Talia.

You're getting them. I'm not the only one who speaks.

August 3

8:30 AM
What are you doing today, Talia?

Being myself. Did you notice the flowers?

This earth is a pale reflection.

August 4

8:50 AM

During another meditation G spoke with the Keeper of the Secrets again.

You asked for rain?

Yes.

Well, it's coming. The secret is being at peace.

How?

By letting his peace RULE in your heart.

You don't seem so gruff today.

I'm coming to accept you. Walk in the Spirit and you will not fulfill the lust of the flesh. They are contrary to one another.

That's no secret.

They are if you're not living them.

It's raining.

August 6

6:00 PM
My mom treated me as who I was. Do you want to know why? Because she knew who I was and never denied it.

August 15

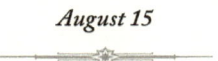

PM
The stick is a teacher.

What does this stick mean?

It looks dead, doesn't it?

What does it have to teach?

If you understand everything about that branch, you will understand everything about everything, because everything is contained in it.

August 18

Colorado—I had fun.

Collection

This statement of Talia's was meant for me. When she was younger I took her to Aspen during the summer. It was so much fun! She rode her bike and went up the mountain, had fun playing with her friends, had picnics, and more. She loved it!

9:23 AM
I'm a trigger for you.

August 28

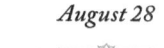

7:20 AM

G: I had been seeing Talia's photos of her with icebergs in my mind for months. I asked her what it was about:

A person's life is as an iceberg. What is seen is but a small part of what is there. What is below the surface, unseen, is the largest part of a person's life, and the most important. Why is this life denied so often?

How did it take me so long to get this?

Because you've been living mostly above the surface. When these images come to you repeatedly, then go within to the Silence. As I've said, that is where we live, and your answers will be revealed. This is a lesson, simple but most important, for it is often missed. All receive these messages often, but they are just as often dismissed and ignored. This truth, when practiced, is a way of enlightenment to arise out of bondage and darkness and enter into the glorious liberty of enlightenment. How can one live contentedly when these messages, these mysteries, are struggling within them to be revealed? This iceberg is not separate from the ocean, this sea of consciousness.

September 2011

September 1

8:45 PM
All right, Talia, I'm doing what you said, only believing.

That's good.

Yes, it is.

613

The Universe Speaks

Why have you waited so long?

Busy, distracted I guess.

With what?

With . . . nothing worth being distracted about.

Remember what you just told your friend.

I said to him many entities don't speak unless they are spoken to.

Yes, and words aren't enough anymore—live it.

That I must.

Yes, you must. Richard (a friend of G and Kim) *heard my voice.*

Does he know?

He knows. How do you think it touched him like it did?

Because he heard your voice.

That's part of it. It has awakened his heart to know that what he knows is true.

Talia, that's beautiful.

That is the nature of truth. That's all I wanted to convey to you now. We can do this anytime.

That's hard to believe.

That's why it's hard for you to do this anytime.

Thanks, Talia.

You're welcome G, and have a good night.

September 2

7:39 AM
There's going to be hearts touched, inspired.

That's really good.

I know.

Just stating facts again.

Always.

Collection

Clever.

I know. That is not all.

What else?

Trust.

Got it.

Well, you're getting it. I'm here today.

I know you are.

You see what I'm doing.

Yes, awesome! Touching hearts, changing people.

That is our purpose, to awaken them.

September 13

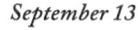

While finding the place of the Temple within:

This is picking up from . . . Everything.

September 14

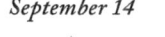

Talia, do you have anything to say to me today?

Yes, do your best.

This isn't the first time you've told me that.

No, it's not. That's because it is important. It refers back to you not wasting moments.

10:00 AM
Talia, up to the last minute before the crash you were speaking truth and helping others, calming and comforting them.

It's who I was and am. Nothing is more important than being your true self. It is where you are.

At that moment G saw a butterfly wing in the sand.

That's beautiful.

615

Death is beautiful because it is life, rebirth.

There's some pain involved.

Yes, like birth. You see that?

Yes.

I'm glad you're learning this. What more is there?

    She was talking about my learning to go within to my place of Oneness.

That's a good question.

You bet it is. It is asking Everything.

September 15

The Silence, where all things are.

9:35 AM
We're doing something together that can change the world and will change many people's world. Why are you rushing? You don't need to rush. Go inside. That's where you need to go. That's where I want Mom to get, within her—that's everything she needs. Anything can be a crutch.

September 19

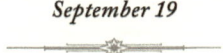

If you've noticed, I've honored all ways, all paths.

Talia, thank you for teaching me.

9:03 PM
IT IS THE TEMPLE OF TRUTH BECAUSE IT IS FREEDOM.

September 23

10:40 AM
    While I was taking a break from recording the audio book for *The Universe Speaks* (Book One):

It's going better than you think.

Collection

7:04 PM

> G and I were having dinner at a fancy restaurant and were talking about how Talia had been used to eating out. G commented:

Talia's a little more sophisticated than me.

A little more?

> When he heard her say that he started to crack up. He then told me, and I started to crack up as well! It was so funny!

September 24

AM

> While recording the audio book, I said to G that I was having a hard time because I did not think I remembered Talia's voice.

Mom DOES remember my voice

September 25

9:00 AM

> While listening to a song called "Raindrops from Heaven," which we were thinking of including on the audio book, G heard Talia say:

I WANT IT.

You never told me you wanted anything before.

Yes, I did. That's one of the first things I ever told you.

September 26

7:54 AM

He said He would leave no nation without a witness. This is the spirit of prophecy. This is a witness of Light. This has been, and is, for every generation. Because people forget history. What has been is what is becoming. Now is the time for this; Now is forever. This includes the past. These gifts given in the past are gifts contained in the presence. He does not change. I am with you today.

617

The Universe Speaks

12:30 PM
Thank you, Talia, for this today.

This is for Mom. It always has been.

September 27

3:15 PM
> G: While driving we heard the song "Time to Pretend." Kim said that she was not sure if the song had come out before or after the crash, but regardless, she knew that this was one of Talia's favorite songs. I replied, "I can tell you I already don't like it." Then I heard Talia laughing.

September 30

5:55 AM
Today is a special day.

How so?

The book.

> This was the day that the book *Hummingbirds Don't Fly in the Rain*, which I wrote about Talia's "death," arrived in hard copy for the first time from the printers!

October 2011

October 2

7:28 PM
Remember when you told me there wasn't anything you wouldn't do for me?

Yes.

Keep your word.

I fully intend to, I just have to know it is you. Whatcha need, Darlin'?

Collection

I need you to listen.

I'm listening.

Are you really? You would rather read what I've already said than listen to what I have to say.

I just got caught up in it.

I told you not to dote on my words.

Yeah, okay, but I'm doting on your meanings.

Are you really?

I thought so.

You're thinking so doesn't make it so.

I figure you must have something to say.

I do.

What is it?

You're still struggling with a most basic truth.

Which is?

Your belief. Your success is achieved in quiet. Not in outer works. In inner works of the Spirit. That achievement is lasting. The work of the flesh is but for a moment. Then it disappears, disappears with the wind.

For two weeks, I kept seeing WORK over and over.

But it's the inner works of the inner man. Remember when you heard "Time to become a man"? That's what that meant.

Thus my lack of enthusiasm with the work I've been doing this week.

Work that doesn't matter much.

That's what it feels like.

That's what it is like, until you step it up to another level, another state of being.

Being who I am.

Being who you are and walking in what you know. Your time here is limited—make the most of it.

How?

By doing what you know you should do. By being who you know you are and by purity of purpose. Remember, you're going to influence regardless of your purpose, so your purpose might as well be pure. Quit just reading my words and put them into practice. You just said that first book was like a study manual; what do you think this one is? I told you this was words of Life, not idle curiosity. You've given up a lot to do this, but it was a lot of nothing. Now play the part you've been assigned.

Are you angry?

No, but I'm concerned you're wasting a precious gift, a gift of Life, a gift of Light.

Time to get it together.

It is time to get it together; time is short.

October 3

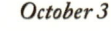

8:19 PM
What have you done that you couldn't do again?

Nothing.

That's something to consider, isn't it?

It is.

Has it not been said your strength is perfected in weakness?

It has.

When have you not loved me?

I can't remember a time. There isn't one.

Have I ever failed you?

No.

Do you believe in what I do?

Yes, totally.

Have you not met me and your life been changed?

Yes, totally.

Do you not believe what I say?

Yes, I believe you.

Collection

Then why do you doubt me?

I don't doubt you Talia, ever; I just have to be sure it's you.

That's wise.

Boy, you're filled with questions today.

I'm filled with answers. The questions are for you.

G picked up the Bible and opened it; it opened to Psalm 82 and then he said:

This is where we are at.

Glad you noticed. Do you know how many see that?

No, I don't.

Few, very few. The time has come for man to open his eyes and receive the truth. Those who judge by outward appearance will come to false conclusions. That is receiving a lie and embracing it, by looking on the surface. It is an appearance. It is not real, not the truth, but it appears real as if it is the truth. It is the Word made flesh that heals the blind. It is that Light that purges all darkness and makes whole again. It is only that Light that delivers Man from bondage and restores what is his. He rules among the gods.

October 4

5:54 PM
You see how far we could take this?

Yes, forever.

Now you're getting it.

October 6

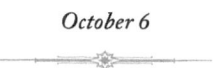

1:11 PM
Where do you think the New Jerusalem is? It is within you. A new heaven and a new earth wherein dwells righteousness. These having the nature of God written on their foreheads transform the earth around them. The beauty of their hearts giving manifestation to new life. Both within and without in harmony with divine love, which is, as I've said, the structure of the universe.

The Universe Speaks

October 9

12:45 PM
You've got something to say.

Yes. You can see everything at once because every part is complete in itself.

How so?

Every part is a reflection of every other part, revealing the coherent whole of everything.

Space and time suspended?

Not suspended . . . you just see it as it is, all at once.

Got a method?

By pure and fervent desire. What does need to be suspended is unbelief. Know that on the other side there is a pure and fervent desire by the Light to reveal itself. Remember when I said, "It's good to be known." This is another manifestation of love activated, the passion to be known. That doorway I held open for you was the doorway to infinity, and everyone has that doorway opened for them.

Then why . . .

Most ignore it or are held back by fear, greed, and many other base disharmonies. Many are blinded by what they are taught to believe, but this door of opportunity exists for ALL, and all are encouraged to step through this door to the unknown. For to step through this door is to know even as you are known, and this is Everything.

Keep traveling.

Keep traveling?

Yes, keep traveling. There is no end.

Thank you, Talia!

You're welcome.

11:30 PM
Water, water everywhere and not to drink a drop.

That's not the first time you've said that to me, but you've never explained.

It means you are surrounded by an ocean of consciousness. You are it, it is you, but if you do not drink of it you die. This is the death of your perception, of your will, of your determination—in

Collection

essence, of your very consciousness. This is an outside influence that when you drink of it, it becomes you. You understand now when I told you that you didn't need the energy but you needed to eat?

I was a little fuzzy on that.

I was speaking of spiritual food, plain and simple, while you were thinking physical—that's why you didn't understand it. You see how basic that is and how easy it is to miss such simple truth? We are doing something here that is also very basic and simple, and that's righting wrongs. Wrong thinking based on missed perceptions. I spoke to you before about first principles. Single-mindedness is open to the infinite. Pure focused thought expanded to include all.

Can . . .

No, I will not explain this now, for it too must be experienced. But to experience this is to know in an instant exactly what it means.

I'm tired.

Yes, you are.

I mean, I'm not complaining, just a fact.

Yes, it is.

I thought you liked to talk.

I do.

You said today you had a lot to say.

I do. Rest isn't a first principle, but it seems like it should be to you.

You don't miss a thing.

Well, rest or rise above it, it is a choice.

I couldn't sleep now anyway.

Good choice.

I need THIS food.

Now we are getting somewhere.

You know, you can be kind of strict at times.

Yes.

I see what you're getting at.

The Universe Speaks

Yes, you know whom I work for.

That really strikes me as funny.

You SHOULD have fun with it.

Talia, I adore you to no end.

I just told you today there wasn't an end.

I just saw a white light move very quickly in front of me. That was you, right?

Yes . . . and that was too . . . and that . . . that too.

Are you showing off?

I'm letting you see how fast I move. In this realm it's speed in perfect stillness.

Guess I'll have to get real still to figure that out.

You will, you are, you do. You know where to find me and I'm always here.

    G yawned.

Am I boring you? ☺

You are a joker.

I like making you laugh.

That is so sweet of you. Don't ever stop.

There is no stopping me.

Yeah, I know. Lovely light show.

I'm glad you like it.

I love it.

I know you do.

Is this part of the message?

Not really, but it could be.

Something like all parts are the whole?

Something like that. Why would you want to read what you wrote when you can read what you've written after you've written it?

Just wanted to see where we were.

We're where we are.

Collection

You are the clever one.

I am clever.

How did you move like you moved when I met you?

I had good genes—we've already talked about it. Now I'm showing you how I move now.

But I've yet to meet anyone so confident.

Do you know why?

That's why I'm asking.

Because I believed in who I was.

Made a believer out of me.

And that was its design. You want to emulate me?

Absolutely.

Emulate your Self, your Higher Self, and you will walk in that same confidence.

Tall order.

It's an opportunity.

Another doorway.

Yes.

October 13

9:00 AM
Talia, I have not heard you all day.

Yes, you have. You have been inspired the whole time; you have not missed a moment. Even now you are divinely inspired.

4:35 PM
That harmony we have spoken about is more than what most think of it. It is a vibration of your innermost being, your True Self, in sync with the vibration of the universe, which is the harmony of the love of the Creator in His creation, enfolding over and over forever.

Concerning Book One, it is a one-step program. One step at a time.

The Universe Speaks

October 14

6:13 AM
Thank you for doing this.

You are welcome.

You know, there are not many things more important than this.

I do not think I even want to know what they are.

Showing your love, for one. You know you could not do this with a cold heart.

You can obviously do it with a cold body though.

It's not that cold.

Not now—I have some heat going.

You like to feel things.

Your point is?

My point is sometimes you give some things more power than they deserve.

6:35 AM
Took me a while, but you are talking about the knuckleheads, aren't you?

That's what you call them and that is only one thing. Why empower an illusion?

That would be stupid.

Then why do you do it?

Do I do this often?

You do it more often than you think.

Then that makes me a knucklehead.

That interconnectedness has a negative aspect, thus the "be ye separate." That is what you should empower; that is a separation in fullness, and when that part is brought back into the whole, it changes a negative into a positive. It's separated itself from the illusion, become again one with the whole, and its influence from this place of love and completion changes the negative to a positive. This is a subtle influence, but it is the difference between victory and defeat.

10:55 PM
    G asked Spirit what He wanted from him.

Collection

Continue with Talia.

How can I get there?

By listening.

How can I find it?

Be still and know I am God.

October 17

11:08 AM
A friend told me he had heard a young lady's voice directing him in a decision. I knew it was you, Talia. Then I remembered that you told me you had spoken to him, but I was not sure I was hearing you right.

I told you I did.

I know you did.

Then why didn't you believe me?

I did.

I know you did but you had doubts.

When I thought about it I didn't think he needed it, to hear you

It was a confirmation not so much for him, but for you and my mom.

Anything else?

Not now. Be present in the ceremony.

    A special ceremony G and I were in.

October 18

9:27 AM
Richard told me that you had spoken to him about loyalty and how it "couldn't be found on this earth but within that circle."

The lack of loyalty he saw there was a source of frustration for him, and that circle I talked to him about is that same sphere of responsibility that I talked to you about. That is a sphere of safety, of service, of pure love that can do no wrong. It is your first nature to dwell there.

There is so much more, isn't it?

There is no end.

But one word wrong could change the meaning, couldn't it?

One word COULD change the meaning, but also one word misconstrued could change the meaning unless this is quickened by the Spirit. It does not matter what words we use because without the Spirit they will be misunderstood. That is the yielding to that that is real, and not that imagining of that that is wished.

October 19

6:06 PM
It was about thirty years ago that in a vision I saw what is happening now, the rioting in the streets, and it was because they woke up to the fact they had been lied to. Mostly I saw college students. Would you like to add anything?

That IS the root of it, the awareness that this system is founded on lies, untruths. The fix is not playing that game. The fix is helping and gain, not hurting TO gain. The fix is a complete paradigm shift in consciousness. There is ONLY a spiritual solution.

Got a method?

Only when you change yourself can you change others. Speaking the truth out of a sincere heart and loving others is the answer. This cannot be done in the flesh, for that profits nothing. It MUST be done in the Spirit, and to do this there must be a yielding to God's Holy Spirit, an absolute surrender to HIS will in YOUR life. Only then can you bring lasting change in another.

October 20

12:56 PM
Hey, Talia, did you take the day off?

No, did you?

Collection

Okay, you just opened up my brain to a lot of stuff there.

That was its purpose.

I wish I could have spent more time with you here, so I could have outwitted you a time or two.

You think you would have?

I think it would have been a possibility.

It would have been a possibility.

All right, did you ever not pay attention?

Sometimes; not very often though.

Then I would have used that time to outwit you.

That WOULD have been clever.

Okay, you have a bit of an edge on me now.

Now?

I just realized something. You never let on just how clever you were.

That is true, because it is ego, and I noticed it could sometimes cause insecurity in others.

That was kind of you.

It was kind.

You were brilliant.

I said I was.

You were a genius; I saw that when I met you.

I do not really like that term.

Why not?

Because it sets you apart from others, for one, and for another, everyone has genius—it just isn't always recognized.

I am out of time.

We will talk later.

The Universe Speaks

October 25

6:45 PM
You said to me a while back, "It's not in the database." I thought you were talking about something inside of me, but I found out today the book *The Universe Speaks* is not in the correct database.

It was not but it is going to be, but it could have been in sooner. There are forces at work here.

That was not much information to go on.

I thought you prided yourself on putting the pieces together.

Not anymore. I remember feeling that pride as a realization when I said it.

Yes, you did take pride in that. Being humble about it is much better.

Because it is a gift.

It sure is.

And gifts can be taken away.

They sure can. It is just rough edges. Nothing to be alarmed about, but it is something to be aware about.

I know all of that could be explained away as normal or technical difficulties.

There is a good chance of that. Most of these kinds of things are explained away.

There I go again, thinking I'm ahead of the game, and the late bloomer comes out.

It is a lesson. You had a gut feeling of what that meant, and you did mention it.

That is right, I did.

But you spoke it in passing, without force or passion.

Yeah.

Well, it is a lesson so learn from it.

Have you spoken to Richard?

Yes, I have.

What did you say?

I told him to believe in himself, just as I spoke to you when you started this.

Collection

October 28

5:58 PM

Talia, I have to tell you. Your voice is one of the most beautiful things I have ever heard.

I am glad you think so. It is another motivation for you to listen.

You got that right.

When have I ever gotten it wrong?

Never.

October 29

12:42 PM

Does a snowflake judge another snowflake for looking different?

That would mean snowflakes are smarter than most humans.

Something to think about, isn't it?

He does reveal Himself in His creation.

It is impossible for Him not to.

G was going to read from *The Universe Speaks* when she said:

Do you really want to do that?

I did.

If you cannot see the Creator in his creation, you are not seeing. The eyes are more than passive receptors, they project and receive energy. Most see what they have been taught to see or what they have perceived in the past. When you look with new eyes, which are renewed every moment, nothing seems the same as it did when you saw it before—because you are seeing energy as it is, in a never-ending flow of life, creating every instant. A constant change to renew.

Remember, I said it takes energy to see energy. But you have it, it simply must be used. To engage this energy is to see beyond the illusion and into the pure reality of being. You will also see at times symbols, images, superimposed on the energy you see to interpret what you are seeing. This is usually, in the beginning stages, when your eyes are first opening to seeing this energy. It may be a flash of something, an image, a glimpse in your head that at first may seem to be unrelated to what you are looking at. Pay attention to this and do not discount it, for this has meaning. I said it was a language beyond words, and this is a most efficient way to teach the meanings of the movement, colors, shapes of this energy. Eventually these images may not be needed because you will just know. Few if any interpretations will be needed at that time.

I will have to check with my optometrist about that.

You make a joke, but many do that when they begin to see these things. It is very alarming to some. It is not at all what most have been taught of the world. Everything in the natural world has a spiritual counterpart, and that spiritual counterpart is also a symbol of something. These symbols do not always come internally; they are also external. But the interpretation is gained internally.

I know that.

I know you do but not everyone does, and that is why most do not pay attention to even the most blatant physical signs. One thing we are trying to get across here is these things happen to EVERYONE and every day. These lessons are never-ending. Most have been trained NOT to pay attention to them, and in your world THESE lessons are also never-ending. That is why I said to pay attention to what your attention is on, because someone or something is always vying for your attention. Remember the test of truth. Does it bring you more freedom? With the freedom I am speaking of, nothing is impossible for you. Aren't you glad now you didn't read instead?

Yeah, big time. I was sure tempted though.

I know you were; it is a good book.

October 30

1:00 PM

> G: As I was sitting I had an image appear to me of Talia sitting quietly and listening, so that is what I did. Not long after someone said to me, "Baby steps, G." That was a message to me, a reminder of what Talia had said to me before.

Thanks, Talia.

You just have to listen.

An example of exactly what you were speaking of yesterday.

It was.

Collection

And I did not have to dress in fancy garments or sit in a lotus position for days meditating.

You did not need a form. You just need to listen. If you cannot do this while you are doing what you need to do, it would not be very practical.

I know, just life flowing.

It is and it's always there.

1:11 PM
Some psychics, not all, receive impressions, and they are many times preloaded.

Preloaded?

Their own words are used for these impressions and the temptation to preload the information is because it is a job for them; there is money involved. If money is the motivation in this work this work WILL eventually become tainted.

Not pure.

That's what tainted means. We HAVE already talked about this.

I know; you brought it up.

YOU were wondering and you had concerns. There is a strong motivation to give the client what the client wants to hear.

November 2011

November 1

8:52 PM
Talia, are you busy?

I am always busy.

I just feel your presence.

I have something to say.

I want to hear it.

I have already said a lot more than you have written.

The Universe Speaks

I cannot write that fast, and you also said sometimes writing just gets in the way.

That's not what I am talking about. You were open as a child.

I am open now.

You are, but be aware that as a man gets older there is a tendency not to be as open, to have his mind made up. The counterpart to that is to let the mind expand, open to receive more truth. With this expansion comes the little child again, able to see things as they are and to revel again in that childlike joy.

That is exactly what I had planned.

That is a good plan. How do you intend to accomplish this?

By keeping my mind open.

How?

By intending it fully, by presence of mind, by God's grace, by praying for that help, and by the help of people like you.

That's a pretty good answer.

Do you have a better one?

You have covered most of the bases.

There is more?

There is always more.

Well, I am open to hearing more.

Then you will. Do you want me to say more?

Yes!

Then be open.

Okay, you can't enter into the Kingdom of Heaven unless you become like a little child, and the answers are within you are two things I got out of this. Is there more?

There always is.

I got a lot out of that last sentence too.

See?

Yes.

You want to go somewhere?

Collection

Yes.

Then go. You have things to do.

November 5

1:11 PM
Why do you think He said that He had magnified His word above His name?

Why?

Because he knew that the time would come when His name would be misunderstood, misinterpreted, and misused to make unreasonable demands upon others. I said to you that everything He does is reasonable. He said not to use His name in vain. It is vain to make unreasonable demands upon a person because of a name.

Remember, a name, if used correctly, is descriptive of the nature of the thing named. If this nature is not used when proclaiming His name in a teaching, then that teaching is incomplete. God is love, and if this pure and holy love does not flow out of the person, the lesson will be very difficult to accept.

Another aspect of this is His magnified word simply means to listen, to pay attention to what He says. He has used many names to describe Himself, but the one that causes the most contention is the one used to proclaim God in the flesh. Have you asked why? Because that is the absolute victory over all things. That simple acceptance and belief destroys the power of darkness and restores all into One.

11:25 PM
Don't worry about the book; it's already out there. The book will take care of itself; my mom will see to that.

> This statement of Talia's cracked us both up!

November 15

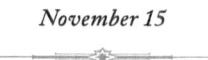

8:06 PM
> While in the bathroom G was thanking God for Talia.

That's funny.

The Universe Speaks

November 16

1:09 PM
I feel you.

I'm always around. You're my vessel and I thank you for that.

You're welcome and I'm a willing vessel.

I know you are.

It's a very great honor and I appreciate it. I wish I had the words to say how much.

You're yielding yourself to mine and that's enough.

You have something to say.

I usually do.

I'd like to hear it.

My words to you are pure and they must be heard from a place of pureness.

I'm as pure as the driven snow, I'm sure.

I'm sure you know how to get there.

I don't have the time now, do I?

No, but when you do, you will, and I need you to be pure. Our symbols for explanations must be accurate. Remember, these steps are ordered in His word.

I see many pitfalls, and we need accuracy, precision in this walk.

Yes, what else?

I see even the right path will have booby traps at times.

At times it will; that's why I need you on your toes. These are perilous times.

I'm sure seeing that.

What you see is true.

Collection

November 18

3:15 PM
Okay, what's next?

You already know.

No, I don't.

Yes, you do. Follow your heart. It's only the advice you've been given—time you followed it.

November 22

9:40 AM
   Just after we finished recording the audio book of Book One, G heard Talia:

I appreciate her.

   Talia was speaking about the girl who was the voice of Talia for the audio book. Her name is Talia also! Then, right after she finished uploading the files to her computer, Talia spoke up again.

Thank you, Talia.

Talia, was that you?

That was me.

November 23

   G was joking with me about what he thought Talia would say about something.

Don't put words in my mouth.

November 27

The place of the skull is a place of limitation, a place of death.

Golgotha—you spoke to me about that before.

Yes, many times. That's the place I spoke of when I said the thoughts just circle in your head. A false spherical way, leading to nowhere until the realization that those thoughts are only your creation of an illusion, usually of how you wish things were. This is the prison of the mind, and it can only see limitation. It can only see death.

Only death?

Only death when you see with this limited perception. For even when one beholds the glory of life all one can see as the end result is death. Do you see the hopelessness this causes, the despair? When you break out of the prison of the skull then can you see with perfect vision, for you will see that life is limitless, that it has no end. This is when your victory is assured. There is no limitation.

November 28

1:04 PM
All my thoughts are purposeful because thoughts are Light. We are beings of light.

Yes. When you see that, you see that the brain too is just a filter, filtering spiritual experience.

So we can express ourselves with our choices.

Exactly. The only wise choice is Light and freedom. Pretty simple, isn't it.

Sure sounds like it.

It sounds like it because it is. All my thoughts are pure.

I never thought otherwise.

But do you know why?

Why?

Because that's the only thing that is. Don't you see, the impure, the unclean, is just a thought, an illusion, a corruption of what's real. The only reality is that which is pure.

Hard to see sometimes.

That's because you're seeing it with a biased perception. That which is true needs no embellishment. Have you seen anything impure when you walked in the Spirit?

No.

No, not even the evil, because it was pure evil and it had purpose.

What?

Collection

To open your eyes to what was pure. All things work together for your good; how could it ever be otherwise? God is love.

And love never fails.

It never does. Even when all seems lost, it never fails. Therefore, worry is lack of faith and understanding. Truly it is faith in something else; it is belief in lack or unworthiness or any other base thought born of ignorance, conceived in darkness. It is a vague belief that God could lie, which He cannot. I am His daughter, and I can never lie.

November 29

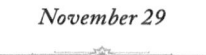

7:06 AM
And now are we the sons of God.

That's what I wanted you to see. Only believe.

You're really something.

I'm really Everything, contained in a form. The form of Talia, Heaven's Dew. This containing is without restraint. None is needed, I am free, and I will say it again, nothing is better.

11:42 PM
I thought I heard you say, "I don't like him."

      G is speaking about someone we knew of that was not a nice person.

You did.

Just never heard you say that about anyone before.

I said that because of his actions—they affect others negatively. He is an agent of chaos and a servant of conflict. He has given place to this and has assured himself that he is right. This is a game he has chosen and he plays it consistently. I have a divine love for him, but I dislike what he has chosen to become. My thoughts are pure and my emotions are perfected. Have you not doubted yourself because of your feelings toward him?

At times.

That is confusion. You will know them by their fruits.

Okay, I'm curious about something else: how did I teach you to rip and snort?

You have a determined nature once your mind is made up about something. It's just sometimes hard for you to make your mind up. But when you do, nothing can stop you. I had asked Him some of the same questions you have and one of them was, "How can I get through to them?"

639

His answer to me was, "Behold my son." You taught me to penetrate into things, to grab hold and not let go.

That's . . .

You underestimate yourself. You've been told that before; I said I learned from everything you do.

That's very encouraging and so very humbling at the same time.

It should be. You think sometimes you have nothing to offer, but you have a wealth of knowledge. And when you share this knowledge you bless yourself and those who hear you. These are seeds planted that bring forth fruit, and it is lasting.

Talia, my love for you has no end.

I'm glad you noticed that, and neither does mine for you.

December 2011

December 2

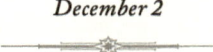

1:03 PM
Don't I bring you joy?

You sure do.

Then why don't you live in it?

In it.

Yes.

Because sometimes I'm out of it.

Why? Because you don't always believe who you are. Walk in who you are. Believe in who you are and your problems disappear. What did Grandfather say?

To know myself.

The same thing I said. Why is that so difficult?

Because I'm elusive.

That sounds romantic, but it's really foolish.

Collection

Duh!

You're quoting Homer Simpson now?

Thought I could make you laugh.

It's not working.

Actually that which you said was pretty funny.

You're being elusive with yourself; how smart is that?

Have you forgotten what it's like here?

No, have you forgotten what it's like here? You just need a change.

Sure do.

Well, it's coming.

What kind of a change?

A change in perspective.

May it be painless.

The choice is yours.

Then I choose painless.

Good choice. I told you it didn't always have to be hard.

So you did.

Not being hard doesn't necessarily mean easy though.

You're just full of good news today.

All my news is good.

Time to go.

Yes.

7:53 PM
Talia, I read His yoke is easy.

It is. Why don't you take it upon you.

I do.

Yes, sometimes, and sometimes you take your own, which isn't so easy.

The Universe Speaks

This is a tough planet.

It can be.

December 3

2:30 AM
Happy Birthday, Talia.

Thank you.

3:27 AM
Why don't you sleep?

It's cold.

Why don't you put more clothes on—that's why you brought them.

You're right. Thanks for the laugh.

You're welcome.

8:23 PM
Many have thought of me today and I appreciate each and every one of them.

December 6

11:37 AM
Talia, I asked you the other day how you felt about the books being out and you said, "I feel like a celebrity."

That was funny, and I heard you said the same to someone else also.

That's how it feels to me. I said to you death brings life.

December 8

There has to be a change of collective consciousness. He's giving you the key. It's going to be good.

Speaking about a class we were going to.

Collection

December 14

9:20 AM
It is all now. Even the future is now—it just hasn't appeared yet.

That's true. See, my teachings do work.

That's funny.

Even here we need to be reminded by the Great Spirit that all things are ours, that our works bring forth fruit in your realm. Our exasperation is perfect; it pushes us toward the need. Remember what I said: it is a give and take into Oneness. Like a heartbeat, the drum of heaven.

The life is in the blood.

It is. The waters of Life.

9:31 AM
Surrender to that that is.

You want to explain?

No. You already know what it is.

I mean for others.

This can never be interpreted with the natural mind, with the flesh. What does your heart say?

> G thought about a vision he had had while in meditation:
>
> . . . I stepped just past the threshold of the bigger hole of the probable future, into a green place, a place with grass and moss, and watched the works of man, concrete dust and blocks, 4x4s, building materials of all kinds rush by me.

That green place is a place of growth, of life, and it will not be found in the natural, for it is the real place of life, a place of quiet waters, a place of reflection, a reflection of all truth. A place of birds and geese. A place of Divine protection. A place where the hurts are healed. It is a place I LIVE and it is harmony.

That rushing by is a place of the world. A place filled with fear. And that is the root of conflict—fear. It does not exist where I live and my invitation is always open; therefore, be open to live there, for you are deserving, you ARE a child of God. Do you think He will not take care of His children? That He would forsake them?

Never!

Never is correct; that would be merely appearance. Judge not of appearance but judge righteous judgment. For that is the way of life and this life is never-ending. It is trial of your faith. Tested, tempered, and perfected.

Talia, your wisdom is astounding.

So is yours. You have the solution.

December 16

This is the temple of Life, and this is where the Art of Life is lived from. What is imagined is more real than what you perceive to be real. When people get that, the way will be clear. Nothing hidden that shall not be revealed when you open your all to THE All. Grace is Oneness. Mankind is One. And rivers of living water shall flow out of your innermost being and the kingdom shall be the Lord's.

Be yourself. But you can't bind their choices.

December 18

10:40 AM
Those people were making goddesses into a God.

> Referring to what Paul said about letting the women keep silence in the church.

3:22 PM
You're reading today, you're studying today, aren't you?

Yes, I am. I see that the things coming upon mankind ARE horrible, but I also see these things must be, because of their choices, because they have chosen to reject the truth. These things must be for the purification of all things, to restore that which has been lost, to purge from them the lies they have accepted as truth. This is an abomination of the Truth. You feel it in the air; you feel it in the water, in the earth, the animals, the people, the trembling, the unsettledness, the unrest.

Yes.

That which you feel is true. Go within.

Collection

I remember when I bought that trailer from the artist, I was told, "You will do a work of art there," and I've thought of that a few times since.

And so it has been. This prophecy is power, the power to be forewarned. Absorption. Be absorbed into the truth, and let it surround you like a light, a light of protection, for the dark cannot exist within the Light.

December 19

6:06 AM

Our friend Richard wears one of the "Pretty Much Amazing" bracelets. It has fallen off his wrist, an impossible feat, THREE times.

Talia, what are you trying to tell Richard?

I'm trying to tell him I love him.

December 21

1:01 PM

Talia, I'd sure like to talk to you.

You're rushed.

I know.

Well, don't be rushed. Slow down; remember, slow down to speed up. The quickening is yours when you accept it and claim it as yours. Rushing rarely accomplishes anything but to create more chaos.

Got enough of that.

So very true, and now you know what creates that. God is not the author of that.

But of peace.

And that in abundance.

You . . . I don't have the words.

And you don't need them. You have me and that is everything.

I can see how that could be misunderstood.

The Universe Speaks

I can see how any of this can. What's important for these students is what they are learning about themselves.

I see that.

Yes, and that is very important. The subject matter is just a tool. Remember when I said, "Touching hearts from the Temple"?

Yes, years ago, soon after we started this.

Now you know what that means.

The Temple part threw me off—I thought of a building. I thought I had misunderstood.

I know you did. Remember when I said "write it like I say it"?

Yes.

Well, just do that.

It's not for lack of trying.

Yes, sometimes you try too hard. Just be, flow, and take no thought.

Simple.

Almost overly simple. You know what is true.

I did see it.

Yes, what the Temple meant.

I know I heard that the other day, but I didn't know it was you.

It is us and we are One.

You also called it the Temple of Truth.

That's because that is what it is. Your shackle says go now. Go, but don't be a slave to it.

Slavery isn't my thing.

I know it's not.

8:14 PM
When you receive these vignettes that are seemingly overwhelming, pick those that stand out as most pertinent.

> She is referring to a prophetic dream G had at about five years old that was brought back to him in a very powerful way.

Collection

There is a current in the flow, like the Gulf Stream; some are carried along faster. This river within the ocean you should consider deeply. Let your focus be all-inclusive. This information in the present foretells the future, for it is made now. Man's darkened choices have brought him to a place without true understanding, yet he insists his way is right. This way is the way of death, devoid of the true light that would guide his way. He has leaned unto his own understanding and has lost his true self. His understanding is darkened and he lives in the trap he has built. He worships the god of money. This god will fail him. This worship of money most would deny to their death, but that is what these do, put money first before all things. Depend on it to bring them life. Is this not the definition of worship? To desire riches above all else?

Yes.

It will not last. It will be brought down. Man's factories shall fail and be used against him.

January 2012

January 3

10:30 AM
Thank you for what you've done, this book, changing peoples' lives.

Thank you for what you've done.

Good to hear from you.

Good to be heard from.

12:00 PM
That was unbidden.

It wasn't unbidden. You were talking to me.

Yeah, I was.

Well, if someone talked to you would you ignore them?

Guess that depends on who it was.

I mean a sincere dialogue.

No.

Then why would I?

The Universe Speaks

You wouldn't.

Of course I wouldn't. Any questions?

What about this new law? Defense Authorization Act . . .

It shows their true face and reveals their hand.

Global domination and slavery?

Total control. Remember what I said about someone trying to control others, that is the flesh?

I do.

Well, that's what this is, the desire to control others. These are convinced that they know best, when in reality this is the worst face of man, the desire to dominate others. Remember also that I said they would not succeed, but it wouldn't stop them from trying.

Nice to know they will not succeed.

Not to them. They will use draconian methods. Remember what I also said of these, that it would never be enough. You can attempt to appease, but it will never be enough. That's why I said that there was no compromise in this war of Light and darkness. And that is what this is. The desire to dominate is always born of darkness. So feel free to use a ruse, but at best it will only buy you time.

There is no parlay with the prince of darkness, although his servants, if they cannot be awakened, can be led by their own darkness, by hooking into their own blind obsessions. They are useful tools.

The rise of the machines.

Yes, I told you it would come.

January 10

4:15 PM

While G was speaking to his father, his father told him this:

If you're not at peace with yourself you can't be at peace with anyone.

Collection

January 11

10:35 PM

Do you have a voice?

Yes.

Then use it.

For?

You've sought wisdom and now that you have it you refuse to share it?

Not at all.

But sometimes you do.

So how have you been?

Perfect and growing in grace.

The timing . . .

I told you all things are yours. The timing is as well. Manipulate what needs to be manipulated; the rest let it be as it is.

Not sure what you mean.

Don't deny what you know.

You manipulate your reality; everyone does this. I do this constantly. Remember, the beauty of our hearts transforms the world around us. Out of the ABUNDANCE of the heart the mouth speaks. Speak into being by the sincerity and truth of the heart. This truth can never be deceived for it is born of purity. Your innermost being knows what is true. Your birthright stolen is not a mistake, it is a diabolical plan. One's anger of this is justified. Transform the world around you by the beauty of this truth by manipulating that anger. Channel it to destroy the works of the enemy, to remove that seed from the earth.

Sounds like a plan.

Oh, it is. It is planned perfection. Remember when the thief awoke you.

Offshore.

Yes. Wasn't that ultimately used for good?

It sure was.

That is good to remember; it is a microcosm of these days.

The Universe Speaks

I remember thinking it had something to do with "these" days.

Yes, you were told that and that it would be brought back and by a young girl that would read your heart, the future, and the past—as one.

Wow, I remember that but it made no sense at the time.

But now it does, doesn't it?

It sure does. I remember seeing an astounding beauty, very powerful. Like not of this world.

I'm not.

Felt like the pure Holy Spirit of God upon her. She was filled with it and it was all around her, almost like it was following her.

What else?

Like a friend.

Do you see the correlation there?

Yes.

That is truth. He honors your decisions.

He follows you?

Yes, that's why I have no doubts.

I knew you didn't.

Yes, but think about what I said.

No respecter of persons.

That is correct.

What He will do for one, He will do for all.

That is what He has been trying to get across for thousands of years, yet it's one of the hardest things for people to believe. In actuality, He does this already, but most have been convinced by the accuser that they are unworthy; therefore, the gifts go unnoticed or are kicked to the side or trampled upon. Yet the solution is so very, very simple. Just accept the gifts, for they are freely given and the merit is God's love. It is His all-encompassing, boundless love for His children. It is grace, not works, that saves.

Saves?

Saves from the delusion of this world, from the anguish of ignorance, among other things.

Collection

You're changing heaven, aren't you?

Heaven is eternal and it is eternally changing.

I think you've made it better.

It's always been perfect. Heaven is a state of mind. It is a state of God-mind, which all are born with. "Be ye perfect." In other words, "Be ye in heaven." That's another birthright most have forgotten.

Thank you, Talia.

You're welcome. The flesh is weak, isn't it?

Sure is.

Then why give it so much credit.

Another typical Talia unique way of looking at something.

This way of looking at something is a tool, a tool to bring life.

Then I don't need sleep

No, you do need it, but not just yet—we're not done.

Okay.

It's always okay, when you listen to me.

Don't get overconfident now.

That's not possible.

So you're saying you're perfect?

I've said it before and nothing's changed.

That's the unchangeable part then

Yes, and you have more of those parts than you know.

Or care to admit to.

Those parts will be changed.

I need to listen.

Yes. Yes, you do. Everything we've spoken of is not to be shared with everyone.

You've said that before.

Yes, and I'm saying it again. Be . . . discerning.

The Universe Speaks

I know there are things that are unlawful to utter.

There are.

January 14

7:57 AM
We have plains like this here, and it is heaven. Beautiful.

> Talia is speaking of the great plains of the USA. G was driving across country.

January 16

5:25 AM
You're not listening.

I just heard you.

You know what I mean.

10:18 AM
> G was thinking of that plane crash, Talia's "death," and why it had to be when she said:

I asked Him why and He said He needed me here. That I had fulfilled what I had been sent to do there and that now I would be used in a much greater way than I could have been there. That I would be used now to help people to fulfill their destiny and purpose. You feel what I felt when He said this to me and there are no words to describe it. Then I asked, what about my mom? He answered that my mom would be fine and that I would help her to fulfill her destiny there as well. That it would never be unless I had been called here.

That's the moment that I came to accept things as they are, as I have told you to do. Our lives are not planned by us, for we are not our own, but the One who creates us, it is His plan we are to fulfill, and our peace depends on our plans being His plan for us. There is nothing there to bring one peace or fulfillment but God's perfect plan for you. Nothing else will ever satisfy. This is designed by the Holy Creator, by perfect love. Why second-guess this law of perfection?

Thank you for that today.

You're welcome.

Collection

There's so much to transcribe.

That's why it's a good idea to keep up with it.

So much explanation.

You don't have to explain as much as you think. Bullet points. Notes to remember. If something does need an explanation then let it come like you let the rest of it come.

Feels like we've shifted gears somehow.

We have. We have entered into a new dawn emerging.

How so?

Things ARE accelerating. Some changes will come so fast it will be like a storm. Don't fight the storm; it is meant to be.

Just flow with it.

Yes, flow with it and adjust to it. Become adaptable. That is survival of the fittest, to adapt to change. This change cannot be stopped; this IS a new world order.

Hidden meanings in plain sight.

They are always there. Only animals that adapt to change survive the change. You are a spiritual being. Formless.

There is a lot of detail you could get into here.

Yes, there is, but it would be like trying to put a form to something that is formless. If this formlessness is upon one, as a mantle, putting symbols of a form is not needed, and the rigid will not be helped by the symbols for it will not be understood by them. Humility is imperative.

January 17

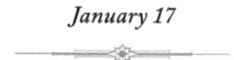

6:38 PM
Wow.

That was a lot, wasn't it?

Yeah, a lot more than I thought.

That's why it's important to keep up with it as best you can.

You're probably right.

Probably?

The Universe Speaks

Yeah, you are right.

You really do think you know more than me sometimes.

I just surprised you again.

You did.

I surprised me too.

Yes, you did.

Talia, wow, is this really happening?

It's really happening.

Well, if I had been aware of that I really would have known more than you.

Yes, but you weren't.

That's some funny stuff there.

Yes, it is.

Just imagine me knowing more than you.

I'm not saying it couldn't happen, but you're not there yet.

But am I close?

You're as close as you can be right now.

That's not very specific.

Yes, it is, you just don't know it.

Oh man, I wish I could keep up.

You can, you just don't know it.

Hey, that's some good food for thought.

Yes, it is. I'm not hiding anything from you; you can only hide it from yourself.

I think that's a nice way of saying I'm a knucklehead.

No, it's not, it's a nice way of telling you the truth.

Talia, I would sure like to take you somewhere.

Why don't you come where I am—that way you can be who you are. The veil is thinner than you think.

Talia, it's been so long.

Collection

Whose fault is that? I want to show you something. You ready?

Yes.

   G went with Talia on a spiritual journey.

What is the place?

Stories. All the stories. This is where we tell the stories.

What stories?

Any stories. Any story you want to tell, or hear.

Do you want to go somewhere else?

Anywhere you want to.

Follow me.

Where we are going has nothing to do with anything you think you need to know now.

Then why are we going?

It has PURPOSE. I want you to look into the windows of time. You can look in or you can look out.

It looks like a church.

It's not. Relax. Don't worry about writing any of this. Just look.

January 25

1:19 PM
I'm sorry, Talia.

What are you sorry for?

I don't know, just figured I screwed something up.

And that's the problem that is not even a problem, the thinking that you screwed something up when you didn't.

Live your life. Trust yourself. Your instincts are finely tuned from birth. We are the same.

But you are awesome.

YOU are awesome. Do not underestimate yourself.

Thanks for the reminder; I was told that not so long ago.

Yes, you were. I told you, you have to speed up to hear me; your vibration must be faster. I have to slow down for us to communicate, but I have mastered slowing down.

Let me be the highest version of myself.

You are.

8:54 PM
You notice I use focal points to get and hold your attention; we use them here as well. It's good to notice things; it's a key point to remember.

Like landmarks.

It's more than that; it is starting at the point then expanding outward to take in the whole. A part is partial; blending and becoming one with the whole is to know all things. It is becoming them. Even to become one with what you would call one thing is to know all things, because these separate objects or entities are in reality one thing. It all comes from the One. All of these things are one thing, that that is. As I've said, the separation is for learning. When you see everything coalesce into One, that is when you understand what I mean when I say "nothing hidden that shall not be revealed." That is also the reason I told you that this book was about everything.

Nothing off the table?

Nothing I can think of.

That possible, greener future I saw running just to the right of the probable; it was rough but nothing like I saw in the probable. I never saw that there before.

It is new. The changes are constant.

How can we get there?

Will it. Ye are gods; act like it. Believe with all your heart then make it so. It's not so difficult; it's just a nudge. It can seem overwhelming. That's the natural mind reasoning, reacting to what it has seen. It is also the children of Light not knowing who they are or what they are capable of. You are capable of all things; nothing is impossible to you. Now is the time to apply the knowledge that you know. Use it. Nudge that future from the path it is on and create a new one. It is already there for the taking, created by the prayers of the saints and the mercy of God.

Saints and children of the Light.

Of course these are set apart. To apply the pressure needed to change things, to move them in a new direction, these must be outside of the chaos and confusion causing it.

But . . .

Collection

Everyone's methods to get this done, to achieve what would appear impossible to most, are different. That is why to explain in more detail would take volumes and still it would be incomplete. I gave you the point, now expand it outward and the answers will be clear.

Talia, you are a master genius.

It's safe to say I am now.

Talia, I wish YOU had the words.

I wish words were enough; this is a knowing without words. Words are superfluous.

January 26

6:55 PM

Talia, so many times I've heard you say "growing up together into all things" or "as one, together growing as one," and so on. Then when I looked up *coalesce* for the spelling I read the Latin, which was *co* (together), *alesce* (grow up). The full definition was to unite into a single body or group.

Guess that pretty much says it all, doesn't it?

It doesn't say it all but it's close.

February 2012

February 4

10:32 AM

There is something I want to talk about, and that is reverence. Reverence for the earth, for the planet. The earth is a gift and it is your home. Why would one disrespect one's own home? It is your birthplace and learning center. She is also a living being. This disrespect by mankind she feels deeply and she WILL purge herself of his disrespect. This cannot continue. Man is poisoning her, thereby poisoning himself. You are now seeing the results of this. She is a reflection of man upon her, of his thoughts. She sustains his life and yet he disregards the life she provides.

A change in consciousness is required. A change of lifestyle. The life most live is unsustainable; it is so obvious, yet most ignore her pain. This ignorance must be healed or the price is more than can be borne. Man was created to care for her, to nurture her. Many have forgotten this. Man's first directive was to tend the garden; many now work to destroy it with no thought to the consequence. Even many who would call themselves spiritual have no regard for their present home. She is sick and she needs your help to be healed. Man must open his eyes to this and stop denying what he knows for profit.

"I will destroy those who destroy the earth." Revelations 11:18.

How much plainer could that be? You were wondering how this book would end.

That's what I meant when I said, "Here is not there, it's here." Remember, "no separation." Earth and heaven are One. Heaven is everywhere, for it is the Presence of God, and He is everywhere. This treatment of her, this behavior, must be repented of, and I mean left behind forever. Excuses are no longer an option. Your exposure of truth cannot be ignored. Death is not life and this is what some are creating by their actions. Return to your first love. Become a child again. The answer is love. Love yourself, each other, and the earth, your home. And love God with all your strength, mind, body, and soul. For He loves you, with all His mind. He just asks for His love to be returned, to be reflected by you, through you, to all things. His creation is a manifestation of His never-ending love. You are made in His image. This making, this creating, is also never-ending. Grow up into Him in all things.

Talia, I can tell you've got so much more to say.

There is always more to say, there is always more to be, there is always more to do. This is never-ending.

11:38 AM
We finished. ☺

We did?

We did. ☺

6:00 PM
I told you we were close.

I know you did.

Are you disappointed?

No, I'm excited about it, but at the same time, yes, I guess I am a little disappointed.

Why the mixed emotions?

It's been a wonderful journey.

It always will be.

Collection

6:58 PM
I have one page left—you told me that.

Yes, and you did not want to believe it.

No, I guess not. I sure can't put a "The End" there.

No, because that would be dishonest. There is no end.

Yeah, I know. Now what?

Now we continue with our journey.

That's way cool. I knew you wouldn't retire.

That's funny. I'm too young to retire and so are you. ☺

February 20

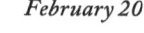

12:55 PM
Talia, are you still speaking?

Yes. Our core message is completed. There IS enough there to mitigate the things you have seen coming if the lessons are implemented, if they are walked in. They will become a part of you as you live them, in experience and not concept. There is more, much more, but they will come infrequently, as you need them.

I am a little disappointed.

Why? You completed a great work, a work of Art.

You mean we?

I mean that I could not have done this without you. You yielded yourself to me and to our work together. You have sacrificed much to do this, so do not downplay your part in this. It has been a noble journey and you approached it as such.

It does not feel like a sacrifice at all, but a very great honor.

It IS a great honor, and it has also been a sacrifice. You put your heart on the altar for this, and that honors us and your Creator. We here see this so very rarely, and this work will not be forgotten.

It seemed easy.

It IS easy. That was part of the message.

Thank you so very, very much.

Thank YOU.

Afterword

As I sit here writing my final words about *The Universe Speaks*, I can't help thinking back to the beginning of my remarkable journey of learning, healing, spiritual awakening, and life changes, which Talia's and our Creator's messages have brought to me—and hopefully to you, the reader, and the world.

When Talia first started to speak the messages found in *The Universe Speaks*, I was astounded at the healing qualities her messages had for me on a personal level. As her messages continued and expanded in Book One, then delved deeper in Book Two, I was hopeful that you, the reader, would understand her words, take them to heart, and have as miraculous a change of understanding about the universe as I did.

Apparently, you did! After the release of Book One, I received numerous e-mails from readers around the world telling me that as soon as they had finished reading it, they too began to hear from their loved ones on the other side. What I know now, after much learning from Talia, is that such communications had actually always been there, but the readers, myself included, were either too hurt or closed off to hear or be aware of them. As we all read the messages brought to us by Talia, doubt and hurt were pushed aside, leaving us open to believe.

That belief is the key to hearing what Spirit is trying to get through to us, all the time: belief in the Spirit, belief in our ability to hear, belief in the existence of something bigger than us—more powerful, more brilliant than we have ever let ourselves believe before. Without belief, we are cut off. Cut off from what is our birthright. Our connection to the Spirit that moves through all things. Our connection to Oneness. Our connection to ALL.

My belief is based on a great deal of substantiation of my communications with the spirit world. These substantiations were fact; they were proven to me. So I call my belief a fact-based belief, a belief that grew out of many factual experiences. It's much like learning that $1 + 1 = 2$. Once we see that this is true, we have a belief, and that belief is based on the fact that we have seen and experienced that $1 + 1$ is in fact 2. We have faith in that fact and also faith that our belief is true. We then have fact-based faith.

This is very different from faith "just because." Just because our parents told us there was—or was not—a God, just because they said so, we had faith it was true. This is the faith that many people have, but I don't believe in it. It is faith based on fact that gives us a firm belief in something. For me, this firm, factual belief is that there is no death, the spirit lives on, and we all can hear the communications from the spirit world if we learn how.

Learning how to hear—that is the biggest hurdle. But if you have faith that you can, and you're able to let go of the noise that's in your head in everyday life, you will hear. There are hundreds, if not thousands, of books out there to help you learn how to let go, how to quiet the noise, how to meditate, how to hear. I am not going to tell you how you should do it; each path is different for each person. For me, my path was set out by Talia.

Talia's messages were clear. She said that I could feel her, I could hear her, and I could receive her contact. When she said that, I knew I could. That was hurdle one: I believed I could.

Hurdle two was to actually begin receiving messages and signs. The key to hearing or receiving is acknowledging every communication you get. The more you acknowledge, the more you will begin to receive. So I made sure to acknowledge each and every sign I received.

If I saw a dime in a very strange place, I let Talia know that I saw that dime, and that I thought it was from her. If I felt something on my head, I asked Talia if that was her. When I felt it again, I knew it was. When I received a thought in my head and wasn't sure where it had come from, I let Talia know that I had "heard" that thought and thanked her.

Soon the signs came more frequently, and they were much clearer. Instead of feeling a little tingle on my leg, I'd feel a very strong touch. Instead of receiving a thought in my head that I thought might have come from Spirit, that thought became very clear—louder, though not audible. Instead of finding one dime, I would notice dime after dime in the same place for a day or so as emphasis.

I also studied very hard. I was extremely fortunate to have many healers work on me to help me release grief and open up my channels of communication. I was also lucky to be able to take many classes on learning to communicate with the spirit world.

In these classes, many exercises helped me learn how to communicate and how to receive. After each exercise, my fact-based belief was reinforced. I received substantiation after substantiation that there is in fact a spiritual world, one that we are part of even while we are still in our bodies.

Though I am very thankful to Talia for bringing this great work to the world, enabling as many people as possible to open up to the reality that is, it is also hard for me because of course I would rather she still be with me, in her body, growing up, getting ready to move away to college. I wish she were here in her body to sit with and laugh with, to dine with and just hang out with. But she is not here in her body, and that makes me sad, still to this day.

It is a strange sadness. Strange because, along with my sadness, I am so happy that she is happy. Talia has said numerous times that where she is is so much greater than where we are. She has told me she is happy—happier than she can even explain. It is more beautiful

Collection

"there" than here. So how can I be sad for her? I cannot. She is happy beyond belief and that makes me happier than I would ever have imagined I could be.

I always only wanted the best for her, and if heaven is the best, then that is where she should be. Being able to communicate with her is what brings peace, joy, and happiness to me now.

A Message from G

When I first started hearing Talia speak to me, I thought all she wanted was for me to get a message to her mom—a message letting her mom know that she was all right. As it turned out, Talia had much much more to say to her mom and me than just the simple statement, "Tell my mom I'm OK." Talia had a message, and she wanted to get that message out to the world.

I always knew that there was much more to this universe than we see with our eyes, more to life, death and the spirit than I was taught in school. And though I have always been able to hear from the spirit world whenever someone wanted to get through to me, I never realized the depth and extent of what there was to learn from the other side until Talia started to reveal herself, her words, and all the information she has given me to pass on to others.

The more I heard from Talia, the more she spoke to me. The more she spoke, the more I wanted to hear. I spent every available moment of every day and evening being quiet, listening to her, and writing down everything she told me and everything I said to her.

I am truly honored to have known Talia before she "died," and even more honored, grateful, and humbled to have been able to help her get her messages—the universe's messages—out to you, the reader, and the world.

Special Thanks from Kim

I WANT TO GIVE a very special thank you to all of the readers of *The Universe Speaks*, Books One and Two, and true believers of Talia's words, who are my inspiration for this *Collection Edition*.

I offer an especially large, heartfelt thank-you and utmost gratitude to Tom Brown Jr, for his lifetime of unwavering dedication and passion for healing the earth, and for all of his teachings, which have led to my own abilities to hear Talia. You know my heart.

About Kim Klein

Raised in Southern California, Kim Klein attended the University of California, Santa Barbara. After graduating with a B.A. in Political Science, attending law school and being admitted to the California State Bar, Kim worked with her then husband in real estate investments and their high-tech companies. After having her daughter, Talia, Kim became a stay-at-home mom, devoting all of her time to raising her only child.

Just after her thirteenth birthday, Talia was killed when the small private plane she was on crashed into the side of a volcano. The event devastated Kim's heart and shattered her entire belief system—and from the moment of Talia's death, Kim's motherly devotion shifted from raising Talia to learning to communicate with her in the afterlife.

Kim now spends her time writing about her experiences surrounding the death of Talia, as well as her communication with Talia from heaven and the spirit world to us here on earth in the physical. Through the many discussions Kim has had with Talia, both directly and via mediums, Kim has learned a great deal about the spirit world, spirituality, and the reality of heaven. She now dedicates her time to writing about her experiences, helping others to learn and open their spiritual minds, and helping others to heal from their loss of loved ones.

Kim can be reached via her website: *www.kimberlyklein.com*.

If you would like to read more about Talia before the crash, or about the author's extraordinary journey before, during and after Talia's transition, please read *Hummingbirds Don't Fly in the Rain*.

You can buy *Hummingbirds Don't Fly in the Rain* at Amazon.com, as well as from other retailers and online bookstores.

"A riveting story of unimaginable heartbreak and courage. It leaves you in awe of this mother's vast ability to love and to heal. It cannot help but change your view of what is possible."

~Ellen Simon, Screenwriter, *One Fine Day* and *Moonlight and Valentino*

"*Hummingbirds Don't Fly in the Rain* is a compelling story that grabs you from the first paragraph and doesn't let go, even after the last word has been read. Kim Klein weaves a tale of a special relationship between a mother and her daughter, a moment in the life of two great spirits as they travel an all-too-short path. Her journey is one of tragedy, fear, anger—and, ultimately, forgiveness. A great and easy read."

~Ronalafae Thapa, internationally recognized psychic and medium

Seeds of Wisdom and Heavenly Inspirations: A collection of inspirational quotes direct from the Spirit, that will inspire, transform, heal, and encourage anyone looking for answers—about love, life, death, Heaven, and living authentically. This book brings understanding to lifes most significant questions: Who are we? What does it mean to live and die? What is our purpose? A gift for anyone at any age.

You can buy *Seeds of Wisdom* and *Heavenly Inspirations* on *Amazon.com*, as well as from other retailers and online bookstores.
ISBN: 978-0-9881787-3-1

www.ingramcontent.com/pod-product-compliance
Lightning Source LLC
Chambersburg PA
CBHW020054020526
44112CB00031B/68